Charles Whibley, Philemon Holland

History of twelve Caesars

Vol. I

Charles Whibley, Philemon Holland

History of twelve Caesars
Vol. I

ISBN/EAN: 9783337188207

Printed in Europe, USA, Canada, Australia, Japan

Cover: Foto ©ninafisch / pixelio.de

More available books at **www.hansebooks.com**

THE TUDOR
TRANSLATIONS

EDITED BY

W. E. HENLEY

XXI

SUETONIUS
HISTORY OF TWELVE CÆSARS
TRANSLATED INTO ENGLISH BY
PHILEMON HOLLAND
ANNO 1606

With an Introduction by

CHARLES WHIBLEY

VOLUME I

LONDON
Published by DAVID NUTT
IN THE STRAND
1899

TO

THE RIGHT HONOURABLE

CECIL JOHN RHODES

A MAKER OF IMPERIAL BRITAIN

THESE MEMOIRS

OF IMPERIAL ROME

INTRODUCTION

I

HILEMON HOLLAND, 'the Translator Generall in his age,' was born at Chelmsford in 1552. From the Grammar School of his native town he passed in proper course to Trinity College, Cambridge, of which august foundation he was successively scholar and fellow. Thereafter he gave himself to the study of medicine, graduated M.D. in 1595, and settled at Coventry in the same year to the practice of his profession. Materials are lacking wherefrom to compose an accurate biography; anecdote for the most part supplies the place of fact; and it is in his works that we must seek the securest evidence of his talent and dignity. Yet from these scanty branches we may throw the vague shadow of a rarely amiable career.

Philemon Holland's birth and upbringing

We know not what pursuits or ambitions engrossed him before the year of his arrival in Coventry. Perhaps he was of those whose mind and character are not hastily shaped. But he was past forty when he commenced the practice of physic; and it was not until he had completed his tenth

The Coventry of his age

THE HISTORIE OF

INTRODUCTION

lustre that he found the real task of his life. He could not have found a better theatre for his gifts than the Coventry which he loved so well, and which in return generously acknowledged the honour conferred by his presence. It was not then the tourist-haunted city of bicycles and of Peeping Tom; the houses, now the antiquary's delight, were then all fair with fresh stucco and painted beam; in the narrow roadway, shadowed by the upper stories, from which the inmates might exchange handkerchiefs and messages of love, passed the staid scholars and ruffling adventurers of Eliza's glorious age; and upon all smiled—as they still smile—the lofty steeples of Trinity and St. Michael's. Yet it was the Warwickshire of to-day—the land of Shakespeare, and Shakespeare still inglorious! Down the stately avenues, less stately then, but already avenues, went Philemon Holland to the unruined Kenilworth, late witness of Amy Robsart's beauty, and to the enduring splendours of Warwick. Wherever he paid his visits he was welcome, for was he not the scholar of whom all the county was proud? Was he not the kindly physician, who healed not for money, but for healing's sake?

A healer of the sick

So he tended the sick in charity, and grew poor. Wherever the pestilence raged, or fever burned, there went Holland, bringing with him the comfort of medicine and good counsel. But his worldly wisdom was not equal to his skill, and his reputation dwindled as his generosity increased. The great houses which received him as an eminent wit and renowned scholar were not disposed to trust his knowledge of physic, and Holland, still meeting the attack of poverty and disease, was driven for his own

TWELVE CÆSARS

safety to another profession. He became an usher, and for thirty years he instructed the youth of Coventry in sound theology and polite learning. The building wherein for so long he worked and taught still stands, though turned to baser uses; and the mere fabric, which now echoes to the raucous sound of popular psalmody, helps us to reconstruct the life of the ancient scholar. With the outward seeming of a Gothic church, the old school preserves its character of austere simplicity. Once were ranged within its walls the worn benches of poor and patient scholars. There in a corner stood the priceless library—now fallen into unutterable decay—whose volumes, then consulted by learned men, were presently torn for fire-lighting and meaner offices, and whose slim catalogue, written in a princely hand and bound in vellum, one would like to believe the handiwork of Holland. Pursuing scholarship, he cherished the fine ambition of making other scholars. Though he was but an usher in a free school, it was a distinction to be trained by his intelligence, and we hear of many a great nobleman whose tottering steps were first guided by the erudite Philemon. Thus George, Lord Berkeley, was at the age of twelve placed under his charge, and Lucius Cary, the great Lord Falkland, was a constant visitor at the school. Now Falkland's youth had been wild; he had been apt, saith report, 'to stab and do bloody mischief'; but he, too, falling under the sway of Holland, grew into a grave student. 'I have heard Dr. 'Ralph Bathurst say'—it is Aubrey who speaks—'that, ' when he was a boy, my Lord Falkland lived at Coventry ' (where he had then a house), and that he would sett up ' very late at nights at his study, and many times came to

INTRODUCTION

His career as usher

Some of his scholars

THE HISTORIE OF

INTRO-
DUCTION

'the library at the schoole there.' And though Holland did not live to witness his scholar's glorious death, he must have enjoyed a proper satisfaction in training the finest wit and most polished cavalier of his time.

The old library

Nor was Lord Falkland ill advised to resort to the library of Coventry School, for it was so well furnished, that it could hardly be matched outside London and the greater cities. But, alas! the eighteenth century respected not the patience and generosity of the past. The noble volumes, printed at the great presses of Europe, were heedlessly mutilated, and served as missiles for an idle generation of schoolboys, who knew not the example and the severity of Philemon Holland. The few poor relics which survive are a sad proof of excellence wantonly outraged, and if to-day they are beyond the reach of worse mutilation, the harm already done is irreparable. But in Holland's time the books were still fresh upon their shelves, and it is small wonder that in a panegyric of Coventry, presently quoted, he praises the city of his adoption for 'maintaining a faire Librarie, not exampled (without offence 'to others be it spoken) in many cities of the Realme.'

His honours and privileges

So for twenty years he taught school, a simple usher, yet dignified high above his common office. In 1612 he received the freedom of the city, an honour not generally conferred upon those who impart the elements. Five years later a yet higher privilege was reserved for him. King James paid a visit to his loyal citizens of Coventry, and Philemon Holland, who had already addressed a pious dedication to his Majesty, was appointed to receive the king in an appropriately pompous oration. That he acquitted himself

TWELVE CÆSARS

with glory is recorded in the Annals of Coventry, and assuredly he cut a very handsome figure. He was 'in a suite of black satten,' says the chronicle, and thus sumptuously arrayed at the cost of the city, which was so little niggardly that it spent upon its representative's apparel the round sum of £11, 1s. 11d. The oration is compacted of the familiar commonplaces. The orator compliments his sovereign in the well-known terms of extravagant adulation. He welcomes the king to Coventry on his 'safe returne out of your Noble united Realme of Scotland,' and though the piece lacks its author's characteristic ingenuity, it afterwards made a brave show on the bookseller's list,[1] and at any rate Philemon dressed the part admirably 'in black satten.'

But this was an interlude of greatness, and Holland awaited promotion for twenty years. Indeed, when at last promotion came, it found him unwilling or incompetent, and surely it should not have tarried so long. The doctor, in truth, had been famous beyond the limits of Coventry for a quarter of a century, when the following order of the Council House was signed on January 23rd, 1627-8: 'It is this ' daie agreed that Mr. Doctor Holland shalbe head Schoole-' maister of the free Grammar Schoole, of this Citie, so long ' as Mr. Maior and his brethren of this house please.' Doubt-

Introduction

His tardy promotion

---

[1] 'A Learned, Elegant, and Religious Speech, delivered unto his most ' excellent Majestie, at his late being at Coventry. By Philemon Holland, ' Dr. of Physicke, the Right Honourable Recorder his Deputie for the Time. ' When as his Royall Majestie was graciously pleased to grant and command ' the erecting of a Military Garden therein: And sithens, to enlarge the afore- ' said Cities Charter. . . . London. Printed by John Dawson for John ' Bellaine, and are to be sold at his shop at the two Greyhounds in Corne- ' hill, neere the Royall Exchange. 1622.'

THE HISTORIE OF

INTRO-DUCTION

less Mr. Mayor and his brethren would have pleased until the end, but Holland himself found his new office irksome. The honour, which might have flattered the scholar twenty years earlier, came too late. He was well past seventy; and however great was his ardour to frame scholars, he could not or would not govern the fortunes of a school. Ten months sufficed to weary him, and on November 26th, 'Doctor Holland came to this House'—so say the Annals —'and desired to leave the place of head Schoolemaister 'of the ffree Grammar Schoole of this Citie, and wished 'that in convenient tyme this House would provide another.' Whether or no he resumed his ancient office of usher is unknown; but it is certain that henceforth he fell upon poverty, and that the declining years of his life were spent in painful embarrassment.

His straitened old age

Disabled by age from travelling abroad, he could neither practise physic nor attend his pupils. He had sustained, moreover, a great charge of children, and his straitened circumstances were but the unhappy consequence of his lifelong devotion to charity and sound learning. Coventry came to his aid—in 1632—with an annual stipend of £3, 6s. 8d., not princely nor even sufficient, but at least a welcome recognition of his worth. Moreover, an appeal to his University was not unheard, and Henry Smyth, Master of Magdalen, and Vice-Chancellor, published in 1635 the

The University's answer to his appeal

quaint licence which here follows:—'In consideration of 'the learning and worthy parts of Dr. Philemon Holland, 'and in consideration of his want of means to relieve him 'now in his old age, I have given leave that he should 'receive such charitable benevolence as the Master and

TWELVE CÆSARS

INTRODUCTION

'Fellows in every College shall be pleased to bestow upon 'him.' The Vice-Chancellor was further persuaded to record that not only had Holland translated divers works, but that 'for sixty years he had kept good hospitality, *sit tota Coventria testis*,' and that therefore he was worthy an amiable consideration. One hopes that the appeal was generously answered, and that he who had done so much for learning received from the learned a generous recompense.

And so death found him, a grave and dignified scholar, full of years, and honoured in an honourable poverty. In the year 1637 'this eminent Translator,' to use Fuller's phrase, 'was translated to a better life.' Coventry proved her respect by a monument in Trinity Church, and it is to the city's eternal glory that she recognised a great man and worthy citizen in this simple maker of mighty folios. Nor was he ever behind in gratitude, and when—in 1609—he dedicated his *Ammianus Marcellinus* 'to the right wor- 'shipful the Mayor, and his Brethren, the Aldermen, etc., 'of the Citie of Coventry,' he composed such an eloquent tribute to his patrons as nobly repaid their respectful consideration. Therein he applauds the chief magistrate and grave senators of Coventry, first for their wise and moderate government of the place, 'which hath afforded unto him both quiet repose and meanes also to follow his studies'; and secondly, for the affectionate love they have always borne to good literature, a love 'testified by courteous 'entertainment of learned men; by competent salaries 'allowed from time to time to such professors as have 'peaceably and with discreet carriage bestowed their talents 'among you; by exhibitions given to poor scholars in the

The translator translated

The ties which bound him to Coventry

xiii

THE HISTORIE OF

INTRO-
DUCTION
'Universitie; by erecting also of late, and maintaining a fair Librarie, not exampled (without offence to others be it spoken) in many cities of the Realme.' Such the city and such the citizen, well matched in appreciation and attainment, in generosity and gratitude.

His portrait
A portrait published in a version of the *Cyropædia* shows us what manner of man the translator was in his old age. White hair and beard frame an oval face, and a large ruff encircles the scholar's neck. Small eyes, a fat nose, a lofty brow, an air of gravity—these are the outward characteristics of Philemon Holland. A quill-pen, held in his right hand, is a proper symbol of his devotion to letters.

and character
And as his portrait shows him, so we know him to have ambled through life. Always a recluse, shut up with his pens, which became fabulous, and his books, which were all of serious import, he went seldom abroad; and though his reception of James I. was a public triumph, his attempt to govern the Free School was, as we have seen, a dismal failure. In brief, he had no talent for affairs: his were the quieter virtues of kindliness and scholarship; so long as his strength endured, he carried healing and hospitality to the poor; and even when old age chained him to his bed, he preserved the vigour of his mind. His godson, after the gossiping fashion of the time, confided to Anthony à Wood

Philemon Angel's testimony
a sketch of manifest truth. 'His intellectuals and his 'senses,' wrote Philemon Angel, 'remained perfect until 'the eighty-fourth year of his age; and more especially 'his sight so good, that he never used spectacles in all his 'life; he was always of a spare and temperate diet, and 'seldom drank between meals. And was always of a peace-

TWELVE CÆSARS

'able and quiet spirit; and his life so innocent that he was **INTRO-**
'never in all his days either plaintiff or defendant in any **DUCTION**
'suit at law in any court (though he suffered sometimes
'by it). As a scholar he was a most reserved man, most
'indefatigable in his study, saying often, that there was
'no greater burden than idleness.' He drank not between
meals, and never wore spectacles—these are the details, so
well understood in the heyday of biography, which mark off
a man from all his fellows. But, indeed, Philemon Holland **The pedant**
might well interest the biographers, for he seemed the charac- **of his time**
teristic pedant of his generation, not dry and crotchety as the
pedant of to-day, but ripe and eloquent and quickened by
a sturdy love of noble words. Assuredly he was a scholar
dear to Aubrey and Anthony à Wood, such a one as for
Fuller was a true worthy; and since he makes no claim
upon our interest save by his scholarship, he represents his
age and his profession better than North, or any other of
his contemporaries.

He was, moreover, a man of clear opinion and wise view. **His**
Being a brave and loyal subject of Elizabeth, he was, for all **patriotism**
his seclusion, a sound patriot. 'Howsoever I have faulted,'
he writes in the Preface to his *Livy*, 'otherwise by over-
'sight, set against it my affection and desire to do some good
'whiles I live to my sweet native country.' If he faulted,
he faulted generously, and he needs no forgiveness at our
hands; but with these words he strikes the note of love for
his country which was struck as well by the captains as by
the poets of his time, and which has found its sincerest and
most glorious echo in these our own years. Again, he displayed a cunning ingenuity in unravelling the difficulties of

THE HISTORIE OF

His simple theology — dogma, then as now a delicate office. Science and theology were already at war, and though Holland, being a physician and a classic, might have been expected to flout orthodoxy, he deferred in all respect to the authority of divines. He prefaced his translation of Pliny, the most popular of his works, with an apology for his author's paganism. There is one scruple, he confesses, which troubles him not a little. He fears that Pliny, attributing so much to Nature, may seem to derogate from God, to the heathen ἄγνωστος; and since he would neither corrupt men's manners, nor prejudice the Christian faith, he conferred with sundry divines, who strengthened him in his purpose. Wherefore he resolved to finish the work which he had begun, that he might not 'defraud the world of so rich a gem for one small blemish appearing therein.' Such was his view of theology, a cautious mixture of common-sense and modesty. Nor does it differ widely from the prudence of to-day, which would claim a respect for both the houses. No doubt he himself was ranged on the side of science; but with a wise forethought he saw the danger of disturbing belief, and it was only after taking counsel with eminent divines that he deemed himself justified in dressing Pliny in an English habit.

'The Translator Generall in his age' — But before all things he was, in Fuller's phrase, 'the Translator Generall in his age.' North and Adlington are each the heroes of one book. Philemon Holland is a legend; as it were, translation made concrete. He won as great a fame by his splendid versions as have other men by their own invented fables. Epigrams were composed upon his fair achievements; his prowess was celebrated in

TWELVE CÆSARS

adulatory verses, and the single pen wherewith he indited a whole work has grown into a sort of fairy-tale. Moreover, the fairy-tale, like every piece of folk-lore, has its variants. The translator's son informs the world that *Plutarch's Morals* all fell upon paper from one quill, while Aubrey prefers to believe that it was the *Livy* which was thus honoured. Whichever be the truth, the story is found in all the books of anecdotes, further embellished with a quatrain, more amiable than accomplished. Thus it runs:— {INTRODUCTION. The fairy-tale of his pen}

> 'This booke I wrote with one poore Pen
> Made of a grey Goose Quill:
> A Pen I found it, us'd before,
> A Pen I leave it still.'

The pen's destiny also is variously described. Aubrey implies that it was presented to the Lady Harington, who 'embellished it with silver, and kept it among her rare κειμήλια'; while Henry Holland declares that it was 'begged by an ancient gentlewoman (mother of a noble 'Countesse yet living) who garnished it in silver, and kept 'it as a monument.' Fuller, on the other hand, gives a variant of his own, precise and circumstantial as the others. 'This Monumental Pen,' writes the author of the *Worthies*, 'he solemnly kept and showed to my reverend Tutor, 'Doctor Samuel Ward. It seems he leaned very lightly 'on the Neb thereof, though weightily enough, in another 'sense, performing not slightly, but solidly what he under- 'took.' If he kept it, you may be sure that he kept it 'solemnly,' and you smile at the moral tag which he as well deserved as Fuller could ill have avoided. But, indeed, his pen was something better than a mere piece {Its destiny}

THE HISTORIE OF

INTRO-DUCTION of folk-lore; in Holland's hand it was a cunning instrument. Once upon a time there existed in the library of Coventry School a manuscript of Euclid's *Harmonics* in the Doctor's own handwriting. And so beautiful was it, says rumour, that Baskerville, the prince of printers, imitated it for his own peerless Greek fount. But to-day it is impossible to confirm the rumour or to admire the caligraphy. For the only trace of Euclid's *Harmonics* is an entry in an ancient catalogue.

Holland's part in the re-birth of England 'The Translator Generall in his age'! And thus he lays claim to the genuine spirit of Elizabeth's reign. Thus he played his part in the re-birth of England. He, too, no less than Drake and Raleigh, was a gentleman adventurer; he, too, set sail to cross unknown seas to discover mysterious continents. **A literary captain** A literary captain, a scholarly pirate, he plundered strange realms, and never did he return from a voyage without a costly spoil. In his enterprise were displayed the recklessness and curiosity of a valiant generation, nor is it least characteristic of him that he regarded his conquests and the conquests of others as new-made citizens or the prisoners of peace. Livy, said he, has twice been 'enfranchised' by the French; and when he offers the proper meed of praise to Sir Thomas North, 'Plutarch,' he exclaims, **An apology for translation** 'has newly come to London.' And it was no mean task—the task of translation, to which he set himself; and, in truth, it needed no apology. Yet he spoke up for it with a wise enthusiasm in his preface to *Pliny*. 'All men,' said he, 'cannot *aut facere scribenda, aut scribere legenda.*' It was not for him to perform mighty deeds, nor to record the deeds of living heroes. So there remained only to give

TWELVE CÆSARS

another dress to the works of others, and this he did with an eloquence and a spirit which no man has ever surpassed.

    Though his own age accepted the gift he gave, there were yet cavillers, and Fuller was but a mouthpiece when he declared that 'some decry all Translators as Interlopers, 'spoiling the Trade of Learning, which should be driven 'among scholars alone.' But Fuller found a ready answer: 'This opinion,' said he, 'resents too much of envy, that 'such gentlemen who cannot repair to the Fountain, should 'be debarred access to the Stream.' So it was that Montaigne, who had no Greek, gave 'prick and praise unto Jacques Amyot'; for the wisdom of Plutarch was Montaigne's daily sustenance, and it was only in his compatriot's version that he could read the *Parallel Lives*. And nobly he justified his own lack of knowledge. 'We that are in the number of 'the ignorant,' wrote he, in a sort of apology, 'had been 'utterly confounded, had not his book raised us from the 'dust of ignorance. . . . Even Ladies are therewith able to 'confront Masters of Arts. It is our breviary.' Thus North's *Plutarch* was a breviary unto Shakespeare; thus Holland's masterpieces were breviaries unto many generations, and they have descended to us rich treasuries of sound English and wise interpretation.

    For Holland possessed all the rare and various gifts of the translator. To him no language came amiss; he had a marvellous skill in Latin and Greek, while Italian and French were as familiar as his own tongue. So while North could only rely upon Amyot, Holland could supplement a loyal study of the original with the borrowed wisdom of

Sidenotes: INTRODUCTION — Fuller's answer to the cavillers — and Montaigne's — Holland's various gifts

THE HISTORIE OF

INTRO-DUCTION

His skill in languages

foreign commentators. Wherefore, with a certain irony, he thus forestalls his critics. 'Have I varied in some places ' from the French or Italian?' he asks; 'censured I look to ' be, and haply reproved : but like as Alcibiades said to one, ' πάταξον οὖν καὶ ἄκουσον, i.e., strike hardly (*Euribiades*) ' *so you heare me speake*: even so say I; Find fault and spare ' not; but with al, read the original better before you give ' sentence.' None knew more clearly than he that few of his critics could read the original either better or worse, and he was right to entrench himself behind the original against the attacks of French or Italian. But he had a still higher qualification for his task than a knowledge of Greek and Latin. He was a master of robust and varied English. Like the best of his contemporaries, he ignored the commonness of speech. No man ever spoke as Holland wrote. Even when he is most familiar his periods pass like a pageant or march as armed men.

A master of English

His versions not literal

But well as he knew his original, majestically as he handled his own tongue, he made no attempt to fit the one to the other. His was not the ingenuity which would echo a foreign phrase in native English, and tried by the strictest standard of perfect consonance his translations fail of their effect. He did not put Livy and Suetonius in an appropriate dress; rather he took Suetonius or Livy, and tricked them out in the garb of his own time. So that he gives us not an accurate reflection of the original, but a quick vision of Livy or Suetonius as they might have been had they been born in Elizabethan England. His commentary upon his own style is an astounding piece of criticism, and at the same time an intimate revelation of

TWELVE CÆSARS

seventeenth-century prose. 'According to this purpose and
'intent of mine I frame my pen,' so he writes, 'not to any
'effective phrase, but to a mean and popular style, wherein,
'if I have called again into use some old words, let it be
'attributed to the love of my country-language: if the
'sentence be not so concise, couched and knit together as
'the original, loth I was to be obscure and darke: have I not
'Englished every phrase aptly? each nation hath several
'manners, yea, and terms appropriate by themselves.'

There in a nutshell is Holland's theory of style and translation. He believed (what man ever knew himself?) that he was writing in a mean and popular style! And so ill-grounded was his belief, that you have but to compare his magnificent periods with the pamphlets of his time, to realise the splendour of his manner, the effectiveness of his phrase. His love of old words, on the other hand, is apparent and honourable. Old they were then! How much older and more dignified do they appear to-day! And how severe a reproach is this one phrase of an ancient master to those shallow, ignorant critics—loquacious in our midst—who assert that no word is admissible in written English which they themselves do not employ in their ill-done, ungrateful task of journey-work! But when, again, Holland confesses his prose less concise than the original, he puts his finger upon a true quality, whether a vice or virtue. Never is he 'knit together' with the precision of his Latin or his Greek. He embroiders his author with a freedom and liveliness which are delightful and (maybe) inapposite. When he is at work, Pliny and Plutarch are poured into the same mould, and, different as is the prime

THE HISTORIE OF

material, they both take on the admirable shape of their doughty translator. Thus it is that Holland based his practice upon his theory; and whether or no you approve the reasoning, you must needs acknowledge the splendour of the result.

In brief, he translated well, because he wrote admirably. His style was so much a part of himself, that he sacrificed in his versions the subtlety of imitation. His prefaces are master-pieces of good judgment and sound English. Here, for instance, is a sketch of Padua, the birthplace of Livy, fashioned with all his plenitude of phrase and sound: ' My ' purpose is not here to enter into a large field and rhetori-' cal discourse of his praises in regard of any gifts of fortune ' wherewith he was plentifully enriched: namely the place ' of his nativity, a city more ancient by 400 years than ' Rome, flourishing in martial puissance, able to set out and ' maintain 100,000 fighting men for the wars; in stately ' port at home; having a nobility of 400 in number; in ' gorgeous and costly buildings; in traffic and frequent ' affluence of merchants thither; as also, that Venice was a ' Colony deducted and drawn from thence; and which is not ' the least, how at this day the famous University there, ' affordeth excellent professors in all kind of learning.'

In such terms he set forth the excellences of the city, and it is not surprising that his translations are brilliant with purple patches. Turn, for instance, to Hannibal's passage of the Alps, and you will find not Livy but a masterpiece of English. Or, if you be so minded, glance at Plutarch's essays *On Curiosity* or *On Superstition*, and you will delight not in the cold phrase of Plutarch, but in a piece of learned

TWELVE CÆSARS

English, which seems the near forerunner of Burton's own *Anatomy*. And thus we arrive at the best measure of his talent: with leisure and opportunity he might have been a Montaigne or a Burton. He, too, might have woven the woof of research into the web of fancy. He, too, might have lived in a tower, or a college room, and eked out a sluggish imagination with apt quotings from recondite or forgotten authors. All the materials of an original masterpiece are there—style, erudition, curiosity; but he preferred the pedestrian office of the translator, and he succeeded so well that in his own lifetime he conquered an easy fame, and that immortality, the shyest of the demons, has not remained deaf to his call. *INTRODUCTION — His possibilities*

Thomas Fuller, who occupied himself most amiably with Philemon Holland, declared that 'the Books alone of his 'Turning into English will make a Country Gentleman a 'competent library for Historians.' Nowadays it is something of a disgrace in a book to be indispensable to a gentleman's library; but in Fuller's day, culture was not yet the possession of the people, and the compliment was sincerely paid. The works of Holland might then, and still may, complete a noble bookcase. His originals, as they were admirably turned, were wisely chosen. First came the monumental *Livy*—in 1600—dedicated in terms of customary adulation to Queen Elizabeth. He modestly describes his performance as the first fruits of a few years' 'study,' and he begs the most gracious Lady to accept them 'for the benefit enjoyed of life and liberty.' Thereafter he acclaims 'the 'incomparable perfections resplendent in your Royal person: 'the wonder of the World.' But no man had more securely *Fuller's opinion — The Livy — Its dedication*

THE HISTORIE OF

Introduction

The Pliny

the gift of Euphuistic English, and his dedications are one and all noble exercises in the art of adulation. Within a single year came the vast folio, *Pliny*, whose bulk alone is an eloquent tribute to the author's energy and patience. Inscribed in the general terms of flattery to the Right Honourable Sir Robert Cecil, it was prefaced by admirable discourses upon theology and the art of translation. The author precisely chimed with the curious spirit of the age, and it is no wonder that this one of Holland's works was the most popular.

Plutarch's Morals

Then followed a third vast folio, the *Morals of Plutarch*, addressed in a piece of amazing prose to James I., whom he describes as his 'dear Lord and dread Sovereign.' The opening is so fantastic and withal so characteristic of the writer, that it stands here as a specimen of Jacobean extravagance. 'In this general joy of affec-
'tionate and loyal subjects,' thus begins the learned doctor, 'testified by their frequent confluence from all
' parts, longing for nothing so much as the full fruition
' of that beautiful Star, which lately upon the shutting in
' of evening with us after our long Summer's day, immedi-
' ately by his radiant beams maintained still a twilight from
' the North, and within some few hours appeared bright
' shining above our Horizon, suffering neither the dark night
' and confused CHAOS of ANARCHY to overspread and sub-
' vert, nor the turbulent tempests and bloody broils of
' factious sidings to trouble and subvert our state: I also
' for my part could not stay behind, but in testimony of
' semblable love and allegiance shew myself; and withal,
' most humbly present unto your Highness this PHILOSOPHY

TWELVE CÆSARS

'of Plutarch.' In such terms did conscious merit address itself to the throne of royalty, when James I. was king; and that such extravagance is not permitted to-day, is due not to a lofty regard for the literal truth, but to a pitiful incapacity to frame so grandiose a period.

But Holland never fell below the proper level of eloquence, and his *Suetonius* (1606), of which more presently, was dedicated with a rare propriety to the Lady Harington. Nor even now have we completed the tale of his works. Such trifles as *Ammianus Marcellinus*, Camden's *Britannia*, and the *Cyropædia* were also Englished after his imperial manner. And we must not forget his single incursion into what for him must have appeared light literature. Once even he condescended to translate that strange compost of medicine and superstition, *Regimen Sanitatis Salerni*, or, in his own phrase, 'the Schoole of Salernes Regiment of 'Health, containing most learned and judicious directions, 'and instructions, for the Preservation, Guide and Govern-'ment of Man's Life.' The book's simple rules, which you may be sure the old scholar followed himself, are translated into a simple doggrell. Here is a sample:—

> 'Shun Busie cares, rash angers, which displease,
> Light supping, little drink, do cause great ease.'

It is poor stuff, and the Doctor too willingly indorses the mediæval nostrums. But this was the mere diversion of a serious mind, and does not lighten by an ounce the writer's grave reputation. He still remains the first translator of his age; and if the Bible is the Shakespeare of translation, then Philemon Holland is the ingenious Ben Jonson of a splendid craft.

THE HISTORIE OF

II

The Suetonius

But the *Suetonius*, here reprinted, is the finest fruit of his toil, and the reason is not far to seek. Holland did not so much translate as compose an original work upon a given theme, and Suetonius was a theme which appealed to his profoundest sympathy. Indeed, the author of the *Twelve Cæsars* was quickened by the self-same spirit which quickened the biographers of Holland's own time. His genius was a genius of anecdotage, and nothing was essential to his purpose save such facts as appear trivial to the pedantic historian. We may ransack antiquity in vain to find his equal, but we shall easily recognise in the *Athenæ Oxonienses* the love of scandal and intimate infirmities, which gives a very present life and energy to his immortal book. As we read the *Twelve Cæsars*, we forget that they were Emperors; we are persuaded at every line that they were men, and, maybe, monsters of iniquity. For to Suetonius the greatest hero was made of common (or of uncommon) clay; or at any rate he assumed the heroism as familiar, and explained with infinite pleasure and circumstance that Emperors are memorable for intrigue, infirmity, and crime. He was possessed, in truth, with the indefatigable curiosity of the modern journalist; nothing was sacred from his prying eye; and he gathered in his facts with the reporter's own superficial love of facts for their own sake, and without the lightest regard to their social or historical import.

Holland's sympathy with his author

The curiosity of Suetonius

Yet it is not for us to resent the shamelessness of his method. Many a vice is converted by the centuries into

TWELVE CÆSARS

a shining virtue, and Paul Pry, an odious figure to-day, may appear to-morrow the fearless benefactor of posterity. Time has the trick of hallowing even gossip, and there is no detail so trivial and so impertinent but it appears interesting, nay sacred, in the biography of a man long since dead. Thus we are constrained to admire in the past that which we deprecate in the present; and if the present eavesdroppers make conquest of immortality, our remote descendants will no doubt welcome their indiscretions as an invaluable commentary, though they too will deplore most strenuously their own contemporary gossips.

And there is a perfect logic in the apparent contradiction. We lose the habit of censoriousness with the years, and we palliate in the dead those vices and follies for which we would cut a living man. Moreover, the libel law looks not beyond the grave; and though at the moment of writing his book Suetonius deserved the pillory, he has won at last an admiring appreciation. But it is his conspicuous merit that he drew a series of individual portraits; there is not one of his Emperors who is not separated from his fellows rather by the peculiar frailties of his temper than by any public achievement. 'Art,' says M. Marcel Schwob in a luminous essay on Biography, 'is opposed to general ideas; it desires only the unique'; or in other words, *il ne classe pas, il déclasse*. Conquest does not set a peculiar stamp upon a man; intellect defies the resources of skilful portraiture. And these truths were ever present to Suetonius, who selected for his illustration the facts which the more princely historian rejects with scorn. For instance, his admiration of

THE HISTORIE OF

INTRO-DUCTION Augustus is generous and sincere; he applauds his administration, and gives full credit to his sense of justice; but, having finished with his public life, he bids us pay a visit (as it were) to the man himself, and reveals to us not only his thought but the ordering of his daily life.

Augustus the man All thought of the politician, the prig, the literary patron, vanishes in an instant. No longer are we contemplating the hero who found Rome brick and left it marble; but a Roman citizen of the first century, whose trivial tastes and fancies seem worth recording. Thus (we are told) he slept always on a low bed, and wore no apparel **His apparel** that was not of housewife's cloth, spun at home by the women of his family. In the winter he clad himself stoutly against the cold, putting on as many as four coats, and a waistcoat of wool; and he had so great a fear of the sun, that even at home he always kept upon his head a broad-brimmed hat. Careless of elegance as he was in his dress, he chose his shoes with much circumspection, underlaying the soles that he might appear taller than he **His diet** was. At table, though he ate little meat, he was a gross feeder—bread, small fishes, cheese, and green figs being most to his taste. But it was not his custom to wait for the meal-time; rather he would eat whenever his stomach called for food. A small drinker, he delighted most in Rhætian wine; and he seldom drank between meals. He preferred a sop of bread soaked in cold water, or a piece of cucumber, or a young lettuce-head, or some new-gathered apple, sharp and tart.

His appearance, if not precisely handsome, was surely

TWELVE CÆSARS

distinguished. 'He had a pair of clear and shining eyes,' says Suetonius in the English of Holland; 'wherein also (as he would have made men believe) was seated a kind of divine vigour: and he joyed much, if a man looking wistly upon him held down his face, as if it were against the brightness of the sun. But in his old age he saw not very well with his left eye. His teeth grew thin in his head, and the same were small and ragged. The hair of his head was somewhat curled and turning downward, and withal of a light yellow colour. His eyebrows met together; his ears were of a mean bigness; his nose both in the upper part, bearing out round, and also beneath somewhat with the longest. Of colour and complexion, he was between a brown and a fair white. His stature but short.' There he is painted, with all his imperfections, by the hand of a faithful artist, who knew not how to conceal the truth. It may be something of a shock to hear that the Divine Augustus saw not well with his left eye, that his teeth were small and ragged; yet it is to his greater glory that he should be drawn as a man, than represented in the guise of a graven image with a marble intelligence and a mechanical gesture.

INTRODUCTION
The Emperor's aspect

But the portraiture of Suetonius does not cease here: he heightens the effect by a hundred other intimate touches. For instance, the Celestial Bear (says he) was marked upon the Emperor's breast, and he was not very sound in his left hucklebone. Moreover, the forefinger of his right hand was so weak, that at times he could scarcely write, even with the help of a finger-stall of horn. And no less curious is Suetonius when he records the qualities of the Augustan

His intimate peculiarities

THE HISTORIE OF

INTRODUCTION

His tricks of speech

mind. He saves from oblivion a dozen tricks of style and speech, which seem to bring the man even more vividly before us than his limping leg or failing speech. Thus, when the Emperor pointed to those who would never pay their debts, he was wont to say, 'They will pay at the Greek Calends.' For Augustus, too, loved his little joke. And did he wish to express the speed of something over-hastily accomplished, 'It was quicker done,' he would exclaim, 'than asparagus is boiled.' Again, he would substitute *baceolus* for *stultus*, *vacerrosus* for *cerritus*; and while others employed the phrase *male se habere*, he by a euphemism would say *vapide*. Trivial differences are they all, but it is by trivial differences of speech that the individual is recognised, and it is to great purpose that Suetonius has preserved these subtle traits that the more earnest chronicler proudly despises.

The Imperial view of style

But Augustus, amid the manifold duties of an empire, found time also for the cultivation of literature, and his views concerning the Latin tongue, if not always wise, were stoutly maintained. He preferred prepositions to case-endings, we are told, and for the sake of clarity he would repeat his conjunctions very often. So he forestalled the development of language, and by an act of prophecy compelled Latin to initiate a practice which all the modern tongues have followed. Moreover, being a practical politician, rather than an artist in speech, he detested 'the stinking savours of dark and obscene words.' Strange expressions, either new or old, were distasteful to him; and it was one of his pastimes to gibe his friend Mæcenas, that prince of dilettanti, for his *myrobrechos cincinnos*, and even to compose parodies of his conceited style. Little concern

TWELVE CÆSARS

have these entertaining details with politics; but they are the very elements of character; and so it is that while Pericles is a splendid abstraction, the Roman Emperor appears, after nineteen centuries, an intelligent and wayward human being.

Augustus is treated no better than the rest, and there is not one of the Twelve who does not masquerade before us in dressing-gown and slippers. And what a magnificent material did Suetonius choose whereon to exercise his genius! It was a period of colossal enterprise and savage lust. The old austerity was dead, and the modern world had not yet learned the lesson of restraint. The vastest empire, save one, which a triumphant energy has ever fashioned, had succeeded to the policy of small states. A hundred wealthy colonies poured into Rome a willing tribute. Military glory was aided by an unparalleled talent for administration. As no land seemed too distant to subdue, so none was too wild for civilisation. The progress of victorious armies was marked by the more lasting achievements of peaceful ingenuity. The modern general lays his railroad as he goes; the Roman warrior, inspired by a similar wisdom, threaded the desert by an imperishable highway. Wherever a river was to be spanned, he threw across it a bridge which has defied the shocks of storm and tide. He carried the gift of pure water from hill to hill on the giant aqueducts which attest to-day the Roman omnipotence. The known world was but a network of Imperial roads, and an army might march without impediment from York to Jerusalem. Meanwhile the wealth of tribute gave the Emperors means and opportunity to indulge their vices and

INTRODUCTION

Suetonius's material

The vast empire

The vaster vices

xxxi

THE HISTORIE OF

<small>INTRO-
DUCTION</small>
pamper their appetites. And surely they rose one and all to the height of the occasion. The masterpiece of Suetonius might bear for a sub-title: 'the grosser Passions delineated,' for, in truth, there is no passion, no vice, that does not find itself personified in one or other of the Twelve. To us it appears remarkable that so much wickedness should be concentrated in so few monarchs. But lack of habit accounts for much, and may be it is natural that the Romans, for centuries accustomed to the Republican ideal, should interpret callously the advantages of a tyranny. Here were a set of men, trained to believe in equality, suddenly raised to the summit of divine honours. And with the aid of that monstrous corruption which is the birthright of Cosmopolis, they invented vices, as their generals annexed provinces.

<small>Even Julius
besmirched</small>
So Suetonius spared no single one of the Emperors. He lays a blasphemous hand on the great Julius himself. If he does not see in this splendid hero the greatest general, the wisest statesman, the finest historian that the world has known, he yet esteems his virtues, and does all the justice of which his unemotional temper is capable to his illustrious qualities. But the chance of scandal cannot be resisted, and Suetonius omits not even the scurrilous verses of the time. However, it is with Tiberius that the biographer finds his real talent. The description of the voluptuary's *sæva ac lenta natura* ($\pi\eta\lambda\grave{o}\nu$ $\alpha\H{\iota}\mu\alpha\tau\iota$ $\pi\epsilon\phi\nu\rho\mu\acute{\epsilon}\nu o\nu$) is nothing less than stupendous. The Emperor who appointed a new officer of state, *a voluptatibus*, easily surpassed the Marquis <small>The insanity
of Tiberius</small> de Sade in ingenious cruelty. Whether or no the sojourn at Capri be faithfully described, it remains an insurpassable record of wild insanity, until at the last the Emperor ceases

TWELVE CÆSARS

to be human. Tacitus himself had no love of Tiberius, yet his loftier portrait is also more convincing. The man of weak will and clear perception is a psychological possibility; and while in the page of Tacitus Tiberius is a figure of austere tragedy, in Suetonius he is but a bogey of disgust, a common epitome of the vices. INTRO-
DUCTION

And so the vain and brutish Caligula, who believed that in gathering shells he was wresting the spoils of Ocean, who designed a horse for the consulship, and who could scarcely dine without the excitement of carnage, is followed by the stealthy Claudius, who, despite his erudition and tact of government, loved nothing so much as the contemplation of dying gladiators, and who died in a welter of blood. Then comes Nero, fit subject for Suetonius, professional poisoner and amateur of the arts, who delighted in gold fish-nets and silver-shod mules, who sang his own songs 'with a small and rusty voice,' and who really believed that with his death there died an artist. So Galba's misery is matched by the gluttony of Vitellius, and even the wisdom of Vespasian is balanced by a hungry covetousness. Titus escapes easily with the semblance of too fine a virtue; and since Suetonius is resolved that the Emperors shall be remembered by vice or triviality, Domitian is sent down to posterity as the fly-catcher. The excesses
of the others

Meanwhile, under Claudius and Nero, the mighty Empire grows in strength, and Suetonius does not note it. In his page the drum is not beaten, the trumpet blares not. When he might present to the world a great historical drama, he prefers to play the tragi-comedy of cruelty and lust. The triumph of engineers is as little to him as the courage of No history
of drum and
trumpet

e   xxxiii

THE HISTORIE OF

<small>INTRO-
DUCTION</small>

<small>Tacitus and
Suetonius</small>

<small>The sagacity
of the *Annals*</small>

armies. True, he records without sequence or statistics the mere events of each reign; but his curiosity is for passion, not statesmanship, and he is only himself when, forgetting the march of Empire, he sits him down to enumerate the follies and vices of his heroes. Tacitus, of course, invites a comparison, and in these two—Suetonius and Tacitus—are illustrated the opposing methods of history. The author of the *Annals*, that he may set forth his country's omnipotence with a proper reverence for truth, is deaf to the frail, delightful voice of hearsay. Though he has no ardent love for his Empire, yet he understands its strength and its weakness, and he displays its achievements with an absolute regard for the claims of proportion. A rarely wise man, he knows most things, and what he does not know he easily divines. And as you read him, you recognise that he is not only relating the story of one period: he is opening a treasure-house of political sagacity, from which the statesmen of all ages may enrich themselves. More than this, he is a master of style and irony; with four words he can sketch a situation or enunciate a policy. He who wrote, 'They make a solitude and call it peace,' has nothing to learn in the art of expression, and it is the good fortune of the world that the most puissant writer of all time should have elected to write the history of the most puissant age. But Tacitus merely affords a general confirmation of Suetonius. His material is so far loftier, that they rarely meet upon a common ground. The one strikes the stars, while the other crawls upon the earth. Yet for the very reason that they live and work at different levels, the one supplements the narrative of the other. To doubt the

TWELVE CÆSARS

infinite superiority of Tacitus would be to laugh at the truth. One might as well prefer a common memoir to the Hamlet of Shakespeare. Tacitus is a philosopher, with a godlike understanding, who compels conviction while he dazzles the judgment. He lectures you in the staid and noble dialect of omniscience, and to miss a phrase is to confuse the argument. Suetonius, on the other hand, has no ambition of politics or philosophy. He is but a shambling old gossip, who sits over the fire and entertains the first comer with the stories his grandfather told him when he was a boy. (*Sed avum meum narrantem puer audiebam*, says he, in the phrase of the true gossip.) For our guidance he provides nothing, for our amusement much; and it is small wonder that while we render all our respect to Tacitus, we turn more often to Suetonius, that he may beguile our leisure. We cannot always rest at the cold and splendid altitudes of thought; it is seldom that we cannot enjoy a crack across the hearth with a master of scandal.

The question arises: Was Suetonius moved by malice or by love of truth in the selection of his material? And the answer comes that he is never convicted of the worse motive. At the same time, it is evident that he had a natural love for whatever was curious and abnormal. Let us suppose that all facts are of equal value, and we must confess that the historian's interest is mirrored in his choice. So Suetonius found food for reflection in the decaying morality of the Empire, and he reported that which he heard and knew with a perfect impartiality. He held a brief for nobody; and if he ever felt the prick of political animosity, he is careful to conceal the wound. Averse from

INTRODUCTION

The gossip of the Twelve Cæsars

Suetonius not malicious

THE HISTORIE OF

<small>INTRO-
DUCTION</small>

flattery, he closed his history at the death of Domitian; and there is not a single word in his book that impugns his honesty.

<small>His passion
for accuracy</small>

He had, on the contrary, a passion for accuracy, and while he suppresses his judgment he parades his facts. As a writer, he is clear rather than distinguished, and his single preoccupation is to express his meaning with a just simplicity. Where Latin fails him, he falls back upon Greek; and as he was a master of both tongues, he could at will double his vocabulary.

<small>The man
himself</small>

Of the man we know little enough, and that little wholly to his credit. By profession an advocate and writer, he discharged the office of secretary to Hadrian, and left behind him one immortal work. His peace was disturbed by an unhappy marriage, on which account he demanded, with faulty logic, the *jus trium liberorum*. These scanty rumours, with two passages in Pliny, complete our poor information. But Pliny's affection may be cited for the confusion of those who are persuaded by his outspokenness to belittle his character and flout his sincerity. 'He was my comrade,' says Pliny, 'and the companion of my school-days.' And thereafter, in a letter to Trajan, Pliny declares him the most upright, honest, and learned man that ever he had met, and that he loved him the more the more closely he came to know him. So once again we must separate the man from his work, and feel no surprise that an amiable scholar should have recorded faithfully and without shrinking the vices and frailties of the Roman Emperors.

<small>Pliny's
eulogy</small>

Such the writer and such the book which Philemon Holland elected to translate in the plenitude of his talent.

TWELVE CÆSARS

As has been said, he rather transformed than translated it; for, however akin to his own curiosity was the matter of this amazing book, the curt, crabbed, even brutal style of Suetonius was wholly alien from Holland's elaborate eloquence. For Holland (as we have seen) loved to adorn a simple statement, to turn it about in a dozen different attitudes, to trick it out with the rich frippery of Elizabethan English. Nor did he scruple to embellish and increase his author beyond recognition. In mere bulk his version must surely double the original. Here is one instance of many: 'Jacta est alea,' exclaimed Cæsar as he crossed the Rubicon. 'The dice be thrown,' translates Holland; 'I have set up my rest; come what will of it.' It is magnificent, but it is not the polite echo of the accurate translator. However, Holland's object was to employ all the resources of his own splendid prose; and he employs them to such admirable purpose, that you may read his *Suetonius* in perfect forgetfulness of the Latin and in perfect satisfaction with the rise and fall of the majestic periods. The masterpiece is dedicated 'to the Right Honorable and Vertuous Ladie, the Ladie Harington,' and the inscription proves that Holland had no ill thought of the book's brutality, though he does presently declare that Suetonius penned the lives of Princes, *eadem libertate qua ipsi vixerunt*. 'If haply in pro-
' secuting this point,' says he, ' he hath recorded aught that
' may be offensive to chaste and modest minds, ye shall do
' well to glance over with your eye such places lightly, as
' I with my pen touched unwillingly.' Furthermore, he tells us that the work was composed during the last pestilence in Coventry, 'for being altogether restrained then from free

Side notes: INTRODUCTION — Holland's version — Its embellishment — Its dedication

TWELVE CÆSARS

<small>INTRO-
DUCTION</small>

'practise of my profession abroad, and no less impatient of 'idlenesse at home, I could not readily think of a better 'course to spend that vacation, than in an argument having 'a reference to mine old grammatical Muses, and according, 'in some sort, with my later studies in Physic.'

<small>The
translator's
erudition</small>

So he composed the work for 'the benefit of young scholars,' and truly the pathology of the Cæsars might most properly call forth his medical knowledge. Moreover, he equipped his version with a set of notes which are often inapposite, but always erudite with the quaint erudition of his century. Alone of the Elizabethan translators, he can refer with confidence to original authorities, and sprinkle his pages with quotations from Josephus and Aulus Gellius. Nor does he neglect such more modern writers as Beroaldus and Casaubon, and he never lets slip a vague chance of discoursing upon his own art of medicine. But author and theme are perfectly matched, and it is a genuine pleasure to read Suetonius's masterpiece of familiar scandal echoed thus pompously in the sounding prose of Philemon Holland.

CHARLES WHIBLEY.

NOTE

This Edition of the Twelve Cæsars is reprinted from the Editio Princeps of 1606

THE HISTORIE OF
TWELVE CÆSARS
EMPEROURS OF ROME
WRITTEN IN LATINE BY
C. SUETONIUS TRANQUILLUS
AND NEWLY TRANSLATED INTO ENGLISH
BY PHILÊMON HOLLAND
DOCTOR IN PHYSICKE

TOGEATHER WITH A MARGINALL GLOSSE, AND OTHER BRIEFE ANNOTATIONS THERE-UPON

1606

References in *letters* (ᵃ ᵇ ᶜ etc.) are to the Annotations at the end of the volume. References in *figures* (¹ ² ³ etc.) are to Notes at the foot of the page, which are printed in the original edition as a marginal gloss.

TO THE READERS

HAT yee may with better contentment reade these Historicall reports of the twelve first Ceasars, which Suetonius hath delivered most truely, compiled as compendiously, and digested right methodically, I have thought it good with some few advertisments præmised, to commend the same unto you.

First therefore, whereas by the judgement of the best learned, and the Analogie of other Histories, hee seemeth to affect nothing so much as uncorrupt and plaine trueth, (the principall vertue of an Historiographer) forbearing to meddle with those Emperours[1] in whose daies he flourished; because he would not thrust himselfe into danger by revealing, nor betray the libertie of a writer in concealing the faults, much lesse incurre the note of Flatterie, extolling above measure the good parts of Princes then living; and to that purpose penned their lives, who were lately deceased, as one said very well, *eadem libertate qua ipsi vixerunt*: if happlie in prosecuting of this point, he hath recorded ought that may be offensive to chast and modest mindes, yee shal do well to glaunce over with your eye such places lightly, as I with my pen touched unwillingly.

Secondly, forasmuch as he continueth in generall the Narrations of the said Princes, from before their Nativitie unto their Death and Funerals: and in the severall discourses, of their ages, affaires, vertues, vices, feature and lineaments of bodie, first, after an uniform maner, proposeth throughout certain heads summarily, and then exemplyfieth

---

[1] Nerva, Trajanus, and Hadrianus, whose secretarie he was.

THE HISTORIE OF

TO THE READERS

the same in due order by perticulers (a most lightsome method and way of teaching) keeping him selfe still to the Subject matter, without any digressions at all: my advise is, that for your more expedite course in reading the whole, yee direct your minde thereunto. Now, for that his Julius Ceasar sorteth not with the rest, but appeareth ἀκέφαλος, as whose aunceestours, birth, childhoode, etc. be not set downe, (which maime I impute rather to the injurie of time, than unto the purpose or oversight of the Authour) I have in some sort supplyed that defect, with the labours of Lewis Vives, Torrentius and others, which I finde præfixed in the last and best Editions.

Thirdly, considering that brevitie is many times the mother of Obscuritie, may it please those among you, who are not so conversant in such concise writings, as admit not one word superfluous, to have recourse, for the clearing of some doubts unto the margin, as also to those briefe Annotations, which for their sakes, out of mine owne readings, together with the select observations of Beroaldus, Sabellicus, Torrentius and Casaubonus I have collected. Which also will ease them of many difficulties that his succinct style and termes, not elswhere obvious, interlaced, may otherwise breed.

Finally, if there happen to occur some Errata, that might escape either my pen in writing, or the ordinarie diligence of meane Correctors in the printing, ye will of your judicious candour, I hope, either passe them over with connivency, if they be literall, or else taxe with some easie censure in case they bee materiall: so long as for your full satisfaction, ye may with small paines before yee begin either to read or judge, correct what is amisse, according to the Examen and Review annexed to the end of all. Farewell.

TWELVE CÆSARS

To the Right Honorable and Vertuous Ladie
THE LADIE HARINGTON

MADAME, the late pestilence in Coventrie, which occasioned my translation etc. of this Historie, moved me also, in part, to addresse the same unto your Honour.

For being altogether restrained then, from free practise of my profession abroad, and no lesse impatient of idlenesse at home, I could not readily thinke of a better course to spend that vacation, than in an Argument having a reference to mine old Grammaticall Muses, and according, in some sort, with my latter studies in Physick. What howres, therfore, either the doubtful or diseased estate of my neighbours, together with the meditations of mine owne mortalitie would afford, I employed gladly in the said Subject.

Againe, for as much as the selfe same cause debarred me from accesse unto your house at Combe (a dutie that otherwise the vicinitie of our aboad did require) I fully resolved at the

THE HISTORIE OF

THE EPISTLE DEDICATORY

finishing of those my Sedentary labours, to present the same to your view: therby to sheild my selfe (whom it pleased you beforetime to grace with kind entertainment) from the just imputation of rude negligence in that behalfe. But now, since the same citie so dangerous the yeare before, is become a retyring place of safety for your Houshold, and hath to mee alreadie yeelded fit opportunitie to excuse my former absence personally by word of mouth, I have presumed nevertheles to dedicate the same unto your Honour, as a token of my thankefulnesse for your bounteous favour, farre above the proportion of my deserts, and an earnest penny of that propense minde, which I carie to honour your name, in the best maner I could devise.

And verily calling to my remembrance how courteously you have vouchsafed heretofore to accept even at second hand my travailes in this kinde, and with good words testified oftentimes the contentment you received therin, I had no reason to doubt the like acceptance of that which out of a loving and devote heart I offer first unto your selfe.

Lastly, when I consider, how together with sincere pietie, rare wisdome, and other eminent vertues, there is seated in your person a singular

TWELVE CÆSARS

affection to advance good literature, with an extraordinarie respect of learned men, I knew no means out of my small fortunes to do you greater honour, than by entituling you as Patronesse of that, which may benefit young Scholers, my countrimen, that would be learned: to give knowledge unto the word, that all the profit or pleasure whatsoever, which shall grow unto them, from these endeavours of mine, are derived immediatly from you and for your sake bestowed upon them.

These motives, right Honorable, as well of my first enterprise, as of chusing your Patronage, if it please you to approve, (the onely thing that I humbly crave at your hand for this present) I shall not only thinke my pains well taken and choise as well made: prising your acceptance to the worth of a competent guerdon: but also continue my hearty prayers unto the Almightie for your perfect health, proceeding in a vertuous course of life, with increase of true Honour here upon earth, and after the revolution of many new yeares, for eternall happinesse in the highest Heaven.

Your Honours most readie at command,

PHILEMON HOLLAND.

THE HISTORIE OF

THE TABLE

	PAGE
A SUPPLEMENT TO THE BEGINNING OF C. JULIUS CEASAR, DICTATOR . .	9
CAIUS JULIUS CESAR, DICTATOR . .	15
OCTAVIUS CÆSAR AUGUSTUS . .	81
TIBERIUS NERO CÆSAR . . .	170
ANNOTATIONS UPON C. JULIUS CÆSAR, DICTATOR	231
ANNOTATIONS UPON OCTAVIUS AUGUSTUS CÆSAR	249
ANNOTATIONS UPON TIBERIUS NERO CÆSAR	274

TWELVE CÆSARS

A SUPPLEMENT TO THE BEGINNING OF C. JULIUS CEASAR DICTATOR

HE Julian linage, as most men are perswaded, is descended from Ascanius Jülus, the sonne of Æneas by Creusa: which Jülus, after he had left Lavinium, built long Alba: wherein also he reigned. Others, grounding upon a more assured evidence, have thought it good to derive the same rather from Jülus the son of Ascanius. For when after the death of (this) Ascanius, the Kingdome of the Latines was devolved againe¹ upon Sylvius the sonne of Æneas and Lavinia, the charge of Religion and sacred ceremonies of the Latin and Trojan Nation both, remained yet still in the race and progenie of Jülus: out of which are sprung the Julii. These (Julii) with certaine other most noble families of Latium, Tullus Hostilius King of the Romanes, after he had rased Alba, translated to Rome, and raunged among the Nobilitie. Late it was, ere they rose and mounted to high place of Magistracie; but were reckoned almost in the last ranke of the Patritians of aunceint Nobilitie: and of them, the Jüli bare the principall name. For C. Julius, (sonne of Lucius) surnamed also Jülus, was Consull together with P. Pinarius Mamercinus Rufus, in the yeare after the foundation of Rome citie 264². And seaven yeeres after³, his sonne⁴, with Q. Fabius Vibulanus (Consull) the second time. Againe, some space of time comming betweene,

---

¹ Or returned unto. annexed unto Titus Livius. Cassiodorus and others.
² Or rather 265, according to the Chronology
³ By the computation of Dionysius, T. Livius,
⁴ C. Julius, or Jülus.

THE HISTORIE OF

A SUPPLE- MENT

Vopiscus Julius, sonne of Caius and Nephew of Lucius, bare the Consulshippe with L. Æmilius Mamercinus [1] third time Consull, in the yeere 280 [2]. I finde likewise, that in the yeere 302 [3] Caius Julius, sonne of Caius, and nephew of Lucius, was a decemvir for the enacting and penning of Lawes, and that in the former Election of that Magistracie: as also, that Caius Julius sonne of Caius and Nephew of Caius, became Consull with Marcus Geganius Macerinus, in the yeare 306 [4], and the selfe same man a second time, with Lucius Verginius Trirostus in the yeere 318 [5]: and immediately in the yeere next following [6], a third time, with the same Verginius now twice Consull. And thus much for the Jüli. For to reherse and collect all them of that familie, together with the honorable places of everie one, which were many in number, and of sundry kindes, is not our purpose: and besides, the thing it selfe is apparent and upon record in the publick Registers.

Moreover, I have observed in the Julian line, a certaine house also of the Mentones: and among them, one Caius Julius, colleague in the Consulshippe with T. Quintus Pennus Cincinnatus, in the 322 yeere after the foundation of the citie. I finde likewise, Caius Julius Denter to be master of the Horsemen, when Caius Claudius Crassus Sabinus Regillensis was Dictator, for to hold their solemne assembly of Election, in the yeare 405. There were besides of these Julii, others going under the name of Libones: and of the same race one triumphed; to wit, Lucius Julius, sonne of Lucius and nephew of Lucius, companion in the Consulate with Marcus Attilius Regulus, in the yeere 486 [7]. But, as touching Caius Julius sonne of Lucius, and surnamed Cæsar Strabo, whom Suetonius also ment in the 55 chapter of Julius Cæsar, and Cicero praiseth in his *Brutus*, and in the second booke of his *Oratour*, I doubt, whether this addition (Strabo,) should not be taken as a by-name. For otherwise there is in our hands a peece of silver coine, with the inscription of Lucius Julius, sonne of Lucius, and surnamed Strabo.

---

[1] Al. Mamercus.   [2] Or 281, after the Chronologie aforesaid of Dionysius.
[3] More truly 303.   [4] 307, by Livius accoumpt.   [5] 319.   [6] 320.
[7] 487.

TWELVE CÆSARS

The Epigramme of the former is extant among the Antiquities of Rome citie, in this maner.

A SUPPLEMENT

C. Julius, L. F. Cæsar Strabo, Æd. Cur. Q. Trib. Mil. Bis XVIR AGR. D and. ADTR. IVD. Pontif.

To conclude, I have met with writers, who reckoned also among the Julii certaine Annales[1]: which, for mine owne part verily, I could never yet light upon, in searching the Records and Chronicles. But in the eight booke of the *Familiar Epistles* (of Cicero) and namely in the seaventh letter there, of M. Cælius unto Cicero, there is mention made among others, of one L. Julius, sonne of Lucius, Pomp.[2] Annalis: where the writing (as I suppose) is not very certaine and cleerely acknowledge. For besides that the better corrected Copies call him Villius, (for Julius) Livie also hath expresly and plainely written in his fortieth booke, that one Lucius Villius a Tribune of the Commons, made a Law which provided and ordained, in what yeere of mens age they might sue for everie kinde of Magistracie, and be capable thereof. Whereupon, unto that familie was given this surname, to be called Annales. Thus farre Livius. Hereunto may be added this moreover; that the Kinred Julia, is reckoned in the Tribe Fabia (and not Pomptina), as we have noted in the fortieth chapter of Augustus. I am of opinion therefore, that safer it is to account the Annales among the Vilii, and not the Julii. But thus much hereof, by the way, and as it were passing by; now proceede we to the rest.

In the linage Julia then, there was a familie also of the Cæsars. But what the reason should be of that surname, it is not certainely knowne; no more, than who he was, that first bare the saide surname. For, before Cæsar the Dictator, and his father and grandfather, there were Julii named Cæsares. As for example: He, who (as Livie witnesseth in his 27 booke) was in the second Punick warre sent from the Senate to Crispinus the Consul, about the nomination of a Dictatour. As for the terme Cæsares, those usually the Romane tongue surnamed so, who were borne,

[1] So surnamed.   [2] Haply Pomptinas of the tribe Pomptina.

THE HISTORIE OF

A SUPPLEMENT

either by ripping their mothers wombes[1], or with a bush of haire growing on their heads[2], or else grey-eied[3]. Some adde moreover the tale of an Elephant slaine in Africk, which the inhabitants there call Cæsar: and upon that verie cause, this surname first befell unto Cæsar the Dictatours Grandsire. But Spartianus and Servius, the Authors hereof, are of the meanest credite and authoritie. For not his progeny alone, of all the Julii, had this surname, but many others besides of his house and kinred, both long before and also together with him.

Consuls before Julius Cæsar the Dictator, there were, Sext. Julius, sonne of Caius, nephew of Lucius, together with Lucius Aurelius Orestes, in the yeere after the foundation of Rome 596[4]: also Sext. Julius sonne of Caius, nephew of Sext. was colleague with L. Marcius Philippus in the beginning of the Sociall warre in the yeare after the cities foundation 662[5], and in the next yeere after, Lucius Julius sonne of Lucius, and Nephew of Lucius, bare the Consulate with Pub. Rutilius Lupus. Neither before these, were anie of the Cæsars renowmed or advanced to the highest Office of State[6]. Many yeeres after, out of the same familie, Lucius Cæsar, son of Sextus and cosin Germane[7] to that C. Julius Cæsar, who begat the Dictatour, and attained only to the Preturship, who also died at Pisæ without any evident sicknesse, even as he did his shoes on in a morning, that L. Cæsar I say came to be Consull.

Well, Cæsar the Dictator was borne at Rome (when Caius Marcius and Lucius Valerius Flaccus were Consuls) upon the fourth day before the Ides of Quintilis, which moneth after his death, was by vertue of the Law Antonia called for that cause, Julie. His bringing up hee had with his mother Aurelia, daughter of Caius Cotta, and his aunt by the fathers side Julia, the wife of Marius. Whereupon grew the love that he tooke (a Patritian though he were) to the Plebeian Faction, and the hatred he bare to Sulla. The Greeke and Latine tongue, the precepts also and rules of Oratorie, he learned of M. Antonius Gnipho, a French

---

[1] *Cæso matris utero.* [2] *Cum cæsarie.* [3] *Oculis cæsiis.* [4] 597, after the above said Chronologie. [5] 663. [6] Consulship. [7] *Frater patruelis.*

TWELVE CÆSARS

man borne. Who being of an excellent wit and singular memorie, courteous besides in his behaviour, and of a kinde and gentle nature, taught the Greek and Latine, Grammer, and Rhetorick withal, first in the house of Caius Cæsar his father, afterwards in his owne; and got much thereby, such was the bountie of his scholars, considering that hee never compounded with them for any wages or reward. Now, was this Cæsar wonderous docible and apt to learne, yea and framed naturally for eloquence.

A SUPPLE-
MENT

His Latine speech was trimly garnished, (through Domesticall acquaintance) by his mother Aurelia, a woman that spake the Romane tongue purely and elegantly: like as the Muciæ, Læliæ, Corneliæ, and other right honorable Dames did, in whose families there arose Oratours of great name.

THE HISTORIE OF CAIUS JULIUS CESAR
DICTATOR

1

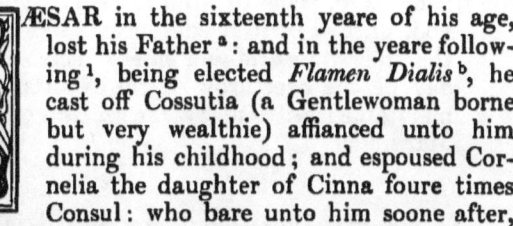ÆSAR in the sixteenth yeare of his age, lost his Father ᵃ: and in the yeare following ¹, being elected *Flamen Dialis* ᵇ, he cast off Cossutia (a Gentlewoman borne but very wealthie) affianced unto him during his childhood; and espoused Cornelia the daughter of Cinna foure times Consul: who bare unto him soone after, his daughter Julia: neither could he by any meanes be forced by Sulla the Dictatour, to put her away ² ᶜ: whereupon, deprived of his sacerdotall dignitie, loosing the dowrie in the right of his wife, and forfeiting all his heritages ᵈ descended unto him from his linage and name, hee was reputed one of the contrarie Faction ³: in so much as he was constrain'd to hide his head ⁴; and (albeit the quartaine Ague hung sore upon him) to change almost every night his starting holes wherein hee lurked; yea, and to redeeme himselfe with a peece of money out of the Inquisitours hands that made search for him ᵉ: untill such time, as by the mediation of the religious vestall virgines ᶠ, by the meanes also of Mamercus Æmilius and Aurelius Cotta, his neere kinsfolke ⁵ and allied unto him, hee obtained pardon. Certaine it is, that Sulla, when he had denied a good while

---

¹ *Sequentibus Coss.* For at Rome they reckoned the yeares according to their Consuls: whose office ordinarily continued one yeare, and began with the yeare, upon the first day of Januarie.   ² Or Divorse.   ³ Of Marius.
⁴ To flie into the Sabines Countrie.   ⁵ For Aurelia was his mother.

THE HISTORIE OF

CAIUS JULIUS CESAR
A.U.C. 670.

the request of those right worshipfull persons, and his singular good friends intreating in his behalfe, and yet they persisted earnest suiters still for him, being thus importuned and at length overcome, brake forth aloud into these words, either in a Divine prescience, or some pregnant conjecture, 'Goe to' (quoth hee) 'my Masters: take him to you, since yee will needes have it so: but know this withall, that he whose life and safety yee so much desire, will one day be the overthrow of the Nobles, whose side yee have maintained with mee: for in this Cæsar there be many Marii.'

2

The first time that Cæsar served in the Warres, was in Asia, and that in the domesticall retinue [a] of M. Thermus the Pretour [1]: by whom being sent into Bithynia for to levie a Fleet, he made his aboade with K. Nicomedes: not without a foule rumour raised, that he prostituted his bodie to be abused by the King: which rumour he augmented himselfe, by comming againe into Bithynia within fewe dayes, under a colour of calling for certaine money, which should be due to a Libertine [b] and Client [c] of his. The rest of his soulderie he caried with better fame and reputation: and at the winning of Mitylenæ, Thermus honored him with a Civike guirland [d].

3

A.U.C. 676.

He was a Souldiour also under Servilius Isauricus [2] in Cilicia, but it was not long: for upon certaine intelligence given of Sulla his death, and the hope withall of the new dissention that was stirred and set on foote by M. Lepidus [a], he returned in all hast to Rome. And notwithstanding hee was mightily solicited by many large offers and faire promises, yet forbare he to joyne in societie with Lepidus partly distrusting his nature,[3] and in part doubting the present oportunitie, which he found nothing answerable to his expectation.

[1] M. Minutius Thermus.   [2] Surnamed so of the people in Cilicia named Isauri, whom he subdued.   [3] So variable and indiscreet.

TWELVE CÆSARS

4

Howbeit when that civill discord and sedition was appeased ᵃ, hee judicially accused for extortion ¹ Cornelius Dolobella, a man who had beene Consull, and triumphed. But seeing that the Defendant was found unguiltie and acquit, hee determined to retire himselfe unto the Citie of Rhodes, as well to decline the hatred of the world ², as by occasion of that leasure and repose to learne the Art of Oratorie under Apollonius Molon ³ a most renowmed Rhetorician in those daies. As he crossed the seas thitherward (being now Winter time ⁴) his fortune was about the Isle Pharmacusa to be taken by Rovers, and with them he remained in custodie (not without exceeding indignation ⁵) for the space well neere of xl. dayes, accompanied with one Physician ⁶ and two Groomes of his chamber. For, his companions and the rest of his servants ⁷ belonging to his traine, he had sent away ⁸ immediatly at the very first, to procure him money with all speed for his ransome. After this, upon the payment unto them of L. talents being set a shoare, he delayed no time, but presently put his Fleet to Sea againe, embarked, and never gave over pursuing the said Pirates, untill he had over-taken them: and no sooner were they within his power, but as hee often times had threatned in mirth, hee put them all to death. Now whiles Mithridates wasted the Countries next adjoyning, because he would not be thought to sit still and doo nothing in this dangerous and doubtful state of confederate Nations and Allies to the Romaines, he left Rhodes whether he had directly bent his course, gathered a power of Auxiliarie Souldiers, expelled the Governour under the King out of the Province, and so kept the Cities and States in their allegeance, which were wavering and at the point to revolt.

CAIUS JULIUS CESAR

---

¹ Whiles hee governed his Province. ² For calling into question so honorable a person. ³ Moloni, not Molonis, as Plutarch taketh it, that is, the son of Molon. ⁴ *Hibernis mensibus*, that is, In the Winter monethes which were Decemb. Januar. Febr. ⁵ Some reade *dignatione* in a divers sense. ⁶ *Medico, vel amico*, that is, a friend. ⁷ Or the rest of his companions and servants. ⁸ To the Cities of Asia, a Province adjoyning.

THE HISTORIE OF

CAIUS JULIUS CESAR

5

In his Militarie tribuneship [a], which was the first dignitie after his returne to Rome, that befell unto him by the voyces and election of the people, hee assisted with all his might those Patrones of the Commons [1], who stoode out for the restitution of their Tribunes authoritie; the force and strength whereof Sulla had abated. Hee effected moreover thus much, by vertue of an Act proposed by Plotius [2 b], that L. Cinna his wives brother, and they, who together with him in the time of the civill discord above-saide, tooke part with Lepidus, and after the Consuls death [3], fled unto Sertorius, might returne safely into the Citie, and enjoy their freedome. As touching which matter, himselfe made an Oration before the body of the people.

6

Being Questour [4] hee made as the auncient manner was Funerall Orations out of the publique Pulpit called *Rostra*, in the praise of Julia his Aunt by the Fathers side, and of his wife Cornelia, both late deceased. And in the commendation verily of his said Aunt, speaking of the pedigree and descent by both sides, namely of her selfe, and also of her Father, hee maketh report in these termes: 'Mine Aunt Julia' (quoth he) 'by her Mother is lineally descended from Kings, and by her Father united with the race of the immortall Gods: for, from Ancus Marcius are derived the Marcii surnamed *Reges, id est*, Kings, which name my mother was stiled with: and from Venus the Julii draw their originall, of which house and name is our familie. So then, in this stock there concur and meete together, as well the sanctitie and sacred Majestie of Kings, who among men are most powerfull, as the religious Cæremonies and service of the Gods, in whose power Kings themselves are.' In the place of Cornelia departed, hee wedded Pompeia, daughter of Q. Pompeius, and Neece to L. Sulla. But her afterward hee divorced, suspecting that she had beene naught with

[1] C. Cotta, M. Crassus, and Cn. Pompeius, who were the chiefe. [2] A Tribune of the Commons. [3] Lepidus. [4] Treasurer.

TWELVE CÆSARS

P. Clodius, of whom there went so constant a report abroade, how at the celebration of certaine publique Divine ceremonies, he being disguised in womans aparel had accesse secretly unto her, that the Senate by Decree directed a Commission to Justices Inquisitours, for to sit upon the pollution of those sacred Rites and Mysteries [1].

CAIUS
JULIUS
CESAR

7

During his Questureship, it fell unto him by lot to execute his Office in the farther Province of Spaine [2]: where, when as by the commaundement of the Lord Pretour [3], he rode his circuit to keepe the Assises [4], and came to Gades, beholding advisedly the Image or pourtracture of K. Alexander the Great in the Temple of Hercules there: at the sight thereof hee fetched a deepe sigh, yea, and as one displeased and yrked with his owne sloathfulnes, in that hee had performed yet no memorable Act at those yeeres [5], wherein Alexander had conquered the whole world, hee presently made earnest suite for his discharge and licence to depart, thereby to take the first oportunitie of all occasions to compasse greater enterprizes at home within the Citie: and being moreover much disquieted and dismayed with a dreame the night before (for he imagined in his sleepe that he had carnall company with his owne Mother) the Divinours and Wizards incited him to the hopes of most glorious atchievements, making this exposition of his dreame, that thereby was portended unto him the Soveraigntie of the whole world, considering that his Mother whom hee saw under him betokened nought else but the subjection of the earth, which is counted the Mother of all things.

A.U.C. 687.

8

Departing therefore thence before his time was fully expired, hee went unto the Latine Colonies [a], which were now devising and in counsell to sue for the freedome of the Citie of Rome, and no doubt had solicited and excited them

---

[1] Of the Goddesse Bona : which were celebrated in Cæsars house, being the Pontifex.   [2] Called Betica.   [3] Antistius Vetus.   [4] In head shire Townes which were called *Conventus*. Plin.   [5] That is, 33. C. Philip. 5.

THE HISTORIE OF

CAIUS JULIUS CESAR

to attempt some tumult and trouble in the State, but that the Consuls for the avoiding of this very danger, kept back the Legions for a while which were enrolled for to be sent into Cilicia.

9

A.U.C. 688.

And yet for all that, soone after he projected greater designes within the Citie. For, not many daies before he entred upon his Ædileship, suspected he was to have conspired with M. Crassus (a man of Consular degree[1]) with P. Sulla likewise and P.[2] Autronius, (who after they were Consuls elect stoode condemned for suing indirectly and by corruption for that place) to set upon the body of the Senate in the beginning of their yeare; and that after they had massacred whom it pleased them, M. Crassus should usurpe the Dictatourship; himselfe be chosen by him Maister of the Horsemen: and so when they had setled the State at their pleasure, Sulla and Autronius should be restored againe unto their Consulship. Of this conspiracie, Tanusius Geminus maketh mention in his Storie, M. Bibulus in his Edicts, and C. Curio the Father in his Orations. Cicero likewise seemeth to signifie as much in a certaine Epistle unto Axius wherein hee reporteth that Cæsar established in his Consulship that Kingdome and roiall government, which he plotted and thought upon when hee was Ædile. Tanusius writeth farther, that Crassus either repenting himselfe, or else upon feare, was not present nor kept the day appointed for the said massacre, and therefore Cæsar neither gave that signall which by agreement hee should have given. Now agreed it was as Curio saith, that he should let his gowne fall from his shoulders. The same Curio yea and M. Actorius Naso doo write, that he conspired also with Cn. Piso a noble young Gentleman, who being in suspition for a conspiracie within the Citie, had the Province of Spaine extraordinarily and without his owne suite bestowed upon him; and complotted it was, that both hee in forraine parts abroade and himselfe also at Rome should at once make an insurrection for to alter the State; and that, by the occasion and meanes

[1] That had been Consul.   [2] Or L. rather.

TWELVE CÆSARS

of the Lambranes[1] and inhabitants beyond the Po. But the designement both of the one and the other was defeated and frustrate by reason of Piso his death[2].

CAIUS JULIUS CESAR

10

When he was Ædile, besides the *Comitium*[a], the Market-place, and statelie Halls of Justice, hee beautified the Capitoll also with faire open Galleries built for the present occasion to stand onely during the publique shewes and plaies: wherein if the number of Images, Statues, and painted Tables fell out to be greater than was needefull, part of that furniture and provision might be set forth to the view of all men. As for the chasing and baiting of wilde beasts, the Stage plaies and solemne sights, he exhibited them both jointly with his companion in Office, and also severally by himselfe. Whereby it came to passe, that howsoever the charges of these Solemnities were borne in commune by them both, yet he alone went away with all the honour and thanke thereof: neither did M. Bibulus his Colleague dissimule the matter, but utter as much, when he said that the same befell unto him which befell unto Pollux: 'For like as' (quoth he) 'the Temple erected in the Common Market place of Rome unto both the Twin-brethren[3], beareth the name of Castor alone: even so my munificence in expence and Cæsars together in setting out these games and plaies, goeth under the name of Cæsar onely.' Cæsar over and above, did exhibit another shew of Sword-fight even at the sharpe: but hee brought into the place fewer couples of champions by a good many than he purposed[4]: for, buying up (as he did) such a sort of Fencers from all parts out of every Schoole, and putting his adversaries of the other faction in great affright thereby, hee gave occasion unto the State to provide by a speciall Act in that behalfe, for a certaine set number of Sworde-plaiers, above which no man might retaine anie at Rome.

A.U.C. 689.

[1] So called of a river, neere into which they dwelt beyond the Po.
[2] Who was slaine by Spanish Horsemen, of whom hee had the conduct.
[3] *Geminis fratribus*, that is, Castor and Pollux, who commonly be called *Gemini fratres*. [4] And yet hee exhibited 320 paire, as Plutarch writeth

THE HISTORIE OF

11

Thus when he had gained the harts and favour of the people, he gave the attempt by some of the Tribunes[1], and sued to have the Province of Ægypt by an Act of the Commons conferred upon him: taking occasion to make suite for this extraordinarie Governement, for that the Alexandrianes had driven their King out of his Roialme[2], whom the Senate had styled with the title of Allie and Friend, an Act of theirs generally misliked. Howbeit hee could not carie it, by reason that the faction of the Nobles crossed him. Whose authoritie because hee would by way of quittance infringe and impaire by all meanes possible; the Tropæes and victorious Monuments of C. Marius for subduing K. Jugurtha, the Cimbrians and the Teutons, which before time had beene demolished and cast downe by Sulla, he erected and set up againe[3]: also in sitting upon a Commission for the examination of murderers[4], hee reckoned those in the number of them, who in the time of the Proscription, had received money out of the publique Treasurie for bringing in the heads of Romaine Citizens[a], notwithstanding they were excepted by vertue of the Lawes Corneliæ[b].

12

Moreover, he suborned one and set him on[a], to endite C. Rabirius of high treason[b], by whose helpe especially some yeares before the Senate had repressed and restrained the seditious Tribuneship of L. Saturninus: and being by lot chosen a Judge Delegate[5] to passe sentence of the prisoner, so willing he was to condemne him, that when Rabirius appealed unto the people[c], nothing did him so much good as the rigour of the Judge[6].

---

[1] That hee might governe it and place the King againe in his roiall Seate. [2] Ptolomeus Auletes the Father of Cleopatra, who many yeares after by Gabinius was restored to his Kingdome. [3] As Torrentius saith. [4] This is by the figure *Prolepsis* to be understood of Cæsar when hee was Prætour of the Citie: as who favoured the Faction of Marius both then and before, howsoever it may seem that Suetonius speaketh this of him being Ædile, or presently after his Ædileship: which by Torrentius leave, may well stand with the truth. [5] In place of the Pretor. [6] Cæsar.

TWELVE CÆSARS

CAIUS
JULIUS
CESAR
A.U.C. 691.

13

Having laied a side all hope of the foresaid Province [1], he stood to be the Highest Priest, not without excessive and most lavish largesse. Wherein, considering how deeply hee engaged himselfe in debt, the same morning that hee was to goe unto the assemblie for the Election, when his Mother kissed him he told her (by report) afore-hand, that he would never returne home but Pontife. And so farre over-weighed he two most mightie Competitours [a], who otherwise for age and dignitie much outwent him, that in their owne Tribes hee alone caried more voices, than both of them in all throughout [2].

14

Being created Pretour [3], when as the Conspiracie of Catiline was detected, and all the Senate generally awarded no lighter punishment than death [4], for as many as were parties and accessarie in that Action; hee onely gave his sentence, That their goods should be confiscate, and themselves put into severall free Cities and Burrowghes under the people of Rome, and there to bee kept in ward: and furthermore hee put them in so great a fright that gave sharper censure (intimating eft-soones and setting before their eyes the exceeding great hatred of the Romaine Communaltie, which in time to come they should incurre) that Decimus Silanus Consul elect was not abashed nor unwilling to mollifie his owne award [5], with a gentle exposition (because it had been a shame to alter it and eate his owne words) as if it had beene taken and construed in an harder sence, than hee meant it. And verily prevailed hee had, and gone cleare away with it (for many there were alreadie drawne to his side, and among the rest, Cicero [6] the Consuls brother [7]) but that a speech made by M. Cato emboldened the whole house, and confirmed all the Senatours in their former sentence,

---

[1] That is, Egipt and the restoring of the king afore said.   [a] Which were 35.   [3] But not entred yet into the Office.   [4] *Ultimum supplicium.*   [5] As if he ment by *ultimum supplicium,* imprisonment or some lesse punishment then death.   [6] Quintus Cicero.   [7] M. Cicero.

THE HISTORIE OF

CAIUS JULIUS CESAR

who now were at the point to yeeld unto him. And yet for all this, he ceased not to hinder their proceedings, untill such time as a troupe of Romaine Knights, who stood round about the place in Armes for guard and defence[1], threatned to dispatch him out of the way, in case hee continued still in his obstinate contumacie, holding and shaking their drawne Swords so neere unto him, as that his next fellowes forsooke him as he sate with them, and very few taking him in their armes and putting their Gownes betweene[2], hardly and with much a doo saved him from violence. Then was hee scared in deede, in so much as hee not onely condiscended unto them, but also for the rest of that yeare[3] forbare to come into the Senate house.

15

A.U.C. 692.

The very first day of his Pretourship, he convented Q. Catulus before the body of the people to receive their order upon a matter to be discussed by them [a], as touching reedification of the Capitoll, having withall promulged a Lawe [b], by vertue whereof hee transferred the charge of that worke unto another[4]. But not able to match the Nobles and better sort [c], nor to make his part good with them drawing in one line, as they did, whom hee sawe in great frequencie to runne by heapes together, so fully bent to make resistance, that presently they left their officious attendance upon the new Consuls [d], hee gave over this action.

16

But, whereas Cecilius Metellus[5] a Tribune of the Commons, proposed most turbulent and seditious Lawes, malgre his Colleagues with all their opposition, he shewed himselfe a stout abbetter and maintainer of him: most stifly bearing him out in the cause, so long untill both of them were by an injunction and decree of the Senatours remooved from the administration of the Common-wealth. Howbeit presuming

---

[1] Of Consul and Senate.   [2] Plutarch nameth Curio for one of them.   [3] Of M. T. Cicero the Consul his yeere which now drew to an end.   [4] That is, to Cn. Pompeius.   [5] Surnamed Nepos (as Valerius witnesseth) for his riotous life and behaviour.

TWELVE CÆSARS

neverthelesse to continue in his magistracie, and to execute his jurisdiction, when he understood once that some were ready to prohibite him by force and Armes, hee sent away his Serjeants, cast off his embrodered purple Robe [a], and retired privily to his owne house, minding there to keepe himselfe quiet in regard of the troublesome time. And when two daies after, the multitude flocked unto him willingly and of their owne accord, promising after a very tumultuous manner their helpe and assistance in the recoverie of his former place and dignitie, he repressed them. Which thing happening thus beyond all expectation, the Senate which was hastily met together about that riot and uprore, gave him hartie thankes; and that by the principall and noblest personages among them, sent for him into the Curia [b], and after they had in most honourable termes commended him, they restored him fully to his Office, and reversed their former Decree.

17

He fell againe into another newe trouble and daunger, being called into question as one of Catilines conspiracie, both before the Questor Novius Niger in his house, and that by L. Vettius who appeached him [1]; and also in the Senate, by P. Curius: unto whom for that he detected first the plots and designments of the Conspiratours, were rewards appointed by the State. Curius deposed that he knew so much by Cattiline: and Vettius promised to bring forth even his owne hand-writing which he gave unto Catiline: But this was such an indignitie as Cæsar in no wise thought tollerable; whereupon, craving the testimonie of Cicero by which he proved, that himselfe merely of his owne accord had given some information unto him of the said Conspiracie, he prevailed so much that Curius went without those rewards. As for Vettius, after his goods were arrested and stresses taken, his houshold-stuffe rifled, himselfe evill entreated, beaten, and in the open assemblie of the multitude even before the *Rostra* wel neere pulled in peeces, him he clapt up in prison. After the same sort he served Novius

[1] *Indice*, some read *Judice*, that is, as if Judex were his surname.

THE HISTORIE OF

CAIUS JULIUS CESAR

the Questour, because hee suffered him, a superiour Magistrate of State ᵃ, to be accused and defamed in his house.

18

A.U.C. 693.

After this Pretourship of his¹, having the Government of the farther Province in Spaine allotted unto him, hee tooke order with his Creditours (that were in hand to stay him) by the meanes of certaine sureties ᵃ who came in and undertooke for him: and before the Governours of the Provinces were disposed-of by the State, with Commissions sealed for their jurisdiction and other affaires, with allowance and furniture also set out for them accordingly, he contrarie to all right and custome put himselfe in his journey: were it for feare of some judiciall proceeding intended against him whiles he was a private person, or because he might more speedily succour the Allies of the Romaines, who craved helpe, it is uncertaine. Well, when he had setled the Province in peace, he made as great hast to be gone: and not expecting a Successour hee departed, as well to ride in Triumph as to take upon him the Consulship. But after the Writs and Proclamations were out for

A.U.C. 695.

the great Assemblie to Election (of Consuls) when he might not be pricked nor propounded (Consull) unlesse hee entred the Citie in qualitie of a private Citizen, and many withstoode him ² labouring as he did to be dispensed-with for the Lawes, forced he was for feare of being put by the Consulship to forgoe his triumph ᵇ.

19

Of the two Competitours with him for the Consulship, to wit, L. Luceius and M. Bibulus, hee made choise of Luceius to be his Companion in Office; upon this compact and condition, That since hee was a man not so gracious, but better monied than himselfe, he should of his owne purse pronounce in the name of both, and promise to deale monies among the Centuries ᵃ. Which devise being known, the Nobles ³ and great men who were afraide, that being once a soveraigne

---

¹ *Ex prætura*, whereby it appeareth he was *Prætor Urbanus*. ² Cato, and his followers. ³ *Optimates*.

TWELVE CÆSARS

Magistrate[1], and having a collegue ready at his beck to agree and consent with him, he would both dare and do any thing; perswaded with Bibulus to make promise of as great a Donation as the other did: and the most part of them contributed their monies thereunto: yea, Cato himselfe verily was not against it, but saide, This Largesse stoode with the good of the weale publique. Heereupon created Consul hee was with Bibulus. For the same cause, the saide Nobles and principall persons of the Citie gave order, that the Consuls for this yeere following, should have the Provinces[b] and Commissions of least affaire and importance, to wit, the looking unto Forrests and Woods[c], unto Lanes and Pathes[d]. Cæsar taking this wrong and disgrace most to the heart, made court all that ever he could unto Cn. Pompeius, who had taken offence against the Senatours, for that having vanquished K. Mithridates, his Acts and Decrees were no sooner ratified and confirmed. He reconciled also unto Pompeius, M. Crassus, an olde enemie ever since that Consulship, which they bare together with exceeding much jarring and disagreement: hee entred likewise into a Societie[e] with them both, upon this contract, That nothing should be done or passe in the administration of the Common-weale, that displeased any of them three.

20

When he was entred into this Honourable place of Consulship; hee (first of all that ever were) ordained, That all Acts, as well of Senate as People, should day by day as they were concluded[a], bee recorded also and published. Hee brought-in likewise the ancient custome againe, that in what moneth hee had not the Knitches of rods with Axes borne before him[b], a publique Officer called Accensus[c] should huisher him before, and the Serjeants or Lictours follow after behinde. Having promulged the Lawe *Agraria*, as touching the division of Lands among the Commons, when his fellowe Consull withstoode and resisted his proceedings, hee drave him out of the Common-place, by violence and force of Armes. The morrow after, when the saide Bibulus

CAIUS
JULIUS
CESAR

[1] Consull.

THE HISTORIE OF

CAIUS
JULIUS
CESAR

had made his complaint in the Senate of this outrage, and there would not one be found that durst move the house about so great a garboile and hurliburly as that was, nor give his censure thereof (as often times in lighter tumults[1] and stirres there had passed many Decrees) hee drave him to such a desperate feare, that untill hee went quite out of his magistracie, hee kept close within house and never prohibited any proceedings else[2], but by way of Edict[3]. From that time forward, Cæsar alone managed all the affaires of State, even as hee would himselfe: in so much as divers Citizens pleasantly conceited, when so ever they signed, subscribed, or dated any writings to stand upon record, would merily put it downe thus, Such a thing was done, not when Cæsar and Bibulus, but when Julius and Cæsar were Consuls: setting downe one and the same man twice, by his name and surname: yea, and soone after, these verses were commonly currant abroad,

> *Non Bibulo, quidquam nuper, sed Cæsare, factum est:*
> *Nam Bibulo fieri Consule, nil memini.*
>
> Cæsar of late did many things, but Bibulus not one:
> For nought by Consul Bibulus, can I remember done.

The Stellat champian fields held consecrated and religious by our Auncestors, together with the Campane territorie, reserved to yeeld rent and pay tribute for a Subsidie to the Common-weale, hee divided without casting lots[4], among twentie thousand Citizens who could shew three children or more[d]. The Publicanes[e] making request for some easement hee relieved[5], by striking of a third part of their rents, and warned them openly, that in the setting and letting of the new commodities and revenues of the Citie, they should not bid and offer too much. All other things likewise he gave and graunted, according as every mans mind and desire stood thereto, and no man gaine-said him: but, went any about

---

[1] *Turbis alias culpis*, that is, Trespasses or offences. [2] *Obnunciaret*, by pronouncing out of the Augurs learning, that the day was *nefastus et non comitialis*, that is, no Law-day. [3] *Per edicta*, some read, *per lictores*, that is, by his Serjeants and Officers. [4] At the discretion of xx. men deputed Commissioners for that purpose. [5] For that they had taken things at too high a rate.

TWELVE CÆSARS

to thwart him, he was soone frighted away. M. Cato, when hee seemed to interrupt and stop his proceedings, hee caused to be haled violently out of the Senate house by an Officer, and committed to prison. As L. Lucullus stoutly withstood his doings, he put him into so great a feare of sundry Actions and criminations, that hee was glad to come and fall downe before him at his knees. When Cicero pleading upon a time in Court, had lamented the wofull state of those times: the very same day, at the ninth houre thereof[1], hee brought P. Clodius his enemie to be adopted into the house and name of a Commoner; one who long before had laboured in vaine to goe from the Nobles, and be incorporate among the Commons. Last of all, it is credibly reported, that he induced by rewards, against all those in generall of the contrary faction, an appeacher[2], to professe that he was sollicited by some for to murder Pompeius; who being produced forth by him before the body of the people, nominated (as he had instructions, and as it was agreed betweene them afore) those that set him a worke: but when one or two of them were named to no purpose, nor without pregnant suspition of some fraudulent practise; he despairing the good successe of so rash and inconsiderate a project, poysoned the partie whom he had suborned[3], and made him away for telling any more tales.

CAIUS
JULIUS
CESAR

21

About the same time, hee tooke to wife Calpurnia the daughter of L. Piso, who was to succeede him in the Consulate; and affianced his owne daughter Julia unto Cn. Pompeius, rejecting and casting off her former spouse Servilius Cæpio[4], by whose helpe especially a little before he had impugned Bibulus. After this new contracted affinitie, hee began (in Counsell) to aske Pompeius opinion first[a]; whereas before, hee was wont to begin with Crassus: notwithstanding also the custome was, that the Consul should

---

[1] Three a clock in the after-noone. [2] *Indicem*, others read *Judicem*, *id est* Vettius Judex. L. Vettius according to Dion and Appian. [3] *Id est* Vettius Judex aforesaid: For, dead hee was found in prison by night. [4] Whom hee promised in mariage the daughter of Cn. Pompeius.

observe that order all the yeere following, in asking the Senatours sentences, which he began with, the first day of Januarie.

22

Being backed therefore by the favour and assistance of his wives Father [1] and Sonne in Law [2], out of all that choice of Provinces hee chose especially the Gaules, the wealth and commoditie whereof might fit his hand, and minister matter sufficient of triumphs [a]. And verily at the first by vertue of the Law Vatinia [b] he tooke upon him the government of Gallia Cisalpina [c] together with Illyricum. Soone after by the meanes of the Senate, that also which was called Comata [d]: for, the nobilitie feared, least if they had denied him it, the people would have bestowed the same also upon him. With joy whereof he grew so haughtie and proud, that he could not hold and temper himselfe, but after some fewe daies make his boast in a frequent Senate house, that he had gotten now what he desired in despite of his adversaries, and full sore against their wills; and therefore from that time forward, would insult upon all their heads [e]: whereupon, when one by way of reproach denied that and said, That it was no easie matter for a woman so to doo: he answered againe, as it were alluding merily to another sence, That, even in Assyria there some time raigned Queene Semiramis: and that the women named Amazones [f] held in times past a great part of Asia in subjection.

23

When hee had borne his Consulship, C. Memmius and L. Domitius Pretours for the time being, put to question his Acts passed the former yeere [3]: whereupon hee referred the examination and censure thereof unto the body of the Senate, but seeing they would not undertake the thing, after three daies spent to no purpose in vaine brables and altercacions, he departed into his Province. And immediately his Questour [4] for to prejudice him [a], was drawne into trouble

---

[1] Piso.   [2] Cn. Pompeius.   [3] Whether they should be repealed or stand in force.   [4] When he was Consul.

TWELVE CÆSARS

and indited upon certaine crimes. Within a while himselfe also was brought judicially to his triall, and accused by L. Antistius a Tribune of the Commons: but by appealing unto the Colledge of the Tribunes, hee prevailed through their favour thus much (in regard of his absence about the affaires of Common-weale) that he should not be liable to the accusation. For his better securitie therefore against future times, he travailed much to obligue and make beholden unto him the Magistrates every yeare: and of those Competitours who sued for any honourable Office, to helpe or suffer none other to come unto the place, but such as covenanted with him, and undertooke to defend and maintaine him in his absence[1]. For assurance of which their covenant, he stuck not to require of some an oath, yea, and a bill of their owne hands.

CAIUS JULIUS CESAR

24

But when L. Domitius a Candidate for the Consulship[a] threatned openly, that were he once Consul, he would effect that which he could not while he was Pretour, yea, and take from him his Armies, hee made meanes to draw Crassus and Pompeius unto Luca a Citie within his Province: with whom hee dealt effectually, that for to give Domitius the repulse, they should both sue for themselves to be Consuls the second time, and also labour that his government might be prorogued or continued for five yeares longer; and he effected both. Upon this confidence hee presumed to assume unto those Legions which hee had received from the State, others beside, maintained partly at the Cities charges, and in part with his owne private purse. And one Legion above the rest, enrolled from out of the Countries beyond the Alpes, hee termed by a French word, for named it was *Alauda*[2]. Which, being trained in militarie discipline, armed also and set out after the Romaine fashion, hee afterwards enfranchized throughout and made free of Rome.

A.U.C. 698.

---

[1] For that hee was extraordinarily absent, longer than the Law *Sempronia* did permit.   [2] The bird *Galerita* or *Cassita*, so called of a crest, upon the head. This Legion it should seeme ware Plumes of feathers in their crests of Helmets, whereupon it tooke that name.

THE HISTORIE OF

CAIUS
JULIUS
CESAR

Neither from this time forward forbare he any occasion of warre, were it never so unjust or dangerous: picking quarrels as well with confederate Nations, as those that were enemies, savage and barbarous; whom he provoked to take Armes: in so much as the Senate one time decreed to send certaine Embassadours for to survay and visite the State of the Gaules: yea, and some were of opinion[1] that he should be delivered unto the enemies hands. But by reason that his affaires sped well and had good successe, hee obtained in regard thereof solemne Supplications [b] both oftner, and to hold more daies than ever any man did (before himselfe).

25

During the time of his (provinciall) government, which continued nine yeares space, these, in manner, were the Acts which hee performed. All that part of Gaule, which from the Forrest and Mountaine Pyrenæus, the Alpes, and the hill Gebena, is enclosed within the Rivers Rhene and Rhosne, containing in circuit 3200 miles, not accounting the associate Cities and States who had deserved well of the people of Rome, hee reduced into the forme of a Province, and imposed upon them a payment of tribute yeerely. The Germanes inhabiting beyond the Rhene, he of all the Romaines first assailed by meanes of a bridge which he built over the said River, and those he grievously plagued and gave them manie great overthrowes. He set upon the Britaines also, a people before time unknowne, whom hee vanquished and compelled both to pay money, and also to deliver hostages. In so many prosperous battailes and fortunate exploits, he tasted of adverse fortune thrice onely and no more: once in Britaine, when his Fleete had like to have beene lost and cast away in a violent tempest: a second time in Gaule, where a Legion of his was discomfited and put to flight, neare unto Gergovia: and last of all, in the marches of Germanie, when Titurius and Aurunculeius his Lieutenants were forlayed by an ambush and put to the sword.

[1] Namely Cato, Plutarch.

TWELVE CÆSARS

26

CAIUS
JULIUS
CESAR

Within the compasse of which very same time, hee lost by death, first, his Mother [1], then his daughter (Julia): and not long after his Neece [2] by the said daughter. And in this meane while, the Common-wealth being much troubled and astonied at the murder of Clodius [3], when the Senate thought good there should be but one Consul created, namely Cn. Pompeius, hee dealt with the Tribunes of the Commons (who intended that hee should be the Colleague in Office with Pompeius) to propose this rather unto the People, That they would grant leave unto him in his absence, whensoever the terme of his government drew toward an end, to sue for his second Consulship: because he might not be constrained upon that occasion, and whiles the warre was yet unfinished, to depart out of his Province. Which when he had once obtained at their hands, reaching now at higher matters, and full of hopes, there was no kind of largesse, no manner of dutifull Office either in publique to the whole Citie, or privately unto any person that he omitted and left undone. His Forum or stately Hall he began to build with the money raised of the spoiles gotten in warres: the very plot of ground whereon it should stand, cost him *Millies sestertium* [a] and above [4]. He pronounced also a solemne Sword-fight and Feast unto the people, in the honour and memoriall of his Daughter, a thing that never any man did before him. And to cause an expectation of these solemnities in the highest degree, the viands and whatsoever pertained unto the feast, albeit he had agreed with Butchers and Victualers for the same at a certaine price, he provided neverthelesse by his houshold-servants [5]. All the notable and well knowne sword players, when and wheresoever they fought so, as upon the mislike and displeasure of the beholders they were in danger to be killed in the place at their commaundement, he tooke order and charged they should be had away

A.U.C. 700.

---

[1] Aurelia a Dame of singular chastitie.   [2] *Neptem, alii nepotem*, that is, Nephew.   [3] By Milo.   [4] That is, a hundred millians of Sesterces, and 20, as Plinie writeth, lib. 36, cap. 15, if Glareanus readeth truly, *Millies ducenties*.   [5] *Domesticatim.*

E

THE HISTORIE OF

CAIUS JULIUS CESAR

by force and reserved for himselfe. As for new-Fencers and young beginners, hee trained them neither in any publique Schoole, nor under professed Masters of that Facultie, but at home in private houses, by Gentlemen of Rome, yea, and Senatours, also, such as were skilful in their weapon and in feates of Armes, praying and beseeching them earnestly (as appeareth in his Epistles unto them) to take the charge of every one severally, and to have a speciall care to instruct each one, and give them rules in their exercises. The legionarie Souldiours pay in money he doubled for ever. And so often as there was plenty of corne, hee gave them their allowance of it without stint and measure, and other-while he bestowed upon every one a slave or bond-servant, yea and possessions by the poll.

27

Moreover, to retaine still the bond of acquaintance, affinitie, and good will of Pompeius, Octavia his sisters Neece[1] wedded unto C. Marcellus, hee affianced and made sure unto him: but withall, he craved his daughter to wife, promised in mariage before unto Faustus Sulla. Having thus obligued and brought to his devotion all those about him, yea, and the greater number of Senatours, by crediting out his money unto them, either gratis, or upon a slight consideration: those also of other sorts and degrees, either invited kindly by himselfe, or resorting unto him of their owne accord, hee gratified with a most magnificent and bounteous congiarie[a]. The freed men besides, yea, and the Servants and Pages belonging to every one, according as any of them were in favour with their Lord and Maister[2], tasted of his liberality. Moreover, there was not a man sued in Court judicially and in danger of the Law; there was not any deeply engaged and endebted unto their Creditours; there were no prodigall young spend thrifts, but he was their onely supporter, and most readie at all assaies to help them: unlesse they were those that either had committed such grievous crimes, or were so low brought, or had

[1] So, hee was great Unkle unto her, like as he was to Octavius Augustus, the Emperour.   [2] Or Patrone.

TWELVE CÆSARS

been so excessive in riot as that they could not possibly be relieved by him. For such as these, hee would say in plaine termes and openly, there was no other remedie but civill warre.

CAIUS JULIUS CESAR

28

No lesse carefull and studious was he to allure unto him the hearts of Kings, yea, and whole Provinces throughout the world: unto some, offering in free gift the deliverie of Captives and prisoners by thousands at a time: unto others, sending aide secretly and under-hand without authoritie or commission of Senate and people, whether and as often as they would: and more than this, adorning with goodly building and excellent peeces of work the mightiest Cities in Italie, Gaule, Spaine, yea, and of Asia and Greece. This he did so long, untill all men now were astonied thereat: and when they cast with themselves whereto this might tend, at last M. Claudius Marcellus the Consull, after a preface and preamble made to his Edict, namely, That he would speake as touching the maine point of the Common-weale, proposed unto the Senate, That for as much as the warre was now ended, and peace abroad established, there might be one sent to succeede him, before his time was fully expired; also, That the victorious Armie ought of right to bee dismissed and have their discharge from warfare. Item, that in the High Court and assembly for the Consuls election his name should not bee propounded, considering Pompeius afterward had annulled that Act of the people [1a] (by vertue whereof it was graunted that he might be chosen Consul in his absence). Now it had fallen out so, that hee making a Law as touching the right of Magistrates, in that Chapter and branch thereof, wherein he disabled those who were absent for being capable of honours and dignities, forgat to except Cæsar: and soone after, when the said Law was once engrossed and engraven in brasse, and so laid up in the Treasurie, corrected his error and oversight. Neither was Marcellus content to deprive Cæsar of his Provinces, and to put him by the priviledge of a former Act passed in especiall favour of him, but he made

A.U.C. 703.

[1] *Ei plebiscito.*

35

THE HISTORIE OF

CAIUS JULIUS CESAR

a motion moreover, that those inhabitants, whom by the Law Vatinia Cæsar had planted in the Colonie of Novocomum, should leese the freedome which they had, as Citizens of Rome: for that this prerogative of theirs had been graunted by ambitious meanes, and beyond that prescript number which was appointed and warranted by the Decree in that behalfe.

29

A.U.C. 704.

Cæsar highly displeased and troubled at these proceedings, and judging it, (as he was heard by report many times to give out) an harder matter for him a principall man of the Citie, to be deposed and thrust downe from the highest and first place of degree into the second, than from the second into the lowest and last of all, withstood him with all his might and power, partly by the opposition and negative voice of the Tribunes, and in part by Servius Sulpitius the other Consull. Also in the yeare following when C. Marcellus who succeeded his cousen Germain by the fathers side Marcus, in the consulship, assaied to bring the same about, he bribed and made sure unto him, with a mightie summe of mony, Æmilius, Paulus companion with him in office, and C. Curio a most violent Tribune, to sticke unto him, and defend his honor. But seeing all things carried still against him more obstinately than before, and the new Consuls elect take the contrarie side and bent another way, he wrote unto the Senate, and by his letters humbly besought them, not to suffer the benefit granted unto him by the people to be taken from him: or if they did, yet to give order that other Generals likewise as well as hee, might leave their Armies: presuming confidently, as men thinke, upon this, himselfe should be able whensoever he pleased to assemble together his souldiers more easily then Pompeius to levy new. But with his adversaries he wold have treated by way of Capitulation in these termes, that after he had discharged and sent away 8 Legions, and given over the province of Gaule beyond the Alpes, he might be allowed 2 legions with the province on this side the Alpes: or if not so, yet at least wise one, together with Illyricum, until such time as he were created consul.

TWELVE CÆSARS

CAIUS JULIUS CESAR

30

But perceiving that the Senate came not betweene nor interposed their authoritie to stop the course intended against him, and his adversaries denied flatly to admit all manner of capitulating and composition concerning the common-wealth, he passed into the hither part of Gaule, and having kept the Assizes there and executed his provinciall jurisdiction stayed at Ravenna, with full resolution to be revenged by open warre, in case there had passed from the Senat, any sharp and cruell decree, touching the Tribunes of the Commons opposing themselves in his behalfe, and quarrell: and verily this was the colour and occasion which he pretended of civill warre: yet men thinke there were some other causes and motives thereto. Cn. Pompeius was wont to give out that for as much as Cæsar was not able of himselfe and with his owne private wealth, either to consummate and finish those stately workes and ædifices which he had begun, or to satisfie the expectation of the people which he had raised and wrought of his comming, therefore he intended to trouble the state and set all on a garboyle. Others say, that he feared least he should be compelled to give an accoumpt of those things which in his first Consulship he had done against the sacred Auspices, the lawes, and prohibitions of the Tribunes [a] (in the name of the people) considering that M. Cato had threatned and professed eftsoones, and not without an oath, that no sooner should he and his armie be parted, but he would judicially call his name in question and bring him to his answere: also for that it was commonly spoken abroad that if he returned ones in qualitie of a private person, he should after the example of Milo plead before the judges, with a guard of armed men about the Court and Tribunall. And this seemeth to bee more probable by that which Asinius Pollio writeth, who reporteth, that in the battaile of Pharsalia, when he beheld his adversaries before his face, slaine and put to flight, he uttered this speech word for word. 'Loe, this was their own doing: this would they needes have, and I Caius

37

THE HISTORIE OF

CAIUS JULIUS CESAR

Ceasar after so many worthie exploites atchieved should have beene a condemned man, had I not craved helpe of mine armie.' Some are of opinion, that being so long inured and acquainted with soveraigne command, and weighing his owne puissance and the power of his enemies, in ballance one against the other, took the occasion and opportunitie to usurpe that absolute dominion, which in the verie prime of his years he aspired unto; and of his mind, it seemeth Cicero was, who in his 3 book of duties writeth, that Ceasar had alwaies in his mouth, these verses of Euripides,

Εἴπερ γὰ, ἀδικεῖν χρή, τυραννίδος πέρι
Κάλιστον ἀδικεῖν, τᾶλλα δ' εὐσεβεῖν χρεών.

Which Cicero himselfe translated thus,

*Nam si violandum est ius, imperii gratia
Violandum est, aliis rebus pietatem colas.*

For if thou must do wrong by breach,
Of lawes, of right and equitie,
Tis best thereby a Crowne to reach,
In all things els keepe pietie.

31

A.U.C. 705.

When word therefore was brought unto him, that the Tribunes inhibition and negative voice was put down, and themselves departed out of the Citie: having immediatly sent before certaine Cohorts privily, because no suspition might arise, he dissimuled the matter, and was present in person to behold a publike Game, viewed, and considered the plot forme according to which he was about to build a Schoole of sword fencers, and according to his usuall manner gave himselfe to feast and banquet often. After this presently upon the Sun-setting, he tooke up certaine Mules from the next Bakersmil-house; set them in their geires to his wagon, and as closely as possibly he could with a small retinewe and companie about him put himselfe in his Journie; and when by reason that the lights were gone out, he had lost his way, after he had wandred a long time, at the length meeting with a guide by that time it was day, he passed on foote through most narrow crosse lanes and by-pathes untill he recovered the right

TWELVE CÆSARS

way againe. Now when he had ones overtaken his Cohorts, at the river Rubicon, which was the utmost bound of his province, he rested and stoode still a little while: then casting in his mind, how great an enterprise he went in hand with, he turned unto them that were next unto him and said, ' As yet my maisters wee may well returne backe; but passe we once over this little bridge, there will be no dealing but by force of armes and dint of sword.'

CAIUS
JULIUS
CESAR

32

As he thus staied, and stood doubtfull what to doe, a strang sight he chanced to see in this manner. All of a suddaine their appeared unto him a certaine man of an extraordinary stature and shape withall, sitting hard by and piping with a reed. Now when besids the shepheards and herdmen many soldiours also from their standing wards ran for to heare him, and among them the Trumpetters likewise, he caught from on of them a Trumpet, leapt forth to the river, and begining with a mightie blast to sound the battaile, kept on his pace to the very bancke, on the other side. Then Ceasar, ' Let us march on,' quoth he, ' and goe whither the tokens of the Gods and the injurious dealings of our enemies call us. The die be throwne: I have set up my rest. Come what will of it.'

33

And thus having conveyed his armie over the river, he joyned with the Tribunes of the commons, who upon their expulsion out of the Citie were come unto him, and in a ful and frequent assemblie, with shedding teares and renting his garment down the brest, besought the faithfull helpe and assistance of his soldiers. It is supposed also that he promised unto every on of them a knights living: which happened upon a vain and false perswasion, for when in his speech and exhortation unto them, he shewed ever and a non the (ring) finger of his left hand ᵃ, and therwith avouched and promised for the satisfaction and contentment of al those by whose meanes he should maintaine his honour and dignitie, that he would willingly plucke the ring from off his owne finger[b]: those that stood hinmost in the assembly, who might better see than heare him speak, took that for spoken which they imagined by bare sight, and so the speech went for currant, That hee promised them the dignity of wearing the ring (of gold) together with 400000 (sesterces)[c].

34

The order, proceeding a final complement of those Acts, which from thence forth he atchieved, summarily goeth in this maner. He seized into his hands and held Picenum, Umbria, and Hetruria. L. Domitius, who in a factious tumult was nominated to be his successor, and kept Corfinium with a garison, he subdued and forced to yeeld: and when he had dismissed him, hee marched along the coast of the Adriatick sea[1], to Brundis, whether the Consuls and Pompeius were fled, intending with all speed to crosse the narrow Seas: whose passage after he had assaied by all manner of lets to hinder and stop (but in vaine) he turned his journey and took the way directly to Rome. And when he had curteously moved the Senatours to give him meeting in the Senate house, there to treat and consult as touching the State of the Common-weale, he set upon the most puissant forces of Pompeius, which were in Spaine under the conduct of three Lieutenants, M. Petreius L. Affranius and M. Varro: having given out before among his friends and openly professed, that he was going to an Armie without a Captaine[a]; and would returne from thence to a Captaine without an Armie[b]. And albeit the besieging of Massilia, which Citie in his journey forward, had shut the gates against him, and exceeding scarcity of corn and victuals was some impeachment and stay unto him, yet within a short time he overcame and subdued all.

35

From hence having returned to the City (of Rome) againe, and passed over into Macedonie, after he had held Pompeius besieged for the space wel-neare of 4 moneths, and that within most mighty trenches and strong rampiers, he dis-

---
[1] That is Venice-gulf.

TWELVE CÆSARS

comfited at the last in the Pharsalian battel and put him to flight: and following him hotly in chase as he fled to Alexandria, so soone as he understood that he was slaine, and perceived likewise that King Ptolomæus laid wait for his owne person also, he warred upon him: which, to say a truth, was a most difficult and dangerous peece of worke, by reason that he managed it, neither in place indifferent, nor time convenient, but in the very Winter season, and within the walls of a most wealthy and politick enemie, being himselfe in distresse and want of all things, and unprovided besides to fight. Having atchieved the victory, he graunted the kingdome of Ægypt unto Cleopatra and her younger brother, fearing to reduce it into the forme of a Province, least at any time, beeing governed under some L. President of a more stirring spirit and violent nature than others, it might give occasion and yeeld matter of rebellion. From Alexandria he went over into Syria, and so from thence into Pontus, upon the urgent newes as touching Pharnaces; whom, notwithstanding he was the sonne of that great Mithridates, and taking the opportunitie of the troubles and civill warre among the Romanes, made warre, yea, and now bare himselfe presumptuous and overbold for his manifold victories and great successe, yet within 5 dayes after his arrivall thither, and 4 houres after he came into sight of the enemie, he vanquished and subdued in one onely battaile: eft-soones and oftentimes recounting the felicity of Pompeius, whose hap it was, to win his principall name for warfare, of so cowardly a kinde of enemies. After this, he defeated Scipio and Juba, repairing the reliques of that side in Africk, and the children of Pompeius in Spaine.

36

In all the civill warres, hee sustained no losse or overthrow but by his owne Lieutenants: of whom, C. Curio was slaine in Affrick: C. Antonius yeelded himselfe into the hands of his enemies in Illyricum: P. Dolabella in the same Illyricum lost his fleete, and Cn. Domitius his armie in Pontus. Himselfe fought his battailes alwaies most fortunatly, and

THE HISTORIE OF

CAIUS JULIUS CESAR

never was so much as in any hazard, save only twice: once before Dyrrachium, where being discomfited and put to flight, when he saw that Pompeius followed not on in chase, he said of him, That hee knew not how to use a victorie. A second time, in Spaine, at the last battaile that ever he fought, what time, being in great despaire, hee was of mind even to have killed himselfe.

37

Having finished all his warres, he rode in 5 triumphs: to wit, when he had vanquished Scipio, 4 times in one and the same moneth, but certaine daies betweene: and once againe, after hee had overcome the children of Pompeius. The first and most excellent triumph that hee solemnized, was that over Gaule: then followed the Alexandrine; after it the Pontick; next thereunto the Affrican: and last of all the Spanish: every one set out diversly, with variety of Ordinance, provision and furniture. On the day of his Gaules triumph, as he rode along the Velabrum[1], he had like to have beene shaken out of his Chariot, by reason that the Axel-tree brake. Hee mounted up into the Capitoll by torch-light, having xl. Elephants on his right hand and left, bearing branches[a] and candlesticks. In his Pontick triumph, among the Pageants and shewes of that pomp, he caused to be caried before him the title and superscription of these three words, *Veni, vidi, vici*, I came, I saw, I conquered: signifying, not the acts atchieved by warre, as other Conquerours, but noting his expedition in despatching the warre[2].

38

Throughout the Legions of old Souldiers, he gave in the name of pillage, unto every footman (over and above the 2000 *sestertii*[a], which he had paied at the beginning of the civill tumult) 4000 *sestertii*[3 b]: and to the horse-men 24000 a piece[4 c]. He assigned lands also unto them, but not lying all

---

[1] A streete in Rome. [2] *Sicut cæteri*. [3] Or rather *vicena*, that is 20000. [4] Rather *quadragena*, that is 40000. By which reckoning the proportion to horsemen was double.

TWELVE CÆSARS

together, because none of the owners should be thrust out (of their livings). Among the people (of Rome) beside x. *modii*[d] of corne, and as many pints of oyle[e], he distributed and dealt 300 Sesterces[f] also by the poll, which hee had in times past promised, with an overdeale of 100[g] a peece to boote, for time[1]. Hee remitted moreover one yeeres house rent, unto all tenants in Rome, if it amounted to 2000 *Sestertii*[h] and not above: but to those in Italie, if the said rent exceeded not 500[1]. Furthermore, hee made them a generall great feast, and distributed a dole of raw flesh[2]: yea, and after his victorie in Spaine he gave them 2 dinners: for, deeming the former of them to have been made niggardly and not beseeming his liberality, he bestowed upon them 5 daies after, another, and in most large and plenteous manner.

CAIUS
JULIUS
CESAR

39

He exhibited shewes of sundry sorts (as namely) a sword-fight of Fencers at sharpe: hee set forth Stage Plaies likewise in severall quarters and Regions[a] of the Citie throughout, and those verily acted by Plaiers in all languages[3]: semblably, the solemne games *Circenses*[b], hee shewed; and brought foorth Champions also to performe their devoir, and represented a naval-fight. At the saide solemnity of sword-plaiers, there fought to the uttrance in the Market place of Rome, Furius Leptinus, descended from the race of Pretours, and A. Calpenus, one who had beene sometime a Senatour, and a pleader of causes at the barre. There daunced the Pyrrhick[c] warlike daunce, the children of the Princes and Potentates of Asia and Bithynia. During the Stage plaies aforesaid D. Laberius[d] a Gentleman of Rome acted his owne Poem or Enterlude: for which, being rewarded with 500 thousand Sesterces, and a ring of gold, he passed directly from the Stage by the *Orchestra*[e], to take up his place among the Knights in the 14 foremost seates.

A.U.C. 708.

---

[1] That is, for bearing so long.   [2] *Viscerationem:* which as some thinke Persius calleth ἀρτοκέας, and is expounded εὐφρασία, whereupon the *Genius* of such merriments, is named Εὐφραδής.   [3] To gratifie all strangers that conflowed to Rome.

THE HISTORIE OF

CAIUS JULIUS CESAR

At the Games *Circenses*, against which the Cirque was enlarged on both sides and moted round about, there drave the Steedes drawing Chariots foure and two together, yea and mounted the vaunting Horses from one to another, the greatest gallants and bravest young Gentlemen of the Nobilitie. The warlike Trojan Game¹ was performed by a two-fold troupe of greater boyes and lesse. The hunting or baiting of wilde beasts was presented five daies together. And the last day of all, there was a fight betweene two battailes of 500 footmen, 20 Elephants, and 30 horsemen on a side, put to skirmish one against the other. For, to the end that they might have more scope to bicker together, the goales ᵍ were taken up and remooved: but in steed of them were pitched two Campes¹ confronting one another. As for the Champions ʰ above-said, they having a place for to exercise their feats of Activitie set out and built for the present time, strove for the prize or best Game three daies together in the Region of Mars field. To set out the *Naumachie* or naval battaile, there was a place digged for a great poole, in the lesse *Codeta*ⁱ; wherein certaine gallies as well with two ranks of Oares as with three; the ships of Tyros also and of Ægypt encountred, being manned with a great number of fighting men. To behold these sights and shewes, such a number of people resorted from all parts, as most of the strangers either within the streetes of the Citie or in the high waies without, were faine to abide within booths pitched of purpose: yea, and often-times very many were in the presse crowded and crushed to death; among whom were two Senatours.

40

Turning after this to set the State of the Common-weale in good order, he reformed the Kalender, which long since through the Prelates default, by their liberty of interlacing (moneths and daies) at their pleasure, was so confused, that neither the feastivall holidaies of harvest fell out in Sommer, nor those of the vintage in Autumne. And he framed the whole yeare just unto the course of the Sunne, that it should

¹ Or tents.

TWELVE CÆSARS

containe 365 daies; and by abolishing the leape moneth, one day every fourth yeare might be inserted betweene ᵃ. Now to the end that the computation of the times to come, might from the new Kalends of Januarie[1] agree the better, betweene November and December, he put two other moneths. So as, that yeare wherein all this was ordained, had 15 monoths, reckoning the ordinarie interlaced moneth, which by course and custome fell just upon the said yeare.

CAIUS
JULIUS
CESAR

41

He made up the full number of the Senatours ᵃ, and chose unto that place new *Patritii* ²ᵇ. The number of Pretours, Ædiles, Questors, and of other inferiour Magistrates hee augmented ᶜ. Such as were displaced and put downe by vertue of the Censors Office, or otherwise by sentence of the Judges condemned for unlawfull briberie, and suing indirectly for any Office, hee restored to their former roomes. In the election of Magistrates he parted with the people thus farre forth; as (excepting the Competitours of the Consulship) for all the number besides of Candidates, the one halfe should be declared those whom the People were disposed to propound, the other halfe, such as himselfe would nominate. Which nomination passed by certaine bills sent about unto the Tribes, in a briefe kind of Writ, after this manner: Cæsar Dictatour unto this or that Tribe (greeting) I commend unto you, such an one and such an one, that by vertue of your voices and suffrages they may have and hold the dignitie they sue for. He admitted unto honorable places the children of those who had been proscript and outlawed ³. He reduced all Judgements unto two sorts of Judges, namely of the Knights degree and the Senatours: as for the Tribunes of the Treasurie or chamber of the Citie, which had been the third, he utterly abolished ⁴. The generall survay and numbering of the people he held, neither after the accustomed manner ᵈ, nor in the usuall

[1] *Calendis Januariis novis.*   [2] According to the Law Cassia.   [3] Contrary to the Law Cornelia.   [4] Disabled them for being Judges.

THE HISTORIE OF

CAIUS JULIUS CESAR

place, but streete by streete, and that by the Land-lords and owners of messuages and tenements standing together[1]: and whereas 3020000 Citizens received allowance of corne from the State [o], he brought and reduced them to the number of one hundred and fiftie thousand. And to the end that no new conventicles and riots at any time might arise about this review, he ordained, That every yeare, in the place of those that were deceased, the Pretour should make a new supply and choise by casting lots, out of such as had not beene reckoned and enrolled in the former survey.

42

Moreover, when as to the number of 80000 (Romaine) Citizens were bestowed in sundry Colonies beyond the Sea; hee made a Law for the more frequent inhabiting of the Citie (of Rome) thus exhausted and dispeopled; That no Citizen above 20 yeares of age, and under 40 (unlesse he were a sworne souldiour to the State [a], and so bound by his oath) should remaine out of Italie above 3 yeares together. Item, That no Senatours sonne, except hee lodged within the house or Pavilion, or belonged to the familiar traine of a chiefe Magistrate [b], should travaile (forth of Italie). Item, That no Grasiars should keep and reteine fewer than a third part of free borne young men, among the keepers of their cattell. All professours of physick at Rome, and teachers of the liberall Arts, he enfranchized Citizens: that both they themselves might more willingly dwell in the Citie, and others beside desire there to inhabite. As touching money lent out; when he had quite put down the expectation of cancelling debts [c], (a thing that was often moved[2]) hee decreed at length; That all debtours should satisfie their Creditours in this manner: Namely by an estimate made of their possessions, according to the worth and value as they purchased them before the civill warre, deducting out of the principall whatsoever had beene paide

[1] As who best knew the number of their tennants and inhabitants in their houses.   [2] Either by the Tribunes of the Commons, or the debters themselves.

TWELVE CÆSARS

or set downe in the Obligations for the use: by which condition, the third part wel-neare of the money credited forth, was lost. All the Societies and Colledges, saving those that were of auncient foundation, he dissolved. The penalties of hainous crimes he augmented: and whereas the rich and wealthier sort fell to wickednes so much the sooner, because they went into banishment[1], and saved their whole patrimonies and estates: parricides[d] therfore and wilfull murderers (as Cicero writeth) hee deprived of all their goods; other manslaiers besides he fined with the losse of one halfe.

CAIUS JULIUS CESAR

43

He ministred Justice and decided matters in Law, most painfully and with passing great severitie. Such as were attaint and convict of extortion[a], hee removed even from their Senatours place and degree. He brake the mariage of a man that had beene Pretour, marying a wife presently after two daies that she was divorced and went from a former husband, albeit there was no suspition at all of adulterie and naughtinesse. Hee ordained customes and imposts of forraine merchandize. The use of Licters, likewise the wearing of purple cloathes[2] and of pearle he tooke away, saving onely in certaine persons and ages, and upon special daies. The Law *Sumptuaria*[b], to represse excessive cost in fare, he executed most of any other: and for this purpose, he set certaine Watchmen and Warders in sundry places about the shambles and markets where victuals were sold, to lay hold upon all cates and viands contrarie to the prescript rule of the Law in that behalfe, and to bring the same unto him. Otherwhiles also, he sent secretly his owne Officers and Souldiours, to fetch away such meates out of the very dining Parlors and banquetting roomes, even when they were set upon the bord, if happily they had any way escaped the hands of the foresaid warders.

[1] In the free State before the Emperors, Citizens of Rome might depart before sentence pronounced, and so avoid both condemnation and losse of goods.   [2] Or scarlet in graine.

47

THE HISTORIE OF

CAIUS
JULIUS
CESAR

44

For, as concerning his purpose to adorne and beautifie the Citie of Rome with gallant works, as also to maintaine and amplifie the Empire, hee had more matters in his head and greater every day than other. Principally his intent and meaning was, to build so stately a temple in the honour of Mars, as the like was no where to be seene; having filled up and laid levell that huge pit, wherin he had exhibited the shew of a Naval battel: and also to erect an exceeding great Theater, fast adjoyning to the Mount Tarpeius. Item, to reduce the whole corps of the civill Law to a certaine meane and mediocrity: and out of that huge and diffused number of Lawes, to choose out the best and necessarie points, and those to bring into as few volumes as possibly might be. Item, to erect publiquely the greatest Libraries that he could, as wel of Greeke as Latine Authors: committing unto M. Varro [a] the charge, both to provide the said books, and also to digest and place them in order. Item to lay the Meeres and Fennie Plashes Pomptinæ drie: to draw and let forth the lake Fucinus: to make a cawsie or high-way, from the Adriatick Sea, by the ridge or side of the Apennine hill, as farre as to the river Tibris, and to digge through the Isthmus [b]. Moreover, to bridle the Dakes who had invaded Pontus and Thracia: and soone after, to make warre upon the Parthians by the way of Armenia the lesse: but not to give them battell before he had made triall of them [c]. Amid these purposes and designes, death prevented him. Concerning which, before I enter into speech, it shall not be impertinent to deliver summarily those points which concerne the shape, feature, and proportion of his body: his habite and apparell: his fashions and behaviour: and withall, what may touch both his civill and also his martiall affaires.

45

Of stature he is reported to have beene tall; of complexion white and cleare; with limbs well trussed and in good plight; somewhat full faced; his eies black, lively,

48

TWELVE CÆSARS

and quick; also very healthfull, saving that in his latter daies he was given to faint and swoune sodainly; yea, and as he dreamed, to start and be affrighted: twice also in the midst of his martiall affaires[1], he was surprized with the falling sicknes[a]. About the trimming of his body, he was over-curious[2]: so as he would not onely be notted and shaven very precisely, but also have his haire plucked, in so much as some cast it in his teeth, and twitted him therewith. Moreover, finding by experience, that the deformity of his bald head was oftentimes subject to the scoffes and scornes of back-biters and slaunderers, hee tooke the same exceedingly to the heart: and therefore he both had usually drawne downe his haire that grew but thin, from the crowne toward his forehead: and also of all honours decreed unto him from the Senate and People, he neither received nor used any more willingly, than the priviledge to weare continually the triumphant Lawrel guirland. Men say also, that in his apparel he was noted for singularity[3], as who used to goe in his Senatours purple studded robe, trimmed with a jagge or frindge at the sleeve hand: and the same so, as hee never was but girt over it, and that very slack and loose: whereupon, arose (for certaine) that saying of Sulla, who admonished the Nobles oftentimes, To beware of the boy that went girded so dissolutely[b].

CAIUS
JULIUS
CESAR

46

He dwelt at first in the Suburra[4]; but after he was high priest, in the streete Sacra, in an edifice of the Cities. Many have written, that he was exceedingly addicted to neatnesse in his house, and sumptuous fare at his Table. The Mannor house which he founded out of the very ground, and with great charges finished in the territorie Nemorensis, because it was not wholly answerable to his minde, he demolished and pulled quite downe: although as yet he

---

[1] *Inter res gerendas vel agendas*, that is, *cum aciem ordinaret*, Plutarch. Whiles he was setting his Armie in battaile ray.   [2] Or fantasticall.   [3] His attire different from others, or of a new fashion which the Greekes call ἐσθῆτας ἐξάλλους καινοφανεῖς.   [4] A streete in Rome much frequented.

THE HISTORIE OF

CAIUS JULIUS CESAR

was but of meane estate and deepely endebted. Finally, this speech goeth of him, That in his expeditions he caried about with him pavements of checker worke made of quarels square cut[1], so as they might be taken asunder, and set againe together.

47

He made a voyage (as they say) into Britaine, in hope of pearles: and otherwhiles, in comparing their bignesse, would with his owne hand peise them to finde their weight. For to get and buy up pretious stones, engraved and chased peeces, Images, and painted Tables of antique worke, he was ever most eager and sharp set. Slaves likewise, if they were any thing fresh and new come, trimly set out with all, and fine, he procured at an exceeding price, such as himselfe also was ashamed of: so as he forbad expresly the same should be brought in any of his reckonings and accoumpts.

48

It is reported of him, that in all the Provinces which he governed, hee feasted continually, and furnished two Halls or dining chambers ordinarily; the one, wherein either Gaules in their warlike habite[2], or Greeks in their cloakes; the other, in which the gown'd Romaines, together with the more noble and honourable personages of the Provinces sat. The domesticall Discipline of his house hee kept so duly, so precisely, and with such severity, in small matters as well as greater; that hee bound with fetters and yrons his Baker for serving up secretly unto his guests other bread than to himselfe: and a freed man of his owne (whom otherwise he did set very great store by) he put to death, for dishonouring by adulterie a Romaine Gentleman's wife, albeit no man made complaint thereof.

---

[1] The paving tiles of marble, etc., whereof such floores are made. [2] Thus Turnebus expoundeth it: but it may be meant of the meaner sort of his *Cohors prætoria*, who were *Sagati* or *palliati*: to put a difference betweene them and the persons of better quality, who were *Togati*.

TWELVE CÆSARS

49

His good name for continencie and cleane life, nothing verily blemished, save onely the aboade and inward familiaritie with Nicomedes: but a foule staine that was, which followed him with shame for ever; yea, and ministred taunting and reproachfull matter unto every man. I omit the notorious verses of Calvus Licinius.

Bithynia quicquid,
Et pædicator Cæsaris[1]*, unquam habuit.*
Looke what it was that Bithyne Land had ever more or lesse;
And he that Cæsar did abuse, in filthie wantonnesse.

I let passe the invectives and accusatorie actions of Dolabella and Curio the Father: in which, Dolabella for his part, termeth him the Kings Concubine in the Queenes place, and the inner roome of his Licter: and Curio nameth him Nicomeedes his filth and harlot[2], yea and the Bithynian Brothel house. I overpasse likewise those Edicts of Bibulus, wherein he published his colleague, and made him knowne, by the name of the Bithynian Queene: saying moreover, That before, he had loved the King, and now cast a fansie to the Kingdom. At which verie time, as M. Brutus makes report, there was one Octavius also, a man upon distemperature of his braine given to jest and scoffe over broadly, who in a most frequent assembly, after he had called Pompeius, King, saluted him by the name of Queene: C. Memmius likewise layd in his dish, that he stood with the rest of the stale Catamites as Cup-bearer, to serve Nicomedes with wine at a full feast, where sate at the Table divers Merchants and Occupiers, Citizens of Rome, whose names he putteth downe. But Cicero, not contented herewith, that in certaine Epistles he had written, how by the Guard or Pensioners of the said King being conveied into his bed-chamber[3], hee lay downe upon a bed of gold, arraied in purple: and so the flower of youth and maidenhead of him, who was descended from Venus*, became

---
[1] That is, K. Nicomedes. [2] *Stabulum.* [3] *Deductum,* or *Eductum,* that is, brought out of his owne bed chamber into the kings.

THE HISTORIE OF

CAIUS JULIUS CESAR

defiled and desteind in Bithynia. One time also, as Cæsar in the Senate house pleaded to the cause and in the behalfe of Nysa, Nicomedes his daughter, and therewith rehearsed up the gracious favours that the King had done unto him, 'Let be' (quoth he) 'these matters I pray you, and away with them, since it is well knowne, both what hee bestowed upon you, and also what you gave to him.' Finally, in the Triumph over Gaule, his Souldiers among other Sonnets (such as they use to chaunt merily when they followe the (triumphant) Chariot) pronounced also these verses so commonly divulged.

> *Gallias Cæsar subegit, Nicomedes Cæsarem,*
> *Ecce Cæsar nunc triumphat, qui subegit Gallias;*
> *Nicomedes non triumphat, qui subegit* [b] *Cæsarem.*

> Cæsar did subdue the Gaules, and him hath Nicomede.
> Behold, now Cæsar doth triumph, who did the Gaules subdue:
> But Nicomede triumpheth not who Cæsar had subdu'd.

50

An opinion there is constantly received, that he was given to carnall pleasures, and that way spent much: also, that he dishonoured many Dames, and those of noble houses: by name among others, Postumia the wife of Servius Sulpitius; Lollia, wife to A. Gabinius; Tertulla, M. Crassus his wife, and Mutia the wife of Cn. Pompeius. For, certaine it is, that not onely the Curiones, both Father and Sonne, but many others also reproached Pompeius, that for whose cause, he had put away his owne wife after she had borne him three children, and whom hee was wont with a deepe sigh and groane to call Ægisthus [1]; his daughter (I say) afterwards, hee espoused; upon a desire of power and greatnes by that mariage. But above the rest, he cast affection to Servilia the mother of M. Brutus; for whom both in his last Consulship [2] he had bought a pearle that cost him sixe millions of Sesterces [3]: and also unto whom during the civill

---

[1] That is, Adulterer: for that Ægysthus committed adultery with Clytemnestra the wife of Agamemnon. [2] *Proximo, alii legunt primo,* that is, first, *cum Bibulo.* [3] 46875 pounds sterling, or 150000 French crowns, according to Budæus.

TWELVE CÆSARS

warre, over and above other free gifts, hee sold in open port sale, faire Lands and most goodly Manors at a very low price: what time verily, when most men mervailed that they went so cheape, Cicero most pleasantly and conceitedly, 'That yee may know' (quoth hee) 'shee hath the better pennyworth in the purchase, *Tertia deducta est*'ᵃ. For it was thought that Servilia was bawd also to her owne daughter Tertia, and brought her to Cæsar his bed.

CAIUS JULIUS CESAR

51

Neither forbare he so much as mens wives in the Provinces where he was governour, as appeareth even by this his Distichon, taken up likewise by his Souldiours at the Gaule Triumphᵃ.

Urbani, servate uxores; mæchum calvum ad ducimus,
Auro in Gallia stuprum emisti, hic sumpsisti mutuum.

52

He was enamoured also upon Queenes, and among them he loved Eunoe, the Moore, wife of Bogudes (King of Mauritania) upon whom, as also upon her husband, he bestowed very many gifts and of infinite value, as Naso hath left in writing: but most especially hee fancied Cleopatra: for, with her, hee both sate up many times and feasted all night long even untill the breake of day; and also in the same Barge or Galley[1] called *Thalamegos*ᵃ, had passed into Ægypt, almost as farre as to Æthiopia, but that his Armie refused to followe: and in the end having trained her into the Citie of Rome, he sent her back againe, not without exceeding great honours, and enriched with many rewards: yea, and suffered her to call the sonne she bare, after his owne name[2]. Whom verily, some Greek writers have recorded, to have been very like unto Cæsar both in shape and also in gate[3]: and M. Antonius avouched unto the Senate, that by the same resemblance he knew him to be his sonne: averring withall, That C. Matius, Caius Oppius,

---

[1] Of which the Ægyptians Kings had alwaies ready rigged 800, as Appian writeth.   [2] That is Ptolomæus Cæsario.   [3] *Incessu*, in his gang or manner of going.

THE HISTORIE OF

CAIUS JULIUS CESAR

and the rest of Cæsars friends knew as much. Of whom C. Oppius (as if the thing were so pregnant, that it required some Apologie and defence) put forth a book entituled thus: *That he was not Cæsars Sonne, whom Cleopatra fathered upon him.* Helvius Cinna, a Tribune of the Com. confessed unto many persons, That hee had a Law drawne out in writing and in readines, which Cæsar being absent himselfe commaunded him to propose, to this effect, That it might be lawfull for him to marrie what wives[1] and as many as he would[2], for to get children upon. And that no man need at all to doubt how infamous he was, both for uncleannesse of body against kinde[b], and also for adulteries, Curio the Father in a certaine Oration calleth him a woman for all men, and a man for all women.

53

That he was a most spaire drinker of wine, his very enemies would never denie. Whereupon arose this Apophthegm of M. Cato, That of all that ever were, Cæsar alone came sober to the overthrow of the State. For, about his foode and diet C. Oppius sheweth hee was so indifferent and without curiosity, that when upon a time his Host set before him upon the bord olde ranke oile[3] in steed of greene, sweet, and fresh, so that other guests refused it, he onely (by his saying) fell to it and eate therof the more liberally; because he would not be thought to blame his Host[4] either for negligence or rusticitie.

54

From other mens goods he held not his hands, neither when he had the command of Armies abroad, nor when he was in place of magistracie at home: for, in Spaine (as some have recorded) he took money of the Proconsul[5], and the Allies there, and that by way of begging, to help him out of debt: and certaine townes of the Lusitanes[6], he

---

[1] *Quas et quot, ducere vellet*, even an Alien.   [2] For otherwise, πολυγαμία was unlawfull. And Antonius was the first Romaine that had two wives at once.   [3] *Conditum oleum penult. cor.* or *conditum product id est unguentum*, an ointment.   [4] Or friend.   [5] Tubero.   [6] That is in Portugale.

TWELVE CÆSARS

sacked in hostile manner, albeit they denied not to do whatsoever he commanded them; and besides, did set open their gates for him against his comming. In Gaule he robbed and spoiled the Chappels and Temples[1] of the Gods, full of rich gifts and oblations. As for Cities, he put them to the sack, more often for bootie sake and pillage, than for any trespasse committed. Whereupon it came to passe, that he got abundance of gold, so as of it which he had to spare and did set to sale, he sold[2] throughout Italy and in the Provinces after 3000 sesterces of silver the pound weight[a]. In his first Consulship, when he had stollen out of the Capitoll three thousand pound waight of gold, hee bestowed in the place thereof as much brasse guilt. The priviledges of Societie and alliance with the Romanes, as also Kings Titles he gave for summes of money[b]: as who (for example) from Ptolomeus[3] that was but one, tooke away wel-neere 6000 talents[4], in the name of himselfe and Pompeius: but afterwards by most open pilling, poling, and sacriledges, he maintained the charges both of civill warres, and also of his triumphes and solemne shewes[5] exhibited to the people.

CAIUS
JULIUS
CESAR

55

In eloquence and warlike feates together[6], he either equalled or excelled the glory of the very best. After his accusation of Dolobella, he was no doubt ranged in the ranke of the principall Advocates at Law. Certes, Cicero in his Catalogue of Oratours to Brutus, sayeth; 'He cannot see any one, unto whom Cæsar might give place'; affirming withall, 'That hee holdeth an elegant and gay, a stately also, and in some sort a generous and Gentlemanlike kind of pleading': and unto Cornelius Nepos, thus wrote he of the same Cæsar, 'What should a man say more? which of all there Oratours that practised nothing else but Oratorie, will you preferre before this Cæsar? who is there in sentences either quicker or cumming thicker? who for words, yeelded more

---

[1] *Templaque; deorum*, etc. or *templaque; dearum*, etc. the temples, ful of rich gifts and oblations to the Gods.   [2] *Divenderet*, some reade *divideret*, hee distributed and dealt away.   [3] Auletes.   [4] Sc. of silver after 80 pound weight the talent.   [5] *Munerum*.   [6] *Eloquentia, militarique re*, after Lipsus.

THE HISTORIE OF

CAIUS JULIUS CESAR

gallant or more elegant?' Hee seemeth whiles he was yet but young, to have followed that forme of eloquence onely, which Strabo Cæsar professed: out of whose Oration also intituled, *Pro Sardis*, he transferred some sentences, worde for word, into his owne, called *Divinatio*. It is said, that in his Pronunciation[1], he used an high and shrill voyce; an ardent motion; and earnest gesture, not without a lovely grace. Some Orations he left behind him (in writing). Among which certaine goe under his name, but untruely as namely that *pro Q. Metello*: which Augustus deemeth (and not without good cause) to have beene written rather by Notaries, who either tooke not his words aright, or wrote not so fast, as he delivered them, than penned by himselfe. For in certaine copies I find that it had not so much as this Inscription, *Pro Metello*: but *quam scripsit Metello*[2]: being (as it is indeede) a speech comming from the person of Cæsar, cleering Metellus and himselfe, against the criminations and slaunders of common backebiters to them both. The Oration likewise, *Ad Milites*[3], in Spaine, the same Augustus hardly thinketh to be his: and yet there be 2 of them extant: the one, was pronounced at the former battaile: the other, at the latter: when, by the report of Asinius Pollio, he had not so much as any time to make a speech; the enemies ran upon him and charged so suddainly.

56

He left Commentaries also of his owne Acts, to wit, as touching the Gaule-warre, and the Civill warre with Pompeius. For, of the Alexandrine, African, and Spanish warres, who was the writer it is uncertaine: whilest some thinke it was Oppius; others, Hirtius; who also made up and finished the last of the Gaule-war, which was unperfect. As concerning those Commentaries aforesaid of Cæsar, Cicero in the same booke[4], writeth thus: 'Hee wrote Commentaries exceeding well, I assure you, to be liked: (naked they be, straight and upright, yea and lovely too, being devested, as it were, of all ornaments and trimme attire of Style) but

---

[1] Take it generally for the whole Action. [2] Which he wrote for, or to Metellus. [3] *Orat. apud Milites.* [4] *Ad Brutum.*

TWELVE CÆSARS

while his mind was, that other disposed to write a complet historie, should furnish and serve themselves with matter there ready to their hands, happilie, to some foolish folke he did some pleasure, who are willing to curle and frizle the same with their crisping pins, but surely the wiser sort he skared altogither from writing.' Of the same Commentaries, Hirtius giveth this report, 'They are' quoth he, 'in the judgement of all men so approved, that it seemes he hath prevented writers, and not given them any helpe.' And yet, our admiration of this matter is more than all mens beside. For, whereas others doe know onely how well and purely they were penned, wee note also with that facilitie and expedition he wrote them. Pollio Asinius[1] thinketh they were compiled with smal care and diligence: with as little regard also of sound truth: seeing that Cæsar received hand over head, and beleeved most things lightly: namely such as were by others atchieved; and even those Actes which himselfe exploited either of purpose or for default of memorie hee put downe wrong: he supposeth also that he meant to have written the same a new and corrected them. He left moreover ii. books, *de Analogia*: and as many *Anticatones*[2] besides a Poeme, entituled *Iter*; of which books the formost[3] he made in his passage over the Alpes, what time as having ridde his Circuits and finished the Assises, he returned out of the hither province of Gaule to his armie: those next following[4,5], about the time of the battaile at Munda. And the last of all[5], whiles he travailed from the Citie of Rome into the farther province of Spaine, and performed that journey within 24 dayes[6]. Extant, there bee also Epistles of his written unto the Senate: which (as it seemeth) he was the first that turned into pages and leaves, even to a forme of a Memoriall[7]: whereas before time, the Consuls and generalles, never sent any letters but written overthwart the paper. Missives likewise there be of his written to Cicero, and to familiar friends as touching home-affaires. In which, if any matters of secrecie were to

CAIUS
JULIUS
CESAR

---

[1] Asinius Pollio. [2] Against Cicero in the dispraise of Cato Uticensis in whose commendation Cicero had written before. [3] *De Analogia.* [4] *Anti-Catones.* [5] *Iter.* [6] Or rather 27. [7] A Booke of remembrance.

THE HISTORIE OF

CAIUS JULIUS CESAR

be carried, he wrote them by privie markes[1]: that is to say, placing the letters in such order, as there could not one word be made of them. Which if a man would descypher and find out, he must of Necessitie exchaunge everie fourth letter of the Alphabet, to wit, d for a and the rest likewise[2]. Furthermore there be certaine workes of his abroad in mens hands written when he was a boy and a very youth: as namely, *The Praises of Hercules*, *The Tragœdie of Œdipus*: as also, *Collects of Sayings and Apophthegms*: all which pamphlets, Augustus forbad to be published, in a certaine Epistle of his; which beeing verie briefe and plaine; he sent to Pompeius Macer whome hee had appointed for the disposing and ordering of his Libraries.

57

In handling his weapon[3] most skilfull he was, and in horsemanship as cunning: but what paines he would take, it is incredible. In the marching of his armie, his manner was to be formost: sometime on horsebacke[4], more often on foote: bare headed, whether the Sunne shone, or the Clouds poured raine. He made exceeding long Journies with incredible speede: even an hundred miles a day riding in some hired wagon[5], if he were lightly appointed otherwise and without cariages. Were rivers in his way to hinder his passage? crosse over them he would; either swimming, or els bearing himselfe upon blowed lether bottles[6]: so that, verie often he prevented the letter-cariers, and messengers of his comming.

58

In performing his expeditions and martial exploites doubtful it is, whether he were more warie or adventurous. He neither ledde his armie at any time through wayes

---

[1] In manner of Cyphres. [2] c for b etc. [3] Or bearing armes. [4] Or riding an horse. [5] Or carroch with fowre wheeles, *i.* τετράκυκλον, or πετοριτον, *Gracè.* [6] In imitation hereof the Romains devised *Ascogephros*, quasi ἀσκογεφύρας, *i.* bridges founded upon such leather bottles blowne with wind, or lightly stuffed with straw.

dangerous for ambushments, before he had throughly vewed and descried the situation of the quarters: nor put over his fleete into Britaine, untill he had beforehand in proper person[1] sounded the havens, and tryed the manner of sayling, and arrivall to the Iland. Howbeit, the same man, (as circumspect as he was) upon newes brought unto him, that his Campe was beleagured in Germaine; passed through his enemies *Corps de guard* in French habite, and so came unto his owne men. From Brindis to Dirrhachium, he sayled over sea in winter [2], betweene ii. Fleetes of the enemies riding opposite one to the other: and whiles his own forces which he had commanded to follow streight after him, lingered still behinde; having sent messengers oftentimes to call them away but all in vaine, at last himselfe secretly in the night went abourd into a verie small botoum, with his head hooded: and neither discovered who he was, nor suffered the pillot to give way unto the Tempest that came full affront the vessell, before hee was well nere overwhelmed with the waves.

59

No religious feare of divine prodigies could ever fray him from any enterprise, or stay him if it were once in hand. As he sacrificed upon a time, the beast made an escape and ran away: yet for all that differred not he his journey against Scipio and Juba. He fortuned also to take a fall then, even as hee went forth of the ship to land: but turning this foretoken to the better presage, 'I take possession,' quoth hee, 'of thee, O Afrike.' Moreover, in verie skorne, and to make but a mockerie of those prophesies, whereby the name of Scipions was fatall to that province, and held luckie and invincible there, he had with him in his Campe the most base and abject fellow of all the Cornelian family, and who in reproch of his life was surnamed Saluito[3].

---

[1] Yet himselfe writeth that he sent C. Vossenus before.   [2] *Hieme*, or in a tempestuous and stormie season, as Virgil and others use the word.   [3] Or Salutio. Read Plinie, *Natur. Hist.* lib. 7. cap. 12.

THE HISTORIE OF

CAIUS
JULIUS
CESAR

60

He fought not often[1] set fields appointed before hand, but uppon the present occasion offred; many times he struck a battaile immediatly after his journy, otherwhiles in most foule and stormie wether, when no man ever thought he would once sturre. Neither held he off, and detracted fight, but in his latter dayes: being then of this opinion that the oftener he had gotten victorie, the lesse he was to venture and make tryall of fortune; also, that a victorie could gaine him nothing so much, as some disasterous calamitie might take from him. No enemie put he ever to flight, but he discamped him and drave him out of the field. By this meanes he gave them whom hee had once discomfited, no time to be thinke themselves. In any doubtfull and dangerous service, his manner was to send away the horses, and his owne with the first: to the ende, that when all meanes of flight were gone, they might of necessitie be forced the rather to stand to it and abide to the last.

61

The horse he used to ride upon was strangly marked, with feete resembling verie neere a mans, and the hoves cloven like toes, which horse was foaled about home: and when the Soothsayers of their learning had pronounced, that he presaged unto his owner the Empire of the whole world, verie carefull hee was to reare him and nourish him. Now when as the beast would abide no man els to ride him, himselfe was he that backed him first. The full pourtraict and proportion of which horse, he dedicated also afterwards before the Temple of Venus Genitrix[a].

62

Many a time himselfe alone renued the battaile when it was discomfited, standing in their way that fled and holding them one by one backe: yea and by wreathing their throats he turned them againe upon the enemies. Thus dealt he I

---

[1] *Non sæpe.* Some read, *non tantum*, *i.* not onely etc. but also.

TWELVE CÆSARS

say with his own soldiers, when they were many times verily so fearefully maskared, that a Standerdbearer threatned as he staied him[1], to smite him with the footepoinct[2] of the speare that carried the Ægle[a]: and another left behinde him the Ensigne in Ceasars hand as he deteined it.

CAIUS JULIUS CESAR

63

Of his constant resolution these be no lesse tokens, if not greater (which I shall now reherse). After the battaile of Pharsalia, when he had sent his forces before into Africke, and himselfe crossed the seas through the streight of Hellespont in a small passengers barke[3], where he met with L. Cassius one of the adverse part, with x. strong war-ships armed with brasen beakeheads; he avoided him not, nor gave way: but affronting him, began to exhort him for to yeld: and so upon his humble supplication received him abourd.

64

At Alexandria being busie about the assault and winning of a bridge where by a sodaine sallie of the enemies he was driven to take a boat, and many besides made hast to get into the same, he lept into the sea, and by swimming almost a quarter of a mile recovered cleare the next ship: bearing up his left hand all the while, for feare the writings which he held therein should take wet, and drawing his rich coate armour after him by the teeth[a], because the enemie should not have it as a spoyle.

65

His soldiers hee allowed for good, in regard neither of manners and behaviour[4], nor of welth and outward estate[5], but onely of bodily strength: and he used them all with like severitie: with like indulgence also and sufferance. For

---

[1] *Aquilifer.* Some read *Aquilifero*, as if Cæsar threatned the Standerdbearer. See Valer. Max. lib. 3. cap. 2. [2] Wherewith it was pitched into the ground. [3] *Vectoria navicula*, a ferrie boat. If you read *victor*, *i.* being conquerour, distinguish there. [4] This seemeth strang and contrary to the Romane disciplinae. [5] *a fortuna*, πλουτίνδην, others read, *a forma*, *i.* beauty, favour, and feature of body.

THE HISTORIE OF

CAIUS JULIUS CESAR

he awed and chastised them not in all places nor at all times: but only when the enemie was very neere at hand: and then especially was he most severe, and precise in exacting and executing of discipline: in so much as hee would not give them warning of the time, either of journey or of battaile, but kept them readie, intentive and prest to be led forth upon a suddaine, everie minute of an houre, whether soever he wold; this did he also many times without any cause, especially upon rainie daies and festivals. And admonishing his soldiers ever and anon, to observe and have an ey unto him, he would suddainely in the day-time or by night, withdraw himselfe out of the way: yea and stretch out his journy more then ordinarie; even to tyre them out who were late in following after.

66

As for his soldiers that were terrified with the rumor of their enemies, his manner was to animate and encourage them, not by denying or diminishing,[1] but by augmenting the same to the highest degree, even above the truth. And thus upon a time, when the expectation of Juba his comming was terrible, he called his soldiers togither: and in a publike speech unto them, 'Be it knowne unto you all,' quoth he, 'that within these very fewe dayes the King will bee here with a power of 10 Legions of 30000 men of armes[2]: an hundred thowsand light armours[3] and three hundred Elephants. Forbeare therefore some of you to enquire or imagine further of the matter: but give credite unto me, that know this for a truth: or else verely I will embarque you in the oldest ship I can get, and cause you to be carried away with any winde, into what Landes and Countries it shall be your fortunes to fall upon.'

67

As touching his soldiers trespasses and delinquencies, he neither observed and tooke knowledge of them all, nor yet

---

[1] *Minuendo*, or *inhibendo*, *i.* suppressing, which might seeme good pollicie.
[2] Fotemen heavily armed.   [3] Footemen lightly armed.

TWELVE CÆSARS

punished them fully to the proportion [1]. But as he made streight inquisition after those who trayterously forsooke their colours, and were mutinous, and proceeded against them with rigour: so, at others he would winke. Sometimes also, after a great battaile and victorie obtained, he released them all of militarie duties; permitting them in all licentiousnesse to roist and royot wantonly here and there: beeing wont to give it out, That his souldiers (perfumed though they were with Odours: and besmeered with sweete oyles) could fight valiantly. Neither called he them in his publike oration, plaine soldiours, but by a more pleasing name, Fellow-soldiers. Furthermore he maintained them so trim and brave, that he stucke not to set them out in polished armour, damasked with silver and gold: as well for goodly shewe, as because they should in battaile take better hold and keepe the same more surely for feare of damage and losse. Moreover he loved them so affectionately, that when he heard of Titurius his overthrow [2], he suffred the haire of his head and beard to growe long, and would not cut the same before he had revenged their death. By which meanes, he both had his soldiers most devoted unto him, and also made them right valorous.

CAIUS
JULIUS
CESAR

68

When he was entred into the Civill warre, the Centurions of everie Legion presented unto him one horseman a peece, provided out of their owne private stocke [a]; and generally all his soldiers offred their service freely, without allowance of corne or wages out of his purse: considering that the welthier sort had taken uppon them the finding and maintenance of the poorer. Neither all that long time of solderie, was their any of them that once revolted from him; and verie many being taken prisoners (by the enemies) and having life granted unto them upon condition, they would serve as soldiers against him, refused it. Hunger and other extremities which necessarily follow warre, not onely whilst they were beseeged, but also when themselves beleagured

[1] *Pro modo*, or, *pro more*, *i.* after the manner of militarie discipline.   [2] And the Legions with him, A.U.C. 700.

THE HISTORIE OF

CAIUS JULIUS CESAR

others, they indured so resolutely, that during their strong siedge and fortification against Dyrrachium, Pompey, when he saw what kinde of bread made of a certaine Herbe [b] they lived upon, said, He had to deale with wild beasts, commanding withall, the same quickly to be had away, and not shewed to any one: for feare, least his owne soldiers hearts should be utterly daunted, seeing once the patience and constancie of their enemies. And how valiantly they bare themselves in fight, this on thing may testifie that having taken one foyle in a battaile before Dyrrachium, they voluntarily offered to be executed therfore [c]; in so much as their Generall was more troubled about comforting then punishing them. In all other battailes, they fewer in number by many parts, easily vanquished infinit forces of their enemies. To conclude, one cohort [d] and no more of the 6 Legion, which had the keeping of a skonce [1], made good the place and held out for certaine houres against foure of Pompeis Legions: and were in manner all of them throughout shot into their bodies with a multitude of their arrows: of which were found one hundred and thirtie thousand within their trench and rampires. And no mervaile, if a man consider their several facts singly by them selves, either of Cassius Scæva a Centurion, or of C. Acilius a common soldier: to say nothing of many more. Scæva, when his eie was smitten out, his thigh and shoulder shot through, and his buckler perced likewise with the shot of 120 arrowes [2] yet defended the guard of the fort committed to his charge, and kept it still. Acilius in a fight at sea before Massilia, after his right hand was quite cut off, wherwith he had caught the Poope of his enemies ship, following herein that memorable example of Cynecirus among the Greekes, leapt notwithstanding into the saide shippe, shoving and driving before him with the bosse and pike of his buckler those that he met in his way.

69

In ten yeeres space during the Gaule-warre, they never so much as once mutinied: in the Civill warres some times

---

[1] Or fort, at the Siege of Dyrrachium.   [2] Plutarch, 130.

TWELVE CÆSARS

they did : yet so as they were soone reclaimed and came againe into order: not so much by the remisse indulgence as the authoritie of their Captaine: for, never would he yeeld one jot unto them in these their seditious tumults: nay, hee alwaies withstood and crossed them: and verily the 9 Legion at Placentia, (notwithstanding Pompeius yet was in armes with his power in the field) he casherde ful and wholy, and sent away with shame: yea and after many humble prayers and supplications with much a do restored he them to their places again, and not before execution done upon the offenders.

70

As for the soldiers of the tent Legion, when as in Rome they earnestly called for their discharge from warfare, and required their rewards even with mightie threats, and that to the exceeding danger of the whole Citie, at what time also, the war was verie hote in Afrike, he neither would admit them into his presence, nor yet dismisse them albeit his friends seemed to scare him from taking that course: but with one onely word, wherby he named them *Quirites*ª, insteed of *Milites*, he did so gently turne and winde, yea and bring them to his bent, that forthwith they made answere, They would be his souldiers still: and so of their owne accord followed him into Africk, notwithstanding he refused their service. And yet for all this, he ammerced and fined the most mutinous sort of them with the losse of a third part, both of the pillage and also of the Lands appointed for them.

71

In affectionate love and faithfull protection of his dependants, he was not wanting in his verie youth. When he had upon a time defended Masintha a noble young Gentleman against King Hiempsal[1], so earnestly, that in the debate and altercation between them he flew upon Juba the Kings sonne and caught him by the beardª: after that the said Masintha was pronounced definitively the Kings Tribu-

[1] Who laid claime unto Masintha as his Tributarie.

CAIUS
JULIUS
CESAR

THE HISTORIE OF

CAIUS
JULIUS
CESAR

tarie[1]: he forthwith both rescued him out of their hands that would have haled him away: and also kept him close a long time in his owne Lodging; and soone after his Pretorship there expired, when he went into Spaine, tooke the young gentleman away with him in his own litter among others his followers, and favorites, and those officers that attended upon him with their knitches of rods.

72

His friends he used at all times with so great curtesie and tender respect, that when C. Oppius who accompanied him in his journey through a wild forest fell suddainely sicke, he gave him rowme in the onely Inne that was, while him selfe lay all night upon the ground [2] without doores [3]. Moreover, being now become Emperour and Lord of all: some of them he advanced even from the lowest degree unto the highest place of honour. And when he was blamed and reproved therefore, he professed openly, That if he had used the helpe of robbers by the highway side, of cutters and swasbucklers in maintaining of his owne dignitie, he would not faile but requite them and be thankefull even to such.

73

He never entertained malice and hatred against any man so deepely but willing he was to lay downe the same upon occasion offered. Notwithstanding C. Memmius had made most bitter invectives against him, and hee againe written unto him as bitterly, yet soone after, when the said Memmius stoode for the Consulship, hee friended him all that he could with his good word and procured him voyces. When C. Calvus after certaine Libels and defamatorie Epigrams against him, dealt by the mediation of friendes for a reconciliation, he of his owne accord wrote first unto him. As for Valerius Catullus (by whose verses concerning Mamurra he could not chuse but take knowledge that he was noted and branded with perpetuall infamie) when he excused him-

---

[1] *Stipendiarium quoque pronuntiatum*: how ever some read *pronuntiavit*: as if Cæsar had averred openly that he was his waged soldiour.   [2] In a pallet or mattrice upon the ground.   [3] Under the Jetty of the house.

TWELVE CÆSARS

selfe unto him and was readie to make satisfaction [1], he bad him to supper that verie day: and as he used before time, so he continued still to make his fathers house his lodging.

CAIUS
JULIUS
CESAR

74

Moreover, in his revengements hee was by nature most milde. Those rovers by whome he was taken prisoner, after he had forced to yeeld, because he had sworne before that he would hang them upon a crosse, he commanded that their throats be first cut, and then to be crucified [2]. Cornelius Phagita, whose for-laying him by night, he lying sicke and latitant hardly had escaped (although he gave him a good reward [3]), but had like to have beene brought unto Sulla, he never could find in his heart to hurt. Philemon a servant and secretarie of his, who had promised his enemies to take his life away by poyson, he punished onely by simple death, without any other torment. Being cited and called much upon to beare witnesse against P. Clodius, for being naught with his wife Pompeia, who was accused besides for the same cause to have polluted the sacred Ceremonies [4], he denied that he ever knew any thing of the matter, or was able to bring in evidence, albeit both his mother Aurelia, and Julia his sister, had simply related all upon their credites even before the same Jurie and Judges. And being demanded therupon, wherefore then he had put away his wife? 'Because I deeme,' quoth he, 'that those of my house ought to be cleere as well of suspition as of crime.'

75

The moderation and clemencie which he shewed as well in the menaging of the civil war, as in his victorie, was admirable. When Pompeius denounced in minatory terms, that he would recken him for an enemie, whosoever he was, that failed to maintaine the Common-wealth: he for his

---

[1] By saying *Nollem factum*, etc., I am sorrie for it: and I would I had not so done.   [2] Where note, that crucifying was a painefull death.   [3] 2 Talents, Plutarch.   [4] Of *Bona Dea*, in whose chappell it was thought he did the deede disguised in womans apparell.

THE HISTORIE OF

CAIUS JULIUS CESAR

part pronounced openly, That he wold make sure account of them to be his, who stoode indifferent betweene and were Neuters. And so many, as upon the commendation of Pompeius before time, he had given any charg or place of command unto, in his armie under him, he granted them all free leave and libertie to depart unto him. Upon Articles and conditions of yeelding moved and propounded to Pompeius at Ilerda, whiles between both parts there passed reciprocall dealing and commerce continually: when Afranius and Petreius had taken within their Campe certaine of Ceasars soldiers, and (which they repented soone after) put them to the sword, he would in no wise imitate the same perfidious treachery of theirs practised against him. At the battaile of Pharsalia he cryed out, 'Spare all Citizens'; and afterwards granted unto everie one of his owne soldiers (none excepted) this favour to save each of them one of the adverse part, whom he would: neither were any found or knowne slaine, but in the verie medly, except Afranius, Faustus, and L. Ceasar the younger: and even these verely, men thinke, were not with his good will put to death. Of whom notwithstanding: both the former, to wit, Afranius and Faustus, after pardon obtained had rebelled and entred into armes againe, and L. Ceasar for his part, when in cruell manner by fire and sword he had made havock of his freed men and bondservants, spitefully slew the verie wild-beasts also which Ceasar had provided against the solemnitie of a publike shew to be exhibited before the people. To conclude, in his very latter daies he permitted al those also whom beforetime he had not pardoned to return into Italy, to govern as magistrates in the Citie, and to command as generals in the field. Yea the very Statues of L. Sulla and Pompeius which the commons had overthrown and cast up and down, he erected again in their due places. And if after this, there was any plot intended or word spoken against him by his adversaries to his hurt, he chose rather to represse than to revenge the same. And so, diverse conspiraces detected and night conventicles, hee found fault with no farther then thus, by giving notice in some edict and proclamation, that he had intelligence therof. And as for such as gave out bitter speeches of him, he thought it sufficient in an open assemblie to give them an Admonition, not to persist therein. Finally, when in a most slaunderous booke written by A. Cæcina, and certaine verses as rayling and reprochfull as it, devised by Pitholaus, his credite and reputation was much cracked and empaired he tooke the matter no more to the heart, than one Citizen would have done at an others hand[1].

CAIUS JULIUS CESAR

76

Howbeit, the rest of his deedes and words overweigh and depresse his good parts downe: so as he might be thought both to have abused his soveraintie, and worthily to have beene murthered. For, he not only tooke upon him excessive honours, to wit, continued Consulship, perpetuall Dictature, and Presidency of Manners[2]; and more than so, the forename of Emperour[3], the Surname Father of his Countrie; his statue among the Kings, an eminent seate of Estate raised above the rest in the *Orchestra,* among the Senatours: but hee suffered also more stately dignities than beseeming the condition of a mortall wight to bee decreed and ordained for him: namely, a golden Throne in the Curia, and before the Tribunal[4]: a sacred Chariot [a] and therein a frame carrying an Image[5], at the solemne pomp of his Games *Circenses*: Temples, Altars, his owne Images placed neere unto the Gods: a sacred Bed-loft[b] for such Images to be bestowed upon: a *flamin*[c], certaine *Luperci*[6][d]: and the denomination of one moneth[e] after his owne name. Besides, no honourable offices there were but he tooke and gave at his owne pleasure. His third and fourth Consulship in name onely and title he bare: contenting himselfe with the absolute power of Dictatourship decreed unto him with his Consulares all at one time: and in both yeeres, he substituted two Consuls under him for the three last moneths: so as, in the meane time, he held

---

[1] *Civili animo tulit.*   [2] *i.* Censorship in deed though not in name.
[3] *Imperatoris, i.* Soveraine and absolute commander.   [4] In the forum.
[5] Of himselfe, as a God.   [6] Juliani.

THE HISTORIE OF

CAIUS
JULIUS
CESAR
A.U.C. 709.

no Election but of Tribunes and Ædiles of the Commons. In steed of Pretours he ordained Provosts, who should administer the affaires of the Citie even whiles he was present[1]. And upon the very last day of the yeare, to wit next before the Kalends of Januarie[2], the place of a Consulship being vacant by the suddaine death of a Consull he conferred uppon one that made suite to enjoy the same but a few houres[1]. With semblable licentiousnesse despising the custome of his Countrie, he ordained majestrates to continue in office many yeares together. To x. men of Pretours degree he graunted the Consulare Ornaments. Such as were but enfranchized Citizens, and divers mungrell Gaules no better then halfe Barbarians, he admitted Senatours[3]. Furthermore, over the Mint and receipt of the City-revenewes, he set certaine peculiar servants of his owne to be rulers. The charge and commaund of three Legions which he left in Alexandria, he committed wholly to a sonne of Rufinus his freed man, a stale youth and Catanite of his owne.

77

Neither did some words of his which he openly delivered, bewraie lesse presumptuous Lordlines, as T. Ampius writeth. For example, That the Commonwealth was now no more any reall thing [a], but a name onely, without forme and shape: That Sulla was altogether unlettered and no Grammarian [4 b], in giving over his Dictature. That men ought now to speake with him more consideratly, and to hold every word that he saith for a Law. Nay he proceeded to this point of Arrogancie, that when upon a time in a certaine Sacrifice, the South-sayer brought him word of unlucky Inwards in the beast, and such as had no heart at all, he made answere and said, That those which were to follow afterwards should prove more joyfull and fortunate if it pleased him [5]: neither was it to be taken for a prodigious and strange token, if a beast wanted an heart.

[1] *Etiam præsente se:* some read *absente te*: cleane contrarie. [2] The last of December. [3] Made free Citizens of Rome. [4] *Nam Grammatici est dictare.* [5] Should signifie better fortune.

TWELVE CÆSARS

78

But the greatest envie and inexpiable hatred he drew upon himselfe by this occasion most of all[1]. What time as al the Senatours in generall came unto him with many and those most honourable decrees, he received them sitting still[2] before the Temple of Venus Genitrix. Some thinke, that when he was about to rise up, Cornelius Balbus stayed and helde him backe: others are of the mind, that he never went about it. But when C. Trebatius advertised him to arise unto them[3], he looked backe upon him with a strang kind of looke: which deede of his was thought so much the more intollerable, for that himselfe, when Pontius Aquila on of the Colledge of Tribunes[a], stood not up nor did reverence to him as he rode in Tryumph and passed by the Trybunes Pues, tooke such snuffe and indignation therat, that he brake out alowd into these words: 'Well done Tribune Aquila, recover thou then, the common-welth out of my hands': and for certaine dayes togither, never promised ought unto any man without this Proviso and Exception, 'If Pontius Aquila will give me leave [b].'

79

To this contumelious and notorious behaviour[4] of his toward the Senate thus despised, he adjoyned a deede much more arrogant: for when as in his returne from the solemne Sacrifice of the Latine Holie dayes, among other immoderate and new acclamations of the people, one out of the multitude had set upon his Statue, a Coronet of Laurell tied about with a white band[5]; and Epidius Marullus, a Tribune of the Commons together with his colleague Ceasetius Flavus commanded the said band to be plucked of, and the man to be had away to prison, he taking it to heart, either that this overture to a kingdome sped no better, or, (as he made semblance and pretended himselfe) that he was put by the glorie of refusing it, sharpely rebuked the

---

[1] *In expiabilem* or *exitiabilem*, *i.* deadly, and that which brought him to mischeife. [2] Not so much as rising up unto them. [3] Saying with all, What, Sir. Remember you are Cæsar. [4] Or gesture. [5] Resembling a Diademe.

THE HISTORIE OF

CAIUS JULIUS CESAR

Tribunes, and deprived them both of their authoritie. Neither for all this, was he willing afterwards to put away the infamous note of affecting and seeking after the title of a King: albeit he both made answere unto a Commoner [a] saluting him by the name of a King, That he was Cæsar and no King: and also at the *Lupercalia*, when Antonius the Consul imposed the Diademe oftentimes upon his head before the *Rostra*, did put it backe againe, and send it into the Capitoll to Jupiter Optimus Maximus [b]. Moreover sundrie rumours ran rife abroad, that he would depart (for ever) to Alexandria [c] or to Ilium [d], having at once translated and remooved thither the puissance and wealth of the Empire: dispeopeld Italie with mustring of soldiers; and withall betaken the administration of Rome-Citie unto his friends: as also, that in the next Session of the Senate, L. Cotta on of the Quindecimvirs [e] would move the house to this effect, That for as much as it was contained in the Fatall bookes of Sybilla, that the Parthians could not possiblie be vanquished but by a King, therfore Ceasar should be stiled King.

80

This gave occasion to the Conspiratours for to hasten the execution of their designe, least of necessitie they should be driven to assent thereto. Their counsels therefore and conferences about this matter, which before time they held dispersed here and there, and projected oftentimes by two and three in a companie, they now complotted altogither, for that by this time the very people joyed not in the present state, seeing how things went; but both in secret and openly also distasted such soveraintie, and called earnestly for protectors and maintainers of their liberties. Upon the admission of Aliens into the order of Senatours, there was a Libell[1] proposed in this form *Bonum Factum* [a] etc., That no man would shew the Senate-house to any new Senatours. And these verses were commonly chaunted:

[1] Or Bill.

TWELVE CÆSARS

Gallos Ceasar in Triumphum ducit, Iidem in Curia[1] *Galli Bracas*[2][b] *deposuerunt, latum clavum sumpserunt.*

The French in triumph Ceasar leads, In Senate they anon
No sooner laid their Breeches of, but purpled robes put on.

CAIUS
JULIUS
CESAR

As Q. Maximus substituted (by Ceasar) to be a Consul for 3 Moneths entred the Theater, and the Sergant commanded[3] (as the manner was) that the people should observe and regard him according to his place[c], they all with one accord cryed out, That he was no Consul. After that Cæsetius and Marullus the Tribunes aforesaid, were removed out of their office, at the next Solemne assembly, held for Election, verie many voices were found declaring them ii. Consuls. Some there were who subscribed under the Statue of L. Brutus these words, 'Would God thou were alive'[d]. Likewise under the Statue of Cæsar himselfe,

Brutus for expelling the Kings, was created Consul the first[e].
This man for expelling the Consuls is become King, the last[f].

There conspired against him more than three-score, the heads of which conspiracie were C. Cassius, Marcus[5] and Decimus Brutus; who having made doubt at first whether by dividing themselves into partes[6], they should cast him downe the bridge[f], as he called the Tribes to give their voices at the Election in Mars fielde, and so take him when hee was downe and kill him right out: or set uppon him in the high streete called *Sacra via*[7]: or else in the very entrance to the Theater; after that the Senate had summons to meete in Counsell within the Court of Pompeius upon the Ides of March[8], they soone agreed of this time and place before all others.

81

But Cæsar surely had faire warning of his death before

[1] Or rather, *Idem in curiam*, for the same Cæsar brought them into the Senate.   [2] *Bracas*, or *trousses*, or *Brachas*, some take them for mantels.   [3] *Histor*.   [4] *Postremus* or *Postremo*, at last.   [5] M. Brutus.   [6] Some upon the bridge others under it.   [7] In which Cæsar dwelt after he had beene high priest.   [8] 15 of March in honor of Anna Perenna. And because the plaies were exhibited in Pompeis Theatre. Therfore the Senate met also in his *Curia*.

THE HISTORIE OF

CAIUS
JULIUS
CESAR

it came, by many evident prodigies and strang foretokens. Some few moneths before, when certaine new inhabitants, brought by vertue of the Law Julia[1] to dwell in the Colonie Capua, overthrew most auncient Sepulchers for to builde them houses to their landes; and did the same so much the more diligently and with better will, for that in searching they light upon manufactures and vessels good store of Antique worke: there was found in that verie monument, wherein by report, Capys the founder of Capua lay buried, a brasen Table with a writing upon it in Greeke words and Greeke letters to this effect: 'When the bones and reliques of Capys happen to be discovered, it shall come to passe, that one descended from Julus shall be murdered by the hands of his neere kinsfolke, and his death soone after revenged with the great calamities and miseries of all Italie.' And least any man should thinke this to be a fabulous tale and forged matter, know he that Cornelius Balbus a verie inward and familiar friend of Cæsar is the author thereof. And the verie day next preceeding his death, those troupes of horses which in his passage over the River Rubicon hee had consecrate and let go loose ranging here and there without a keeper, (as he understood for certaine) forbare their meat and would not to die for it, touch any, yea, and shed teares aboundantly. Also, as he offered sacrifice, the Soothsayer Spurina warned him to take heede of danger toward him, and which would not be differred after the Ides of March. Now, the verie day before the said Ides, it fortuned that as the birde *Regaliolus*[2a] was flying with a little branch of Lawrell, into the Court of Pompeius, a sort of other birdes of diverse kindes from out of the grove hard by, pursued after and there pulled it in peeces. But that night next before the day of his murder, both himselfe dreamed as he lay a sleepe, one while, that he was flying above the clouds: another while, that Jupiter and he shooke hands: and also his wife Calpurnia, imagined, that the Finiall of his house fell downe, and that her husband was stabbed in her verie bosome: and sodainely withall the chamber

[1] Which him selfe promulged.   [2] Or *Regaviolus*, quasi *rex avium*.

TWELVE CÆSARS

doore of it selfe flew open. Hereupon, as also by reason of sickelinesse, he doubted a good while whether he should keepe at home and put off those matters which he had purposed to debate before the Senate, or no? At the last, being counselled and perswaded by Decimus Brutus, not to disappoint the Senatours who were now in frequencie assembled and stayed for his comming long since, he went forth when it was well neere eleven of the clocke. And when one met him by the way[1], and offered him a written pamphlet, which layd open the conspiracie, and who they were that sought his life, he shuffled the same among other skroes and writings which he held in his left hand as if he would have red it anone. After this when he had killed many beasts for sacrifices and could speede of the Gods favour in none, he entred the *Curia*[2] in contempt of all Religion; and therewith laughed Spurina to scorne: charging him to bee a false Prophet, for that the Ides of March were come: and yet noe harme befell unto him; albeit hee aunswered, That come indeede they were, but not yet past.

CAIUS JULIUS CESAR

82

When they saw once that he had taken his place[3], and was set, they stood round about him as serviceable attendants readie to do him honor: and then immediatly Cimber Tullus[4]: who had undertaken to begin first, stepped neerer unto him, as though he would have made some request. When Ceasar seemed to mislike and put him backe, yea and by his gesture to post him of unto another time, he caught hold of his gowne at both shoulders: whereupon as he cried out, 'This is violence,' Cassius[5][a] came in 2, full a front, and wounded him a litle beneth the throat[6]. Then Cæsar catching Cassius by the arme thrust it through with his stile or writing punches[b]; and with that being about to leape forward[7] he

A.U.C. 710.

---

[1] *Ab Obvio quodam, vel Ovio,* 1, one Ovius. [2] Of Pompeius. [3] Conspicati, or *conspirati, i.* the conspiratours stood round about him. [4] Who before had beene his great friend and sided with him. [5] *Alter Cassius* or *alter e Cassiis* one of the *Cassi, vel alter, Casca.* [6] *Jugulum,* or the chanell bone. [7] Out of his chaire.

THE HISTORIE OF

CAIUS
JULIUS
CESAR

was met with another wound and stayed. Now when he perceived himselfe beset on everie side and assailed with drawne daggers he wrapped and covered his head with his gowne: but withall he let downe the large lap[1] with his left hand to his legges beneath, hiding thereby the inferiour part also of his bodie, that he might fall more decently[c]: and so, with 3 and 20 wounds he was stabbed: during which time he gave but one grone, without any worde uttered, and that was at the first thrust; although some have written, that as M. Brutus came running upon him he said, Καὶ σὺ τέκνον[2]; i. 'And thou my sonne'[d]. When all others fled sundrie waies, there lay he a good while dead, untill three of his owne pages bestowed him in a licter: and so with one arme hanging downe[3], carried him home. Neither in so many wounds, was there, as Antistius his Physitian deemed, any one found mortall, but that which he received second, in his breast[4]. The conspiratours were minded to have dragged his Corps, after hee was thus slaine, into the River Tiberis; confiscated his goods, and repealed all his acts: but for feare of M. Antonius the Consul and Lepidus, Maister of the Horsemen, they held their hands and gave over those courses.

83

At the demand therefore of L. Piso whose daughter he married, his last will and Testament was opened and red in the house of Antonius: which will, upon the Ides of September[5] next before, he had made in his owne house at Lavicium and committed to the keeping of the chiefe vestal Virgin[D]. Q. Tubero writeth, that from his first Consulship unto the beginning of the Civill war, he was ever wont to write downe for his heire, Cn. Pompeius, and to reade the saide will unto his soldiers in their publike assemblie. But in this last Testament of his, he ordained three Coheires,

---

[1] Which they were wont to cast over their shoulders. Senec. *de Benefico*. Or tucke up slack above the wast.   [2] Some read: Καὶ σὺ εἶ ἐκνων.
[3] Some expound this of the licter as if one corner thereof hung downe, carried as it was by three.   [4] Whereby it seemeth he had one given him in his neck before: which the Author hath omitted.   [5] 13 of September.

TWELVE CÆSARS

the nephewes all of his sisters¹. To wit C. Octavius², of three fourth parts, L. Pinarius, and Q. Pedius of on fourth part remaining. In the latter end and bottome of this Testamentarie Instrument, he adopted also C. Octavius into his house and name ; and many of those that afterwards murdered him, he nominated for guardiers to his sonne³, if it fortuned he had any borne. Yea and Decimus Brutus to be one of his second heires in remainder. Hee bequeathed in his legacies unto the people ⁴ his hortyards about Tiberis to ly common ; and three hundred Sesterces ⁵ to them by the Poll.

CAIUS
JULIUS
CESAR

84

The solemnitie of his Buriall being proclaimed, there was a pile of wood for his funerall fire reared in Mars field, neere unto the Tombe of Julia ⁶. Before the *Rostra* was placed a chappell ⁷ all guilt resembling the Temple of Venus Genetrix, and within it a Bedsteed ⁸ of Ivorie, richly spred with cloth of gold and purple, and at the head thereof a *Tropee* ⁹ supporting the Robe wherein he was slaine. Now because it was thought, that those should not have day enough who came to his offerings and brought their oblations, commandement was given, that without observing the strict order ¹⁰, every man might bring which way and by what streete of the Cittie he would, his gift into Mars field above said. During the Games and playes then exhibited there were chaunted certaine verses fitly applyed as well to moove pittie as hatred withall of his death, and namely out of the Tragedie of Pacuvius, entituled, *The judgement of Armour* ᵃ :

> *Men' Men' servasse, ut essent qui me perderent ?*
> Alas the while, that I these men should save :
> By bloudy death, to bring me to my grave ᵇ ;

¹ So hee was there great Unkle.   ² Afterwards Augustus, sonne of Atia Julius Cæsars sisters daughter.   ³ As *Posthumus*, *i.* borne after his death.   ⁴ Of Rome.   ⁵ 46s. 10d. ob. starling.   ⁶ His owne daughter, wife to Pompey, who died of childbirth, and by speciall privilege, was enterred in Mars field.   ⁷ Or Herse.   ⁸ Or Bierre.   ⁹ *Appion*, a pole.   ¹⁰ Which was, That the magistrates and Senatours shold go before without their badges and robes of dignitie : the knights and gentlemen follow in murning weed : then the soldiers, carrying the heads or points of their weapons downeward : last of all, the common people marshalled according to their Tribes.

THE HISTORIE OF

CAIUS
JULIUS
CESAR

as also another out of that of Accius[1] to the same sence. Insteed of a laudatorie oration, Antonius the Consul pronounced by the publike Crier, the Act of the Senate, wherein they decreede for him all honour, both divine and humaine: likewise the solemne oth wherewith they all obliged themselves to defend the life and person of him and none but him: whereunto he added some few words of his owne. The fore saide Bed[2], the Magistrates for the time being, and such as had borne office of State alreadie, had conveied[3] into the forum before the *Rostra*; which when some intended to burn within the cell of Jupiter Capitolinus, others in the Court of Pompeius[4]: all of a sodaine there were ii. fellowes with swords girt to their sides: and carrying ii. Javelins, who with light burning Tapers, set it on fire: and with that immediatly the multitude that stood round about gat drie sticks together and heaped them thereupon, with the Tribunall seats and other pues[5], of inferiour Magistrats, and whatsoever beside was readie and next at hand[c]. After them, the Minstrels and stage players disrobed themselves of those vestiments which out of the furniture of his Tryumphs they had put on for the present use and occasion, rent the same in peeces and flung all into the flaming fire. The olde Legionarie soldiers also did the like by their armour, wherein they bravely went to solemnize his funerall. Yea and most of the Cittie Dames did no lesse by their Jewels and Ornaments which they had about them: their childrens pendant brooches also and rich coats embrodred and bordred with purple. In this exceeding sorrow and publike mourning, a number there were besides from forraine Nations: who everie one after their Countrie manner, lamented round one after another, by companies in their turnes: but above all other the Jewes[6]: who also for many nights together frequented the place of his sepulture and where his bodie was burnt.

---

[1] Or Atius, who wrote a Tragedie bearing the same title. [2] Or Bierre. [3] *Detulerant*. [4] Where he was murdered. [5] Or Benches. [6] They affected Cæsar (it should seem) in regard of many benefits, and namely for bringing Pompeie to confusion who had forced their cheife Citie.

TWELVE CÆSARS

CAIUS JULIUS CESAR

85

The common people streight after his funerall obsequies went with burning fire-brands and torches to the dwelling houses of Brutus and Cassius: from whence being hardly repelled, they meeting with Helvius Cinna by the way, and mistaking his name, as if he had beene Cornelius Cinna (one who the day before had made a bitter invective as touching Cæsar and whom they sought for) him they slew: set his head upon a speare, and so carried it about with them. After this they erected in the Forum a solide Columne[1] almost 20 foote high, of Numidian Marble: with this title graven therupon; *PARENTI PATRIÆ.* 'To the father of his Countrie.' At which piller for a long time they used still to sacrifice, to make vowes and prayers, to determine and end certaine controversies interposing alwaies their oth by the name of Cæsar.

86

Cæsar left behind him in the minds of certaine friends about him, a suspition, that he was neither willing to have lived any longer, nor cared at all for life: because he stood not well to health, but was evermore crasie: and thereupon neglected as well all religious warnings from the Gods, as also what reports soever his friends presented unto him. There be that thinke, howe trusting upon that last Act of the Senate, and there oth aforesaid, he discharged the Guard of Spaniards from about him, who armed with swordes, gave attendance upon his person[2]. Others contrariwise are of opinion; that seeing as he did how he was forelaied on everie side, and confessing it were better once for all to undergoe those imminent daungers, than alwaies to stand in feare thereof, he was wont to say: It concerned not himselfe so much as it did the state, that hee should live and bee safe: as for him, he had gotten long since power and glorie enough: marie the Common-wealth (if ought but well came to him) should not bee at quiet, but incurre the troubles of Civill warre, the issue whereof would be farre worse then ever it had beene.

[1] Or Piller.   [2] *Insectantium.*

THE HISTORIE OF

CAIUS JULIUS CESAR

87

This one thing verily, all men well neere are agreed upon, That such a death befell unto him as himselfe in manner wished. For not onely uppon a time when he had read in Xenophon[1], how Cyrus beeing at the point of death gave some order for his funerall, hee setting light by so lingering and slow a kind of death, had wished to die quickely and of a suddaine; but also the verie daie before he was killed, in a certaine discourse mooved at supper in Marcus Lepidus house uppon this point, What was the best ende of a mans life? preferred that which was sodaine and unlooked for.

88

He died in the 56[2a] yeare of his age and was canonized among the Gods, not onely by their voice who decreed such honour unto him, but also by the perswasion of the common people. For at those Games and playes which were the first that Augustus his heire exhibited for him thus deified[3], there shone a blazing starre for seven dayes together, arising about the eleventh houre of the day; and beleeved it was to be the soule of Cæsar received up into heaven. For this cause also uppon his Image there is a starre set to the verie Crowne of his head. Thought good it was to damme up the Court where in hee was murdred[b]: to name the Ides of March *Parricidium*[c], and that the Senate should never meete in Counsell upon that day.

89

Of these murderers, there was not one in manner that either survived him above three yeares, or died of his naturall death. All stood condemned: and by one mishap or other perished: some by ship-wracke, others in battaile: and some againe[4], shortened their own daies, with the verie same dagger, wherewith they had wounded Cæsar.

[1] *Cyripædia*, 8. [2] In the 8 Septimane. [3] Consecrate. [4] Cassius: as Plutarch reporteth, and Brutus according to Dion, and the ii. Cascaes. A notable judgement of Almightie God upon the unnatural murderers of their Soveraine.

TWELVE CÆSARS

THE HISTORIE OF OCTAVIUS CÆSAR AUGUSTUS

1

HAT the principall name and linage of the Octavii, dwelt in times past at Velitræ, there be many evidences to shewe: for, both a street in the most frequented place of the said towne long since carried the name Octavius, and also there was to be seene an Altar there consecrated by one Octavius [1], who being Generall of the field in a warre against the borderers, when he happened to be sacrificing to Mars, upon newes brought that the enemie gave a suddaine charge, caught the Inwards of the beast sacrificed halfe raw as they were, out of the fire [2]; cut and offered them accordingly: and so entred into battaile and returned with victorie. There is beside, a publike Act extant upon record, wherein decreed and provided it was, that everie yeare after, the inwards in like manner should bee presented unto Mars, and the rest of the sacrifice remaining, carried backe unto the Octavii.

2

These Octavii [3], being by K. Tarquinius Priscus naturalized Romaines soone after translated and admitted by Servius Tullus, into the Senate among the Patritians, and Nobles, in processe of time ranged themselves with the commons, and with much adoe at length, by the meanes of Julius of

[1] Or to Octavius: *Octavio Consecrata*.   [2] Where they were a boyling or rosting.   [3] *Ea gens inter Romanos allecta*.

THE HISTORIE OF

OCTAVIUS CÆSAR AUGUSTUS sacred Memrie returned to the Patritian degree again: the first of these that by the peoples election bare any Magistracie, was C. Rufus: who having beene Questor begat Cn. and C. From them descended two families of the Octavii, and those for their estate of life farre different. For Cn. and all the rest from him one after another, attained to places of highest honour: but Caius and his posteritie everie one even unto the father of Augustus, (such was either their fortune or their will,) staied in the order and degree of gentlemen, and rose no higher. The great Grandfather of Augustus, in the second Punike war [1], served in qualitie of a Militar Tribune [2], in Sicilie, under Æmilius Papus Lord generall. His father contenting himselfe with bearing office like another Burgesse in his owne Bourrough, being left welthie by his father, grew to a good estate, and lived to be an olde man, in much peace and tranquilitie. But of these matters let others make report. Augustus himselfe writeth noe more but thus. That the house from whence he came, was of Romaine Gentlemen, welthie and ancient withall, wherein the first that ever came to be Senatour was his father. M. Antonius hitteth him in the teeth with his great Grandfather: saying he was but a Libertine borne, and by occupation a roper [3], and come out of a Village of the Thurines: also that his Grandfather was no better then a verie banquer [4]. Neither have I founde any more, as touching the Auncestours of Augustus by the Fathers side.

3

Octavius his father, from the verie beginning of his age, was of great welth and reputation; so that I cannot but mervaile, that hee also hath beene reported by some a banquer or monie changer: yea and one of the dealers of monie [a] and servitours employed in Campus Martius, by those that stand for offices: for having beene from his verie cradle brought uppe in wealth highly and plentifully, he both

---

[1] Against Anniball and the Carthaginians.   [2] Colonel of 1000 footmen.
[3] A seller of ropes: *restionem*, not *Restionem* with a capital *R*, as if it were a proper name.   [4] *Argentarium* an exchanger of monie for gaine.

TWELVE CÆSARS

attained unto honorable dignities with facilitie, and administred the same with credite and reputation. Presently uppon his Pretourshippe, the province of Macedonie fell unto his lot. And in his journey thither, the fugitives, to wit the reliques of Spartacus and Catilines forces, who then helde the Thurine teritorie hee defaited; having commission extraordinarily given unto him in the senate so to doe: this province hee governed with noe lesse justice then fortitude. For having discomfited in a great battaile the Bessi and the Thracians, he dealt so well with the Allies and confederats of that Kingdome: that there be certaine letters of M. Tullius Cicero extant, wherein he exhorteth and admonisheth his brother Quintus, (who at the same time, little to his credite and good name, administred the proconsulship of Asia) for to imitate his neigbour Octavius, in doing well by the Allies, and winning their love thereby.

OCTAVIUS CÆSAR AUGUSTUS

4

As he departed out of Macedonie before that he could professe himselfe to be a suiter for the Consulship, he died a suddaine death: leaving these children behind him alive, namely two daughters Octavia the elder, which hee had by Ancharia: Octavia the younger, and Augustus likewise, by Atia. This Atia was the daughter of M. Atius Balbus, and Julia the sister of C. Cæsar. Balbus by his fathers side was an Aricine, a man that shewed Senatours Images and armes in his house: by his mother linked to Magnus Pompeius in the neerest degree of consanguinitie. And having borne the office of Pretorship he among the xx. Commissioners devided by vertue of the Law Julia, the lands in the territory of Capua among the Commons. But M. Antonius, despising the parentage and petegree of Augustus by the mother side also, twitteth him and layeth in his dish, that his great Grandsire was an African borne: saying on while, that he kept a shop of sweete oyles, Ointments and perfumes; another while, that he was a baker in Aricia: Cassius verily of Parma, in a certaine Epistle taxeth Augustus as being the Nephew not of a Baker onely, but also of a banker, in

THE HISTORIE OF

OCTAVIUS CÆSAR AUGUSTUS these termes. 'Thou hast meale for thy mother. And then comes a banker of Nerulone, who out of a most painefull backehouse in Aricia knedeth and mooldeth it with his hands sullied by telling and exchanging monie[1].'

5

A.U.C. 691. Augustus was borne, when M. Tullius Cicero and Antonie were Consuls, the ninth day before the Calends of October[2], a little before the Sun rising, in the palatine quarter[a] of the Citie, at a place called Capita Bubula[3]: where now it hath a sacred Chappel, built and erected a little after he departed out of this world: for, as it is found in the records of the Senate, when C. Lectorius a young gentleman of the Patritian order, pleaded to have some easier punishment for the adulterie, and alledged, over and besides his yong yeares and parentage this also in his plea before the Senatours, that he was the possessor and as it were, the warden and Sextaine of that ground or soyle, which Augustus of happy memorie touched first[b], and requested that it might be given and granted unto the said Augustus as to his domestical and peculiar god: decreed it was that the same part of the house should be consecrated to that holy use.

6

There is yet to be seene the place of his nourcery, within a suburbian house belonging to his Auncesters, neere unto Velitra: a very little Cabin, about the bignes of a Larder or Pantry: the neighbours are possessed with a certaine conceit, as if he had been there also borne. To enter into this rowme unlesse it be of necessitie and with devout chastitie, men make it scrupulous and are affraide: upon an old conceived opinion, as if unto as many as came thether rashly and inconsiderately, a certaine horror and fearefulnes were presented. And verily, this was soone after confirmed by this occasion: for when the new Land lord and possessor of that farme house, either by chance and at unwares, or els to

[1] Al this is spoken allegorically of his base parentage. [2] 23 of September. [3] Oxe or Bull-heads.

TWELVE CÆSARS

try some experiment, went into it, there to take up his lodging, it happened that in the night within verie fewe houres after, being driven out from thence by some sodaine violence, (he knoweth not how,) he was found in manner halfe dead, together with bed and all, before the dore.

OCTAVIUS
CÆSAR
AUGUSTUS

7

Being yet an infant, surnamed he was Thurinus, in memorial of the beginning of his Auncestours: or else because in the countrie about Thurii, when hee was newly borne, his father Octavius fought a battaile against the Fugitives. That he was surnamed Thurinus, my selfe am able to report by a god and sufficient evidence, as having gotten an olde little counterfeit in brasse representing him being a child: which had in yron letters and those almost worne out, this name engraven. This said counterfeit, being given by me unto the Prince[1], is now devoutely kept and worshipped among other his bed chamber Images. Moreover called he is oftentimes in taunting wise by M. Antonius in his Epistles, Thurinus: and himselfe writeth unto him backe againe as touching that point, nothing but this: That he marvaileth why that former name of his should be objected unto him as a reproach. Afterwardes, he assumed the surname of C. Cæsar: and after it of Augustus: the one by the last will of his great Uncle, by the mother side, the other by the vertue of Munatius Plancus his sentence: for when some gave their opinion, that he ought to be stiled Romulus, as if he also had beene A Founder of the Cittie, Plancus prevailed, that he should be called rather Augustus: not onely for that it was a new Surname, but also greater and more honourable, because Religious and holy places, wherein also any thing is consecrated by bird flight, and feeding of them be called Augusta, *ab auctu, i.* of growing, or else *abavium gestu gustuve: i.* Of birds gesture and feeding. Like as Ennius also teacheth writing in this manner:

Augusto Augurio postquam inclyta condita Roma est.
After that Noble Rome was built by sacred flight of Birds.

[1] Hadrian the Emperor.

THE HISTORIE OF

OCTAVIUS
CÆSAR
AUGUSTUS

8

He was 4 yeares old when his father died: and in the xij. yeare of his age he praised in a publike assemblie, his Grand-mother Julia deceased. Foure yeeres after having put on his virill robe ª, he had militarie gifts ᵇ bestowed upon him at the African tryumph of Cæsar, albeit by reason of his yong yeares he had not once served in the warres. Soone after, when his Unkle (Cæsar) was gone into Spaine against Cn. Pompeius children, he followed with in a while, (being as yet not well recovered out of a greevous sickenesse,) even through waies infested by enemies, with verie few in his traine to accompany him, and having suffred shipwracke besides: whereby he mightily won his Uncles love, who quickely approved his towardly behaviour and disposition, over and above his diligence in travaile. When Cæsar, after he had recovered Spaine and brought it to his subjection, intended a voiage against the Daci [1], and from thence against the Parthians, he being sent afore to Apollonia, became a Student there and followed his booke. And so soone as he had certaine intelligence that Ceasar was slaine, and himselfe made his heire: standing in doubt and suspense a long time, whether he should implore the helpe of the Legions or no: at length he gave over that course verily, as too hastie and untimely, but when he was returned againe to Rome, he entred upon his inheritance, not withstanding his mother made some doubt thereof and his father in law Martius Philippus [2] a man of Consular degree much disswaded him therefrom. And from that time having levied and assembled his forces, he governed the common welth first jointly with M. Antonius and M. Lepidus ᶜ for the space almost of 12 yeres, and at the last for. xliiij. yeares by himselfe alone.

9

Having thus laid open the very sum as it were, of his life, I will goe through the parts thereof in particular: not by the times but by the severall kinds therof, to the end the same may be shewed and knowne more distinctly. Five

[1] Otherwise called Getœ. [2] His mothers husband.

TWELVE CÆSARS

civill warres he made, to wit, at Mutine, Philippi, Perusium, in Sicilie, and at Actium. Of which the first and last were against M. Antonius: the second against Brutus and Cassius, the third against L. Antonius brother to the Triumvir, the 4 against Sex. Pompeius, Cn. Pompeius his sonne. Of all these warres he tooke the occasion and quarrell from hence, namely, reputing and judging in his mind nothing more meet and convenient than the revenge of his unkles death and the maintenance of his acts and proceedinges.

OCTAVIUS
CÆSAR
AUGUSTUS

10

No sooner was he returned from Apollonia, but he purposed to set upon Brutus and Cassius at unwares: and (because upon foresight of daunger they were fled secretly out of the way) to take the course of law, and in their absence to endite them of murder. As for the Plaies and games for Ceasars victory because they durst not exhibit them, whose lot and office it was so to do, himselfe set them forth. And to the end that he might go through all other matters also more resolutely; he professed himselfe to labour for the Tribuneship [1] in the rowme of one who fortuned to die: albeit he was one of the Nobility, though not of the Senate. But seeing that M. Antonius the Consul withstood his attempts, where as he hoped he would have beene his principall friend in that suit: and vouchsafed not unto him so much as the assistance of his owne publike authority, or helpe procured from others in any thing, without he agreed and covenanted to yeeld unto him some exceeding consideration: he betooke himselfe unto the protection of those Nobles and chiefe Senatours unto whom he perceived that Antonius was odious: in this regard especially, that he [2] endevored all that he could by force of armes to expell Decimus Brutus besieged at Mutina, out of that province which by Ceasar was granted and by the Senate confirmed unto him. And thereupon by the advice and perswasion of some he set certaine persons privily in hand to murder Antonius; which perilous practise of his being detected and fearing still the like danger to himselfe, he waged the old

A.U.C. 710.

[1] Of the commons.   [2] i. Antonius.

THE HISTORIE OF

OCTAVIUS
CÆSAR
AUGUSTUS
A.U.C. 711.

soldiers with as bountifull a larges as possible he could, for the defence as well of his owne person as of the state. And being appointed to lead this armie thus levied, in qualitie of propretour, and together with Hirtius and Pansa, who had entred upon the Consulship, to aide D. Brutus, he made an end of this warre committed unto him within three moneths, in two fought fieldes. In the former of which, Antonie writeth that he fled, and without coat armour or horse appeared at length after two dayes and shewed himselfe. But in the battaile next following, well knowne it is, that he performed the part not onely of a Captaine but also of a soldier: and in the very heat and midst of the medly, by occasion that the Standerd bearer of his owne Legion was grievously hurt, he supported the Ægle with his owne shoulders [1] and so carried it a good while.

11

During this warre, when Hirtius had lost his life in the conflict, and Pansa soone after of his wound, it was bruited rifely abroad, that both of them were by his meanes slaine: to the ende that having defaited Antonius, and the Common-wealth beeing bereift of both Consuls, he alone might seize uppon the victorious armies. And verily the death of Pansa was so deepely suspected that Glyco the Physitian was committed to ward and durance, as if he had put poyson into his wound. Aquillius Niger addeth moreover and saith, that the one of the Consuls, to wit, Hirtius, was in the verie confused medly of the battaile killed by Augustus himselfe.

12

But so soone as he understood that Antonie after his flight was intertained by M. Lepidus: that other Captaines also and armies consented to take part with the side [2]: he forsooke without all delaies the cause of the Nobles and principall Senatours: and for the better pretence of this change and alteration of his minde, craftily and unjustly

---

[1] As massie and heavie as it was.   [2] *Propartibus:* of Pompeius and the common wealth. If you read *pro patribus, i.* with the Nobilitie.

TWELVE CÆSARS

alleadged the words and deedes of certaine of them: as if
some ^a had given it out of him: That he was a boy; others ^b,
that he was to be adorned, and honoured¹: that neither
himselfe nor the olde beaten soldiers might be rewarded
according to their desarts. And the better to approove his
repentance of the former side and faction that he tooke:
he fined the Nursines, in a great summe of monie, and
more than they were able to pay; for that upon the
Monuments or Tombe of those Citizens that were slaine
in the battaile at Mutina (which at their common charges
was reared) they wrote this Title, That they died for the
Libertie and Free-dome of their Cittie.

OCTAVIUS
CÆSAR
AUGUSTUS

13

Being entred into Societie with Antonie and Lepidus, hee
finished the Philippian warre also, (although he was but
weake and sickely,) and that with two battailes: in the
former being discamped and driven out of the field, hardly
hee escaped by flight and recovered the Regiment or wing
of Antonius. Neither used he moderately the successe of
his victorie, but when hee had sent the head of Brutus to
Rome for to bee bestowed under the Statue of Cæsar, he
dealt cruelly with the Noblest and most honourable prisoners,
and not without reproachfull words: so farre forth verily,
that to one of them, making humble suite and prayer for
his Sepulture, he answered, (by report) in this wise: That
it would be anone, at the dispose of the foules of the Aire:
and when others, to wit, the Father, and sonne ^a together
intreated for their lives; he commanded them either to cast
lots or trie by combate whether of them should have life
granted; and so beheld them both as they dyed, whilest the
father who offred himselfe to die was slaine, and the sonne
voluntarily take his death. Whereuppon the rest, and
amongst them M. Favonius that worthie follower of Cato,
when they were brought forth with their yrons and chaynes
to execution, after they had in honorable termes saluted
Antonius by the name of Emperour², openly reviled and let
flie at him most foule and rayling words. Having parted

A.U.C. 712.

¹ *Et tollendum.*   ² Soveraine commander.

THE HISTORIE OF

OCTAVIUS CÆSAR AUGUSTUS

betweene them their charges and offices after this victorie, when Antonius undertooke to settle the East in good order, and himselfe to bring the olde Soldiers backe into Italic, and to place them there, in the lands and teritories belonging to the free Townes and Burowghes, he kept himselfe in favour neither with the said old soldiers, nor the former possessors of those lands: whilest the one sort complained, that they were disseized: and the other, that they were not well entreated according to their hope, for so good deserts.

14

A.U.C. 713.

At which verie time, he forced L. Antonius (who confidently presuming upon the Consulship which he then bare, and his brothers power withall, went about to make an insurrection and alteration in the state) to flie unto Perusia, and there for verie hunger compelled him to yeeld: but yet not without great jeopardie of his owne person, both before and after the warre: for when at a certaine solemne sight of stage plaies, he had commanded an ordinarie and common soldier who was set within the 14 ranks [a], to be raised by an officer, and thereupon a rumor was carried and spred by his malicious ill willers and back-biters, as if presently after torture he had put the same soldier to death. There lacked verie little, but that in the concourse and indignation of the militarre multitude, he had come to a mischiefe and beene murdered. This onely saved his life: that the man for a while missed, sodainely was to be seene againe alive and safe without any harme done unto him. About the walls of Perusia, as hee sacrificed, he had like to have been intercepted by a strong companie of sword fencers that sallied out of the Towne.

15

A.U.C. 714.

After he had forced Perusia, he proceeded to the execution of verie many, and ever as any went about either to crave pardon or to excuse themselves, with this on word he stopped their mouthes, 'Die yee must.' Some write, that iij. hundred of both degrees (to wit Senatours and Knights)

TWELVE CÆSARS

chosen out of them who had yeelded, were killed as sacrifices[1] upon the Ides of March[2], at the Alter built in the honor of Julius (Cæsar) of famous memorie. There have been others who wrote, that of verie purpose he tooke armes and made this warre to the end that his close adversaries and those who rather for feare, then of good will held in, upon occasion given and opportunitie by L. Antonius there leader, might be detected: that having once vanquished them and confiscated their goods, the rewards promised unto the olde soldiers he might the better performe.

OCTAVIUS CÆSAR AUGUSTUS

16

The warre in Sicile he began betimes and with the first, but drewe it out a long time; as being often intermitted: one while, for the repairing and rigging of his fleete which by two ship-wrackes in tempest, (and that in summer time[3]) he had lost: another while by occasion of peace made at the earnest cry of the people, for the provision of their victuales cut off and kept from them: and the famine thereby dayly growing: untill such time as having built newe ships, manumised and set free xx. thowsand slaves, and those put to the ore for to learne to row gallies, he made the Haven Julius at Baiz by letting the sea into the Lakes, Lucrinus and Avernus. In which when he had trained and exercised his sea forces whole winters, he overcame Pompeius betweene Milæ[4] and Naulochus[5]: at the verie houre and instant time of which Naval battaile, he was suddenly surprized with such a sound sleepe, that his friends were faine to waken him and raise him out of bed for to give the signall. Wherupon occasion and matter was ministred (as I thinke) to Antonius[6], for to cast this in his teeth, that he could not so much as with his eyes open see directly before him the battaile set in ray, but lay like a sencelesse blocke on his backe, looking onely into the skie aloft[7]: nor once arose and came in sight of his soldiours, before that M. Agrippa had

A.U.C. 717.

A.U.C. 718.

---

[1] Brained with an axe: and not beheaded. [2] On which day Julius Cæsar was murdred. [3] When commonly it is calme in those Seas. [4] A port town in Sicilie. [5] An harbour neere Messanah. [6] Marcus, the Triumvir. [7] For Gods helpe.

THE HISTORIE OF

OCTAVIUS CÆSAR AUGUSTUS put his enemies 12 ships to flight. Others blame and charge him both for a speech and deede also of his: as if he should crie out and say, That seeing his owne regiment of ships were cast away by tempests, he would even against the will of Neptune obtaine victorie. And verily the next day of the Circensian Games [a], he tooke out of the solemne pompe there shewed, the Image of the said God: neither in any other warre lightly was hee in more and greater dangers. For having transported one armie into Sicilie, when he sailed backe againe for to waft over the rest of his forces from the continent and firme land [1], he was at unwares overtaken and surprised by Demochares and Apollophanes the Lievetenants and Admirals of Pompeius, but at the length with verie much ado, he escaped with one onely barke. In like manner as he travailed by land unto Rhegium [b] neere Locrie, kenning a farre of Pompeis [2] gallies sayling along the coasts, and weening them to be his owne, he went downe to the shore, and had like to have been caught and taken by them. And even then as he made shift to flie and escape through by-waies and blind-lanes: a bond-servant of Æmilius Paulus a companion of his, taking it to the heart that his Maisters father Paulus, was in times past by him proscribed and outlawed, and imbracing, as it were, the good occasion and opportunitie of revenge now offered, gave the attempt to kill him. After the flight of Pompeius [3], when M. Lepidus one of his Collegues [4], whome hee had called forth of Afrike to his aide, bearing himselfe proude uppon the confidence of xx. Legions, challenged a soverainetie over the rest [5], and that, with terrour and menaces: hee stript him of all his armie, and uppon his humble submission and supplication, pardoned his life, but confined him for ever to Circeii. The Societie of M. Antonius [5] wavering alwaies in doubt-full tearmes and uncertaine, and notwithstanding many and sundrie reconciliations, not well knit and confirmed, he brake of quite in the ende: and the better to proove and make good that he had degenerated [c] from the civill

---

[1] Of Italie.   [2] Sext.   [3] Sext.   [4] In the Triumvirate.   [5] M. Antonius and Octavius Augustus.   [6] Some Critickes begin here a newe Chapter.

behaviour and modestie of a (Romaine) Citizen, he caused OCTAVIUS
the last will and testament of the said Antonie, which he CÆSAR
had left at Rome ᵈ, and therein nominated even the Children AUGUSTUS
of Cleopatra among his heires to be opened and red in a
publike assemblie. Howbeit when hee was judged by the
State an enemie, hee sent backe unto him those of his neerest
acquaintance and inward friendes and among other C. Sosius,
and T. Domitius¹ᵉ, being Consuls at that time still. The A.U.C. 722.
Bononians also, for that of olde they were dependantes of
the Antonii and in there retinue and protection, hee by a
publicke Act acquit and pardoned for not entring into a
confederace with all Italie, on his side ᶠ. Not long after, he
vanquished him in a Navall battaile before Actium ᵍ, what A.U.C. 723.
time by reason that the fight continued untill it was late in
the evening hee was forced to lodge all night conqueror as
he was, on ship board.

17

When he had retired himselfe from Actium into the Iland
Samos for his winter harbour, being disquieted with the
newes of his soldiers mutinie demanding rewardes and discharge from service; those I meane, whom after the victorie
atcheived hee had from out of the whole number sent before to Brindis, he went againe into Italie: but in crossing
the Seas thither, twice was he tossed and troubled with
Tempests: first betweene the promontories or Capes of
Poloponensus and Ætolia: againe, about the Mountaines
or Cliffes Ceraunii. In both which places, part of his
pinnaces were cast away and drowned: and with all, the
verie takling of that shippe wherein he embarked was rent
and torne asunder: yea, and the rudder thereof quite
broken. Neither staied he at Brindis above 27 daies, that A.U.C. 724.
is to say untill hee had setled his soldiers and contented
them in their desires and requests: but fetching a compasse
about Asia, and Siria, sailed into Ægypt. Where after hee
had laied seige unto Alexandria, whether Antonie and
Cleopatra were together fled: he soone became Mais. of
that Cittie. And as for Antonie, who now (all to late)

¹ Cn. Domitius.

THE HISTORIE OF

OCTAVIUS CÆSAR AUGUSTUS made meanes for conditions of peace hee enforced to make himselfe away, and saw him dead[1]. And to Cleopatra whom most gladly he would have saved alive for to beautifie his tryumph hee set the Psylli[a] to sucke out the venime and poyson within her bodie: for that supposed it was she died with the sting of the Serpent Aspis[b]. This honour he did unto them both, namely to burie them in one sepulcher: and the Tombe by them begun, he commanded to be finished. Young Antonie the elder of those twaine whom he had by Fulvia, he caused to be violently haled from the Statue of Julius Cæsar of famous memorie, unto which, after many prayers but all in vaine, he was fled as to sanctuarie, and so killed him. Likewise Cæsario whom Cleopatra gave out openly that she had conceived by his father Cæsar[2], he fetched backe againe from the place whether he was fled, and put him to death. The rest of the Children of Antonie and the Queene togither, he both saved (no lesse than if they had beene linked in neere Alliance unto himselfe,) and also according to the state of everie one of them, he maintained and cherished respectively.

18

About the same time, when he beheld the Tombe together with the corps of Alexander the great, taken newly foorth of the vaute or secret Chappell where it was bestowed, he set upon it a coronet of gold: and strewing flowers thereupon worshipped it: and being asked the question, whither hee would looke upon the Ptolomes[3] also? he answered that he was desirous indeed to see a King but not the dead[a]. When he had reduced Ægypt in the forme of a province, to the end that he might make it more fruitfull and fit to yeeld corne and victuals for the Cittie of Rome, he skowred and cleansed by helpe of soldiers, all those ditches where into Nilus over-

---

[1] *Viditque mortuum.* In some copies we read thus: *Viditque mortuam Cleopatram, i.* And he saw Cleopatra dead: for he heard onely of Antonies death and saw the sworde wherewith hee wounded himselfe.   [2] His great Unkle indeede but father by adoption.   [3] Or *Ptolemæis, i.* the bodies or Tombes of the Ptolemœes. If you read *Ptolemæum*, it is meant of Lagus.

floweth, which by long time had been choaked with mud. And that the memorie of his Actiake victorie might be more renowmed among posteritie, he built the Cittie Nicopolis over against Actium, and ordained certaine games and plaies there, everie 5 yeeres: and having enlarged the old Temple of Apollo[1], and the place werein he had encamped, he beautified with Navall spoiles and then consecrated it to Neptune and Mars.

OCTAVIUS CÆSAR AUGUSTUS

19

After this, sundry tumults and the verie beginnings of commotions and insurrections, many conspiracies also detected before they grew to any head, he suppressed: and those, some at one time, and some at an other: namely first one of Lepidus the younger: then, another of Varro Murœna, and Fannius Capio: soone after that, of M. Genatius[2]: and so forward of Plautius Rufus and L. Paulus, his neeces husband: and besides all these, that of L. Audasius accused of forgerie, and counterfeit seales; a man neither for yeares able nor bodie sound: likewise of Asimius Epicadus descended from the Parthynes Nations a Mungrell[3a]: and last of all, of Telephus, a base Nomenclator[4], servant to a woman: for free was not Augustus from the conspiracie and daunger, no not of the most abject sort of people. As for Audasius and Epicadus, they had entended to carrie away Julia his daughter and Agryppa, his Nephew (out of those Ilands wherin they abode confined) unto the armies: and Telephus purposed upon a deepe conceite that the soveraintie of dominion was by the Destinies and will of God due unto him, even to lay upon him and the Senate violent hands. And more then that, one time there was taken neere unto his bed-chamber by night, a camp-slave belonging to the Illyrian armie, who had deceived the porters and gotten thither with a wood knife at his side, but whether he were out of his wits, or feigned himselfe mad, it was uncertaine:

[1] Which stood upon the saide promontarie Actium. [2] Or Egnatius.
[3] Begotten betweene a bond slave and a Libertine. [4] Or Prompter of names, emploied in telling of their names who came to salute and bid good morrow, and placing also of guests at the Table, and in no better service.

THE HISTORIE OF

OCTAVIUS
CÆSAR
AUGUSTUS

for nothing could bee wrung out of him by examination upon the racke and torture.

20

A.U.C. 721, 727.

Foraine warres he made in his owne person ij. in all and no more: that is to say, the Dalmatian ᵃ, when he was yet a verie youth: and the Cantabrian, after he had defaited Antonie. In the Dalmatian warre, he was wounded also: for in one battaile he gat a blow upon his right knee with a stone: and in an other, not his leg onely, but also both his armes were hurt with the fall from a bridge [1] ᵇ. The rest of his warres he managed by his Lieftennants: yet so as that in some of them namely the Pannonian and the Germaine, hee would either come betweene times, or else remaine not farre of: making his progresse from the Cittie of Rome, as farre as to Ravenna, or Millaine or to Aquileia.

21

He subdued partly by his owne conduct in proper person, and in part by his Lieftenants having commission immediatly from him and directed by his auspicies, Cantabria, Aquitaine, Pannonia, and Dalmatia together with all Illyricum, Rhætia likewise, the Vindelicis, the Salassians and the Nations inhabiting the Alpes. He repressed also the incursions of the Dakes, having slaine three of their Generals with a great number of them besides. And the Germaines he remooved and set further of; even beyond the river Albis. Howbeit, of these the Suevians and the Sicambrians, because they yeelded themselves, he brought over into Gaule, and placed them in the lands next unto Rhene. Other Nations being mal-content, he reduced unto his obedience. Neither made hee warre upon any people without just and necessarie causes: and so farre was he from desire of enlarging his Empire, or advancing his martiall glorie, that he compelled certaine princes and potentates of the Barbarians, to take an oath in the Temple of Mars the Revenger ᵃ for to continue in their allegiance, and in the protection and peace which they sued for: yea and from some of them he assaied

[1] Or turret of woode.

to exact a new kind of Hostages, even women[1], for that he perceived, that they neglected the pledges of the males. And yet he gave them libertie, as often as they would, to receive their hostages againe. Neither proceeded he at any time against those, who either usually or trecherously above the rest tooke armes and rebelled, to any punishment more greivous then this, even to sell them as captives: with this condition, that they shold not serve in any neighbour Country, nor be manumised and made free within the space of 30[2] yeares. By which fame of vertue and moderation that went of him, he induced and drew the very Indians and Scythians, Nations knowen by report and heere say onely, to make suite of their owne accord by Embassadours, for amitie of him and the people of Rome. The Parthians also, when as he laied claime unto Armenia, yeelded soone unto him: and those militarie Ensignes which they had taken from M. Crassus and M. Antonius, they delivered unto him againe at his demaund: and moreover, offred hostages unto him. And finally when there were many Competitours together at one time claiming a title to the Kingdome, they would not allow of any, but one by him elected.

OCTAVIUS CÆSAR AUGUSTUS

22

The temple of Janus Quirinus[a], which from the foundation of the City before his daies had once and twice beene shut, he in a farre shorter space of time (having peace both by sea and land) shut a third time[3]. Twice he rod on horsebacke ovant.[b] into the City: once presently upon the Philippian warre; and againe, after the Sicilian. He kept three Triumphes riding in his chariot: to wit, the Dalmatian, the Actiak, and the Alexandrian, and these continued all for three dayes together.

23

Of shamefull foiles and grievous overthrowes, he received but two in all: and those in no place else but in Germanie; namely when Lollius and Varus[4] were defaited. That of

A.U.C. 738, 762.

---

[1] Unusuall in those days. [2] Or 20, rather. [3] *Tertio*, or *ter. i.* thrice.
[4] Quintilius Varus.

THE HISTORIE OF

OCTAVIUS CÆSAR AUGUSTUS

Lollius, was a matter of dishonour more than losse and domage; but the other of Varus, drew with it in manner utter destruction; as wherein three Legions with their Generall, the Lieutenants and Auxiliaries [a], all were slaine. Upon the newes of this Infortunity, he proclaimed a set watch both day and night through the City of Rome; for feare of some tumult and uprore: and the commissions of Presidents and Deputies over Provinces, he renewed and enlarged their time of government: to the end, that the Allies of the people of Rome might bee kept in alleageance by governours, such as were both skilfull and also acquainted with them. Hee vowed also the great (Romaine) Games and Playes to the honour of Jupiter Opt. Max. if the Commonwealth turned to better State[1]. This happened, during the time of the Cimbrian and Marsian warre[2]. For, therewith (by report) hee was so troubled and astonied, that for certaine moneths together hee let the haire of beard and head grow still and wore it long, yea and other whiles would runne his head against the dores[3], crying out, 'Quintilius Varus, Deliver up thy Legions againe.' And the very day [b] of this infortunate calamity he kept every yeere mournfull, with sorow and lamentation.

24

In warfare and feates of armes, he both altered and also instituted many points: yea and some he reduced to the auncient manner. Militarie discipline [a] he exercised most severely. He permitted not so much as any of his Lieutenants, but with much adoe and discontentment, to visite otherwhiles their wives; and never but in the winter moneths [b]. A Romaine Knight, for cutting off the thombs [c] of two young men his sonnes, to avoid the militarie oath and warre service, he set in open port sale, himselfe (I say) and all his goods. Whom notwithstanding, because he saw the Publicanes [d]

---

[1] *Si Resp. in meliorem statum vertisset.*   [2] Which also was called *Bellum sociale,* wherein the Associate nations in Italy rebelled: of which Rebellion the Authors were the Marsi.   [3] Upon an opinion of the Painims, that if they did injurie to their owne bodies they should sooner pacific the Gods.

TWELVE CÆSARS

about to buy, and bid very well for him, he appointed and delivered to his owne Freed man, that being confined and sent away unto his living and lands in the Country, he might permit him to live as Free. The tenth Legion, for being stubborne and unwilling to obey, he dismissed all and whole with ignominie: other legions likewise, requiring malapertly their discharge, he cassed without allowance of rewards due for their service. Whole bands or cohorts, if any of them gave ground and reculed, he tithed, that is to say, executed every tenth man of them: and the rest, he allowed barly in steed of wheat to feede upon. Those centurions who forsooke their Stations, he punished with death, even as well as the common soldiers of their bands: and for other kinds of Delinquencie he put them to shame sundry waies, as commanding them to stand all the day long before the Prætorium [1] sometimes in their single coates [2] and ungirt; other-whiles with ten foote perches [3] in their hands; or else carying turfes of earth.

OCTAVIUS CÆSAR AUGUSTUS

25

After the civile warres, he called none of his soldiours either in any publike speech, or by way of edict or proclamation, by the name of Fellow-soldiours [a], but plaine Souldiours. Nay hee would not suffer them otherwise to be termed so much as by his sonnes, or his wives sonnes: thinking it was a more affected manner of Appellation than stoode either with martial Law, or the quietnes of those times [a], or the majestie of himselfe and his house. Libertines [b] he emploied in soulderie unlesse it were at Rome about skarfires by night, (notwithstanding there was feared some tumult and uprore by occasion of great dearth and scarcity) but twice onely: once in garizon for defence of those Colonies which bounded fast upon Illyricum; a second time for keeping the banks of the river of Rhene. And those, being as yet bond, imposed upon men and women of the wealthier sort for to set out, but without delay manumised, he kept

[1] The Generals Pavilions. [2] Or wastcoates, without their *Saga*. [3] Or meeting poles, in token of Regradation or putting downe to a lower place.

THE HISTORIE OF

OCTAVIUS
CÆSAR
AUGUSTUS

with him to serve under one of the formost banners[1] in the vantguard; neither intermingled with such as were Free borne, nor in the same manner armed. As for militarie gifts hee gave unto his souldiours trappers collars and whatsoever stoode upon gold or silver[2], much sooner than Vallar or Mural coronets[c] which were more honourable. These he bestowed most sparily; and when he did, it was without suit made therefore: and many times upon the common and base souldiers[d]. He gave unto M. Agrippa after a navale victory in Cilicia a blew streamer. Those Captaines onely who had triumphed, albeit they were both companions with him in his expeditions, and also partakers of his victories, he thought not meete to be rewarded with any gifts at all: because they also had power to bestow the same upon whom they would. Moreover he deemed nothing lesse beseeming a perfit and accomplished Captaine, than hast-making and rashnesse. And therefore, these mots and sentences were rife in his mouth. Σπούδε βραδέως,

Ασφαλὴς γὰρ ἐς ἀμείνων, ἢ θρασύς στρατηλάτης[e]:

As also, *Sat celeriter fieri, quicquid fiat satis bene*[g]. His saying was, That neither battaile nor warre was once to be under taken, unlesse there might be evidently seene more hope of gaine than feare of domage: for such as sought after the smallest commodities, not with as little daunger, he likened unto those, that angle or fish with a golden hooke: for the losse whereof, if it happened to be knapt or broken off, no draught of fish whatsoever, was able to make amends.

26

He managed magistracies and honorable places of government before due time[3]; some of them also of a new kinde[4]; and others in perpetuity[5]. The Consulship hee usurped and entred upon in the twentieth yeere of his age[a], presenting

---

[1] *Sub primore vexillo* or *sub proprio vexillo*, i. under his owne banner.
[2] *Quicquid auro argentoque; constaret:* or rather, *quanquam auro argentoque; constarent*, i. Albeit they were made of gold and silver.   [3] By the lawes *Annuariæ*, or *Annales*.   [4] As the Triumvirate.   [5] As the Tribunes authoritie and Censureship.

TWELVE CÆSARS

forcibly and in hostile manner his legions before the City, sending some of purpose to demaund it, even in the name of the Armie for him. What time verily, when the Senate made some doubt and stay of the matter, Cornelius a Centurion and the chiefe man of that message, casting of[1] his souldiours Jacket and shewing his swords haft, stucke not to say thus openly in the Senate house, 'This here shall doe the deede, if yee will not'[b]. His second Consulship hee bare nine yeares after: the third, but one yeare betweene: the rest ensuing hee continued one after an other unto the eleventh. Afterwardes having refused many Consulships when they were offered unto him, his twelfth Consulship a greater while after, even 17 yeares, himselfe made suite for: so did hee againe, two yeares after it, for his thirtenth: to the ende that being himselfe in place of the Soveraine and highest Majestrate, hee might bring honorably into the Common Hall, C. and L. his (adopted) sonnes[2]; each of them to commence and performe their first pleadings at their due time[3] in virile gownes. The five middle Consulships betweene, to wit from the sixth to the eleventh he helde the whole yeeres thorough: the other, for the space of sixe, or nine, foure, or three moneths: but the second, very fewe howers: for uppon the very Calends of Januarie[4], when hee had sitten a while upon his curule chaire of estate before the temple of Jupiter Capitolinus; hee resigned up the Office, and substituted another in his place. Neither entred hee upon all his Consulships at Rome: but the fourth in Asia; the fifth, in the Iland Samos; the eigth and ninth at Tarracon.

OCTAVIUS CÆSAR AUGUSTUS

27

The Triumvirate for setling of the Common-wealth[5], hee administred for the space of tenne yeeres: wherein verily, hee stoode against his colleagues proceedings for a good while, that there might be no proscription: but when it

---

[1] Or casting it behind him, *rejecto sagulo*. [2] The naturall sonnes of his daughter Julia and C. Agrippa. [3] The elder in his twelfth, the younger in his thirteenth Consulate. [4] The first of Januarie or Newyeeres day. [b] That was the colour and pretence of it.

THE HISTORIE OF

OCTAVIUS CÆSAR AUGUSTUS was once on foote, hee executed it more sharply than they both. For, whereas they were exorable and would bee oftentimes intreated by favour and prayer, to respect the persons of many, hee alone was very earnest, that none might bee spared: among the rest, hee proscribed C. Toranius also, his owne Tutour and guardian, yea and the companion in the Office of Ædileship with his father Octavius. Junius Saturninus writeth moreover, that after the proscription was ended, when M. Lepidus had in the Senate-house excused all that was past and given good hope of clemencie for the time to come, because there had beene execution enough done alreadie: he on the contrarie side professed openly, That hee had determined no other end of the saide proscription, but that hee might have liberty still to proceede in all things as he would. Howbeit, in testimonie of repentance for this rigour and obstinacie of his, hee honoured afterward with the dignitie of Knighthood T. Junius Philopæmen [1], for that hee was reputed to have in times past hid his owne Patron, that was proscribed. In the same Triumvirate, hee incurred many waies the ill will and heart-burning of the people: for he commaunded that Pinarius a Gentleman of Rome, (what time as he himselfe made a publike speech in an assembly whereunto hee had admitted a multitude of Paganes, that is to say, such as were no souldiours, and espied him there to take notes of something that he delivered before the souldiours, supposing him to be over busie and a spie,) should be stabbed to death even in his sight: yea, and hee terrified Tedius Afer, Consull elect, (because hee had maliciously in some spitefull termes depraved something that he had done) with so great menaces, that in a melancholy hee cast himselfe headlong and brake his owne necke. Likewise, as Q. Gallius the Pretour held under his robe a paire of duple writing tables, when hee came of course to doe his duty and salute him, he suspecting, that he had a (short) sword hidden underneath, and not daring straightwaies to search him farther, for feare something else than a sworde should bee found about him, within a little while

[1] Or Vinius, for so was his Patrone named.

TWELVE CÆSARS

after caused him to be haled out of the Tribunall seate of Judgement, by the handes of certaine Centurions of Souldiours, and put to torture like a bondslave; yea and seeing he would confesse nothing, commanded him to be killed; having first with his owne hands plucked his eies out of his head. Howbeit Augustus writeth, that the said Gallius by pretending to parle secretly with him, laid waite for his life; whereupon hee committed him to prison, and afterwards dismissed and enlarged him onely to dwell in Rome: and that in the end hee perished either by shipwracke, or else by the hands of theeves who forlayed him. Hee received and held the Tribunate in perpetuity. Therein, once or twice, he chose and assumed unto him a colleague, for severall Lustra[1]. Hee tooke upon him likewise the government of manners and Lawes as a perpetuall Censour: in full right whereof, although hee had not the honourable title of Censureship, yet hee helde a survey and nombring of the people thrice: the first and third with a companion in office; the middle by himselfe alone.

OCTAVIUS CÆSAR AUGUSTUS

A.U.C. 731.

28

Twice hee was in minde, to have resigned up his absolute government: first, immediatly uppon the suppressing of Anthonie, mindfull of that which oftentimes hee had objected against him[2], namely, as if it had beene long of him[3], that it was not resigned, and the Common-wealth brought to a free state againe: and secondly, by reason that hee was weary of a long and lingering sicklinesse; what time he sent also for all the Magistrates and the Senate[4], home to his house; and delivered up an Account-booke or Register of the whole Empire[5]. But considering better with himselfe, that were he once a private person, he could not live without daunger; and withall, that it would greatly hazard the Common-wealth, to be put into the hands and dispose of many, he continued in the holding thereof still. And whether the event ensuing, or his will heerein were better,

---

[1] *i.* The space of 5 yeeres. [2] The saide Antonie. [3] *i.* Augustus. [4] *Ac Senatum:* or, *e senatu, i.* out of the Senate. [5] Or of his acts and proceedings in the government.

THE HISTORIE OF

OCTAVIUS CÆSAR AUGUSTUS

it is hard to say. Which will of his, as hee pretended oftentimes when he sate in place, so hee testified also by a certaine edict in these wordes: 'O that I might establish the Common wealth safe and sound in her owne proper seate[1], and thereof reape that fruite which I desire: even that I may be reported the Author of an excellent estate, and carie with mee when I die this hope, that the ground-worke and the foundations of the Common-wealth which I shall lay, may continue and abide stedfast in their place.' And verily what hee wished, himselfe effected and brought to passe[2], having endevoured and done his best every way, that no man might repent of this newe estate. For the Citie beeing not adourned according to the majestie of such an Empire and Subject to the casualties of Deluges and fires, hee beautified and set out so, as justly he made his boast, that where he found it built of bricke, hee left it all of marble. And for the safety thereof, hee performed as much for future posterity as could be fore-seene and provided for by mans wit and reason.

29

Publike works he built very many whereof the chiefe and principal was his Forum or stately Hall of Justice, together with the temple of Mars the Revenger: the temple of Apollo in Palatium; the Temple likewise of Jupiter the Thunderer, in the Capitol. The reason why he built the said Forum, was the multitude of men and their suites: which because ij. would not suffice[a], seemed to have need of a third also. And therfore with great speed erected it was for that publike use, even before the temple of Mars was finished. And expresly provided it was by law, that in it publike causes should be determined apart, and choosing of Judges (or Juries) by it selfe. The temple of Mars hee had vowed unto him, in the Philippian warre which hee tooke in hand for the revenge of his fathers death. He ordained therefore by an Act, that heere the Senate should

---

[1] Base or Piedstall.   [2] As if he had beene a God himselfe, according to the saying, *Sapiens ipse fingit fortunam sibi.*

TWELVE CÆSARS

be consulted with, as touching warres and triumphs: that OCTAVIUS
from hence those Pretours or Governours who were to goe CÆSAR
into their provinces should be honorably attended and AUGUSTUS
brought onward on their way: and that hither they should
bring the ensignes and ornaments of triumph, who returned
with victorie. The temple of Apollo he reared in that part
of the Palatine house, which being smitten with lightning
was by that God required, as the Soothsayers out of their
learning had pronounced: hereto was adjoyned a gallerie,
with a librarie of Latine and Greeke bookes. In which
temple, he was wont in his old age both to sit oftentimes
in counsaile with the Senate, and also to over-see and
review the Decuries of the Judges. He consecrated the
temple unto Jupiter the Thunderer, upon occasion that
he escaped a daunger, what time as in his Cantabrian
expedition, as he travailed by night, a flash of lightning
glaunced upon his licter, and strucke his servant stone dead,
that went with a light before. Some works also he made
under other folkes names, to wit his nephew, his wife and
sister; as the Gallerie and stately Pallace of Lucius and
Caius[1]: likewise the Gallerie or Porches of Livia and
Octavia: the Theatre also of Marcellus. Moreover divers
other principall persons hee oftentimes exhorted to adorne
and beautifie the City, every man according to his ability
either by erecting new monuments, or else by repairing and
furnishing the old. By which meanes many an Ædifice was
by many a man built: as namely the temple of Hercules and
the Muses by Marcus Philippus: the temple of Diana by
L. Cornificius: the Court of Liberty[2] by Asinius Pollio:
a temple of Saturne by Munatius Plancus: a Theatre
by Cornelius Balbus; and an Amphitheatre[b] by Statillus
Taurus: but many and those very goodly monuments by
M. Agrippa.

---

[1] His daughters children by Agrippa. [2] *Atrium libertatis. Atrium,*
quasi *aithrion.* A place where learned men were wont to meete and
conferre, as our Merchants doe in the Royall Exchange, built not unlike unto it with arched walks on every side standing upon pillers: and
as this cloisture was called *Peristylium,* so, the open yard within, *Atrium,* or
Subdival.

O

THE HISTORIE OF

OCTAVIUS
CÆSAR
AUGUSTUS

30

The whole space of the City he devided into wards [a] and strectes. He ordained, that as Magistrates or Aldermen yeerely by lot should keepe and governe the former: so their should be Maisters or Constables elected out of the Commons of every streete, to looke unto the other. Against skarefires he devised night-watches and watchmen. To keepe downe Inundations and Deluges, he enlarged and cleansed the channell of the River Tiberis, which in times past was full of rammell and the ruines of houses, and so by that meanes narrow and choaked. And that the Avenues on every side to the City might be more passable, he tooke in hand himselfe to repaire the high way or Cawsie Flaminia, so farre as to Ariminnum: and the rest he committed to sundry men who had triumphed, for to pave; and the charges thereof to be defraied out of the money raised of spoiles and sackage. The sacred Churches and Chappels decayed and ruinate by continuance of time, or consumed by fire he reedified: and those together with the rest hee adorned with most rich oblations; as who brought into the Cell, or Tabernacle of Jupiter Capitolinus at one Donation, 16000 pound weight of gold, besides pretious stones valued at 50 millions of Sesterces.

31

A.U.C. 741.

But after that hee entred now at length upon the High priesthood when Lepidus was once dead, which he never could finde in his heart to take from him whiles he lived: what bookes soever of prophesies and destinies went commonly abroad in Greeke and Latine, either without authors, or such as were not authenticall and of credite, he caused to be called in from all places, to the number of 2000 and above: and when he had burnt them, he reteined those only of Sibyls prophesies. And even of those also he made some special choice: and bestowed them close in two litle Desks or coffers under the base and piedstoole of Apollo Palatinus. The yeeres revolution reduced as it was into order by Julius of sacred memory, but afterwards through negligence

TWELVE CÆSARS

troubled and confused, he brought againe to the former calcu-   OCTAVIUS
lation. In the dispose whereof, he called the moneth Sextilis   CÆSAR
(rather than September wherin he was borne,) by his owne   AUGUSTUS
name, because in it there befell unto him both his first
Consulship and also notable victories. Of all the Religious
and priests, but especially of the vestall virgins he augmented the number, the dignity and the commodities also.
And whereas in the rowme of any vestall Nun deceased,
there must another of necessity be chosen and taken, he perceiving many to make suite that they might not put their
daughters to the lottery; protested and bound it with an
oath, that if any one of his owne Nieces or daughters
daughters were of competent age he would present her to
the place. Divers aunvient ceremonies also which by little
and little were disused and abolished, he restored againe, as
namely the Augurie[a] of Salvis, the Flaminship of Jupiter, the
sacred Lupercal, the Sæcular playes[b] and the *Compitalitii.*
At the Lupercall Solemnities, he commanded that no beard-
less boyes should runne. Likewise, at the Secular playes, he
forbad young folke of both sexes, to frequent any shew
exhibited by night; unlesse it were in the company of some
aunvient person of their kindred. The Tutelare Images of
crosse-wayes called *Lares Compitales* he was the first that
ordained to adorne twice in the yeere with flowers of the
spring and sommer seasons. The principal honour next
unto the immortall gods, he performed to the memoriall
of those worthy Captaines, who had raised the Romaine
onpire from a small thing to so high and glorious a state.
And therefore both the works and monuments of every of
them he repaired and made againe, reserving their titles
and inscriptions still; and all their Statues also in triumphant forme and shape he dedicated in both the Porches
or galleries of his Hall of Justice. And in a publick edict
he professed thus much, that he devised it to this end,
That both himselfe whiles he lived, and the Princes or Emperours his successors for the ages to come, might be called
upon and urged by their subjects and Citizens to conforme
themselves as it were to their pattron and example. The
Statue likewise of Pompeius, translated out of the Court

THE HISTORIE OF

OCTAVIUS CÆSAR AUGUSTUS wherein C. Cæsar was murdered, he placed over against the princely Pallace of his Theater under an Arch of marble in manner of a Through-fare[1].

32

Many most daungerous enormities and offensive abuses, which either had continued by custome and licentious liberty during the civill warres, or else crept in and began in the time of peace to the utter ruine of the Commonwealth, he reformed. For a number of bold roisters and professed robbers jetted openly with short swords and skaines by their sides, under colour of their owne defence: passengers and waifaring men, as they travailed through the Country, were caught up (by them) as well Free borne as slaves without respect; and kept hard to worke in the Prisons of landed men[2]: many factious crewes also, under the title of a New Colledge had their meetings and joyned in fellowship to the perpetrating of mischiefe whatsoever. Whereupon, he disposed strong guards, and set watches in convenient places: he repressed those Robbers and Hacksters, he visited and surveyed the foresaid prisons: and all Colledges or Guilds save onely those of auncient foundation and by law erected, he dissolved and put downe. The bills[3] of old debts due to the Chamber of the City, he burnt[4], as being the chiefe matter and occasion of malitious accusations. The publike places and houses in the City, whereof the tenure and hold was doubtfull, he adjudged unto those who were in present possession. The debts and actions commenced against such as had been troubled and sued a long time in the Law, by whose mournfull habite and distressed estate their adversaries sought for nothing but pleasure and the fulfilling of their wils, he anulled and denounced this condition withall, that if any one would needes bring them into new trouble againe, he should be liable to the like daunger of punishment or penalty as the molested party was. And to the end that no lewd Act might escape with

---

[1] *Supposuit*: some reade, *superposuit*, *i.* upon such an arched Janus or Through-fare. [2] In manner of Bridewels or houses of correction. [3] Or obligations. [4] *Exussit* or *excussit*, *i.* canciled.

TWELVE CÆSARS

impunity; nor businesse¹ in Court be shuffled over by delaies, he added unto the Terme² time 30 daies ᵃ over and above: which daies the Honoraric Games³ and playes tooke up (before). To three Decuries of Judges he added a fourth out of a lower and meaner degree, which went under the name of *Ducenarii*⁴, and were to judge of smaller summes. As for those Judges hee enrolled and elected them into the Decuries after they were once 30 yeeres of age⁵: that is to say, five yeeres sooner then they were wont. But seeing that most of them refused and were loth to execute this burdensome office of judging, he hardly granted that each Decurie should have their yeeres vacation⁶ by turnes; and that the law matters which were wont to be pleaded and tried, in the moneths of November and December⁷ should be let passe and omitted quite.

OCTAVIUS
CÆSAR
AUGUSTUS

33

Himselfe sat daily in Judgement, yea and other whiles untill it was darke night, lying if he had not his health, in a licter which was of purpose set before the tribunall seate, or else in his owne house: and he ministred justice not onely with exceeding severity, but also with as great lenity. For when upon a time there was one accused for a manifest parricidy, because he should not be sowed up in a leather male or budget ᵃ (a punishment that none suffred but such as had confessed the Fact) he examined (by report) upon interrogatives in this maner, Certes thou never murderedst thy father, diddest thou? Againe, when as a matter was handled before him as touching a forged will, and all the witnesses that set their hands and seales thereto, were attaint by the Law Cornelia ᵇ, he delivered unto the Commissioners who had the hearing and deciding together, of the cause, not onely the two (ordinarie) tables of

---

¹ Or cause. ² Law daies, or pleading time. ³ *Liberalia, Bacchanalia, Prætoria*, or others in the honour of men living which might be well spared.
⁴ For that they were valewed at 200 Sestertia: where as the other were worth 400. ⁵ Or 20 rather, for the ordinarie age was 25 yeares, at which they were eligible. ⁶ *Quarto quoque anno:* everie 4 yeare. ⁷ Uppon certaine dayes of those moneths, during which, there were Sports and Revels and the licentious feast *Saturnalia.*

condemnation and acquitall, but a third also; whereby they might have their pardon, who were certainly knowne to have beene seduced and brought to be witnesses as is before said, either by fraudulent practise or error and oversight. As for the appeales in Court, he yeerely assigned those which were for the City-Suiters unto Pretours of the City; but if they were for provinciall persons unto certaine men of the Consuls degree, such as he had ordained, in every province one, for to be in commission and to determine provinciall affaires.

34

The lawes made before time he revised and corrected: some also hee ordained and established a-new: as namely *Sumptuaria*^a, as touching expenses at the bord: of Adulteries^b and unnaturall filthinesse committed with the male kind[1]: of indirect suite for offices^c: of the mutall mariages of Senatours and Gentlemen with Commoners^d. This act last named, when he had amended and reformed somewhat more precisely and with greater severitie then the rest, he could not carie cleerely and go through with, for the tumult of those that refused so to do, but that part of the penalties at length was quite taken away or els mitigated; an immunity[2] also and toleration (of widow-head) graunted for 3 yeeres[3], and the rewards besides augmented. And notwithstanding all that, when the order of Gentlemen stood out stifly and stoutly, calling in open sight, and publikely for the repealing of the said Statute, he sent for Germanicus his children, and taking some of them himselfe, and bestowing the others in their fathers armes, shewed and presented them unto their view: signifying as well by the gesture of his hand, as by countenance, That they should not be loath nor think much, to imitate the example of that young Gentleman. Moreover perceiving that the force and vigor of that Law was dallied with, and avoided by the immaturity of young espoused wives[4], as also by often changing of mariages[5]: he brought into a narrower compasse the

---

[1] *De pudicitia* or *impudicitia*.   [2] Of living unmarried.   [3] After the decease of a former wife or husband.   [4] Unripe age, *i.* under 12 yeres.
[5] By meanes of divorses.

TWELVE CÆSARS

time of wedding and having such spouses, and also limited divorcements.

OCTAVIUS CÆSAR AUGUSTUS

35

The number of Senatours growing still to a shameful and confused company (for there were not of them so few as a 1000, and some most unworthy: as who after Cæsars death were taken into the house for favour or bribes; whom the common people termed abortive [1], as it were untimely births or born before their time): he reduced to the aunciant stent [2] and honorable reputation: and that in two elections: the former, at their owne choise, wil, and pleasure, whereby one man chooseth his fellow; the second, according to his owne and Agrippaes mind: at which time he is thought to have sitten as president, armed with a shirt of maile or privie coate under his gowne, and a short sword or skeine by his side; having a gard also standing about his chaire of estate, to wit, ten of the stoutest and tallest men that were of Senatours degree, and all his friends: Cordus Cremutius writeth, that there was not so much as admitted then into the Senate-house any Senatour but singly one alone by himselfe, and not before his clothes were well serched and felt, for having any weapon under them. Some of them he brought to this modestie, as to excuse themselves [3]: and yet for such as thus made excuse he reserved still the liberty to weare a Senatours habite [a]: the honor also to sit and behold the Games and plaies in the *Orchestra* [4]; together with priviledge to keepe their place at the solemne publique feasts. Now, to the end that being thus chosen and allowed (as is above said) they might with more religious reverence and lesse trouble execute the functions belonging to Senatours [b]: he ordained, That before any one sat him downe in his chaire, he should make devout supplication and sacrifice with frankincense and wine, at the altar of that God [5], in whose temple they assembled for the time: and that ordin-

---

[1] *Abortivos:* Some reade *orcivos* or *orcinos, velut Orco seu terra natos, i.* obscure and base.   [2] 300.   [3] For taking upon them that dignity.   [4] Among other Senators.   [5] And that they should not need to come and salute him, but save that labour.

THE HISTORIE OF

OCTAVIUS
CÆSAR
AUGUSTUS

arily the Senate should not be holden oftner then twice in a moneth, to wit upon the Calends^c, and Ides^d of the same: and that in the moneths September and October¹, none els should be bound to give attendance, save those that were drawne by lot: by whose number, Decrees might passe. Furthermore, he devised to institute for himselfe, and that by casting lots, a privie Counsell for 6 moneths: with whom he might treat before hand of businesses and affaires to be moved unto a frequent Senate-house fully assembled. As touching matter of greater importance put to question, he demanded the opinion of the Senatours, not after the usuall manner and in order, but as it pleased himselfe: to the end that everie man should bend his mind so intentively thereto, as if he were to deliver his owne advise, rather then give assent unto another.

36

Other things there were besides, wherof he was the author and beginner: and among the rest: That the Acts of the Senate² should not be published nor appeare upon record. Item that no magistrates after that they had left or given up their honorable places, should eftsoones presently, be sent as governours into any provinces. That for proconsuls or presidents, their should be a certaine rate in monie set downe and allowed, for their sumpter-mules, for their tentes and hales: which were wont really beforetime to be set out and allowed for them, at the publike cost of the Citie. Item, that the charge of the Citties Treasure should be translated from the Questours or treasurers of the Citie, unto those that had been pretours, or to the pretours for the time being: lastly, that certaine Decemvirs³ should summon and assemble the Centumvirall court ⁴, and call the Centumvirs to the speare, which they onely were wont to do, that had borne the office of Questourshippe.'

---

¹ Haply, by reason of vintage that was not to be neglected. ² *Acta Senatus* and not *Senatus consulta*: he meaneth *Diurna acta, i.* the proceedings that passed there every day of sitting. ³ Ten men either chosen out of the Centumvirs by lot, or created of purpose.

TWELVE CÆSARS

OCTAVIUS
CÆSAR
AUGUSTUS

37

And to the end that more men might beare their part in administration of the common weale, he devised new offices: to wit, The overseeing of the publike workes, the surveying of the waies, streetes, and causies, of the water courses or conduits, of the channel of Tybris, and distributing corne among the people. Also the provostship of the Cittie: one Triumvirate[1], for chusing Senatours; and another for reviewing and visiting the troupes or cornets of horsemen, so often as need required. The Censours, whose creation was forlet and discontinued, after a long time betweene, he created againe. The number of pretours he augmented. He required also and demanded, that so often as the Consulship was conferred upon him, he might have for one, ij. colleagues or companions in office: but he cold not obtaine it; whilest all men with one voice cried out, That his majestie was abridged enough alreadie, in that he bare not that honourable office by himselfe, but with another.

38

Neither was he more sparing in honorably rewarding martial prowes, as who gave order, that to 30 Captaines and above, there should be granted by publike decree full tryumphs: and to a good many more tryumphall ornaments[a]. Senatours Children, to the end they might be sooner acquainted with the affaires of State, he permitted to put on even at the first their viril gown: to weare likewise the Senatours robe poudred with broad headed purple studs; and to have their places in the Senate house. Also at their first entrance into warfare, he allowed them to be, not onely militarre Tribunes in the legions[2], but also captaines over the horsemen in the wings[3]. And, that none of them might be unexpert of the Camp-affaires: he ordained for the most part over everie wing or Cornet, ij. such Senatours (sonnes) to be provosts. The troupes and companies of Romaine Gentlemen, he often reviewed; and after a long space of

[1] An office which 3 men joinctly bare. [2] Colonels of 1000 fotemen.
[3] Or men of Armes.

THE HISTORIE OF

OCTAVIUS CÆSAR AUGUSTUS

time betweene, brought into use againe the manner of their muster¹ or riding solemnly ᵇ on horse backe, to shew themselves. Neither wold he suffer any on of them during this solemnity, to be unhorsed and arrested by his adversary, that pretended any matter in law against him: a thing that was usually don. And to as many as were known to be aged or to have any defect or imperfection of body, he gave leave to send their horses before, and to come on foote to aunswere when so ever they were cited. And soone after he did those this favour, to deliver uppe their (publike) horses, who being above 45 yeares of age, were unwilling to keepe them still.

39

Having obtained also by the Senate² x. Coadjutours, hee compelled everie Gentleman (that served with the Citties horse) to render an accoumpt of his life. And of such as were blameable and could not approve their living, some he punished, others he noted with shame and ignominie: the most part of them with admonition, but after sundrie sorts. The easiest and lightest kind of admonition, was the tendering unto them in open place and all mens sight, a paire of writing tables³, to read unto themselves presently, in the place where they stood. Some also he put to rebuke and disgrace for taking up of mony upon smal interest for the use, and putting it forth againe for greater gaine and usurie.

40

At the Election of Tribunes⁴ (of the Commons) if their wanted Senatours ᵃ to stand for that office, he created them out of the degree of Romaine Gentlemen: so as, after they had born that magistracy, they might remaine ranged in whether degree⁴ they would themselves. Now, when as many of the Romain Gentlemen, having wasted and decaied their patrimonie, and estate in the civil wars, durst not out of the 14 formost seats behold the publike plaies and games, for

---

¹ *Transvectionis.*   ² *A senatu* or *senatoribus*, *i.* out of the Senatours degree.   ³ Wherein were written al their faults.   ⁴ *Demarchia.* Dion.
⁵ Of gentlemen or of the Senatours.

TWELVE CÆSARS

feare of the penalty by the law (Roscia and Julia) caled *Theatralis*, he pronounced openly and made it knowne, that such gentlemen were not liable thereto if either themselves or their fathers [1] before them, were ever at any time valued to the worth of Romaine Gentlemen [2]. He made a review of the people of Rome, street by street: and to prevent that the common people shold not be often called away from their affaires by occasion of the dole and distribution of corne, he purposed to give out thrice a yeare, tiquets or talies for to serve 4 moneths: but when the people were desirous of the old custom he granted them again to receive the same upon the Nones [b] of every moneth [3]. The ancient right and libertie also, in Elections and Parliamentes he brought in again: and having restrained the indirect suing for dignities by manyfold penalties, upon the day of such elections he distributed out of his own purse among the Fabians and Scaptians [c], who were of the same Tribes, wherein himselfe was incorporate, a thousand Sesterces a peece, because they should not look for ought at any of their hands who stood for offices. Moreover supposing it a matter of great consequence to keepe the people incorrupt and cleare from all base mixture of forain and servile blood, he both granted the freedom of the City of Rome most sparily, and also set a certain gage and limitation of manumising and enfranchising slaves. When Tiberius made request unto him by letters, in the behalfe of a Grecian, his client to be free of Rome: he wrot backe unto him, That he would not grant it unlesse he came personally himselfe, and could perswade him, what just causes he had of his suite: and what time as Livia intreated the like for a certaine French-man, tributarie to the Romains: he flatly denied the freedome of the Citty, but offred in lieu thereof immunitie and remission of Tribute; avowing, that he would more easily abide that somewhat went from the publike treasure and chamber of the Cittie, than have the honour of the Romaine Citie to be made vulgar, and common. Nor content, that he had by diverse straight edicts and provisoes kept many slaves from

OCTAVIUS
CÆSAR
AUGUSTUS

---

[1] *Parentibus*: comprehending all auncestours. [2] 400 *Sestertia* or 400000 *Sestertii*, *i*. 3215 l. sterling. [3] *Nonis cuiusque Mensis*.

THE HISTORIE OF

OCTAVIUS CÆSAR AUGUSTUS

all manner of freedome, but more a great deal from ful freedom in the best condition; as having precisely and with much curiositie put in caveats both for the number and also for the condition and respect otherwise of those that were to be made free: he added thus much moreover: That no slave, who had ever beene bound and imprisoned, or examined by torture should obtaine the freedome of the Cittie, in any kind of enfranchisement what soever. The olde manner of going and wearing apparell also, he endevoured to bring into use againe. And having seene upon a time assembled to heare a publike speech, a number of Citizens cladde all in blacke clokes[1] or sullied gownes[2], taking great indignation thereat crying out with all: Beholde, quoth he,

Romanos rerum dominos gentemque togatam.
The Romaines[3], Lords of all the world, and longe rob'd Nation.

He gave the Ædiles in charge not to suffer any person from thence forward, to abide or stay, either in the Common place or the Cirque, but in a gowne [d], laying a side all clokes or mantills thereupon.

41

His liberality unto all degrees of Citizens he shewed often times as occasions and opportunities were offred: for both by bringing into the Cittie in the Allexandrine Tryumph the treasures of the Ægyptian Kings he caused so great plentie of monie, that usurie fell, but the price of Landes and Lordships arose to a verie high reckoning: and also afterwards, so often as out of the goods of condemned persons there was any surplusage of monie remaining above their fines; he granted for a certaine time the free lone and use thereof to as many as were able to put in securitie for the principall, by an obligation in duple the summe. The substance and wealth of Senatours hee augmented, and whereas the valew thereof before amounted to the summes of 800000 Sesterces[4]:

---

[1] By blacke he meaneth clokes or gownes of a selfe russet colour, for their gownes should be white and faire, not sullied. [2] By the trope *Ironia*, meaning those that were in clokes or foule gownes. [3] The Ptolomæes.
[4] Duple the worth of Gentlemen.

TWELVE CÆSARS

OCTAVIUS CÆSAR AUGUSTUS

he taxed or sessed them at 1200000: and looke who had not so much, he supplied and made it up to the full. He gave Congiaries[1] often times to the people, but lightly they were of diverse summes, one while 400, another while 300, and some times 200 and fiftie Sesterces: and he left not so much as boyes under age, whereas they had not wont to receive such congiaries, unlesse they were above eleven yeares olde. Hee measured out also to the people by the Poll, Corne in times of scarcitie oftentimes at a verie lowe price, and otherwhiles freely, without payinge therefore: and as for the Tickets, of monie, he dupled the summe in them conteined.

42

And that you may know, hee was a prince more respective of thrift and holesomenes, than desirous of popularitie, praise, and honour: when the people complained of the want and dearth of wine, he checked and snibbed them with this most severe speech, That his sonne in lawe Agrippa had taken order good enough that men should not be athirst, by conveighing so many waters into the Cittie. Unto the same people demanding the congiarie; which indeede was by him promised, he aunswered; That his credite was good, and he able to performe his word: but when they earnestly called for one which hee had never promised, hee hit them in the teeth by an edict or proclamation with their dishonestie, and impudencie: assuring them, that give it he would not although he had intended it.

And with no lesse gravitie and resolution, when uppon his proposing and publishing of a congiarie, he found that many in the meane time were manumised and inserted into the number of Citizens, he rejected such, and said, they should not receive any, unto whom he had made no promise: and to all the rest hee gave lesse than he promised: that the summe which he had appointed, might hould out and be sufficient. When upon a time, there was great barrainnesse and scarcitie of corne, being put to an hard exigent and to seeke a difficult remedie, in so much as he was driven to expell out of the Cittie, all the sort of young slaves pam-

[1] Largesses.

THE HISTORIE OF

OCTAVIUS
CÆSAR
AUGUSTUS

pered and trimmed up for sale, as also whole scholes and companies of Novice-fencers and sword players: all strangers and forainers, except Physitians and scholemaisters: yea and some of the ordinarie houshold servants: so soone as the market began to mend, and victuals grew plentifull, he writeth, That it tooke him in the head to abolish those publike doles of Corne for ever: because upon the trust and confidence of them, tillage was cleane laid downe. Howbeit he continued not in that mind long, as being assured, that the same doles might be set up againe one time or other by the ambitious humour (of Princes his successors). And therefore after this he ordred the matter so indifferently, as that he had no lesse regard of the Citties fermours of tillage, and other undertakers and purveiours of the publike corne, than of the people and commons of the Cittie.

43

In number, varietie, and magnificence of solemne shewes exhibited unto the people he went beyond all men. Hee reporteth of himselfe that he set foorth plaies and games in his owne name foure and twentie times [1]: and for other magistrates who either were absent or not sufficient to beare the charges, three and twentie times. Divers times, he exhibited plaies by everie streete, and those uppon many stages, and acted by plaiers skilfull in all languages not in the Common forum onely, nor in the ordinarie Amphitheater, but also in the cirque. In the enclosure called Septa, he never represented any sportes but the baiting and coursing of wild beasts and the shewes of champions-sight; having built woodden scaffolds and seates for the nonce in Mars field. In like manner, he made the shew of a Navall battaile about the River Tiberis, having digged of purpose a spacious hollow pit within the ground, even there whereas now is to be seene the grove of the Cæsars. On which dayes he bestowed warders in diverse places of the citie, for feare it might be endangered by sturdie theeves and robbers, taking their vantage, that so few remained at home in their houses. In the Cirque he brought forth to doe their devoir, Charioters,

[1] *Quater et vicies.*

TWELVE CÆSARS

Runners, and killers of savage beasts: otherwhiles out of the noblest young gentlemen of all the Cittie. As for the war-like Riding or Turnament called Troie, he exhibited it oftenest of all other, making choyse of boyes to performe it, as well bigger as smaller: supposing it a matter of antiquitie: a decent and honorable maner besides, that the towardly disposition and proofe of noble bloud should thus be seene and knowne. In this solemnitie and sport, he rewarded C. Nonius Asprenas weakened[1] by a fall from his horse, with a wreath or chaine of gold, and permitted both himselfe and also his posteritie to beare the surname of Torquatus. But afterwards he gave over the representation of such pastimes, by occasion that Asinius Pollio the Oratour, made a grievous and invidious complaint in the Senate house, of the fall that Æserninus his nephew tooke, who likewise had thereby broken his legge. To the performance of his stage plaies also and shewes of sworde fight, he employed some times even the Gentlemen and knights of Rome: but it was before he was inhibited by vertue of an Act of the Senate. For after it verily, he exhibited no more, save onely a youth called L. Itius, borne of worshipfull parentage, onely for a shew: that being a dwarfe not two foote high, and weighing 17 l.[2] yet he had an exceeding great voice. One day of the sword fight that he set forth, he brought in for to behould the solemnitie, even through the midst of the Shew place, the Parthians hostages who then were newly sent (to Rome) and placed them in the second ranke or row of seates above himselfe[3]. His manner was moreover, before the usuall daies of such spectacles and solemne sights, and at other times, if any strang and new thing were brought over unto him, and worthie to be knowne, to bring it abroad for to be seene upon extraordinary daies, and in any place whatsoever. As for example, a Rhinoceros within the empaled or railed enclosure called Septa: a Tigre upon

OCTAVIUS CÆSAR AUGUSTUS

---

[1] Or lamed. [2] His lightnes was more to be noted than his short stature: for wheras the full height is 6 foote and the weight somewhat above 100 l. this levity of 2 foot is under that proportion the one halfe. [3] *Superque se:* or behind at his backe higher, and therfore further of: or else in a second seat from him of the one side, but in the same ranke for honor sake.

THE HISTORIE OF

OCTAVIUS CÆSAR AUGUSTUS

the stage: and a Serpent 50 cubits long, within the Hall Comitium. It fortuned that during the great Circeian games which he had vowed before, he fell sicke: whereby he lay in his litter and so devoutly attended upon the sacred chariots called Thensæ. Againe, it happened at the beginning of those plaies, which he set out when he dedicated the temple of Marcellus, that his curule chaire became unjoincted, and thereby he fel upon his back: also at the games of his nephewes when the people their assembled were mightily troubled and astonied, for feare that the Theater would fall: seeing that by no means he cold hold them in, nor cause them to take heart againe, he removed out of his owne place, and sat him downe in that part thereof which was most suspected. The most confuse and licentious manner of beholding such spectacles, hee reformed and brought into order; mooved thereto, by the wrong done to a Senatour, whom at Puteoli in a frequent assemble sitting at their right solemne Games, noe man had received to him and vouchsafed a rowne.

44

Hereupon when a decree of the Senate was passed, That so often as in any place there was ought exhibited publikely to be seene, the first ranke or course of Seates should be kept cleere and wholly for Senatours: he forbad the Embassadour of free nations and confederats to sit at Rome within the *Orchestra*: because he had found, that even some of their libertines kind were sent in embassage. The soldiers hee severed from the other people. To maried men that were commoners, he assigned several rewes by themselves. To Noble mens children under age his own quarter[1]: and to their teachers and governers the next thereto. He made an Act also, that not one of the base Commons wearing blacke and sullied gownes should sit so neere as the midst of the Theatre[a]. As for women he would not allow them to behold so much, as the sword Fencers, (who customarily in the time past were to be seene of all indifferently) but from

---

[1] *Cuneum suum* or a rancke of their owne.

TWELVE CÆSARS

OCTAVIUS CÆSAR AUGUSTUS

some higher loft above the rest¹, sitting there by themselves². To the Vestall Nunnes he graunted a place a part from the rest within the Theatre, and the same just over against the Pretours Tribunall. Howbeit from the Solemnitie of Champions-shew, he banished all the female sex: so farre forth, as that during the Pontificiall Games³, he put of a couple of them who were called for to enter in to combat, untill the morrow morning ᵇ. And made proclamation, that his will and pleasure was, That no woman should come into the Theatre before the fift hower of the day⁴.

45

Himselfe behelde the Circeian Games, for the most part from the upper lofts and lodging of his friendes and freedmen, sometime out of the Pulvinar⁵, sitting there with his wife onely and children. From these shewes and sights he would be absent many houres together, and otherwhiles whole dayes: but first having craved leave of the people, and recommended those unto them, who should sitte as presidentes of those Games in his turne. But so often as he was at them, he did nothing els but intend the same: either to avoide the rumor and speech of men, whereby his father Cæsar (as he said himselfe) was commonly taxed, namely for that in beholding those solemnities he used betweene whiles to give his mind to read letters and petitions⁶, yea and to write backe againe: or els uppon an earnest desire and delight he had, in seeing such pastimes, his pleasure and contentment wherein, he never dissimuled, but oftentimes frankely professed. And therefore he proposed and gave of his owne at the games of prise and plaies even of other men, Coronets and rewards, both many in number, and also of great worth: neither was he present at any of these Greek games and solemnities ᵃ, but he honored everie one of the Actors and provers of Maistcries therein according to

¹ And by consequence farther of.   ² *Spectare concessit solis.*   ³ Which him selfe exhibited being Pontifex Maximus, *i.* the High priest.   ⁴ Eleven of the clok, by which houre all that sight was past.   ⁵ And not, *e pulvinari, i.* The bedloft wher the sacred Images of the Gods were devoutly bestowed, which had beene brought in their Thenses and carried thether, at these solemn games.   ⁶ As if he had no delight in those games.

THE HISTORIE OF

OCTAVIUS CÆSAR AUGUSTUS

their deserts. But moste affectionately of all other he loved to see the Champions at fist fight[1]: and the Latines especially; not those onely who by lawfull calling were professed[2], and by order allowed (and even those he was wont to match with Greeks) but such also as out of the common sort of townes-men, fell together by the eares pell mell in the narrow streets, and though they had no skill at all of fight, yet could lay on load, and offend their concurrents one way or other. In summe, all those in generall, who had any hand in those publike games or set them forward any way, he deigned good rewards and had a speciall respect of them. The priviledges of Champions he both maintained entier, and also amplified. As for sword fencers he would not suffer them to enter into the lists, unlesse they might be discharged of that profession, in case they became victours. The power to chastice Actours and plaiers[3] at all times and in everie place (granted unto the Magistrates[4] by aunctient law) he tooke from them, save onely during the plaies and uppon the stage. Howbeit he examined streightly neverthelesse at all times either the matches or combats of Champions called *Xystici*[b], or the fights of sword fencers. For the licentiousnesse of stage plaiers he so repressed, that when he had for certaine found out, that Stephanio, an actor of Romaine playes had a mans wife waiting upon him shorne and rounded in manner of a boy, he confined and sent him away as banished: but well beaten first with rods through all the three Theatres[5]. And Hylas the Pantomime[6] at the complaint made of him by the Pretour, he skourged openly in the Court yard before his house: and excluded no man from the sight thereof: yea and he banished Pylades out of the Cittie of Rome and Italie, because he had pointed with his finger at a Spectatour who hissed him out of the stage, and so made him to be knowne.

---

[1] *Pugiles*, aunswerable in Greece to the Romaine Gladiatores. [2] And so had learned the skil and feate of fighting. [3] By beating with rods. [4] Pretours and Ædiles. [5] Pompeii, Balbi, Metelli. For so many there were in Augustus dayes, besides the Amphitheatre of Statilius Taurus. [6] A cunning Actour counterfaiting all parts.

TWELVE CÆSARS

46

OCTAVIUS
CÆSAR
AUGUSTUS

Having in this manner ordred the Cittie and administred the civile affaires therin, he made Italie populous and much frequented with Colonies ᵃ to the number of 28, brought thither and planted by him; yea he furnished the same with publike workes and revenues in many places. He equalled it also after a sort, and in some part with the verie Cittie of Rome in priviledges and estimation: by devising a new kind of Suffrages[1] which the decurions or elders of Colonies gave every one in their owne Towneshippe, as touching Majestrates to bee created in Rome, and sent under their hands and seales to the City against the day of the solemne Elections. And to the end, there should not want in any place either honest and worshipfull inhabitants, or issue of the multitude; looke who made suite to serve as men of armes on horse-backe upon the publique commendation of any township whatsoever[2], those hee enrolled and advanced unto the degree of Gentlemen. But to as many of the Commoners as could by goode evidence prove unto him as hee visited the Countries and Regions of Italy[3], that they had sonnes and daughters he distributed a thousand sesterces a piece, for every child they had.

47

As for those Provinces, which were more mighty than other, and the government whereof by yeerely Magistrates was neither easie nor safe, he undertooke himselfe to rule ᵃ: the rest hee committed to Proconsuls by lot: and yet otherwhiles he made exchange of such Provinces: and of both sorts, hee oftentimes visited many in person. Certaine Cities, confederate and in league with Rome, howbeit by over-much libertie running headlong to mischiefe and destruction, hee deprived of their liberties. Others againe, either deeply in debt he eased, or subverted by earthquake he reedified, or able to alledge their merits and good turnes done to the people of Rome hee endowed with the franchises of Latium; or else with freedome of Rome. There is not, I

A.U C. 726.

---

[1] Voices.   [2] *Cuiuscunque oppidi.*   [3] And those were eleven.

THE HISTORIE OF

OCTAVIUS
CÆSAR
AUGUSTUS

suppose, a Province, (except Affrick onely and Sardinia) but hee went unto it. Into these Provinces after he had chaced Sextus Pompeius thither, he prepared to saile out of Sicilie and to crosse the Seas: but continuall stormes and extreame tempests checked him: neither had hee good occasion or sufficient cause afterwards to passe over unto them.

48

All those kingdomes which he wan by conquest and force of armes, unlesse some fewe, hee either restored unto those Princes from whom hee had taken them, or else made them over to other. KK. mere Aliens, Princes, his Associates hee conjoyned also together among themselves by mutuall bonds of alliance, as being a most ready procurer and maintainer of affinity and amity of every one; neither had he other regard of them all in generall than of the very naturall members and parts of his owne Empire. Moreover, he was wont to set Guardians and Governours over the saide Princes, when they were either young and under age, or lunatick and not well in their wits; untill such time as they were growne to ripe yeeres, or began to come againe to themselves. The children of very many of them, he both brought up and also trained and instructed together with his owne.

49

Out of his militarie forces, he distributed both Legions and Auxiliaries by Provinces. He placed one fleete at Misenum, and another at Ravenna, for the defences of the upper[1] and nether[2] Seas. A certaine number of Souldiours he selected for a guard, partly of the City, and in part of his owne person, having discharged the regiment of the Calagurritanes[3], which hee had retained about him, untill he vanquished Antonius; and likewise of the Germaines which hee had waged among the Squires of his body, unto the disasterous overthrow of Varus: And yet he suffred not at any time, to remain within the City more then 3 cohorts, and those without their pavilions. The residue, his manner

---

[1] *Superi*, called otherwise the Adriatich Sea: Venice-gulfe. [2] *Inferi*, otherwise Tusci, or Tyrrheni, *i.* the Tuskane Sea. [3] People of Spaine.

TWELVE CÆSARS

was to send away to wintering places and sommer harbours about the neighbour-townes. Moreover, all the souldiours that were in any place whatsoever, hee tied to a certaine prescript forme and proportion of wages and rewards, setting downe according to the degree and place of every one, both their times of warfare, and also the commodities[1] they should receive after the terme of their service expired and their lawfull discharge: least that by occasion of old age, or for want, they should after they were freed from warfare, be solicited to sedition and rebellion. And to the end, that for ever, and without any difficulty, there might be defrayed sufficient to maintaine and reward them accordingly, he appointed a peculiar Treasurie for soldiors with new revenewes devised for their maintainance[2]. And that with more speede and out of hand word might be brought, and notice taken what was doing in every province, hee disposed along the rode high-waies, within small distance one from another; first, certaine young men as posts; and afterwards swift wagons to give intelligence. This he thought more commodious, and better to the purpose, that they who from a place brought him letters might be asked questions also, if the matters required ought.

OCTAVIUS CÆSAR AUGUSTUS

50

In charters, patents, writs, bils and letters he used for his seale, at the first, the image of Sphinx[a]: Soone after, that of Alexander the great: and last of all, his owne; engraven by the hand of Dioscurides[3]: wherewith the Princes and Emperours his successours continued to signe their writings. To all his missives his manner was, to put precisely the very minutes of houres, not of day onely but of night also, wherein it might be knowne, they were dated.

51

Of his clemencie and civill curtesie[a], there be many, and

---

[1] Fees, pensions, land and living. [2] *Ducentesimis et quinquagesimis rerum venalium. Bonis etiam damnatorum, i.* with the two hundreth peny, and the fiftieth peny of wares sold: with the goods also of condemned persons.
[3] A cunning Lapidarie and graver in pretious stones.

THE HISTORIE OF

OCTAVIUS
CÆSAR
AUGUSTUS

those right great proofes and experiments. Not to reckon up, how many and who they were of the adverse faction, that he vouchsafed pardon and life; yea, and suffred to hold still a principall place in the City: he was content and thought it sufficient, to punish Junius Novatus and Cassius Patavinus, two commoners; the one with a fine of money and the other with a slight banishment: notwithstanding that Junius Novatus in the name of young Agrippa had divulged a most biting and stinging letter, touching him, and Cassius Patavinus at an open table and full feast, gave out in broad termes, That he wanted neither harty wishes nor good will to stab him. Moreover in a certaine judiciall triall, when among other crimes this article was principally objected against Æmilius Ælianus of Corduba, That hee was wont to have a bad conceite[1] and to speake but basely of Cæsar, himselfe turned unto the accuser, and as if he had beene sore offended, 'I would,' quoth he, 'thou wert able to prove this unto me: in faith Ælianus should well know, that I also have a tongue: for I will not stick to say more by him.' And farther than this he neither for the present nor afterwards inquired into the matter. Likewise, when Tiberius grieved and complained unto him of the same indignity in a letter, and that uncessantly and after a violent manner, thus he wrote back againe: 'Doe not my good Tiberius in this point follow and feed the humor of your age[2]: neither set it too neere your heart, That there is any man who speaketh evill of me; for it is enough for us, if no man be able to doe us harme.'

52

Albeit, he wist well enough, that Temples were usually graunted by decree even unto Proconsuls, yet in no Province accepted hee of that honour, but joyntlie in the name and behalfe of himselfe and of Rome. For in Rome verily, he forbare this honour most resolutely: yea, and those silver Statues which in times past had beene set up for him, he

---

[1] *Male opinari.* The same in this Author, that *Male dicere.* [2] Young: imputing his coller and cruelty to the heate of youth and hote bloud: measuring Tiberius by himselfe.

TWELVE CÆSARS

melted every one. Of which¹, he caused golden Tables² to be made, and those he dedicated to Apollo Patavinus. When the people offered and instantly forced upon him the Dictatourship, he fell upon his knees, cast his gowne from off his shoulder, bared his brest, and with detestation of the thing, besought them not to urge him farther.

OCTAVIUS
CÆSAR
AUGUSTUS

53

The name and title of Lord³ᵃ he alwaies abhorred as a contumelious and reproachfull terme. When upon a time, as he beheld the plaies, these words were pronounced out of a Comœdie⁴, O good and gracious Lord⁵: whereupon the whole assembly with great joy and applause accorded thereto, as if they had beene spoken of him: immediatly both with gesture of hand and shew of countenance, he repressed such undecent flatteries: and the next day reproved them most sharply by an edict: neither would hee ever after suffer himselfe to be called *Dominus*, no not of his owne children and nephewes either in earnest or boord. And that which more is, such faire and glavering wordes hee forbad them to use among themselves. Lightly, you should not have him depart forth of the City or any Towne, nor enter into any place, but in the evening, or by night: for disquieting any person in doing him honour by way of dutifull attendance. In his Consulship hee went commonly in the streetes on foote: out of his Consulship oftentimes in a close chaire or licter⁶ᵇ. In generall Salutations and duties done unto him he admitted the very Commons, entertaining the suites and desires of all commers with so great humanity as that he rebuked one of them merily, because in reaching unto him a supplication, he did it so timorously, as if hee had raught a small peece of coine⁷ to an Oliphant. On a Senate-day, he never saluted his Nobles but in the *Curia*ᶜ: and those verily as they sat, every one by name without any prompter⁸: and at his departure out of the house, he used to bid them

---

¹ With the money, for which they were sold. ² *Cortinas*, otherwise called *Tripodas*, standing upon 3 feete: from which Oracles were delivered. ³ *Domini*, or *Sr*. ⁴ Or Enterlude, *Mimo*. ⁵ Or *Sr*. ⁶ *Ad operta*: if *adaperta* the sence is contrarie. ⁷ *Stipem. Quintilianus reddidit assem.* lib. 6. cap. *de risu*. ⁸ Or *Nomenclator*.

THE HISTORIE OF

OCTAVIUS CÆSAR AUGUSTUS

farewell one by one as they were set, in the same manner. With many men he performed mutuall offices yeelding one kindnes for another interchangeably. Neither gave he over frequenting their solemnities and feasts[1] untill he was farre stept in yeeres: and by this occasion, that once upon a day of Espousals[2] he was in the presse and throng of people sore crouded. Gallus Terrinius a Senator, and none of his familiar acquaintance, howbeit fallen blinde and purposing resolutely to pine himselfe to death [d], he visited in proper person, and by his consolatory and comfortable words perswaded him to live still.

54

As he delivered a speech in the Senate, one said unto him, 'I conceived you not': and another, 'I would gain-say you if any place were left for me to speake'[3]. Divers times when upon occasion of excessive altercation and brabbling among the Senatours in debating matters, he was about to whip out of the Senate a pace in a great chafe, some of them would choke him with these words, 'Senatours ought to have liberty to speake their mindes concerning the Common-weale.' Antistius Labeo at a certaine Election of Senatours, when one man chooseth another[4], made choise of M. Lepidus, who sometime was (Augustus) mortall enemie, and then in Exile. Now when he demaunded of the said Antistius, If there were not others more worthy to be chosen? hee returned this aunswere, That every man had his owne liking and judgement by himselfe. Yet for all this, did no mans free speech or froward selfe-will, turne him to displeasure or danger.

55

Moreover, the diffamatory libels of him cast abroad and dispersed in the *Curia*, he neither was affrighted at, nor tooke great care to refute; making not so much as search after the Authors. Onely this he opined, That from thence-

---

[1] As Birthdayes, and Mariage Mihds.   [2] Assurance making of a mariage.   [3] As if Augustus by his absolute power had taken up all.
[4] *Cum vir virum*, not *Triumvirum*.

forth there should be inquisition made, and examination
had of those that either in their owne name or under other
mens, did put forth libels, rimes, or verses to the infamie of
any person. Furthermore, to meete with the spitefull
taunts and skurrile scoffes of some, wherewith he was provoked, he made an Edict against such. And yet, to the
end that the Senate should passe no Act, for the Inhibition
of their licentious liberty ᵃ in their last wils and testaments ¹,
he interposed his negative voice.

OCTAVIUS
CÆSAR
AUGUSTUS

56

Whensoever he was present himselfe at the Generall Wardmotes for Election of Magistrates, he went with his owne
Candidates ᵃ round about to the Tribes, and humbly craved
their voices² according to the usuall custome. Himselfe also
gave a voice in his owne Tribe ³ as one of the ordinary people.
When hee appeared as witnesse in judiciall courts, hee suffred
himselfe right willingly to be examined upon interrogatives,
and also to be impleaded against and confuted. His common
Hall of Justice ⁴ he made lesse, and of narrower compasse ⁵ ;
as not daring to encroch upon the next houses and dispossesse
the owners. He never recommended his sonnes unto the
people, but with this clause added thereto, If they shall
deserve. When, beeing yet under age, and in their purpled
childs habit⁶, al the people generally that sat in the Theater
rose up unto them, and the standers below clapped their
hands, hee tooke it very ill and complained grievously thereof.
His minions and inward friends he would have to bee great
and mighty men in the City ; yet so, as they should have no
more liberty than other Citizens, but be subject to lawes
and judgements as well as the rest. When Asprenas
Nonius ᵇ, a man of neere alliance and acquaintance with him
was accused by Cassius Severus, for practising poison, and
pleaded for himselfe at the Barr, hee asked counsell of the
Senate, what they thought in duty he was to do ? 'For I
stand in doubt,' quoth he, 'least being here present as an

¹ Wherein, the manner was to use broad jests, of any person. Casaubonus.
² Or graces. ³ *In Tribu*, or *in Tribubus*, *i.* among other Tribes.
⁴ Called *Forum Augusti*. ᵇ Than the other. ⁶ *Prætextatis adhuc.*

THE HISTORIE OF

OCTAVIUS CÆSAR AUGUSTUS

advocate, I should acquit the prisoner defendant[1] and so hinder the course of law; againe, if I be absent and faile him, least I might be thought to forsake and prejudice my friend': wherupon, by all their consents, he sat there in the Pues[2] certain houres, but spake never a word nor affourded so much as a commendatorie speech in the defendants behalfe, as the maner of friends was to do in the triall of such cases. He pleaded the causes even of his very clients, and by name, of a certain shield-bearer[3c], whom in times past he had called forth to serve him in the wars: he spake I say in his defence, when he was sued in an action of the case. Of all those that were thus in trouble, he delivered one and no more from making his appearance in Court: and him verily no otherwise, but by earnest praiers and entreating the Accuser before the Judges: and him he perswaded at length to let fal his action. And Castritius it was, a man, by whose meanes he came to the knowledge of Murenaes conspiracie.

57

How much, and for what demerits of his, he was beloved, an easie matter it is to make an æstimate. The acts and decrees of the Senate concerning his honors I passe over, as which may be thought wrested from them either upon mere necessity or bashfull modesty. The Gentlemen of Rome of their owne accord and by an uniforme consent celebrated his birth-feast alwaies for 2 daies together. All States and Degrees of the City, yeerely upon a solemne vow that they made, threw small pieces of brasse-coine into Curtius lake[4] for the preservation of his life and health. Semblably, at the Calends of Januarie every yeere they offred a new yeeres-gift in the Capitol unto him, although he were absent. Out of which masse and grosse sum he disbursed as much money, as wherewith he bought the most pretious Images of the Gods, and dedicated them in divers streets: as namely Apollo Sandaliarius[5], and Jupiter Tragœdus[6], and

---

[1] Or offender. [2] Within the Barr, among the Advocates, as a well willer. [3] Or *Targuatier*, Scutario: some take this for a proper name of some souldiour of his. [4] Into the railed or empaled place named *Septa*, where sometime was that Lake. [5] In the Shoomakers street. [6] In the Tragœdians street.

TWELVE CÆSARS

others besides[1]. For the reedification of his house in Palatine[2] consumed by fire, the old soldiours, the Decuries (of the Judges) the Tribes, and many severall persons by themselves of all sorts, willingly and according to each ones ability brought in their monies together. Howbeit, he did no more but slightly touch the heapes of such money as they lay, and tooke not away out of any one above one single denier[3]. As he returned out of any province, they accompanied him honorably, not onely with good words and lucky osses[4], but also with songs set in musicall measures. This also was duly observed, that how often so ever he entred Rome, no punishment that day was inflicted upon any person.

OCTAVIUS
CÆSAR
AUGUSTUS

58

The surname[5] in his stile of Pater Patriæ, they all presented unto him with exceeding great and unexpected accord. The Commons, first, by an Embassage which they sent unto Antium: then, because he accepted not therof, at Rome as he entred the Theater to behold the plaies, they tendered it a second time themselves in great frequencie, dight with Lawrell branches and Coronets. Soone after, the Senate did the like, not by way of decree nor acclamation, but by Valerius Messalla, who had commission from them all, to relate their minds in this maner. 'That,' quoth he, 'which may be to the good and happinesse of thee and thy house O Cæsar Augustus (for in this wise we think, that we pray for perpetuall felicity and prosperity[6] to this Commonwealth). The Senate according with the people of Rome, do jointly salute thee by the name of Pater Patriæ[7].' Unto whom, Augustus with teares standing in his eyes, made answere in these words, (for I have set the very same downe, like as I did those of Messala[8]) 'Now that I have (mine honorable Lords) attained to the heighth of all my vowes and wishes, what remaineth else for me to crave of the

A.U.C. 758.

---

[1] *Aliaque. In restitutionem*, etc. [2] Mount Palatine. [3] 7d. ob.
[4] *Faustis omnibus*, or, *nominibus, i.* names. [5] Or addition. [6] *Felicitatem Reip. et læta huic: pro, felicitatem et læta Reip. huic.* [7] Father of the Countrey. [8] *Sicut Messella.*

THE HISTORIE OF

OCTAVIUS CÆSAR AUGUSTUS

immortall Gods, but that I may carie with mee this universall consent of yours unto my lives end?'

59

Unto Antonius Musa his Physitian, by whose meanes he was recovered out of a dangerous disease, they erected a Statue, by a generall contribution of brasse, just by the image of Æsculapius. Some housholders[1] there were who in their last wils and testaments provided, That their heires should leade beasts for sacrifice into the Capitoll and pay their vowes, with this title caried before them containing the reason of so doing, Because they[2] had left Augustus living after them. Certaine Cities of Italy began their yeere that very day, on which he first came to them. Most of the Provinces, over and above Temples and Altars, ordained almost in every good Towne, solemne Games and Playes every fifth yeere in his honor[3].

60

Kings his friends and Confederates both severally every one in his own kingdome built Cities calling them Cæsareæ, and jointly altogether intended, at their common charges fully to finish the temple of Jupiter Olympicus at Athens which long time before was begun, and to dedicate it unto his Genius. And oftentimes, the said Princes leaving their realmes, going in Romaine gownes, without Diadems and regall Ornaments, in habit and manner of devoted Clients, performed their dutifull attendance unto him day by day: not at Rome only, but also when he visited and travailed over the provinces.

61

For as much as I have shewed already what his publique cariage was in places of Commaund and Magistracies: in the managing also and administration of the Common-weale throughout the world both in warre and peace: now will I relate his more private and domesticall life: as also what

---

[1] *Patres familias*, good honest Citizens of Rome that were *sui juris*.
[2] *i.* their Fathers, the testatours.   [3] As if he had beene a Demi-God.

TWELVE CÆSARS

behaviour hee shewed and what fortune hee had at home, and among his owne, even from his youth unto his dying day. His mother he buried during the time of his first Consulship, and his sister Octavia in the 54 yeere of his age. And as he had performed unto them both, whiles they lived, the offices of pietie and love in the best manner: so when they were dead, he did them the greatest honours he possibly could.

OCTAVIUS CÆSAR AUGUSTUS
A.U.C. 711, 745.

62

He had espoused, being a very youth, the daughter of P. Servilius Isauricus: but upon his reconciliation unto Antonie after their first discorde at the earnest demaund of both their soldiours, that they might be conjoyned and united by some nere affinitie, he tooke to wife (Antonius) daughter in law Claudia, the naturall daughter of Dame Fulvia by P. Clodius: a young Damosell, scarce mariageable. And upon some displeasure, falling out with Fulvia his wives mother, he put her away, as yet untouched and a virgine: soone after, he wedded Scribonia, the wife before of two husbands, both men of Consular dignity, and by one of them a mother. This wife also he divorced, not able to endure, as hee writeth himselfe, her shrewd and perverse conditions: and forthwith, tooke perforce from Tiberius Nero, Livia Drusilla his lawfull wife and great with child. Her he loved entirely, her he liked onely, and to the very end.

A.U.C. 715.

63

Upon Scribonia he begat Julia: by Livia he had no issue, although full faine he would. Conceive once she did by him; but she miscaried, and the Infant was borne before time. As for Julia, hee gave her in mariage first to Marcellus the sonne of his sister Octavia, even when he was but newly crept out of his childes age. Afterwards, when Marcellus was departed this life, he bestowed her upon M. Agrippa, having by intreatie obtained of his sister, to yeeld up unto him her right and interest in her sonne in Law[1]. For at the same time Agrippa had to wife one of the Marcellæ[2] (her

[1] Her daughters husband. [2] It seemeth the younger.

THE HISTORIE OF

OCTAVIUS CÆSAR AUGUSTUS

daughters) and of her body begotten children. When this Agrippa was likewise dead, he cast about and sought for divers matches a long time, even out of the ranks of Romaine Gentlemen, and chose for her, his wives sonne Tiberius[1]: whom he forced to put away a former wife then with child, and by whom hee had beene a father already. M. Antonius writeth, that he had affianced the said Julia first, to Antonie his sonne: and afterwards to Cotiso King of the Getes: what time Antonie himselfe required to have a Kings daughter[2] likewise to wife.

64

By Agrippa and Julia he had 3 nephewes, Caius, Lucius, and Agrippa: nieces likewise twaine, Julia and Agrippina. Julia he bestowed in mariage upon Lucius Paulus, the Censors sonne: and Agrippina upon Germanicus, his sisters Nephew[3 a]. As for Caius and Lucius he adopted them for his owne children at home in his house, having bought them of Agrippa their Father by the brazen coine and the balance[4 b]. Whom being yet in their tender yeeres, he emploied in the charge of the common-weale: and no sooner were they Consuls Elect, but hee sent them abroade to the government of Provinces and conduct of armies. His daughter and nieces above named, hee brought uppe and trained so, as that hee acquainted them with housewiferie, and set them even to carde, spinne and make cloth: forbidding them streightly either to say or doe ought but openly in the sight and hearing of all men, and that which might be recorded in their day bookes[5]. Certes, so farre forth he prohibited and forewarned them the companie of strangers, that he wrote uppon a time unto L. Tucinius[6], a noble young gentleman and a personable, charging him that he passed the bounds of modestie, in that he came once to Baiæ for to see and salute his daughter: his nephewes, himselfe for the most part taught to reade, to write and to swimme[c], besides the

---

[1] Emperour after him. [2] Iotapas the Median K. of Armenia: or els he meaneth Cleopatra. [3] *Sororis*, or *uxoris*, *i.* his wives nephewe, and both true. [4] *Per assem, vel per as et libram.* [5] Of accompt. [6] Or Vinicius.

TWELVE CÆSARS

rudiments and first introductions to other Sciences. But in
nothing travailed hee so much as in this, that they might
imitate his handwritinge. Hee never supped togither with
them, but they satte at the nether ende of the Table: neither
went hee any Journie, but hee had them either goinge before
in a Wagon, or else about him rydinge by his side.

OCTAVIUS
CÆSAR
AUGUSTUS

65

But as joious and confident as hee was in regard both of
his issewe, and also of the discipline of his house, fortune
failed him in the proofe of all. His daughter and niece
either of them named Julia disteined with all kinde of
leawdnesse and dishonestie he sent out of the way as
banished: Caius and Lucius[1] [a] both, hee lost in the space of
18 monaths, Caius died in Lycia, Lucius at Massilia. His
third nephewe Agrippa, togither with his wives sonne
Tiberius hee adopted [b] his sonnes in the Forum of Rome by
an Act of all the *Curiæ*[2]. But of these twaine within a
small time hee cast out of his favour, yea and confined aside
unto Surrentum, Agrippa, for his base disposition and fell
nature[3]. Moreover he tooke much more patiently the death,
than the reprochfull misdemeanours of his children. For,
at the infortunitie of Caius and Lucius he was not extreamely
dismaied and cast downe: mary, of his daughter and her
leawd pranckes, he gave notice in his absence to the Senate,
and that in writing, which his Questor [c] red openly before
them : and for very shame he absented himselfe a long time
and avoyded the company of men : yea, and that which more
is, once he was of mind to put her to death. And verely,
when as, about the same time a freed woman of his named
Phœbe, one of them that were privie to her naughtines,
knit her own neck in a halter, and so ended her dayes, he
gave it out, that he wisht with all his heart he had beene
Phœbes father[4]. Confined thus when she was, he debarred
her wholly the use of wine, and all manner of delicate trim-

---

[1] ij. of his Nephewes.   [2] These Actes were called *Leges Curiatæ* : made
in a parliament of all the *Curiæ*, in nomber 30, into which Romulus divided
the Cittie. These lawes Sext. Papyrius collected into one Booke, and called
it was *jus civile Papyrianum*.   [3] *Sordidum*, others read *Stolidum*, and
Horridum, i. Sottish and rude.   [4] Or that his daughter had beene Phœbe.

ming and decking her bodie: neither would he permitte any man, one or other, bond or free, to have accesse unto her without his privitie and leave asked: nor unlesse he might be certified before, of what age, of what stature and colour hee was, yea and what markes and skars he caried about him [d]. After 5 yeares ende, he remooved her out of the Iland[1] into the Continent where shee abode at more libertie somewhat, and not so streightly looked unto: for, to call her home againe once for all, he could by no meanes bee intreated: as who, many a time when the people of Rome besought him earnestly and were very instant with him in her behalfe, openly before a frequent assembly of them cursed such daughters and such wives: saying, 'God blesse yee al from the like.' The infant that his niece Julia bare after she was condemned, hee forbad expressely to take knowledge of, and to give it the rearing. As touching his nephew Agrippa, seeing him to proove nothing more tractable, but rather braine sicke every day more than other, he transported him (from Surrentum) into an Iland and enclosed him there besides with a guard of soldiers. He provided also by an Act of the Senate, that in the same place he should be kept for ever. And so often, as there was any mention made either of him or his ij. Julie[2], he used to fetch a sigh and grone againe, and with all to breake out into this speech,

$$\alpha\ddot{\iota}\theta'\ \ddot{o}\phi\epsilon\lambda o\nu\ \ddot{a}\gamma a\mu o s\ \tau'\ddot{\epsilon}\mu\epsilon\nu a\iota,\ \ddot{a}\gamma o\nu o s'\ \dot{a}\pi o\lambda\dot{\epsilon}\theta a\iota.$$

Would God I never had wedded bride
Or else without any childe had died [e].

66

Friendship with any person as he did not easily intertain, so he maintained and kept the same most constantly; not honoring only the vertues and deserts of every man according to their worth, but enduring also their vices and deliquences at least wise if they exceeded not: for out of al that number of his dependants ther wil hardly be any found, during his frendship to have bin plunged in adversity and

---

[1] Pandataria. Tacit. lib. I.   [2] Daughter and neice.

TWELVE CÆSARS

therby overthrown: except Salvidienus Rufus whom he had
before advanced to the dignitie of Consul; and Cornelius
Gallus promoted by him to the provostship of Ægypt, raised
both from the verie dunghill. The one of these for practising
seditiously an alteration in the state: and the other for his
unthankeful and malitious mind he forbad his house and all
his provinces. But as for Gallus, when as both by the
menaces of his accusers, and also by the rigorous Acts of the
Senate passed against him, he was driven to shorten his
owne life: Augustus commended verely their kind harts to
him for being so wroth and grieving so much in his behalfe:
howbeit for Gallus sake he wept, and complained of his owne
hard fortune, in that he alone might not be angrie, with his
friends, within that measure as he would himselfe: all the
rest of his favorites flowrished in power and welth to their
lives end, as chiefe persons every one in their ranke: notwithstanding some discontentment and mislikes came between.
For otherwhiles, hee found a want in M. Agrippa of patience,
and in Mæcenas of Taciturnitie and secrecie; when as the
one[1] upon a light suspicion of his cold love, and affection[2],
with a jelousie besides, that Marcellus should be preferred
before him left all and went to Mitylenæ: the other[3] unto
his wife Terentia revealed a secret [b], as touching the detection
of Murenæs conspiracie. Himselfe also required semblably
mutual benevolence of his friends, as wel dead as living.
For although he was none of these that lie in the winde to
mung and catch at Inheritances, as who could never abide to
reape any commoditie by the last will and testament of an
unknown person; yet weighed he most strictly and precisely
the supreme[4] judgments and testimonies of his friends concerning him, delivered at their deaths: as on who dissimuled
neither his grief in case a man respected him slightly and
without honorable tearmes; nor his joy, if he remembred
him thankfully and with kindnes. As touching either
legacies or parts of heritages, as also portions left unto him
by any parents whatsoever, his manner was either out of
hand to part with the same unto their children, or if they

OCTAVIUS
CÆSAR
AUGUSTUS
A.U.C. 714,
728.

[1] M. Agrippa. [2] *Frigoris:* or *rigoris*, as if Augustus had looked sternely or strangly upon him. [3] Mecænas. [4] Finall or last.

THE HISTORIE OF

OCTAVIUS CÆSAR AUGUSTUS were in their minority, to restore all unto them with the increase, upon the day that they put on their virile gownes, or else whereon they maried.

67

A patron he was (to his freedmen) and a Maist. (to his bondservants) no lesse severe, than gratious and gentle: many of his enfranchised men he highly honoured and imployed especially: by name, Licinius Enceladus, with others. His servant Cosmus, who thought and spake most hardly of him, he proceeded to chastice no farther, than with hanging a paire of fetters at his heeles: as for Diomedes his Steward, who walking together with him, by occasion of a wild Bore running full upon them, for very feare put his Maist. between himselfe and the Beast, hee imputed unto him rather timiditie, then any fault else: and although it were a matter of noe small perill, yet because there was noe prepensed mallice, hee turned all into a jest. Contrariwise, the selfe same man, forced to death Procillus a freed man of his and whome hee set greatest store by, because hee was detested for abusing mens wives. Gallus[1] his scribe[2], had received 500 deniers for making on privie unto a letter of his hands: but he caused his legges to be broken for his labour. The pædagogue and other servitours attendant uppon Caius his sonne, who taking the vantage of his sickenesse and death bare themselves proudly and insolently in his province[3] and therein committed many outrages, he caused to be throwne headlong into a River, with heavie weights about their neckes.

68

In the Prime and flower of his youth he incurred sundrie waies the infamous note of a vicious and wanton life. Sext. Pompeius railed uppon him as an effeminate person. M. Antonius layed to his charge, that he earned his unkles adoption, by suffring the filthy abuse of his bodie. Semblably, Lucius brother to the said Marcus enveied against him, as if he had abandoned and prostituted his youth (deflowred

---

[1] Or Thollus. [2] Clerke or secretary. [3] Lycia.

TWELVE CÆSARS

and tasted first by Cæsar) unto A. Hirtius also in Spaine for 300000 sesterces: and that hee was wont to sindge his legges with red hotte Walnutshels[1], to the end the haire might come up softer: the verie people also in generall one time on a day of their Solemne Stage playes, both construed to his reproach, and also with exceeding great applause verified of him a verse pronounced uppon the Stage, as touching a priest of (Cybele) mother of the Gods playing upon a Timbrell:

OCTAVIUS CÆSAR AUGUSTUS

Videsne? Cinædus orbem digito temperat[a].

69

That he was a common adulterer his verie friends did not denie: but they excuse him for sooth: saying, That he did it not upon filthy lust, but for good reason and in pollicy: to the end he might more easily search out the plots and practises of his adversaries, by the meanes of women and wives, it skilled not whose. M. Antonius objected against him, besides his over hastie mariage with Livia[2], that he fetched a certaine Noble dame, the wife of one who had beene Consul, forth of a dining parlour, even before her husbands face, into his own bed chamber, and brought her thither backe again to make an end of the banquet with her haire all ruffled, even while her eares were yet glowing red: also that he put away Scribonia[3], because she was too plaine and round with him, upon griefe she tooke, that a Concubine was so great and might do so much with him: as also that there were bargaines and matches sought out for him by his friends, upon liking: who stucke not to view and peruse both wives, and young maidens of ripe yeares, all naked, as if Toravius the baud were a selling of them. Moreover he writeth thus much to himself, after a familiar sort, as yet being not fallen out flatly with him, nor a professed enemy: ' What hath changed and altered you ? Is it because I lie with a Queene, she is my wife ? And is this the first time ? Did I not so 9 yeares since ? Alas good sir, you that wold

[1] A kind of Psilothrum.   [2] Whome hee could not forbeare, but mary when she was great with childe.   [3] His owne wife.

THE HISTORIE OF

OCTAVIUS CÆSAR AUGUSTUS

have me company with Octavia my wife onely, tell me true: know you for your part none other women but Drucilla? Go to: so may you fare well and have your health, as when you shall read this letter, you be not redy to deale carnally with Tertulla[1] or Terentilla, or Rufilla, or Salvia Titiscenia, or with all of them. And thinke you it skilleth not, where and whom you lust after and meddle with?'

70

Moreover, much talke there was abroad, of a certaine supper of his more secret, ywis then the rest, and which was commonly called *Dodecatheos*[a]: at which, that their sat guests in habit of Gods and goddesses, and himselfe among them adorned insteed of Apollo: not onely the letters of Antonie, who rehearsed most bitterly the names of every one do lay in his reproach, but also these verses without an author so vulgarly knowne and rife in everie mans mouth:

Cum primum istorum conduxit mensa Choragum,
Sexque Deos vidit Mallia, sexque Deas:
Impia dum Phœbi Cæsar mendacia ludit;
Dum nova Divorum cœnat adulteria:
Omnia se a terris tunc numina declinarunt.
Fugit et auratos Iupiter ipse thronos:

When first the table of these (guests) hired one the daunce to leade [2][b]
And mallia [3][c] six Goddesses and Gods as many saw;
Whiles Cæsar Phœbus conterfaites profanely[d], and in stead
Of supper, new adultries makes[e] of Gods against all law;
All the heavenly powers then, from the earth their eies quite turned away,
And Jupiter himselfe[f] would not in gilt Shrines[4] longer stay.

The rumor of this supper was increased by the exceeding dearth and famine at that time in Rome: and the very next morrow, there was set up this cry and note within the Cittie, That the Gods had eaten up all the Corne: and

---

[1] Tertia, Terentia, Rufa: as lovers use to name their sweete hearts.
[2] *Choragum, Choregon,* or one to provide the furniture of the feasts. [3] Some take this to be the name of one of the 6 goddesses guests: or rather some dame that could skill in bringing such together. [4] *Thronos, altoros,* beds, or *Tholos,* Scutcheons in Architecture.

TWELVE CÆSARS

that Cæsar was become Apollo in deede[1], but yet Apollo the tortor[g]: under which surname that God was worshipped in one place of the Cittie. Furthermore, taxed hee was for his greedie grasping after pretious house furniture and costly Corinthian Vessels: as also for giving himselfe much to dice play. For, as in time of the proscription, there was written over his statue: **OCTAVIUS CÆSAR AUGUSTUS**

> *Pater Argentarius, Ego Corinthiarius.*
> My father was a Banking-monie changer,
> And I am now a Corinth-Vessell-munger.

Because it was thought he procured some to be put into the bill of those that were proscribed, even for the love of their Corinthian-Vesselles: so afterwardes, during the Sicilian warre, this Epigrame of him went currant abroad:

> *Postquam bis classe victus naves perdidit;*
> *Aliquando ut vincat, ludit assidue aleam.*
> Since time he lost his ships at Sea in fight defaited twice;
> That win he may sometime, he playes continually at dice.

71

Of these criminous imputations or malicious slanders (I wot not whether) the infamie of his unnaturall uncleannesse he checked and confuted most easily by his chast life both at the present and afterward. Semblably the invidious opinion of his excessive, and sumpteous furniture: considering, that when he had by force won Alexandria, he retained for himselfe out of al the kings houshold stuffe and rich Implements, no more but on cup of the pretious stone Myrrha[2]: and soone after, all the brasen vessels which were of most use, hee melted everie one. Mary for fleshly lust otherwise and wantonnes with women he went not cleere, but was blotted therwith. For afterwards, also as the report goes, he gave himselfe overmuch to the deflowring of young maides whome his wife sought out for him from all places. As for the rumour that ran of his diceplaying he bashed no whit thereat: and he played simply without Art and openly for his disport, even when he was well striken in yeares: and besides the moneth December[a], upon other play dayes also,

---

[1] Not counterfaite as at the supper over night.   [2] Or Murrha. The Cassidonie.

THE HISTORIE OF

OCTAVIUS
CÆSAR
AUGUSTUS

yea and worke daies too. Neither is there any doubt to bee made thereof. For in a certaine Epistle written with his owne hand: 'I supped,' quoth hee, 'my Tiberius with the same men: there came moreover to beare us companie these guests, Vinicius, and Salvius the father. In supper time[1] we played like olde men[2], both yesterday and to day. For when the dice[3] were cast [b] looke who threwe the chaunce, Canis or Senio, for everie die he staked and layed to the stocke a denier: which he tooke up and swooped all cleane, whose lucke it was to throw Venus.' Againe in another letter, 'We lived full merily, my Tiberius, during the feast *Quinquatria*[c]: for, wee played everie day: we haunted I say and heat the dicing house. Your brother[4] did his deede with many great shouts and outcries: howbeit, in the ende he lost not much: but after his great losses gathered uppe his crummes pretily well by little and little, beyond his hope and exspectation. I for my part, lost 20000 Sesterces in mine owne name: but it was when I had beene over liberall in my gaming, as commonly my manner is. For, if I had called for those loosing-hands which I forgave my fellow gamesters, or kept but that which I gave cleane away, I had wonne as good as 50000 cleere. But I choose rather thus to doe. For my bountie exalteth me unto cælestial glory.' Unto his daughter thus he writeth, 'I have sent unto you 250 deniers: just so many as I had given to my guests a peece, if they would have played togither in supper time, either at cockeall, or at even and odde.' For the rest of his life, certaine it is, that in everie respect he was most continent, and without suspition of any vice.

72

Hee dwelt at first, hard by the Forum of Rome above the winding staires Anulariæ, in an house which had been Calvus the Oratours: afterwards in the mount Palatium: howbeit in a meane habitation, belonging sometime to Hortensius, and neither for spacious receite nor stately setting out, and trim furniture, conspicuous: as wherein the galleries were but

---

[1] Betweene dishes or courses of services.   [2] For *Talorum lusus fuit senilis*.
[3] Or bones.   [4] Drusus Nero.

TWELVE CÆSARS

short, standing uppon pillers made of (soft) Albane stone: and the Refection Roumes without any marble or beautifull pavements. For the space of 40 yeares and more, hee kept on bedchamber winter and summer: and albeit hee found by experience the Cittie not verie holesome in the winter for his health, yet continually he wintred there: if hee purposed at any time to do ought secretly, and without interruption: hee had a speciall roome alone by it selfe aloft which hee called Syracuse[1 a]. Hither would hee withdrawe himselfe orderly, or else make a steppe to some Country house neere the Cittie, of one of his Libertines. Was hee sicke at any time? Then hee used to lie in Mæcenas his house. Of all his retyring places of pleasure, hee frequented these especially, that stood along the Maritime tract, and the Isles of Campania; or else the townes nere adjoyning to the Cittie of Rome, to wit, Lanuvium, Præneste and Tibur: where also within the Porches of Hercules Temple, he sat verie often to minister justice. Large palaces and full of curious workes hee misliked: and verily, those that were sumpteously built he rased downe to the verie ground: his owne as little as they were, he adorned and beautified not so much with trim statues and gay painted Tables, as with open walks[2], pleasant groves[3], and such things, as for their antiquitie and rarenesse were notable: of which sort were at Capreæ the huge members of monstrous fishes[4] and wilde beasts: the bones that are saide to bee of Gyants, and the armour of the demigods and worthies in olde time.

OCTAVIUS
CÆSAR
AUGUSTUS

73

How slenderly provided he was of houshold stuffe and furniture otherwise appeareth by his dining pallets and tables yet remaining: the most part whereof be scarce answerable to the elegancie of a meere private person. Neither slept he by mens saying otherwise than upon a lowbed[5], and the same but meanely spread and laid with Coverlets. He wore not lightly any apparell but of huswifes

[1] Or Technophyon. [2] *Xystis*, admitting the winter sunne. [3] For shade in Summer. [4] *Belluarum*, as whales, whirpooles, etc. [5] Not raysed uppe and swelling high with downe.

THE HISTORIE OF

OCTAVIUS CÆSAR AUGUSTUS

cloth, made within house; by his wife, his sister, his daughter and neipces. His gownes were neither streight and skant, nor yet wide and large. His Senatours robe neither with overbroad studs of purple guarded, nor with narrow. His shoes underlaide somewhat with the highest, that hee might seeme taller than hee was. As for the raiment which hee used abroade, and his shooes, hee had them at all times layed readie within his Bedchamber, against all suddaine occurrents and unlooked for occasions whatsoever.

74

He feasted daily: and never otherwise than at a set table [1]: not without great respect and choise of degrees and persons. Valerius Messalla writeth, that hee never intertained any of his libertines at supper except Meanus, and him naturalized first [2], even after the betraying of Sex. Pompeius fleete; himselfe writeth, that he invited one, in whose ferme hee would make his abode, and who in times past had beene a Spie [3 a] of his. Hee came to the bourde himselfe when he made a feast, sometimes very late, and otherwhiles left the same as soone: and then his guests would both fall to their suppers before he sat downe, and also continued sitting still after hee was gone. The suppers hee made consisted ordinarily of three dishes of meate [4] and when hee would fare most highly of 6 at the most; and as he entertained his guests in no exceeding sumpteous manner, so he welcomed them with all the kindnesse and curtesie that might be. For he would provoke them, if they either sat silent or spake softly to the fellowshippe of discourse and talke: yea and interpose either Acroames [5] and players or else Triviall fellowes [6] out of the Cirque, but most commonly these discoursing poore threedbare Phylosophers [7].

[1] *Cœna recta*, or *recta*, absolutely, in difference of *sportula*. [2] Restored to his blood and created a gentle man, for he was *Donatus aureis annulis ut inter ingenuos haberetur*. Dion. [3] *Speculator*, or a squire of his bodie. [4] *Tribus ferculis*, not such as ours be: but framed in manner of *Tropees*, with devises that some meates might lye flat, others hang thereupon. [5] As minstrels, Musitians, Quiristers, etc. [6] As fortune tellers, juglers, Buffons, etc. [7] *Aretalogos*.

TWELVE CÆSARS

OCTAVIUS
CÆSAR
AUGUSTUS

75

Festivall and solemne daies he celebrated sometimes with unmeasurable expenses, otherwhiles with mirth and sport onely: as the *Saturnalia*, and at other times when it pleased him, hee used to send abroade as his gifts, onewhile apparaile, golde and silver: otherwhile mony of all stampes, even olde peeces currant in the Kings dayes, and strange coynes; sometime nothing but haire clothes, spunges, cole rakes[1], cizars[2] and such like stuffe, under obscure and doubtfull titles symbolizing somewhat else. Hee was wont also to offer sale, by marting in the time of a banquet to his guestes, of such thinges, as were in price most unequall[3], yea and to tender blinde bargaines unto them also of painted Tables, with the wronge side outwarde, and so by uncertaine venturinge uppon their happe, either to frustrate and disappoint, or fully to satisfie the hope of the Chapmen: yet so, as the cheapninge of the thinge should always passe through everie bourde, and the losse or gaine growe to them all as common.

76

As touching diet (for I may not over passe so much as this) hee was a man of verie little meate, and feedinge for the most part grosse. Seconde breade[4] and small fishes: cheese made of cowes milke and the same pressed with the hand[5], and greene figges especially of that kinde which beare twice a yeere, his appetite served unto. His manner was to eate even just before supper, when and wheresoever his stomacke called for foode. His very wordes out of his owne Epistles shewe no lesse, which are these: 'Whiles wee were in a British Waggon[6], wee tasted of bread and Dates.' Againe, 'As I returned homeward in my Licter from the Palace, I eate an ounce weight of bread with a fewe hard coated Grapes[7].' And once more, 'The very Jewe, my Tiberius, observeth not his Fast upon the Sabbath[a] so precisely, as I have this day:

---

[1] Or fire forks.   [2] Or snippers.   [3] A kinde of Lotterie.   [4] Or cheat.
[5] Much like Angelots, *manu pressum, mane pressum, i.* Greene cheese new made.   [6] Or Germain, *essedo.* For they were used in both countries indifferently.   [7] *Uvis duracinis,* or, with hard kernels.

THE HISTORIE OF

OCTAVIUS CÆSAR AUGUSTUS

who in the baines, not before the first houre of the night was past, chewed¹ two morsels of bread, even before I began to be anointed.' Upon this retchlesse neglect of diet², he used divers times to take his supper alone, either before his other guests were set and fell to meate, or else after all was taken away, and they risen: whereas, at a full bourd he would not touch a bit.

77

Hee was by nature also a very small drinker of wine. Cornelius Nepos reporteth of him, that his usuall manner was during the time hee lay encamped before Mutina to drinke at a supper not above thrice. Afterwards, whensoever hee dranke most liberally hee passed not sixe Sextants³; or if hee went beyond, he cast it up againe. Hee delighted most in Rhetian wine; and seldome dranke hee in the day time⁴. In steede of drinke hee tooke a sop of bread soaked in colde water; or a peece of Coucumber, or a young lectuce head, or else some new gathered apple, sharpe and tart⁵, standing much upon a winish liquour within it.

78

After his noones repast hee used to take his repose, and to sleepe a while, in his cloathes as he was, with his shooes on ᵃ, stretching out his feete ᵇ, and holding his hand before his eyes. After supper hee retired himselfe into a little Closet or Studie ᶜ. And there continued hee by a candle farre in the night, even untill he had dispatched the rest of that daies businesse, either all or the most part. From thence, he went directly to his bed: where, hee slept at the most not above seaven houres: and those verily not together but so, as in that space of time hee would awake three or foure times: and if hee could not recover his sleepe thus broken and interrupted (as it happened otherwhiles), hee

---

¹ Or, did eate. ² *Ex hac in observantia, vel, ex hac observantia*: upon this due observing of his, to eate when his stomack called for it, and not els. ³ 6 measures, containing either 2 ounces a peece, or two cyathes, *i.* 3 ounces. In all, at the most not above a good pint, or a small wine quart, called *Sextarius*, consisting of 18 ounces. ⁴ *Interdiu*, as we say, betwixt meales. ⁵ *Acidum*, or *aridum*, *i.* dried, but yet of a winish tast.

TWELVE CÆSARS

would send for some to reade or tell tales[1]: and by their meanes catch a sleepe againe, and drawe the same out often after day-breake. Neither would he ever lie awake without one sitting by his beds side. Much offended hee was with want of sleepe (or waking) early in a morning: and if hee were to bee awakened sooner than ordinarie, either about some worldly affaires of his friends, or service of the Gods, because hee would not prejudice thereby his owne good or health, hee used to stay in some of his familiar friends upper roomes and loft, next to the place where his occasions lay. And even so, many a time for want of sleepe, both as he was caried through the streetes, and also when his licter was set downe, hee would betweene whiles take a nap and make some stay.

OCTAVIUS CÆSAR AUGUSTUS

79

Hee was of an excellent presence and personage, and the same throughout all the degrees of his age most lovely and amiable; negligent though hee were in all manner of pikednesse, for combing and trimming of his head so carelesse, as that he would use at once many Barbers, such as came next hand, it skilled not whom: and one while hee clipped, another while hee shaved his beard; and yet at the very same time, he either read, or else wrote somewhat. His visage and countenance, whether he spake or held his peace, was so mild, so pleasant and lightsome, that one of the Nobles and Potentates of Gaule, confessed unto his Country-men, he was thereby onely staied and reclaimed, that he did not approach neere unto him, under colour of conference as hee passed over the Alpes, and so shove him downe from a steepe cragge to breake his necke, as his full intent was. Hee had a paire of cleere and shining eyes: wherein also, (as hee would have made men beleeve) was seated a kinde of Divine vigour: and hee joyed much, if a man looking wistly upon him helde downe his face, as it were against the brightnesse of the Sunne. But in his olde age he saw not very well with the left eye. His teeth grewe thinne in his head, and the same were small and ragged: the haire of his head

[1] Or, to hold him with talke.

THE HISTORIE OF

OCTAVIUS CÆSAR AUGUSTUS was somewhat curled and turning downeward; and withall of a light yellowe colour. His eye-browes met together: his eares were of a meane bignesse: his nose both in the upper part[1], bearing out round, and also beneath somewhat with the longest[2]. Of colour and complexion, hee was betweene a browne and faire white[3]. His stature but short: (and yet Julius Marathus his freedman writeth in the Historie of his life, that hee was five foote and nine inches high[a]). But as lowe as the same was, the proportionable making and feature of his limmes hid it so, as it might not be perceived, unlesse he were compared with some taller person than himselfe standing by.

80

His body, by report, was full of spottes: having upon the brest and bellie naturall markes which hee brought with him into the worlde; dispersed, for the manner, order, and number, like unto the starres of the celestiall beare[4]; as also certaine hard risings of thicke brawnie skinne, occasioned in divers places by the ytching of his bodie, and the continuall and forcible use of the Strigil[5] in the Baines: which callosities resembled a Ringworme[a]. In his left hucklebone[b], thigh and legge, hee was not very sound: in so much, as many times for griefe thereof he halted on that side: but by a remedie that he had of Sand and Reedes[c], he found ease and went upright againe. Also, the fore-finger of his right hand hee perceived otherwhiles to be so weake, that being benummed and shrunke by a crampe upon some colde, he could hardly set it to any writing, with the helpe of an hoope and finger-stall of horne. Hee complained also of the griefe in his bladder[d], but voiding at length little gravell-stones by urine, he was eased of that paine.

81

All his life time hee tasted of certaine grievous and

---

[1] Toward his forehead. [2] *Deductiore*, or as some expound it, sharp and thin, Lepton. [3] *Inter aquilum candidumque*, somewhat tanned and sunne-burnt, as Casaubon seemeth to interpret it. [4] Charlemaine his waine. [5] Much like a curry comb.

TWELVE CÆSARS

daungerous sicknesses, but especiallie after the subduing of
Cantabria: what time, by reason of his liver diseased and
corrupted by Destillations[1], hee was driven to some extremitie:
and thereby of necessitie entred into a contrarie and desperate course of Physicke[a]: for, seeing that hote fomentations
did him no good, forced hee was by the direction and counsell
of Antonius Musa his Physitian, to be cured by colde. He
had the experience also of some maladies which came yeerely[b]
and kept their course at a certaine time. For about his
birth-day[c], most commonly he was sickish and had a faint-
nesse upon him: likewise in the beginning of the Spring[d],
much troubled hee was with the inflation of the midriffe
and hypochondriall parts[2]: and whensoever the winde was
southerly, with the murr and the pose. By occasion whereof,
his body beeing so shaken and crasie, hee could not well
endure either colde or heat.

OCTAVIUS
CÆSAR
AUGUSTUS

82

In winter time clad he went against the colde with foure
coates, together with a good thicke gowne, and his Wast-
coate or Peticoate bodie of woollen: well lapped also about
the thighes and legges[a]. During Sommer he lay with his
bed chamber dores open, and oftentimes within a cloisture
supported with pillers, having water walming out of a
spring[b], or running from a spout in a Conduit; or else some
one to make winde hard by him[c]. Hee could not away so
much as with the Winter sunne shine: and therefore even
at home hee never walked up and downe in the aire without
a broad brimd Hat[3] upon his head. He travailed in a licter,
and never lightly but in the night. The journeyes that he
made were soft and small: so as if hee went from Rome
but to Tibur or Preneste, he would make two daies of it.
Could hee reach to any place by sea: hee chose rather to
saile thither, than goe by land[d]. But as great infirmities as
he was subject unto, hee maintained and defended his body

[1] *Destillationibus jocinore vitiato.* What if we thus point and read?
Destillationibus, jocinore vitiato: to this sence, That he was much subject
to rhewmes, by occasion that his liver was diseased, to wit, obstructed or
stopped.   [2] Under the short ribs.   [3] Or Bond-grace.

THE HISTORIE OF

OCTAVIUS CÆSAR AUGUSTUS

with as much care and regard of himselfe: but principally by seldome bathing ¹ ᵉ: for, anointed hee was very often and used to sweate before a light fire: and then upon it to be dowssed in water luke-warme, or else heated with long standing in the Sunne. And so often as he was to use the Sea waters hote, or those of Albula ² for the strengthening of his sinewes, hee contented himselfe with this: namely to sit in a wooden bathing Tub, which himselfe by a Spanish name called *Dureta* ᶠ, and therein to shake up and downe his hands and feet one after another, by turnes.

83

The exercises in (Mars) field of riding on horse-backe and bearing armes, he laid aside immediatly after the civile warres, and tooke himselfe, first, to the little tennis-ball ᵃ, and the hand-ball blowne with winde ᵇ. Soone after, he used onely to bee caried ³ and to walke, but so as that in the end of every walke he would take his runne by jumpes, lapped and wrapped within a light garment called *Sestertius* ⁴ or a thinne vaile and sheete of linnen ᶜ. For his recreation and pastime, his manner was sometime to angle or fish with the hooke, otherwhiles to play with cockall bones ᵈ, or trundling round pellets ᵉ, or else with nuttes even among little boyes; whom hee would lay for, and seeke out from all parts, if they were of an amiable countenance and could prattle pretily with a lovely grace ⁵, but principally those of the Moores and Syrians kind. As for Dwarfes, crooked and mishapen Elves and all of that sort, he could not abide such, as being the very mockeries of natures work, and of unlucky presage.

84

Eloquence, and other liberall professions he exercised from his very childhood right willingly, and therein tooke exceed-

---

¹ In hot waters. ² Which naturally were hot standing upon a veine of brimstone. ³ Either on horsebacke, or in a licter. ⁴ Two foote and a halfe square. ⁵ These the Romaines called *Delicias suas*, their playferes and dearlings in an honest sence: not such as the Greeks in an uncleane signification, named *Paidica*, wanton baggages, Catamites.

150

ing great paines. During the warre at Mutina, notwithstanding that huge heape of affaires and occurrents, (by report) he read, he wrote, hee declaimed every day. For afterwards, neither in the Senate-house, nor before the people, ne yet to his souldiours made he ever speech, but it was premeditate and composed before: albeit hee wanted not the gift to speake of a sodaine and extempore. Now, for feare least his memorie at any time should faile him, least also he might spend too much time in learning by rote, hee began to reade and rehearse all out of his written copie. His very speeches also with folke by themselves, even with Livia his wife about any grave and serious matters were never but penned and put downe in writing: out of which hee would rehearse the same, that hee might not speake otherwise *ex tempore* or more or lesse than was meete. His pronunciation and utterance was sweete, carying with it a peculiar and proper sound of his owne: and continually he used the helpe of a Phonascus to moderate his voice: but sometimes when his throate was weakened[1], he delivered his orations to the people, by the mouth of a Crier.

OCTAVIUS
CÆSAR
AUGUSTUS

85

Many compositions he made in prose, of sundry arguments. Of which he would reade some in a meeting of his familiars, as it were in an Auditorie: as namely a Rejoinder, called *Rescripta*, unto Brutus, against Cato[2]. Which volumes, when for the most part, hee had rehearsed, being now well stricken in yeeres and growing wearie, hee made over to Tiberius for to be reade through. In like manner hee wrote certaine Exhortations unto Philosophie, and somewhat of his owne life: which hee declared in thirtie bookes[3], even unto the Cantabrian warre, and no farther. As for Poetrie hee dealt in it but superficially. One Treatise there is extant written by him in Hexametre verses, the argument whereof, is *Sicilie*, and so it is entituled. There is another booke also, as little as it, *Of Epigrammes*: which for the most part hee studied upon and devised whiles hee was in

---

[1] When he was hoarse, by reason of rhewme. [2] *Uticensis*. [3] xxx. *Libris*, or rather xiii. according to Suidas, and all old Copies.

THE HISTORIE OF

OCTAVIUS CÆSAR AUGUSTUS the Baines. For, having in a great and ardent heat begun a Tragædie¹, when he saw his stile would not frame thereto and speede no better, he defaced and wiped it quite out. And when some of his friends asked him, How *Ajax* did? he answered, that his *Ajax* was fallen upon a Spunge² ᵃ.

86

The Eloquence that he followed was of an Elegant and temperate kind: wherein he avoided unapt and unfit Sentences, as also the stinking savours, as himselfe saith, of darke and obscure words: but tooke especiall care how to expresse his minde and meaning most plainely and evidently. For the better effecting whereof, and because hee would not in any place trouble and stay reader or hearer, hee stucke not either to put Prepositions unto Verbes, or to iterate Conjunctions very oft: which being taken away breed some obscurity, although they yeeld a greater grace. As for those that affect new-made words ᵃ, such also as use old termes past date, hee loathed and rejected alike, as faulty, both the sorts of them in a contrary kinde. Those he shooke up divers times, but especially his friend Mæcenas, whose *Murobrecheis cincinnos* ³ ᵇ, for these were his termes, he evermore curseth and taxeth, yea and by way of imitation ᶜ merrily scoffeth at. Neither spared he so much as Tiberius for hunting otherwhiles after old words out of use, and such [as] be obscure and hardly understood. As for Marcus Antonius he rateth him as if he were frantick, for writing that which men may rather wonder at, than understand. And proceeding to mocke his lewd and unconstant humour in choosing a kinde of eloquence by himselfe, he added thus much moreover, 'And are you in doubt to imitate Cimber Annius and Veranius Flaccus ᵈ, so that you might use the wordes which Crispus Salustius gathered out of Catoes *Origines* ⁴? or rather transfer the rolling tongue of Asiatick Oratours,

---

¹ Called *Ajax*. ² Was wiped away or blotted out with a spunge: alluding to Ajax that fell upon his own sword: whereof Sophocles made a Tragædie entituled *Ajax*. ³ Curled lokes or feakes, glib and dropping againe with sweet balmes. ⁴ Censorius, who wrote a booke of Antiquities, so called.

TWELVE CÆSARS

full of vaine words, and void of pithy sentences into our language and manner of speech?' And in a certaine Epistle, praising the ready wit of Agrippina his owne niece[1], 'But you have neede,' quoth hee, 'to endevour that neither in writing nor in speaking, you be troublesome and odious.'

OCTAVIUS
CÆSAR
AUGUSTUS

87

In his daily and ordinary talke certaine phrases hee had which hee used very often and significantly: as the letters of his owne hand writing doe evidently shew: in which, ever and anon, when hee meant some that would never pay their debts, he said, 'They would pay *ad Calendas Græcas*[2].' And when he exhorted men to beare patiently the present state what ever it was, 'Let us content ourselves,' quoth hee, 'with this Cato[3].' To expresse the speedy expedition of a thing done hastily, 'Quicker,' would he say, 'than Sparages can be sodden.' Hee putteth also continually for *Stultus*[4], *Baceolus*[5]: for *Pullus*[6], *Pulleiaceus*: and for *Ceritus, Vacerrosus*; and in steede of *Male se habere, Vapide se habere*: and for *Languere, Betizare*, which commonly we meane by *Lachanizare*[7]. Semblably, for *simus, sumus*; and *domos*, in the genetive case singular for *domus*. And never used hee these two words otherwise, that no man should thinke it was a fault rather than a custome. Thus much also have I observed, especially in his manuscripts, that he never cutteth a word in sunder: nor in the end of any rewes[8] transferreth the overplus of letters unto those next following, but presently putteth them downe even there underneath, and encloseth them (within a compasse line).

88

Orthographie, that is to say, the forme and precise rule of writing set down by Grammarians, he did not so much

---

[1] By his daughter Julia, and M. Agrippa the mother of Caligula. [2] At the Greek Calends, *i.* at latter Lammas, for the Greeks had no Calends, no more than the Latines *Neomenias*, *i.* newe moones to begin their moneths with. And yet the word seemeth to be derived of *Kalo* in Greeke. [3] Read Macrob. *Saturnal.* 2. [4] *i.* A foole. [5] *Vel Bliteolus* a *blito, vel Blacolus*, a *Blax, vel Bateolus*. [6] Or for *Puleium, i. Pulegium, Puleiaceum*. [7] Or *Lachanissare*. [8] Or lines.

U
153

THE HISTORIE OF

OCTAVIUS CÆSAR AUGUSTUS

observe: but seemeth to follow their opinion rather, who thinke, Men should write according as they speake. For, whereas oftentimes he either exchangeth or leaveth cleane out, not letters onely but syllables also, that is a common errour among men. Neither would I note thus much, but that it seemeth strange unto mee, which some have written of him, namely, that he substituted another, in the place of a Consulare Lieutenant (as one altogether rude and unlearned) because hee had marked in his hand-writing, ixi for *ipsi*. And looke how often himselfe writeth darkly by way of ciphring, hee putteth *b* for *a*, *c* for *b*, and so forth after the same manner, the letters next following in steede of the former: and for *x* a duple *a a*.

89

Neither verily was he lesse in love with the studie of Greeke literature: for, even therein also he highly excelled, as having beene brought up and taught under the professed Rhetorician Apollodorus of Pergamus. Whom beeing now very aged, himselfe as yet but young had forth of Rome with him to Apollonia. Afterwards, also when he was well furnished with variety of erudition and learning of Sphærus [a], he entred into familiar acquaintance with Areus the Philosopher and his two sonnes, Dionysius and Nicanor: yet so, as for all that he neither could speake readily, nor durst compose any thing[1]. For if occasion required ought, he drew it in Latine, and gave it unto another for to be translated into Greeke. And, as he was not altogether unskilfull in Poemes, so he tooke delight even in the olde Comœdie [b] also, which he exhibited oftentimes to be acted in publique solemnities. In reading over and perusing Authors of both Languages, hee sought after nothing so much as holsome precepts and examples, serving to publique or private use: and those, when he had gathered out of them word for word, hee sent either to his inward friends and domesticall Servitours, or to the Commaunders of armies and Governours of Provinces: or else for the most part to the Magistrates of the Citie, according as any of them needed admonition.

[1] In Greeke.

TWELVE CÆSARS

Moreover, whole bookes he both read from one end to the other unto the Senate, and also published oftentimes to the people by proclamation: as namely, the Orations of Q. Metellus ᶜ touching the propagation and multiplying of children: those likewise of Rutilius concerning the model and forme of buildings[1]: thereby the rather to perswade them, That hee was not the first that lookt into both these matters, but that their fore-fathers in old time had even then a care and regard thereof. The fine wits flourishing in his daies he cherished by all meanes possible. Such as rehearsed before him their Compositions he gave audience unto, courteously and with patience: not onely verses and histories, but orations[2] also and dialogues. Mary, if any thing were written of himselfe, unlesse it were done with serious gravity and by the best, hee tooke offence thereat; and gave the Prætours in charge not to suffer his name to be made vulgar and stale, in the trivial contentions (of Oratours, Poets, etc.) when they were matched one with another.

OCTAVIUS
CÆSAR
AUGUSTUS

90

For Religious scrupulosity and Superstition, thus by heere-say hee stoode affected. Thunder and Lightning hee was much affraide of: in so much as alwaies and in every place, hee caried about him for a preservative remedie a Scales skinne[3]: yea, and whensoever he suspected there would be any extraordinarie storme or tempest, he would retire himselfe into a close secret roome under ground ᵃ, and vaulted above head: which hee did, because once in times past, he had beene frighted with a flash of lightning, crossing him in his journey by night; as we have before related.

91

As for dreames, neither his owne, nor other mens of himselfe, he neglected. At the battaile of Philippi, albeit hee meant not to step out of his pavilion by reason of sicknesse,

---

[1] As wel to cut of the expenses of sumpteous ædifices as to prevent danger by Skare-fires. [2] Which were not so usually red and rehersed in open audience. [3] Or of a sea calfe, wich as Plinie writeth checketh all lightnings.

THE HISTORIE OF

OCTAVIUS CÆSAR AUGUSTUS

yet went hee forth, warned so to doe by the dreame of his Physitian¹. And it fell out well for him: considering that after his Campe forced and woon by the enemies, his licter was in that concurse of theirs stabbed through and all rent and torne, as if hee had remained there behind lying sicke. Himselfe every spring was wont to see many visions most fearefull, but the same proved vaine illusions and to no purpose: at other times of the yeere he dreamed not so often, but yet to more effect. When as hee ordinarily frequented the temple dedicated to Jupiter the Thunderer in the Capitoll, he dreamed that Jupiter Capitolinus complained, How his worshippers were taken from him perforce: and that hee answered, Hee had placed Thundering Jupiter hard by him, in steede of a Porter²: whereuppon soone after hee adorned the Lanterne³ of that Temple with a Ringe⁴ of belles, because such commonly do hange at mens Gates⁵. By occasion of a vision by night, he begged yearely uppon a certaine day mony of the people ᵃ, and held out his hand hollow⁶ to those that brought and offred unto him brazen Dodkins⁷ or mites called Asses.

92

Certaine foretokens and ominous signes he observed as unfallible presages, to wit, if in a morning his shoes were put one wronge, and namely, the left for the right, he held it unluckie: againe, when hee was to take any long journey by land or sea, if it chanced to mizzle of raine, hee tooke that for a luckie signe betokening a speedie and prosperous returne. But mooved he was especially with uncouth and supernaturall sights. There happened a date tree to spring forth betweene the very joincts of the stones before his dore, which he remooved and transplanted in the inward court of his domesticall Gods⁸; taking great care that it might get roote and grow there. Hee joied so much in the Iland Capreæ, the boughes of a very old holmetree hanging and drouping now for age down to the ground, became fresh

---

[1] *Medici.* Some read, *amici, i.* a friend. [2] Dore keeper. [3] Or top.
[4] Or chime. [5] To raise the porters. [6] As beggers do. [7] Or peeces worth ob. ₰.q. [8] Wherin they stood.

TWELVE CÆSARS

againe at his comming thither, that he would needes make an exchang with the State of Naples, and in lieu of that Iland geve them Ænaria. • Certaine dayes also hee precisely observed: as for example: hee would not take a journey any whither, the day after the *Nundinæ*[a]: nor begin any serious matter uppon the *Nones* of a Moneth: herein verily avoyding and eschewing nought else, as he writeth unto Tiberius, but the unluckie ominousnesse[1] of the name[b].

OCTAVIUS
CÆSAR
AUGUSTUS

93

Of foraine ceremonies and religions, as hee entertained with all reverence those that were aunctient, and whereof hee conceived good reason: so hee despised the rest. For having beene instituted and professed (in the sacred mysteries of Ceres) at Athens, when afterwards he sat judicially upon the Tribunall at Rome to here and determine a controversie as touching the priviledge of Ceres priests in Attica, and perceived that certaine points of great secrecie were proposed there to be debated: hee dismissed the assembly and multitude of people standing all about in the Court, and himselfe alone heard them plead the cause. But contrariwise, not onely when hee roade in visitation all over Ægypt, himselfe forbore to turne a little out of his way for to see Apis[a], but also commended his nephew Caius, because in ryding through Jurie, he did not so much as once make supplication[2] in Hierusalem[b].

94

And seeing we have proceeded thus farre[3], it would not be impertinent to annex hereto, what befell unto him before hee was borne? what happened uppon his verie birth-day? and what presently ensued thereupon? whereby, that future greatnes and perpetuall felicity of his, might be hoped for and observed. At Velitre, part of the (Towne) wall in olde time had beene blasted by lightening: uppon which occasion, answere was given by Oracle, that a Citizen of that Towne should one day be ruler of the world. The

[1] Dusphemian *nominis*.   [2] Or do his devotions.   [3] In the historicall reports of so great and worthy a prince.

THE HISTORIE OF

OCTAVIUS CÆSAR AUGUSTUS

Velitrines, in confidence hereof, both then immediatly, and afterwardes also, many a time warred with the people of Rome, even wel neere to their own finall ruine and destruction. At length (though late it was) by good proofes and evidences it appeared that the said strange accident, portended the mightie power of Augustus. Julius Marathus reporteth, that some sixe moneths before Augustus Nativitie, there happened at Rome a prodigie publikely knowne, whereby foreshewed and denounced it was, that nature was about to bring forth a King over the people of Rome [a], at which the Senate beeing affrighted made an Act, That no man child that yeere borne should be reared and brought up. But they whose wives then, were great bellied (for everie one was readie to drawe the hope unto himselfe), tooke order, that the saide Act of the Senate shold not be brought into the Cittie Chamber and there enrolled. I reade in the bookes of Asclepiades Mendes [1] entituled *Theologoumenon* [2], howe Atia [3], being come at midnight to celebrate the solemne sacrifice and divine service of Apollo, whilest other dames slept, fell fast asleepe also; and sodainely a serpent [b] crept close unto her, and soone after went forth from her: she therewith being awakened purified her selfe, as she would have done uppon her husbands companie with her; and presently there arose to bee seene uppon her bodie a certaine marke or specke representing the picture of a serpent, which never after could be gotten out: in so much as immediatly thereupon shee forbore the publike baines for ever: also, how in the x. moneth after, she was delivered of Augustus: and for this cause he was reputed to be the sonne of Apollo. The same Atia, before she was brought to bed of him, dreamed that her entrails were heaved up to the stars, and there stretched foorth and spred all over the compasse of earth and heaven. His father Octavius likewise dreamed, that out of the wombe of Atia there arose the shining beames of the Sun. The very day on which he was borne, what time as the conspiracie of Catiline was debated in the Senate house, and Octavius by occasion of his wives

[1] Or Mendesius bearing the name of the Cittie Mendes in Ægypt. [2] Of divine discourses. [3] The mother of Augustus.

TWELVE CÆSARS

OCTAVIUS CÆSAR AUGUSTUS

Childbirth came verie late thither, well knowne it is and commonly spoken, that P. Nigidius[1] understandinge the cause of his stay, so soone as he learned the houre also when shee was delivered[2], gave it out confidently, That there was borne the Soveraine Lorde of the Worlde. Afterwardes, when Octavius leadinge an Armie through the secret partes of Thracia, inquired in the Sacred grove of *Liber pater* (according to the rites and ceremonies of that Barbarous Religion), concerning his sonne, the same aunswere hee received from the Priestes there; for, that when the wine was powred uppon the Altars, there arose from thence so great a shining flame, as surmounted the Lanterne[3] of the Temple, and so ascended uppe to Heaven: and that in times past the like strange token happened to Alexander the great, and to none but him, when hee sacrificed uppon the same Altars. Moreover, the night next following, hee presently thought he sawe his sonne[4] carrying a stately Majestie above the ordinarie proportion of a mortall wight, with a Thunder bolt and a Scepter[5] (in his hand) with the Triumphant Robes also of Jupiter Opt. Max. (uppon his backe) and a Radiant Coronet (on his head): over and besides his Chariot dight with Lawrell and drawne with 12 steedes exceeding white. While hee was yet a very babe[6], (as C. Drusus hath left in writing extant,) being by his nource laide in the evening within a Cradell in swadling bands, beneath uppon a lowe floure: the next morning hee could no where bee seene: and after longe seekinge was found at last, lying uppon a verie high Turret just against the Sunne-rysinge. So soone as hee began to speake, hee commaunded the Frogges to keepe silence, that about the mannour of his Grandsires by the Cittie side, chaunced to make a foule noyse: and thereuppon ever after, the Frogges in that place are not able to crouke. About foure miles from Rome, as yee goe directly to Capua[7], it fell out, that sodainely an Ægle snatched a peece of bread out of his hand as hee tooke his dinner within a pleasant grove: and when

[1] A famous Astrologer. [2] And thereby the Horoscope of his Nativity. [3] Or steeple. [4] Octavius. [5] Which properly are attributed unto Jupiter. [6] Augustus. [7] In the way Appia.

THE HISTORIE OF

OCTAVIUS CÆSAR AUGUSTUS

he had mounted up a very great height, came gently downe of a suddaine againe and restored unto him the same. Q. Catulus after the dedication of the Capitol dreamed two nights together: in the former, him thought, that Jupiter Optimus Maximus, whiles many young boyes, Noble mens sonnes, were playing about his Alter, severed one of them from the rest and bestowed in his bosome the publike broade Seale[c] of the State[1] to carrie in his hand. And the next night followinge he saw in another dreame the same boy in the bosome of Jupiter Capitolinus: whome when hee commaunded to bee pulled from thence, prohibited hee was by the admonition of the God, as if the same boy should be brought up for the defence and tuition of the Commonweale. Nowe the morrowe after, chauncing to meete with (young) Augustus, (whome earst hee had not knowne before,) hee beheld him wistly not without great admiration, and withall openly gave it out, That hee was for all the world like unto that boy of whom hee dreamed. Some tell the former dreame of Catulus otherwise: as if Jupiter, (when as a number of those boyes required of him a Tutor) pointed out one of them, unto whome they should referre all their desires: and so lightly touching his lipps, and taking as it were an assay therof with his fingers, brought that kisse backe to his own mouth. M. Cicero having accompanied Caius Cæsar into the Capitoll, happened to report unto his familiar friendes the dreame hee had the night before: namely how a boy of an ingenious face and countenance, was let downe from heaven by a golden Chaine, and stoode at the doore of the Capitoll, unto whom Jupiter delivered a whip[d]: hereuppon espying at unawares (little) Augustus whom (as yet altogether unknowne to most men) his Unkle Cæsar had sent for to the sacrifice, hee avouched plainly, that this boy was very he, whose Image was represented unto him in a vision as he lay asleepe. When hee was putting on his virile gowne, it fortuned that his broad studded Coate[2] with purple, being unstitched in the seames of both shoulders, fell from about him downe to his feete. There were who made this interpretation; That it betookened

[1] Or Citie.   [2] Which Cæsar had given him instead of *Tunica recta*.

TWELVE CÆSARS

nothing else, but that the decree¹ where of that Robe [is] OCTAVIUS
a badge should owne day be subjected unto him. Julius of CÆSAR
sacred memorie being about to choose a plot of ground for AUGUSTUS
to encamp in, about Munda, as he cut downe a wood, chanced
to light upon a date tree which he caused to bee spared and
reserved as the verie presage of victorie: from the root of it,
there sprung immediately certaine shoots which in few dayes
grew so fast, that they not onely equallized but over topped
also and shadowed their stocke: yea and doves² haunted
the same, therein to nestle and breede: notwithstanding
that kind of birde cannot of all others away with any hard
leaves and rough branches. Uppon this straunge sight
especially, Cæsar, by report was mooved to suffer none other
to succeede him in the Empire but his sisters Nephewe.
Augustus, during the time that he was retired to Apollonia,
went up in the companie of Agrippa, into the gallerie³ of
Theogenes the mathematician⁴. Now, when Agrippa, (who
inquired first what his owne fortune should be) had great
matters and those in manner incredible foretold unto him;
Augustus himselfe⁵ concealed the time of his owne nativitie,
and in no wise would utter the same; for feare and bashfulnesse, least he should be found inferiour to the other. But
when, hardly after many exhortations and much a doe,
hee had delivered the same, Theogenes leapt foorth and
worshipped him. Augustus then anone conceived so greate
a confidence in his fortunes, that hee divulged his Horoscope
and the ascendent of his Nativitie: yea and also stamped a
pecce of silver coyne, with the marke of the Celestiall signe
Capricornus, under which figure and Constellation hee was
borne.

95

After Cæsars death, being returned from Apollonia, as he
entred Rome Cittie, sodainely when the skie was cleere and
wether verie faire, a certaine round coronet in forme of a

¹ Senators.   ² Doves are consecrat to Venus, from whence the Julii are
descended. By them therefore and the date tree was præfigured perpetuall
felicitie to that name and familie.   ³ Or schoole.   ⁴ Or astrologer.
⁵ Augustus.

THE HISTORIE OF

OCTAVIUS CÆSAR AUGUSTUS

raine bowe compassed the circle of the Sunne, and therewith soone after, the monument of Julia, Cæsars daughter was smitten with lightening. Moreover in his first Consulship[a], whiles he attended to take his Augurie, there were presented unto him, like as to Romulus, 12 geirs[1]: and as hee sacrificed, the Livers of all the beasts then killed appeared in open view enfolded double, and turned inwardly from the nether fillet; and no man of skill conjectured otherwise, but that prosperitie and greatnes hereby was portended.

96

Furthermore, the very events, also of all his warres hee foresaw. What time as all the forces of the Triumvirs[2] were assembled together at Bononia, an Ægle perching over his tent, all to beat ij Ravens that assailed and fell uppon her of either side, and in the end strucke them both down to the ground: which sight the whole armie marked verie well, and presaged thereby that one day, there would arise betweene the Colleagues of that Triumvirate such discorde, and the like end ensue thereof, as after followed. At Philippi there was a certaine Thessalian[3], who made report of the future victorie: alledging for his author Cæsar of famous memorie, whose Image[4] encountred him as he journied in a desert and by-way. About Perusia when he offred sacrifice and could not speede[5], but demaunded more beasts[a] still to be killed: behold, the enemies made a sodaine sallie forth, caught up and carried away the whole provision of the Sacrifice. The Soothsayers then agreed uppon this point, That those perilous and adverse calamities which had beene threatned and denounced to him that sacrificed, should light all, and returne upon their heads, who gat the Inwards; and so it fell out in deed. The day before he fought the battaile at Sea neere Sicilie, as he walked upon the shore, a fish leapt out of the sea and lay at his feet. At Actium, as hee was going downe to fight the battaile, there met him in the way an Asse with his driver, the mans

---

[1] Or Vulturs. [2] Antonie Lepidus, and Octavius Augustus. [3] And therfore by likelihoode a wizard. [4] Or spectre. [5] *i.* Obtaine the favour of the Gods.

TWELVE CÆSARS

name was Eutychus, and the beasts Nicon ^b. After victorie OCTAVIUS
obtained, hee set uppe the Images of them both in brasse, CÆSAR
within that Temple, into which hee converted the verie AUGUSTUS
place where he encamped.

97

His death also (whereof from hence forth I will write) and his deification after death was knowne before by many signes most evident. When hee had taken a review of the Cittie; and was about the solemne purging[1] therof within Mars field before a frequent assemblie of people: an Ægle there was that soared oftentimes round about him, and crossing at length from him unto a house thereby, setled upon the name of Agrippa, and just upon the first letter[2] of that name; which when he perceived, the vowes which the manner was to be made untill the next *Lustrum*^a, he commanded his colleague Tiberius to nuncupate and pronounce. For, notwithstanding the Tables and instruments^b containing them were now written and in readinesse, yet denied he to undertake those vowes which he should never pay. About the same time the first letter[3] of his owne name, upon a flash and stroke of lightening went quite out of the Inscription that stood uppon his statue: aunswere was made by the Soothsaiers, that he was to live but just one hundred dayes after: which number that letter did betoken; and that it would come to passe that hee should bee Canonized and registred among the Gods, because Æsar, the residue of the name Cæsar, in the Tuskane Language signified God. Being about therefore to send Tiberius away into Illyricum and to companie him as far as Beneventum, when diverse suiters, for one cause or other interrupted him, yea and detained him about hearing and determining matters judicially, hee cryed out alowd (which also within a while was reckened as a presaging osse,) That were he once out of Rome, he would never after be there againe what occasion soever might make him stay. And so being entered upon his journie he went forward as far as to Astura: and so presently from thence (contrary to his usuall maner^c,) with the

[1] Called *Lustrum*.   [2] A.   [3] C, in Cæsar.

THE HISTORIE OF

OCTAVIUS CÆSAR AUGUSTUS

benefite of a forewind and gentle gale tooke water by night and sayled over[1].

98

The cause of his sickenes he caught by a flux of the bellie. And for that time having coasted Campanie and made circuit about the Ilands next adjoyning, he bestowed also foure dayes within a retiring place of pleasure at Capreæ: where he gave his minde to all ease and courteous affabilitie. It happened as he passed by the Bay of Puteoli, certaine passengers and souldiers out of a ship of Alexandria[a], which then was newly arrived, all clad in white, dight also with garlands, and burning frankincense, had heaped upon him all good and fortunate words, chaunting his singular prayses in these terms, That by him they lived, by him they sayled, by him they enjoyed their freedome, and all the riches they had. At which, he tooke great contentment and was cheered at the heart: insomuch as thereupon he divided to everie one of his traine about him 40 peeces of gold[b], but he required an oath againe and assurance of ech one, that they should not lay out that monie otherwise than in buying the wares and commodities of Alexandria[c]. For certaine dayes together that remained, among diverse and sundrie gifts, he distributed among them over and above, gownes and clokes, with this condition, that Romans should use the Greekish habite and speake likewise Greeke; the Greekes also weare Romaine attire and use their language. He beheld also continually the youthes exercising themselves (of whome their remained yet some store at Capreæ) according to the aunciente custome[2]. And even unto them he made a feast in his owne sight, permitting them or rather exacting of them, their olde libertie of sporting, of snatching appels and cates, and of skambling for such small gifts and favours as were sent or skattered abroad. In one word, he forbare no manner of mirth and pastime. The Isle hard by Capreæ[d], he called Apragopolis[e], of the Idlenesse of such as out of his traine retired themselves thither. But one of his beloved minions named Mas-

[1] For Astura was a water towne with a river also of that name running by it. [2] Of the Greeks who sometime inhabited those parts.

TWELVE CÆSARS

gabas¹, hee had wont merily to call κτίστης, as one would say, The founder of that Iland. The sepulcher of this Masgabas (who died a yeare before) when he perceived one time out of his dining chamber to be frequented with a sort of people and many lights: he pronounced this verse a loud which he made *ex tempore*.

OCTAVIUS
CÆSAR
AUGUSTUS

κτίστου δὲ τύμβον εἰσορῶ πυρούμενον,
I see the Tombe of Ktistes¹ all on fire.

And therewith turning to Thrasyllus a companion of Tiberius sitting over against him, and not woting what the matter was, he asked him of what Poets making he thought that verse to be? And when he stucke at the question and made no answere, he came out with an other to it.

Ὁρᾶς φαίσσι Μασγάβαν τιμώμενον,
Thou seest with lights Masgabas honoured.

Of this verse also he demaunded whom he thought to be the maker? but when Thrasyllus returned no other answere but this, That whosoever made them, right excellent they were; he laughed a good and made himselfe exceeding merie. Soone after he crossed over to Naples, albeit even then his guts were greatly enfeebled and the disease² grew variableᵍ: yet for all that, the Quinquennal Gymnick gamesʰ instituted in the honor of him, he beheld to the very end, and so together with Tiberius went to the place appointed. But in his return from thence, his disease increased more and more, so as at length he yeelded to it, at Nola: where, having sent for Tiberius and called him backe from his journey, he held him a great while in secret talke; neither from that time framed he his minde to any greater affaire.

99

Uppon his dying day, enquiring ever and anone, whether there was as yet any sturre and tumult abroad as touching him? hee called for a mirror³, and commanded the haire of

¹ The founder. ² Or if yee distinguish thus, *Morbo variante tamen*, etc., yet by reason that his disease altered, and himselfe was better some time then other. ³ A looking glasse.

THE HISTORIE OF

OCTAVIUS CÆSAR AUGUSTUS

his head to bee combed and trimmed: his chawes[1] also readie for weakenesse to hang or fall, to be composed and set straight. Then having admitted his friends to come unto him, and asked of them whether they thought he had acted well the Enterlude of his life? he adjoyned with all this finall conclusion[2], for a Plaudite,

Δότε κρότον καὶ πάντες ὑμεῖς μετὰ χαρᾶς κτυπήσατε,
Now clap your hands and all with joy resound a shout.

After this he dismissed them all, and whiles hee questioned with some that were new come from the Cittie, concerning the daughter of Drusus then sicke, sodainely amidst the kisses of Livia, and in these words he gave up the ghost, 'Live mindfull Livia of our wedlocke, and so farewell.' Thus died he an easie death and such as he had ever wished to have. For lightly, so often as he heard of any body to have departed this life quickely and without all panges, he prayed unto God, that hee and his might have the like Euthanasia[3], for, that was the verie word he was wont to use. One signe onely and no more he shewed of a minde disquieted and distracted, before he yeelded up his vitall breath: in that he suddainely started as in a fright and complained, That hee was harried away by 40 tall and lustie younge men. And even that also was rather a pregnant presage of his minde, than a raving fitte and idle conceit of light braine. For so many souldiers they were indeede of the Prætorian bande, who carried him forth (dead) into the streete upon their shoulders.

100

A.U.C. 767.

Hee died in that very bed-chamber wherein his Father Octavius left his life before him, when Pompeius and Appuleius, having both their forename Sextus, were Consuls: foureteene daies before the Calends of September[4], at the ninth houre[5] of the day: being 76 yeeres olde wanting

---

[1] Or chaps. [2] As the manner is at the ende of Comædies to call for a Plaudite: hee persisted therfore in the metaphor, and by this plaudite, allegorizeth the end of this life, which hee called before *Mimum vitæ*. [3] Euthanasia. [4] The Nineteenth of August. [5] About three of the clocke after noone.

TWELVE CÆSARS

five and thirtie daies. His corps was conveighed and borne by the Decurions[1] of the free burrowghes and Colonies from Nola to Bovillæ by night, for the hote season of the yeere: whereas till the day time it was bestowed in the Hall of every towne, or else in the greatest temple [a] thereof. From Bovillæ the degree of Romaine Gentlemen tooke charge of it, and brought it into the Citie of Rome, where they placed it within the Porch of his owne house. The Senate both in setting out his Funerals, and also in honouring his memorialls, proceeded so farre in striving, who should shew greater affection, that among many other complements, some were of minde, that the pompe and solemne convoy of his obsequies, should passe forth at the Triumphal gate with the image of victorie, which is in the Court Julia going before: and the chiefe Noble-mens children of both sexes singing a dolefull and lamentable song, others opined, that upon the very day of this funerall, their rings of gold [b] should be layd away and others of yron put on. Againe, divers gave advise, that his bones should be gathered up[2] by the priests [c] of the most aunciant Societies. And one above the rest would have had the name of the moneth August[3] to be shifted and transferred unto September; for that, Augustus was borne in this and died in the other. Another perswaded, that all the time from his very birth unto the dying day, should be named *Seculum Augustum*[4], and so recorded in the Kalendars and Chronicles. But, thought best it was, to keepe a meane in the Honours done unto him. Whereupon, twice, and in two severall places praised hee was in a funerall Oration: once before the temple of Julius late deceased, of sacred memorie, by Tiberius; and againe[5] at the *Rostra* [d] under the Veteres, by Drusus the sonne of Tiberius, and so upon Senatours shoulders was hee borne into Campus Martius, and there committed to the fire and burnt. Neither wanted there a grave personage[6],

OCTAVIUS CÆSAR AUGUSTUS

---

[1] Aldermen, or Senators. [2] A thing against the olde received religion.
[3] Before him called *Sextilis*. [4] The August age. [5] Or before. [6] Dio nameth him Numarius Atticus: and saith, he was hired by Livia for two millians of Sesterces, to sweare that of Augustus, which Proculus had somtime sworn of Romulus.

THE HISTORIE OF

OCTAVIUS CÆSAR AUGUSTUS

one that had been Pretor, who affirmed and bound it with an oath, That he saw his very image[1] when he was burnt, ascending up to heaven. The chiefe Gentlemen of the Knights order, in their single wastcoates[2], ungirt and barefooted gathered up his reliques[e] together, and bestowed them in a stately monument[3][f]: which peece of work himselfe had built between the street Flaminia and the bank of Tiberis in his sixth Consulship, and even then given the Groves growing about it and the walks adjoyning to be common for the use of the people of Rome for ever.

101

His last will and testament made by him when L. Plancus and C. Silius were Consuls, the third day before the Nones of April[4], a yeere and foure moneths before hee died, and the same in two bookes written partly with his owne hand, and in part with the hands of Polbyus and Hilarius his freed men, the vestall virgins[a] who had the keeping thereof upon trust brought forth; together with three other rolls or volumes sealed alike. All which Instruments were opened and read in the Senate. He ordained for his 6 heires; in the first place, Tiberius of the one halfe and a sixt part[b]: and Livia of a third[c]: whom also he appointed to beare his owne name[d]. In a second ranke[5], hee appointed Drusus the sonne of Tiberius to inherit one third part: and Germanicus with his three male children, the other parts remaining. In a third degree[6], he nominated of his owne kinsfolk, Allies and friends, very many. Hee bequeathed as a legacie to the people of Rome[e] 400000 Sesterces[7] an hundred times told. To the Souldiours of the guard[8] a thousand Sesterces a peece. Among the Cohorts of the City Souldiours 500, and to those of the Legionarie cohorts 300 a peece. Which summe of money he commaunded to be paied presently: for hee had so much in store at all times (put up in bagges and

---

[1] Or true Portraict. [2] Or shirts, as some would expound *tunicis*. [3] *In Mausoleo.* [4] The third of Aprill. [5] For default of the other if they dyed. [6] If the second heires failed. [7] Some read *quadringenties tricies quinquies*: and then it is three millions and a halfe more. [8] Or Prætorium band.

TWELVE CÆSARS

OCTAVIUS CÆSAR AUGUSTUS

coffers) lying by him. Sundry parcels gave hee besides by legacie parole. And of some thereof he deferred the payment[1], if the same were above 20000 Sesterces. For paying of which he set a yeeres day at the farthest: alledging for his excuse his meane estate; and protesting, that by this account there would not come to his heires hands, above 150 millions[2]: albeit within the compasse of 20 yeeres immediatly going before, hee had received by the wills and testaments of his friends 4000 millions[3]. All which masse of treasure, together with two patrimonies by his two fathers[4] and other inheritances, hee had spent wel-neere every whit upon the Common-weale. The two Julie, to wit, his daughter and niece[5], (if ought hapned to them[6]) he forbad expresly to be enterred in his owne Mausoleum. Of those three Rolls or Instruments above named, in the first he comprised his owne directions as touching his funerall: the second contained a Register or Index, of those Acts which he had atchieved: and his pleasure was, that the same should be engraven in brazen tables[7], and erected before his Mausoleum. In the third he represented a Breviarie and abstract of the whole Empire: to wit, How many Souldiours were enrolled and in pay, in any place whatsoever? as also, How much money was in the common Treasurie of the City and in his owne coffers? Lastly, what the arrierages were of such revenewes and tributes as were due to the state and unpaid: whereto he annexed also a Shedule, containing the names of Freed men and bond, his receivers, at whose hands the reckoning might be exacted.

[1] *Produxitque quædam ad vicena Sestertia.* So Torrentius expoundeth it. [2] Of Sesterces. [3] *Quater decies millies,* foure thousand millions. [4] Octavius and Julius Cæsar. [5] His daughters daughter. [6] If they died. [7] *Æneis tabulis,* other writers say, Pillers.

THE HISTORIE OF

THE HISTORIE OF
TIBERIUS NERO CÆSAR

1

THE Patritian familie Claudia (for, there was likewise another Plebeian of that name, neither in power nor dignity inferiour) had the first beginning out of Regillum[1] a Towne of the Sabines. From thence they came with a great retinue of vassals to Rome newly founded, there to dwell: induced thereto by the counsell of T. Tatius, fellow in government of the kingdome with Romulus; or (which is the more received opinion) through the perswasion of Atta[a] Claudius[2], a principall person of that house, about the 6 yeere after the kings were expelled: and so, by the Senatours of Rome, raunged they were among the Patritii. Upon this, soone after, they received by vertue of a graunt from the whole City, for their Clients and vassals, lands to occupy beyond the river Anio: and for themselves a place[3] of sepulture under the Capitol: and so forth, in processe of time obtained 28 Consulates, five Dictatures, Censures seaven, Triumphs sixe, and two Ovations. This family being distinguished by sundry fore-names and surnames both, in a generall consent rejected the fore-name of Lucius, after that two of their linage bearing that name were convict, the one of robberie, the other of murder. Among surnames it assumed the addition of Nero[b], which in the Sabine tongue signifieth Strong or stout.

---

[1] Or Regilli.　　[2] Or Clausus.　　[3] *Locum.* Some read *lucum*, not in the strict signification of a sacred Grove, but of a pleasant tuft of trees wherewith monuments were beautified: as you may gather by the Mausoleum of Augustus.

TWELVE CÆSARS

2

Many of these Claudii, as they deserved many waies passing well of the Common-wealth: so, in as many sorts they faulted and did amisse. But to relate the principall examples onely in both kindes; Appius surnamed Cæcus¹ was hee, who disswaded the entring into league and societie with King Pyrrhus, as prejudiciall unto the State: Claudius Caudex ᵃ was the first man that passed over the narrow Seas with a fleete, and drave the Carthaginians out of Sicilie: Claudius Nero surprised and defaited Asdrupal comming out of Spaine with a very great and puissant armie before he could joyne with his brother Annibal. Contrariwise, Claudius Appius ² Regillanus being Decemvir ³ chosen to frame and pen the Romaine Lawes, went about by violence (for the satisfaction of his fleshly lust) to enthrall a virgine Freeborne: and thereby gave occasion to the Commons for to fall away and forsake the Nobles a second time. Claudius Drusus having his owne statue erected with a Diademe in a Towne called Forum Appii ᵇ, attempted with the helpe of his favorites and dependants to hold all Italie in his owne hands. Claudius Pulcher ⁴, when as in taking of his Auspicia ᶜ before Sicilie, the sacred pullets would not feede, caused them, in contempt of Religion, to be plunged into the Sea, That they might drinke seeing they would not eate: and thereupon strucke a battaile at Sea: in which, beeing vanquished, and commaunded by the Senate to nominate a Dictator, scorning, as it were, and making but a jest at the publique danger and calamitie of the State, named a (base) Sergeant of his owne called Glycia ⁵. There stand likewise upon record, the examples of women, and those as divers and contrary. For, two Claudiæ there were of the same house: both shee that drew forth ⁶ the ship with the sacred images of the Idæan mother ⁷ of the Gods sticking fast and grounded within the shelves ⁸ of Tiberis, having before made her praier openly, That as she was a true and pure virgin, so the ship

TIBERIUS
NERO
CÆSAR

A.U.C. 474, 490, 457.

A.U.C. 304.

A.U.C. 505.

¹ *i.* Blind.   ² Or Appius Claudius.   ³ *i.* One of the ten Decemvirs.
⁴ *i.* The Faire.   ⁵ Or Ilycia.   ⁶ Plin. *Nat. hist.* lib. 7, cap. 35.
⁷ Cybele.   ⁸ Or Barr.

THE HISTORIE OF

TIBERIUS NERO CÆSAR
A.U.C. 580.

A.U.C. 695.

A.U.C. 611.

might follow her, and not otherwise: as also another, who after a strange and new manner, being a woman[1], was araigned before the people of high treason, for that when her Coach wherein shee rode could hardly passe forward by reason of a thicke throng and preasse of people, she had openly wished, That her brother Pulcher were alive againe, and might leese a fleete the second time, to the end there might be by that meanes a lesse multitude at Rome. Moreover, very well knowne it is, that all the Claudii, excepting onely that P. Clodius who for expelling Cicero out of Rome, suffred himselfe to be adopted by a Commoner [2d] and one younger also than himselfe, were alwaies Optimates, the onely maintainers or patrons of the dignitie and power of the Patritians: yea, and in opposition of the Commons so violent, stubborne and selfe-willed that not one of them, although he stoode upon his triall for life and death before the people, could finde in his hart so much as to change his weede [6], or to crave any favour at their hands. Nay, some of them there were, who in a brawle and altercation, stuck not to beat the very Tribune of the Commons[f]. Furthermore, a virgine vestale [3] there was of that name, who when a brother of hers triumphed without a warrant from the people, mounted up with him into the chariot, and accompanied him even into the Capitoll: to this end, that none of the Tribunes might lawfully oppose themselves and forbid the Triumph [4].

3

From this race and linage Tiberius Cæsar deriveth his Genealogie, and that verily in the whole bloud and of both sides: by his Father, from Tiberius Nero: by his mother from Appius Pulcher, who were both of them the sonnes of Appius Cæcus. Incorporate hee was besides into the familie of the Livii, by reason that his Grandfather by the mothers side[5] was adopted thereinto: which family (Commoners though they were) flourished notwithstanding and was

---

[1] For, unto this time that sex had not beene endited and attaint of treason. See Valer. Max. lib. 8. cap. 1.   [2] C. Fonteius.   [3] Claudia.   [4] Of so reverent regard were these Nunnes, that no magistrate might either attach or crosse them.   [5] Or mothers grandfather *materno avo*.

TWELVE CÆSARS

highly reputed; as being honoured and graced with eight Consulships, two Censureships, and three triumphs: with a Dictatourship also and Maistership of the Horsemen: renowmed likewise and ennobled for brave and notable men, Salinator[a] especially and the Drusi[1]: as for Salinator, in his Censureship hee noted and taxed all the Tribes everie one and whole bodie of the people, for unconstant levitie, for that having uppon his former consulship condemned him and set a fine uppon his head, yet afterwardes they made him Consul a second time and Censour besides. Drusus, upon the killing of one Drausus the Generall of his enemies in close combat and single fight, purchased unto himselfe and his posteritie after him that surname. It is reported also, that this Drusus beeing propretour, recovered and fetched againe out of his province Gaule, that gold which in times past had beene given unto the Senones when they besieged the Capitol: and that it was not Camillus (as the voice goeth) that wrested the same perforce out of their hands. His sonne[2] in the 4 degree of descent, called for his singular imployment against the Gracchi, Patron of the Senate, left behind him a sonne: whom in the like variance and debate, as he was busie in devising and putting in practise sundrie plots, the adverse faction treacherously slew.

TIBERIUS NERO CÆSAR

A.U.C. 550.

A.U.C. 471.

A.U.C. 433.

4

But, the Father of this Tiberius Cæsar, being Treasurer unto C. Cæsar[3], and Admirall of a fleete in the Alexandrine warre performed very good service for the atchieving of victory, whereupon hee was both substituted Pontifex in steed of Scipio, and also sent with commission to plant Colonies in Gaule, among which were Narbona[4] and Arelate. Howbeit, after that Cæsar was slaine, when as all men for feare of troubles and uprores decreed a finall abolition and oblivion[5] of that fact (and all other quarrels thereupon depending) he proceeded farther and opined, That they should consult about the rewards of such Tyrant-killers. After this, having borne his Pretourship (in the end of which

A.U.C. 463.

A.U.C. 707.

A.U.C. 710.

A.U.C. 713.

[1] Or rather Drusus.   [2] Or Nephew, *abnepos.*   [3] Dictator.   [4] Or Narbo.   [5] This is that *amnestia* which Cicero perswaded unto.

THE HISTORIE OF

TIBERIUS NERO CÆSAR

yeere there arose some discord betweene the Triumvirs) hee retaining by him still the ensignes[1] and ornaments of that office after the time fully expired, and following L. Antonius the Consull and the Triumvirs brother, as farre as to Perusia, when the rest yeelded themselves, continued alone fast, and stuck to the faction (that sided against Octavius) and first escaped to Preneste, then to Naples: where when hee had proclaimed (but in vaine) freedome for all bondslaves[2], hee fled into Sicilie. But taking it to the heart, that hee was not immediatly admitted to the presence of Sextus Pompeius, but debarred the use of his Knitches of rods to bee borne afore him[a], hee crossed the Seas into Achaia, and went to M. Antonius. With whom, by occasion that shortly after, an attonement and peace was made betweene all parties, hee returned to Rome; and at the request of Augustus, yeelded unto him his owne wife Livia Drusilla, who both at that time was great with child, and also had already before brought him a sonne named Tiberius, in his owne house. Not long after, he departed this life, and left his children surviving him, namely Tiberius Nero and Drusus Nero.

5

Some have thought that this Tiberius (Cæsar) was borne at Fundæ, grounding uppon a light conjecture, because his mothers Grandame[3] was a Fundane borne; and for that soone after the image of Felicitie[4], by vertue of an Acte of the Senate was there publiquely set up[a]. But, as the most Authors and those of better credite doe write, borne hee was at Rome in the Mount Palatium, the sixteenth day before

A.U.C. 712.

the Calendes of December[5], when M. Æmilius Lepidus was Consull the second time together with Munatius Plancus, even after the warre at Philippi: for so it standes upon record and in the publique Registers. Yet there want not some who write otherwise: partly that he was borne[6] a yeere

---

[1] To wit, his sixe lictors or vergers' with their Knitches of rods and axes sticking therin. Alexand. ab Alexandr. [2] *Servis ad pileum vocatis:* because the cap or bonet was the badge of freedome. [3] Or his grandame by the mothers side. [4] *Fœlicitatis,* or *Fœcunditatis, i.* fruitfulnes. [5] The sixteenth of November. [6] *Genitum.*

TWELVE CÆSARS

before in the Consulship of Hirtius and Pansa, and partly the yeere next following, wherein Servilius Isauricus and Antonius were Consuls.

TIBERIUS NERO CÆSAR

6

His infancie and childhood both were exceeding forward [1] and the same full of toilesome travaile and daunger, by occasion that every where, hee accompanied his Parents still, in their flights and escapes. And verily, twice hee had like to have descried [2] them with his wrawling at Naples, what time as a little before the forcible and suddaine entrie of the enemie, they made shift secretly to get into a ship: namely once, when hee was taken hastily from his Nources breast: and a second time out of his Mothers lap and armes, by those who as the necessity of the time required, did their best to ease the poore women of their burden and loade. Hee was caried away with them likewise through Sicilie and Achaia: yea, and beeing recommended to the Lacedæmonians (who were under the protection of the Claudii their Patrones) for to take the charge of him in publique, as hee departed from thence by night, hee was in daunger of his life by reason of a light flaming fire, which suddainly from all parts arose out of a wood: and compassed all the companie in his traine so, as that some part of Liviaes apparell and the haire of her head was scorched and sienged therewith. The giftes bestowed uppon him in Sicilie by Pompeia the sister of Sextus Pompeius, to wit, a little Cloake with a button or claspe to it: likewise studds and bosses of golde, continue and are yet shewed to bee seene at Baie. After his returne into the Cittie of Rome, beeing adopted by M. Gallius a Senatour in his last will and testament, hee accepted of the inheritance and entred upon it: but within a while forbare the name, because Gallius had sided with the adverse faction and taken part against Augustus. Being 9 yeares olde he praised his father deceased openly from the *Rostra*. Afterwardes, as hee grewe to be a springall, he accompanied in the Actiacke tryumph the Chariot of Augustus, ryding

---

[1] *Luxuriosam*, *i.* growing a pace to maturity. [2] Or discovered.

THE HISTORIE OF

TIBERIUS
NERO
CÆSAR

uppon the steede drawing without the yoke¹ on the left hand, when as Marcellus the sonne of Octavia rode upon the other on the right hand ʰ. Hee was president also at the Actiack Games and plaies, yea and the Troian Turnament in the Circean solemnities, where he led the troupe of the bigger boyes.

7

After hee had put on his virile robe², his whole youth and all the time besides of the age next ensuing, even unto the beginning of his Empire, hee passed for the most part in these affaires following. He exhibited one sworde fight performed by fencers to the outrance, in memoriall of his father: likewise another in the honourable remembraunce of his Grandfather Drusus: and those at sundrie times and in diverse places: the former in the Forum³ of Rome: the second in the Amphitheatre: having brought againe into the Lists, even those that were freed before time and discharged from that profession: whom hee now hired and bound to fight, with the summe of one hundred thowsand sesterces. Hee did set foorth stage playes also, but whiles himselfe was absent: all with great magnificence, and also at the charges of his mother⁴ and father in Law⁵. Agrippina⁶ the daughter also of M. Agrippa, and neice to Pomponius Atticus a Gentleman of Rome, him I meane, unto whome Cicero wrote his Epistles, hee tooke to wife.

A.U.C. 744.

And when hee had begotten of her a sonne named Drusus, albeit shee fitted him well enough and was besides with Childe againe, enforced hee was to put her away; and foorthwith to wed Julia the daughter of Augustus: not without much griefe and heart breake: considering that hee both desired still the companie of Agrippina and also misliked the conditions and demeanour of Julia, as whom he perceived to have had a minde and fansie unto him whiles shee was the wife of a former husband. Which verily was thought also abroade. But as hee grieved, that after the divorce

¹ Or spirenpole. ² At 17 yeeres of age. ³ Or great market place.
⁴ Livia. ⁵ Augustus. ⁶ Whom Tacitus calleth Vipsania after the surname of her father.

TWELVE CÆSARS

hee had driven away Agrippina, so when hee chaunced but once (as shee mette him) to see her, hee followed her still with his eyes so bent, so swellinge, and staring[1], that streight order was given, and a watch set, shee should never after come in his way nor within his sight. With Julia he lived at the first in great concord and mutuall love: but afterwardes hee began to estraunge himselfe[2], and (that which was the more griefe) hee proceeded to part beddes and to lie from her continually, namely, after that the pledge of love, their sonne beegotten beetweene them, was untimely taken away: who beeing borne at Aquileia died a very infant. His owne brother Drusus[3] hee lost in Germanie, whose bodie he conveyed throughout to Rome going before it all the way on foote.

TIBERIUS NERO CÆSAR

A.U.C. 735.

8

In his first rudiments and beginnings of civile offices, he pleaded at the barre in defence of Archelaus; of the Trallians and Thessalians: all of them in sundrie causes whiles Augustus sat in judgement to heere their tryall: in the behalfe also of the Laodicenes, Thyaterenes and Chians, who had suffered great losse by Earthquake, and humbly sought for reliefe, he intreated the Senate. As for Fannius Cæpio, who together with Varro Muræna had conspired against Augustus, hee arraigned of high treason before the judges, and caused him to bee condemned: and amid these affaires, he executed a duple charge and function[4]: to witte, the purveyance of Corne and Victualles, whereof there happened to bee scarcitie: and the skouringe or riddance of the worke-house prisons[5]: the Lordes and Maisters whereof were become odious, as if they had caught uppe and held to worke not onely waifaring persons, but those also who for feare of taking a militarie oath and to be enrolled, were driven to shrowd themselves in such corners and starting holes.

---

[1] Readie as it were to run out of his head. [2] Or disagree. [3] Who died when he was Consul. [4] Whilest hee was Questour, and but 19 yeares olde. [5] *Ergastulorum.* Such as bridewel and houses of correction.

THE HISTORIE OF

TIBERIUS NERO CÆSAR

A.U.C. 728.

9

His first service in the warres was in the expedition of Cantabria, what time hee had the place of a Tribune Militarie[1]. Afterwardes, having the conduct of an armie into the East parts, hee restored the kingdome of Armenia unto Tigranes, and from the Tribunall seat did put the Diademe uppon his head. Hee recovered also those militarie ensignes which the Parthians had taken from M. Crassus. After this hee governed as Regent that part of Gaule beyond the Alpes, called Comata: which was full of troubles, partly by the incursions of barbarous nations, and in parte through the intestine discorde of Princes and Nobles of the Countrie. Then, warred hee uppon the Rhetians and Vindelici, and so forwarde uppon the Pannonians and Germaines (whom hee vanquished all). In the Rhætian and Vindelicke warres, hee subdued the Nations inhabiting the Alpes: in the Pannonian, he conquered the Breuci and Dalmatians. In the Germaine warre hee brought over into Gaule 40000 that yeelded unto him, and placed them neere unto the Rhene banke, where they had there habitations assigned. For which Acts, hee entred the Citie of Rome both *Ovant* (ryding on horsebacke) and also Triumphant mounted uppon a Chariot: being the first[2] (as some thinke) that was honoured with Triumphant ornaments, a newe kinde of honour and never graunted to any man before: to beare Magistracie hee both

A.U.C. 737, 738, 742, 747. beganne betimes, and also ranne through them all in manner joynctly and without intermission, namely his Quæsture, Præture and Consulate. After some space betweene hee became Consul a seconde time, yea and also received the Tribunitian Authoritie for five yeares together.

10

In this confluence of so many prosperous successes, in the strength also of his yeares and perfect health, hee had a full purpose, sodainely to retire himselfe and remoove out of the way as farre as hee could. Whether it were for the wearinesse

---

[1] Colonell of a thousand footmen. [2] *Primus*, some read *prius*, *i. ante ovationem*, before he had ridden *ovant* or triumphed.

TWELVE CÆSARS

hee had of his wife, whome neither hee durst plainely charge or put awaye, nor was able to endure any longer, or to the ende that by avoyding contempt ᵃ incident to daily and continuall residence, hee might maintaine and increase his authoritie by absenting himselfe, if at any time the State stoode in neede of him, it is uncertaine. Some are of opinion, that considering Augustus his children were nowe well growne, he of his owne accorde yeelded up unto them the place and possession, as it were, of the second degree[1], which himselfe had usurped and held a long time; following herein the example of M. Agrippa, who having preferred M. Marcellus, to bee imployed in publike affaires, departed unto Mitylenæ; least by his presence he might seeme to hinder[2] them or deprave their proceedings. Which cause even himself, but afterwards, alleadged: marie, for the present, pretending the satietie that he had of honorable places, and rest from his travailes, he made suite for licence to depart: neither gave he any eare to his owne mother humblie beseeching him to stay; nor to his father in law, who complained also that hee should be forsaken thereby and left desolate in the Senate. Moreover, when they were instant still to holde him backe, hee abstained from all kinde of meate foure dayes together. At length having obtained leave to be gone, he left his wife and sonne behind him at Rome, and forthwith went downe to Ostia: giving not so much as one word againe to any that accompanied him thither, and kissing very few of them at the parting.

TIBERIUS
NERO
CÆSAR
A.U.C. 748.

11

As he sayled from Ostia along the coast of Campanie, uppon newes that he heard of Augustus weakenesse, he stayed a while and went not forward: but when a rumor began to be spred of him, (as if he lingred there, waiting some opportunitie of greater hopes,) hee made noe more adoe, but even against winde and wether sayled through and passed over to Rhodes: having taken a delight to the pleasant and healthfull situation of that Iland, ever since he arrived there in his returne from Armenia. Contenting himselfe here,

[1] In administration of the common weale.   [2] To darken their light.

THE HISTORIE OF

TIBERIUS NERO CÆSAR

with a meane and small habitation, with a ferme house likewise by the Cittie side not much larger nor of greater receite, he purposed to lead a verie civill and private life: walking otherwhile in the Gymnase[1] without lictor[2] or other officer, performing acts and duties in maner one for another with the Greekes conversing there. It happened uppon a time, when he disposed of the businesses which hee would dispatch one day, that hee gave it out before hand, He was desirous to visite all the sicke[3] in the Cittie. These words of his were mistaken by those next about him. Whereupon all the lazars and diseased persons were by commaundement brought into a publike porch or gallerie and placed there in order according to the sundrie sorts of their maladies. At which unexpected sight, being much troubled and perplexed, he wist not for a good while what to do: howbeit he went round about from one to another, excusing himselfe for this that was done even to the meanest, poorest and basest of them all. This onely thing and nothing else beside was noted, wherein he seemed to exercise the power of his Tribunes authoritie. Being daily and continually conversant about the Schooles and Auditories of professours, by occasion that there arose a great braule among the Sophisters[4] opposite in arguing cases and declaiming one against other, there chaunced to bee one who perceiving him comming betweene and inclining to favorize one part above the other, rayled bitterly at him. With drawing himselfe therefore by little and little, and retyring home to his house, he came forth sodainely againe and appeared with his Lictours: where he cited by the voyce of his cryer to appeare judicially before his Tribunall, that foule mouthed rayling fellow, and so commanded him to be had away to prison. After this, he had certaine intelligence given him that Julia his wife was convict and condemned for her incontinencie and adulteries; also that in his name (by a warrant directed from Augustus) she had a bill of divorse sent unto her. And albeit, he was glad of these tidings, yet he

---

[1] Or publike place of exercises. [2] He was then Tribune of the Commons and Consul the second time. [3] *Ægros*, some read *agros*, as if he minded to walk the fields. [4] Rhetoricians.

TWELVE CÆSARS

thought it his part, as much as lay in him, by many letters to reconcile the father unto his daughter: yea and how ever she had deserved badly at his hands, yet to suffer her for to have whatsoever he had at any time given unto her in free gift. Now, after he had passed through the time of his Tribunes authoritie, and confessed at last, that by this retyring of his out of the way he sought to avoide nought else but the suspition of Jelousie and emulation with Caius and Lucius: hee made suite, That seeing he was now secured in this behalfe, and they strengthened enough and able with ease to manage and maintaine the second place in government, he might be permitted to returne and see his friendes and acquaintance againe, whose presence he missed and longed after. But hee could not obtaine so much: nay, admonished hee was and warned before hand, to lay a side all regard of his friends and kinsfolke, whom he was so willing to leave and abandon before.

TIBERIUS
NERO
CÆSAR

A.U.C. 752.

12

Hee abode therefore still at Rhodes, even against his will: and hardly by the meanes and intercession of his owne mother wrought thus much, that for to cover his ignominie and shame, he might be absent under this pretence, as if he were Augustus his Lieutenant. And then verily, lived he not onely private to himselfe, but also exposed to daunger, and in great feare of some hard measure: lying close and hidden in the uplandish and inward parts of the Iland; and avoyding the offices of them that made saile by those coasts, who had frequented him continually: for as much as no man went into any province that way, as Lord Generall or Magistrate[1], but he strucke a side and turned to Rhodes. Besides, other causes there were of greater feare and trouble presented unto him. For when as he crossed the seas to Samos for to visit Caius, his wives sonne[2], president of the East parts, he perceived him to be more estranged than before time through the slaunders and criminous imputations which M. Lollius companion and governour to the

---

[1] As Prætor, proprætor, proconsul, etc.   [2] The sonne of his wife Julia by Agrippa.

THE HISTORIE OF

TIBERIUS NERO CÆSAR

saide Caius had put into his head. He was drawen also into suspition by certaine Centurions, whom his favour had advanced, and who at the day limited in their pasport were returned to the camp, That he had delivered unto many (of them [1]) Mandates of an ambiguous and duple construction, such as might seeme to sound the mindes of everie one and sollicite them to rebellion. Of which suspition being certified by Augustus, hee never rested to call for, and require to have some one of any degree and order what soever, to observe all his deedes and words.

13

He neglected also his wonted exercises of horse and armour: yea, and having laid by the habite [2] of his native Countrie, hee betooke himselfe to a cloke and slippers [3]. In such a state and condition as this, continued hee almost two yeeres throughout, more dispised and hatefull everie day then other: insomuch as the Meniansians overthrew his Images and statues: and upon a time, at a certaine feast, where familiar friends were met together (by occasion that mention was made of him,) there was one stood up who promised Caius, That in case he did but command and say the word, he would immediatly sayle to Rhodes and fetch unto him the head of that exiled person: for so was hee commonly called. And chiefly upon this which was now no bare feare, but plain perill, enforced he was by most earnest prayers not onely of his owne but also of his mother, to require and seeke for to returne: which he obtained at length with the helpe somewhat of good fortune. Augustus had fully set downe with himselfe to resolve upon nothing as touching that point, but with the wil and good liking of his elder sonne [4]: now was he, as it happened at that time much offended and displeased with M. Lollius, but to his father in law [5] (Tiberius) well affected, and easie to be by him intreated. By the permission therefore and good leave of

---

[1] Or of his friends. [2] The gowne. [3] Pantofles or corke shooes after the greekish fashion. [4] Caius, his nephew or daughters sonne. [5] His mothers husband.

TWELVE CÆSARS

Caius called home he was; but with this condition, That he should not meddle one Jote in the affaires of State.

TIBERIUS NERO CÆSAR

14

Thus in the 8 yeare after his departure, returned he full of great hopes and nothing doubtfull of future fortunes, which he had conceived as well by strang sights, as also by predictions and prophesies even from his very birth. For Livia whiles she went with child of him, among many and sundrie experiments which she made, and signes that she observed (and all to know whether shee should bring forth a man child or no?) tooke closely an egge from under an hen that was sitting, and kept it warme sometime in her owne, otherwhiles in her womens hands by turnes one after another, so long, untill there was hatched a cock-chicken with a notable combe upon the head. And when he was but a very babe, Scribonius the Astrologer gave out and warranted great matters of him, and namely, That he should one day raigne as Monarch, but yet without the royall Ensignes[1]. For as yet, ye must wote, the soveraigne power of the Cæsars was unknowne. Also, as he entred into his first expedition, and led an armie into Syria, through Macedonie: it chaunced that the consecrated Altars of the victorious Legions[2] in time past at Philippi shone out sodainely of themselves all on a light fire[3]. And soone after, when in his journey towarde Illyricum he went to the Oracle of Geryon nere unto Padua, and drew forth his lotte, whereby he was advised that for counsell and resolution in such particulars as he required after, he should throw golden dies[4][a] into the fountaine Aponus, it fell out so that the dies thus cast by him shewed the greatest number[5]: and even at this verie day these dies are seene under the water. Some fewe dayes likewise before he was sent for home, an Ægle, (never seene afore time at Rhodes) perched upon the very top and ridge of his house: and the verie day before he had intelligence given him of his returne, as he was

A.U.C. 755.

[1] i. The Diademe. [2] Under Julius Cæsar or Augustus. [3] *Subitis ignibus* or *Subductis ignibus*, i. When the fire was taken from them. [4] Or Cockals, *talos*. [a] Venus or Cous, which is the best chance.

THE HISTORIE OF

TIBERIUS NERO CÆSAR

changing his apparell, his shirt was seene on fire. Thrasyllus also the Astrologer [b], whom for his great profession of wisedome and cunning he had taken into his house to beare him companie, he made then most triall of; namely, when upon kenning a ship a farre of [1], he affirmed, That joyfull newes was comming, whereas at the verie same instant as they walked togither Tiberius was fully purposed to have turned him headlong downe into the sea, as being a false prophet, (for that things fell out untowardly and contrarie to his former predictions) and one besides who chaunced for the most part to bee privie unto him of all his secrets.

15

Being returned to Rome, and having brought his sonne Drusus solemnly into the Forum [2], he remooved immediatly out of Carina and the house of Pompeius [3] unto Esquilia [4], and the Hort-yards of Mæcenas: where he gave himselfe wholly to quietnesse performing private duties onely and not medling at all in publike offices. After that Caius and Lucius were dead within the compasse of 3 yeares [5], he together with their brother M. Agrippa was adopted by Augustus, but compelled first himselfe to adopt Germanicus his brothers sonne. Neither did he ought afterwards as an housholder [6], nor retained one jote of that right which he had forgon by his adoption. For, he gave no donations, he manumised no person: nor yet made benefite of any inheritance or legacies [7] otherwise then in the nature of *Peculium* [8]: and so he did put them downe in his booke of receits. But from that time forward was there nothing pretermitted for the augmentation of his state and Majestie: and much more after that Agrippa once was in disfavour and sent away: wherby the world tooke knowledge for certaine, that the hope of succession rested onely in him.

[1] Which broght the messenger of his returne. [2] There to commense and shewe the first proofe of pleading at Barre. [3] Which was in the streete Carina. [4] Or Exquilla, an other streete in Rome. [5] Of 2 yeares rather: by Velleius and Dio, and as himselfe hath written in Augustus. [6] One that was *sui juris*. [7] Falling unto him by the Testaments of his friendes. [8] A stocke given and granted unto one by him under whose tuition he is, be hee father or maister.

TWELVE CÆSARS

TIBERIUS NERO CÆSAR

16

Nowe was the Tribunitian Authoritie conferred a second time uppon him, and that for the terme of 5 yeeres; the honorable charge and commission likewise, for to pacifie the State of Germanie was assigned unto him: and the Parthian Embassadours, after they had declared their message at Rome unto Augustus, were commanded to repaire unto him also into his province[1]. But upon the newes that Illyricum revolted, he remooved from thence to the charge of a new warre[2], which, being of all foraine warres the most dangerous since those with the Carthaginians, he menaged with the power of 15 Legions, and equal forces of Auxiliaries, for the space of 3 yeares in great extremitie of all things, but especially in exceeding scarcetie of Corne. And notwithstanding that he was oftentimes revoked from this service, yet persisted he unto the end, fearing least the enemie so neere a neighbour and so puissant with all, should make head and come upon them, if they first did quit the place and retire. And verily, passing well paied and rewarded was hee for this perseverance of his, as having thereby fully subdued and brought under his subjection all Illirycum as farre as reacheth and spreadeth betweene Italie, the kingdome of Noricum, Thracia, and Macedonie: betweene the river Danubius also and the gulfe of the Adriaticke sea.

A.U.C. 757.

A.U.C. 760.

17

Which glorious exploit of his was yet more amplified and encreased by the opportunitie of an occurrent that fell betweene. For, about the verie same time Quintilius Varus together with 3 Legions was overthrowne and defaited in Germanie: and no man made any doubt, but that the Germaines following the traine of this their victorie, would have joyned with Pannonia in case Illyricum had not beene subdued before. For these his noble Acts, a triumph with many great honours was decreed for him: some also delivered their sentence, that he should be surnamed Pannonicus; others would have had the addition of Invincible:

A.U.C. 762.

[1] Germanie.   [2] Out of Germanie.

THE HISTORIE OF

TIBERIUS NERO CÆSAR

and some againe of Pius, in his style. But as touching any such surname, Augustus interposed his negative voyce, promising and undertaking in his behalfe, that he shold rest contented with that[1], which he was to assume after his death. As for the Triumph, himselfe did put it of unto a further day, by occasion that the whole state[2] sorrowed for the overthrow and losse above saide of Varus: neverthelesse, he entred the City in his rich Prætexta or imbrodred purple Robe, with a chaplet of lawrell upon his head: and so mounted up to the Tribunall erected for him in the *Septa*[a], whiles the Senate stoode to give attendance: and there, together with Augustus, in the mids betweene the two Consuls hee tooke his place and sate downe. From whence, after he had saluted the people, hee was honourably conducted round about all the Temples.

18

A.U.C. 763.

The next yeere following, being returned into Germanie, when hee perceived that the Varian defeature aforesaid hapned through the rashnesse and negligence of the Generall, he did nothing at all without the opinion of his Counsell of warre. And whereas hee had used also before to stand upon his owne bothom, and to rest in his selfe-judgement alone, then, contrary to his manner hee conferred with many as touching the menagement of the warre: yea, and he shewed more care and precisenesse in every point than his wont was afore-time. Being about to passe over the Rhene, all his provision of victuals strictly reduced to a certaine rate and stint, hee would not send over the water before he had considered (standing upon the very banke of the river) the lode of every Waggon, that no cariages might bee discharged or unloaden[3], but such as were by him allowed and thought necessary. When hee was once on the other side of Rhene this course and order of life he held: namely to sit uppon a bare banke of turfe, and so to eate his meate: to lie abroad all night, and take his rest oftentimes without tent: to deliver all directions for the day following, as also

---

[1] *i.* Augustus.   [2] Of Rome.   [3] *Deponerentur, vel deportarentur, i.* transported and caried over.

TWELVE CÆSARS

what suddaine service or businesse was to bee enjoyned, by writing; with this caveat and admonition, That whereof any man doubted, hee should repaire unto him at all houres of the night, and seeke for no other expositour but himselfe.

TIBERIUS
NERO
CÆSAR

19

Martiall discipline he required most sharply, bringing againe into use and execution certaine kindes of chastisements and ignominious disgraces which had beene used in auncient times: in so much, as he branded with open shame the Lieutenant of a Legion, for sending a few Souldiours with his owne freed-man over the other side of the river a hunting. As for battailes, albeit hee did put as little as might be upon the hazard of Fortune and chaunce: yet entred he upon them with much more resolution, so often as whiles hee watched or studied by a candle, the light suddainly fell downe and went out, when no body forced it: trusting confidently (as hee said) upon this signe, which both hee and all his Auncestors had tried and found to be infallible during all their warlike conducts and regiments. But howsoever hee sped well and had good successe in this Province, he escaped very faire that hee had not beene killed by a certaine Rhutene [1a], who being among those that were next about his person, and detected by his timorous gesture, was apprehended, and with torture forced to confesse his prepensed designment.

20

Being after two yeeres returned out of Germanie to Rome, hee rode in that triumph which he had differred, accompanied with his Lieutenants, for whom he had obtained triumphall ornaments [a]. And ere hee turned into the Capitoll hee alighted from his Chariot, and bowed himselfe to the knees of his Father [2], sitting then before him as President. A Captaine and Commaunder of Pannonia named Baton, hee rewarded first, with exceeding great Presents, and then remooved him to Ravenna, in thankfull requitall for

A.U.C. 765.

---

[1] *A Rhuteno quodam.*   [2] Augustus Cæsar.

THE HISTORIE OF

TIBERIUS NERO CÆSAR

suffering him upon a time, when with his Armie hee was enclosed within the streights, to passe forward and escape. After this, hee bestowed upon the people (of Rome) a solemne dinner, where they sate at a thousand tables: and gave besides to them three thousand Sesterces a peece for a Congiarie. Hee dedicated also the temple of Concord: likewise that of Pollux and Castor in his owne name and his brothers, all out of the spoile woone from the enemies.

21

A.U.C. 766.

And not long after, when by vertue of an Act preferred by the Consuls, that hee should administer the Provinces jointly with Augustus: and likewise hold the generall review and muster of the people, hee had performed the same and finished it with a solemne purging called *Lustrum*, hee tooke his journey into Illyricum. And being

A.U.C. 767.

incontinently called backe out of the very way, he came and found Augustus dangerously sicke, howbeit yet breathing and alive: with whom he continued in secret talke, one whole day. I wote well, it is commonly received and beleeved, that when Tiberius after private conference was gone forth, these words of Augustus were over heard by the Chamberlaines: *Miserum populum Romanum, qui sub tam lentis maxillis erit:* 'O unhappie people of Rome, that shall be under such a slow paire of chawes ᵃ.' Neither am I ignorant of this also, that some have written and reported of Augustus, how openly and in plaine termes without dissimuling, hee disliked his churlish behaviour and harshnesse of manners so much, as divers times being in pleasant discourse and mery talke, he would breake-of when Tiberius came in place: howbeit, overcome by his wives intreaty and earnest praier he refused not to adopt him; or rather was induced so to doe, upon an ambitious humor and conceite of his owne, that leaving such a successour, himselfe might another day be more missed and wished for againe. Yet cannot I be perswaded otherwise, but to thinke, that Augustus, a right circumspect, considerate and prudent Prince did nothing, especially in so weighty a businesse, hand over head and without advise: but having duly

TWELVE CÆSARS

weighed the vices and vertues of Tiberius, esteemed his vertues of more worth: and namely seeing that both he sware solemnly in a generall assembly of the people, That hee adopted him for the good of the Common-weale[b]: and also commendeth him in certaine Epistles for a most expert and martiall warriour, yea the onely Defender and Protectour of the people of Rome. Out of which, I have thought good to quote some places heere and there for example. 'Farewell most sweet Tiberius, and God blesse your conduct and proceeding, warring as you doe for mee and the Muses[1].' Againe, 'O most pleasant, and (as I desire to bee happy) right valiant man, and accomplished Captaine, with all perfections, adiew.' Also, 'As touching the order and manner of your Sommer-campe, for mine owne part verily, my Tiberius, I am of this minde, That considering so many difficulties and distresses: in regard also of so great sloath and cowardise of Souldiours, no man in the world could performe the service better than you have done. And even they of your traine, who were with you doe all confesse, that this verse may be applied fitly unto you:

TIBERIUS
NERO
CÆSAR

> *Unus homo nobis vigilando restituit rem*[c].
> One man alone by watchfull sight
> Our tott'ring state hath set upright.

'And whether,' quoth he, 'there fall out any occurrent to be considered upon with more care and diligence, or whether I bee displeased and angry at any thing, I have a great misse, I assure you, of my Tiberius: and evermore that verse of Homer commeth into my remembrance:

> Τούτου δ' ἑσπομένοιο, καὶ ἐκ πυρὸς αἰθομένοιο
> ἄμφω νοστήσαιμεν, ἐπεὶ περίοιδε νοῆσαί [2d].
> Whiles this man beares me company (so well he doth fore-see)
> We may ev'n out of flaming fire returne, both I and hee.

'When I heare say and read that you are weakened and growne leane with uncessant and continuall labour, God confound me, if my body doe not quake and tremble. I pray you therefore spare your selfe: least if it come to our

---

[1] Ἐμοὶ καὶ μούσαις or τοῖς σοῖς, *i.* thy friends.   [2] *Iliadiæ.*

THE HISTORIE OF

TIBERIUS NERO CÆSAR

eares, that you are sicke, both I and your mother also die for sorrow, and the people of Rome beside, hazard the Empire. It makes no matter, whether I be in health or no, if you be not well[1]. The Gods I beseech, to preserve you for us and vouchsafe your health both now and ever, unlesse they hate the people of Rome to death.'

22

The death of Augustus hee divulged not abroad, before that young Agrippa was slaine. This Agrippa was killed by a militarie Tribune[2], set and appointed to guard him, so soone as hee had read the writ[3], whereby hee was commaunded to doe the deede. This writ, whether Augustus left behind him when hee died, thereby to take away all matter that might minister tumult after his death: or whether Livia in the name of Augustus endited it, and that with the privity of Tiberius, or without his knowledge, it resteth doubtfull. Certaine it is, that when the saide Tribune brought him word, that the thing was dispatched which he had commaunded, he made answere, That he gave no such commaundement, and added moreover, That he should answere it before the Senate: declining no doubt the envie and hard conceit of men for the present: for within a while after he buried the matter in silence.

23

Having nowe assembled the Senate by vertue and authority of his Tribuneship[a], and begun to make a speech[4] unto them by way of consolation[5]: all on a suddaine, as unable to maister his griefe, he fell into a fit of sighing and groaning: yea he wished, that not onely his voice, but his vitall breath also might faile him: and therewith gave the booke unto his sonne Drusus to read it out. After this, when the last will or testament of Augustus was brought in, and none of the witnesses admitted to come in place, but those onely who were of Senatours degree, the rest standing without

---

[1] *Si tu non valebis:* or, *si tu modo valebis, i.* So you continue well. [2] Colonel. [3] Or warrant. [4] Which hee had penned. [5] For the death of Augustus.

TWELVE CÆSARS

the *Curia* and there acknowledging their hands and seales, hee caused it to be read and pronounced by his freed man. The will began in this manner: 'For as much as sinister fortune hath bereft me of Caius and Lucius, my sonnes, I will that Tiberius Cæsar be mine heire, in the one moity and a sixth part[1].' By which very beginning, their suspition was augmented who thought thus, that seeing he forbare not after this sort to make his preface, hee ordained Tiberius to be his successour upon necessity, rather than any judgement and discretion.

TIBERIUS NERO CÆSAR

24

Albeit hee made no doubt to enter upon his imperiall government immediatly and to menage the same, and that by taking unto him a strong guard of Souldiours about his person, that is to say maine force and the very forme of absolute rule and dominion: yet notwithstanding, he refused it a long time: and putting on a most impudent and shamlesse mind, one while he seemed to rebuke his friends that encouraged him thereto, as those who knew not, what a monstrous and untamed beast an Empire was: and otherwhiles with ambiguous answeres and crafty delaies holding the Senate in suspence when they besought him to take it upon him, yea and humbly debased themselves before his knees: in so much as some of them having their patience moved therewith, could endure him no longer: and one among the rest in that tumult cried aloude, 'Let him either doe it at once, or else give over quite': and another openly to his face upbraided him in these words, Whereas other men be slacke in doing and performing that which they have promised, he was slacke in promising that which hee did and performed. In the end, as if forsooth he had beene compelled, and complaining withall, that there was imposed upon his shoulders a miserable and burdensome servitude, he tooke the Empire upon him: and yet no otherwise, than giving hope, that one day he would resigne it up. His very words are these, 'Untill I come unto that time, wherein yee may thinke it meete to give some rest unto mine aged yeeres.'

[1] That is to say, in 8 parts of twelve, or 2 third parts.

25

The cause of this holding of and delay that he made, was the feare of imminent dangers on every side, in so much as he would often say, Hee held a Woolfe by the eares. For there was one of Agrippaes slaves named Clemens, who had levied and gathered together no small power, for to revenge his Maisters death: and L. Scribonius Libo, a noble man, secretly complotted sedition and rebellion: yea, and a two-fold mutinie of the Souldiours arose, in Illyricum and in Germanie. Both the armies called hard upon him for performance of many matters extraordinarily: but above all, that they might have equall pay with the Pretorian souldiours [a]. And as for the Germanician [b] souldiours, they verily refused him for their Prince and Soveraigne, as not by them ordained: and with all their might and maine urged Germanicus who then was their Generall to take upon him the government of the State, albeit he withstood and denied them stoutly. Fearing therefore the issue and danger of this occurrent most of all, he required for himselfe to have that part of the Common-weale in charge, which it should please the Senate to lay upon him: seeing that no man was sufficient to weld the whole, unlesse he had another or many assistants rather joyned with him. Hee feigned himselfe also to be sickly, to the end that Germanicus might with the better will and more patience abide in expectance either of speedy succession after him, or at least waies of fellowship in the Empire with him. Well, after hee had appeased those mutinies, Clemens likewise by a fraudulent wile he over-raught, and brought to his devotion. As for Libo, because he would not be thought at his entrance newly into the Empire for to proceede rigorously, two yeeres after and not before he charged and reproved him before the Senate, contenting himselfe all that meane space to beware of him onely, and to stand upon his guard. For, as the said Libo was together with him among other Pontifices sacrificing, hee tooke order, that in steed of the (yron) cleaver, there should be closely laid for him a chopping-knife of lead: and when the same Libo requested upon a time to

TWELVE CÆSARS

have secret talke and conference with him, he would not graunt it, without his sonne Drusus might be by: and so long as he walked up and downe with Libo, he seemed to leane upon his hand; and so, held it sure enough all the while untill their communication was ended.

TIBERIUS NERO CÆSAR

26

But being once delivered from this feare he caried himselfe at the beginning very orderly and after a civill sort, yea and somewhat under the port of a private person[1]. Of very many dignities and those right honourable, which by publique decree were presented unto him, he accepted but few, and those of the meanest kind. His birth-day-mind, falling out in the time of the Plebeian games and plaies exhibited in the Cirque[a], hee hardly would suffer to be celebrated and honoured so much as with the addition extraordinarily of one chariot drawne with two Steedes. Hee forbad expresly, any temples, Flamins or Priests to be ordained for him, yea and the erection of Statues and images in his honour, without his leave and permission: the which ranne with this onely clause and condition, That they should not be set up among the images of the Gods, but stand with other ornaments of the house. Hee prohibited also by his negative voice the solemne oath of observing and keeping his Acts inviolably: as also to call the moneth September[2], Tiberius; or October[3], Livius. The forename also in his stile of Imperator[b]; the surname likewise of *Pater Patriæ*: as also a Civick Coronet[c] at the fore gate or porch of his Palace he refused. Nay, the very name of Augustus, hæreditarie though it were, he would not put as an addition to any of his Epistles, but those onely which he sent unto Kings and great Potentates. Neither bare hee more than three Consulships: the first but a few dayes; the second three moneths; the third in his absence no longer than unto the Ides of May[4].

[1] *Paulo minus quam privatum egit:* or, little better than the port, etc.
[2] Or November rather, for in it hee was born, of his own name. [3] Or September, of his mothers. [4] From the Calends or first day of January to the 15 of May.

27

Hee detested flattery and obsequious complements so much, as that hee would admit no Senatour to his Licter side either by way of dutiful attendance, or otherwise about any businesse whatsoever. When a certaine Consulare[1] person was about to make satisfaction unto him, and humbly to entreate and crave pardon by a reverent touching of his knees, he started and fled from him so, as hee fell therewith and lay along upon his backe[2]. Yea, and that which more is, if in any talke or continued speech there passed words of him smelling of flatterie, hee would not sticke to interrupt the speaker, to checke him, and presently to alter and correct such termes. One there was who called him *Dominus*, that is, Sir[3], but hee gave him warning not to name him any more by way of contumely. Another chaunced to say, His sacred businesses: and a third againe, That he went into the Senate, *auctore se*, *i.* by his warrant or aucthoritie. Hee caused them both to change those words, and for *auctore* to say *Suasore*, that is, by his advise and counsell: and in steede of Sacred, to put in, Laborious and painfull.

28

Moreover, against railing taunts, bad reports and rumours, as also slaunderous libels, verses and songs cast out either of himselfe or those about him, he stoode so firme and patient, as that ever and anone he would give out, That in a free state, folke ought to have both tongue and thought free. And when upon a time the Senate called earnestly unto him, That such crimes, and the offenders themselves, might be brought judicially into question; 'Wee have not,' quoth hee, 'so much leasure as to entangle our selves in many affaires. If yee open this window once, yee will suffer nothing else to be done: for under pretence heereof yee shall have the quarrels of every man preferred unto you[4].' There

---

[1] One who had beene Consull: Tacitus saith, it was Quintus Haterius.
[2] Whereby, the said Q. Haterius had like to have beene killed by the guard.
[3] Or Lord.   [4] *Ad vos, vel ad nos,* unto us.

TWELVE CÆSARS

is besides a passing civill Apophthegme[1] of his extant which hee uttered in the Senate. 'If so be,' quoth he, 'that hee speake otherwise of mee than well, I will endeavour to give an account of my deedes and wordes, but in case hee continue so still, I will hate him for it againe.'

TIBERIUS NERO CÆSAR

29

And these things were so much the more remarqueable in him, for that in speaking to them either one by one severally[2], or to all at once in generall, yea and in reverencing them, himselfe exceeded in a manner the measure of all humanity. When he dissented one day in opinion from Q. Haterius in the Senate: 'Pardon mee, I beseech you,' quoth hee, 'if I as a Senatour shall speake ought over-frankly against you': and then directing his speech unto the whole house: 'Both nowe,' quoth hee, 'and many times else, my Lords, this hath beene my saying, That a good and gracious Prince, whom yee have invested in so great and so absolute a power, ought to serve the Senate and all the Citizens generally: often times also, yea and for the most part, every of them particularly. Neither repent I that I have so said, for I have ever found you, and doe so still to be my good, my gracious and favourable Lords.'

30

Furthermore, he brought in a certaine shew of the common Libertie, by preserving entier for the Senate and Magistrates, both their auncient majestie and also their authority: neither was there any matter so small or so great, pertaining to publique or private affaires, but proposed it was at the Counsell-table before the Senatours: as namely, about Tributes, Customes and Revenewes of the State: of Monopolies: of building and repairing any publique works: of enrolling or discharging Souldiours: of setting downe the number as well of Legions as of auxiliarie forces. Finally, who should have their place of commaund and government continued by a new commission: or take the charge of extraordinary

---

[1] Such as might beseeme one Citizen to speake of another, and not a Prince of his subjects.   [2] *i.* The Senatours.

THE HISTORIE OF

TIBERIUS NERO CÆSAR

warres: as also what, and in what forme they thought it good to write againe, and to answere letters sent by Kings. A certaine Captaine over a cornet[1] of horse-men, being accused for an outrage and for robberie, he compelled to make his answere before the Senate[2]. Hee never entred the *Curia* but alone. And being one time brought in sicke within his litter, he caused all his traine and company to void[a].

31

That some Decrees were enacted against his minde and sentence, hee never once complained, nor found himselfe grieved. Notwithstanding hee opined, that Magistrates appointed to any charge, ought not to bee absent; to the end that by their presence they might the better intend their function and calling: yet one Pretour elect, obtained the favour of a free embassage[3][a]. Againe, when he advised in the Otriculunes[4] behalfe a graunt, that they might bestowe the money in paving a cawsie or high-way, which was by legacie given to the building of a new Theater: hee could not prevaile but that the will of the Testator should stand and be fulfilled. When it fortuned upon a time that an Act of the Senate should passe by going to a side, and himselfe went over to the other part where the fewer in number were, there was not one that followed him. Other matters also were handled and debated by the Magistrates and the ordinarie course of lawe, and not otherwise: wherein the Consuls bare so great sway and authority, that certaine Embassadors out of Africk repaired unto them for dispatch, as complaining that they were put-of and delayed by Cæsar unto whom they had beene sent. And no mervaile: for evident it was, that himselfe also would arise up unto the saide Consuls and give them the way.

32

Hee rebuked Generalls of Armies even such as had beene Consuls for not writing unto the Senate of their warre

---

[1] Or wing. [2] Whereas by course he shold have had his triall before the Lord General, or prince himselfe. [3] *Liberam legationem*. [4] Or Trebians.

TWELVE CÆSARS

exploites: also for consulting with him and asking his advise as touching the graunt of militarie gifts[1], as if it lay not in their owne power to give and dispose all. Hee commended a Pretour for bringing uppe againe the aunceint custome, in the entraunce of his government, to make an honourable mention and rehersall of his Auncestours before a frequent assembly of the people. The funerall obsequies of certaine Noble personages, he accompanied with the common multitude to the very fire[a]. The like moderation he shewed in meaner persons and matters both. When hee had called foorth unto him the Magistrates of the Rhodians, for delivering unto him publike letters from the State without the due subscription[b], he gave them not so much as one hard worde but onely commanded them to subscribe and sent them away. Diogenes the professed Grammarian, who was wont to dispute[2] and discourse at Rhodes every Sabbath[3], had put him backe and would not admit him into his schoole comming of purpose extraordinarily to here him, but by his page posted him of untill the 7 day. Nowe when the same Diogenes stood waiting before his gate at Rome to doe his dutie and to salute him, he quit him no otherwise than thus, namely by warning him to repair thither againe 7 yeares after. When the presidentes and governours abroad gave him counsell to burden the provinces with heavie tributes and taxes he wrote backe unto them, That it was the part of a good shepheard to sheare his sheepe and not to slay them.

TIBERIUS NERO CÆSAR

33

By little and little he put himselfe forth and shewed his princely majesty; how ever for a long time, in some variety, yet for the most part, rather mild and gratious than otherwise, and more inclined to the good of the common wealth: and at the first, thus far forth onely interposed he his absolute power and inhibition, That nothing should be done unjustly[4]. Therfore he both repealed certaine constitutions of the Senate, and also very often, when the

[1] As collars, Cheines, speares, chaplets, etc. [2] Or reade a lecture.
[3] Once a weeke or every 7 day.   [4] Beside the rule of law.

THE HISTORIE OF

TIBERIUS NERO CÆSAR

Magistrates were sitting judicially upon the Bench, to decide matters, he would offer himselfe to joyne as it were in counsell, and to be assistant with them, or else just over against them in the fore part (of the Tribunall). And if the rumour went that any defendant were like by favour to escape cleere, all on a sodaine, he would be in place, and either on the ground below, or else from the Tribunall seat of the L. chiefe Justice [a], put the other Judges and Jurie in mind of the lawes, of their conscience and religion, and of the crime whereupon they sat. Also if any thing were amisse and faultie in the publike ordinances and manners of the Cittie, forlet by occasion of idlenesse or taken up through evill custome, he undertooke to reforme the same.

34

He abridged and restrained the expenses of Stage playes and games[1] exhibited unto the people, by cutting short the wages paied to Actours uppon the stage, and reducing the couples of sword fencers to a certaine number. That Corinthian vessels and manufactures grew to an exceeding high rate, and that three barbels were sold for 30000 sesterces, he grievously complained, and gave his opinion, that there should be a gage set, and a mediocritie kept in houshold furniture: as also that the price of victuals in open market should be ordred yeerly at the discretion of the Senate, with a charge given unto the Ædiles for to inhibite victualling houses, tavernes, and thus farre foorth, as they should not suffer any pastry-workes to be set out to sale [a]: and to the end, that by his owne example also, he might put forward the publike frugalitie, himselfe at his solemne and festivall suppers caused oftentimes to be served up to the bord, Viands dressed the day before and those halfe eaten alreadie, saying, That the side of a wild Bore had in it all the same that the whole. He forbad expressely by an Edict, the usuall and daily kisses commonly given and taken: likewise the intercourse of new yeares gifts sent to and fro: namely, that it should not continue after the

[1] Of sword-fencers.

TWELVE CÆSARS

Calends of Januarie. He had wont to bestow for his part TIBERIUS
a new yeares gift foure fold worth that which he received, NERO
and to give the same with his owne hand: but being offended CÆSAR
that a whole moneth together hee was in his other affaires
troubled with such as had not beene with him, nor felt his
liberalitie uppon the verie feast, hee never gave any againe
after the saide day.

35

Wives of leawd and dishonest life, if ther wanted accusers
to call them publikely into question, his advise and sentence
was, that their next kinsfolke should, *more maiorum*[1], agree
together in common, for to chastice and punish. He dispensed with a gentleman of Rome for his oath (who had
sworne before, never to divorce his wife) and gave him leave
to put her away, being taken in adulterie with her sonne in
law[2]. Certaine women infamous for whoredome and filthinesse, began to professe before the Ædiles bawderie: to the
ende, that having by this base trade and occupation lost the
right priviledge and dignitie of matrones, they might delude
the lawes[3] and avoide the penalties thereof[a]. Semblably,
out of the youth of both degrees[4], the leawdest spendthrifts
of all other, because they would not be liable to an Act of
the Senate in that behalfe, for performing their parts in
acting upon the stage, or their devoir within the lists[5],
wilfully underwent the ignominious note of infamie[6]. But,
as well them, as those light women aforesaid he banished
all: that none ever after should by such delusion of the law
seeke evasion. He tooke from a Senatour his robe[7], after
he knew once, that just before the Calends of Julie[b] hee
remooved out of his dwelling house into certaine Hortyardes and gardens[8], to the end that when the said day
was past, he might take his house againe within the Citie
at a lower rent. Another he deprived of his Questureship

---

[1] According to the maner and custome of their auncestours. [2] That
married her daughter. [3] Juliæ, etc., *de Adulteriis*. [4] As well Senatours
as gentlemen. [5] In sword-fight at the sharpe. [6] By committing some
leawd parts. [7] He deprived him from his Senatours place. [8] Without
the Cittie.

THE HISTORIE OF

TIBERIUS NERO CÆSAR

for that having (as it were) by lotterie, chosen and married a wife the one day, he dismissed her on another[1].

36

All foraine ceremonies in Religion: the Ægyptian also and the Jewish rites he prohibited: compelling those who were given to that Superstition[2], for to burne all their religious vestiments: the instruments likewise and furniture what soever thereto belonging. The serviceable youth of the Jewes, under colour of a militarie oth he sent into sundrie provinces which were in a pestilent and unhol-some aire above others[a]: the rest of that Nation or such as were addicted to the like religion, he banished out of Rome, upon paine of perpetuall bondage if they obeyed not. He expelled also Astrologers: but upon their ernest intreatie and promise to give over the practise of that Art, he permitted them there to remaine.

37

A speciall care he had to keepe the peace, and to preserve the state from outrages and robberies, as also from licentious mutinies and seditions. The set guards and garisons of soldiers, hee disposed thicker than the wonted manner was, throughout all Italie. Hee ordained a standing Campe at Rome[3], wherein the Prætorian Cohorts wandering up and downe before that time and dispersed in diverse Innes and Hostelries, might be received. All Insurrections of the people he punished most sharply; hee tooke likewise much paines to prevent such commotions. There happened upon some discord and variance to be a murder committed in the Theatre: but the principal heads of the faction, as also the actours themselves for whose sake the quarrel and fray began, he exiled: neither could he ever be brought for any prayer and intreatie of the people to revoke and restore them. When the Commons of Pollentia would not suffer the dead

---

[1] *i.* The morrow: his levitie was notable as well in making choise so slightly, as in casting her of so quickely, making but a game of mariage.
[2] Romaine Citizens.   [3] Neere unto the wals therof as Plinie writeth, Lib. 4, cap. 5, *Nat. Hist.*

TWELVE CÆSARS

corps of a certaine principall Centurian to be carried with funerall obsequies out of their market place, before they had forcibly extorted out of his heires hands a peece of money to the setting out of a game of Fencers with unrebated swords, he tooke one Cohort from Rome, and another out of K. Cotius[1] Kingdome, dissimuling the cause of this journey, and sodainely discovering their armes and weapons which they closely carried, and giving alarum with sound of trumpets, all at once he put them into the Towne with banner displayed at sundrie gates and so cast into perpetuall prison the greater part of the Commons and Decurions[2]. The priviledge and custome of Sanctuaries, where ever they were, he abolished. The Cyzicenes who had committed some notorious out-rage and violence upon Romaine Citizens, he deprived generally of their freedom, which in the warre against Mithridates they had by their good service gotten. The rebellions of enemies he repressed: not undertaking therefore, any expedition afterwards himselfe, but by his lieutenant onely: and not by them verily without lingring delayes, and driven thereto of necessitie. Kings that rebelliously tooke armes, or were suspected to breake out, hee kept downe with threats rather and complaints, than otherwise by force and open hostilitie. Some of them, whome hee had trained out of their owne Realmes unto him with faire words and large promises hee never sent home againe: as by name Maraboduus the Germaine, Thrasypolis a Thracian: and Archelaus the Cappadocian, whose kingdome also he reduced into the forme of a province.

TIBERIUS NERO CÆSAR

38

For two yeares together after he came unto the Empire, hee never set foote once out of Rome gates. And the time ensuing, hee absented not himselfe in no place unlesse it were in townes neere adjoyning, or as farre as Antium when he travailed farthest: and that was verie seldome and for a few dayes: albeit he promised and pronounced openly oftentimes that hee would visite the provinces also and armies abroade:

[1] A petie king about the Alpes. [2] Senatours, or Aldermen.

THE HISTORIE OF

TIBERIUS NERO CÆSAR

yea and everie yeare almost hee made preparation for a journey, taking up all the waines and wagons that were to be gotten, and laying provision of Corne and victuals in all the good Burroughes and Colonies by the way, yea and at the last suffered vowes to be made for his going forth and returne home: in so much as commonly by way of a jest and byworde, hee was called Callippides ª, who in a Greeke proverbe is noted to bee alwaies running, and yet never gaineth ground one cubit forward.

39

A.U.C. 779.

But being bereft of both his sonnes, of which Germanicus[1] died in Syria, and Drusus[2] at Rome, he withdrew himselfe into Campania, as to a retyring place: and all men well neere, were fully perswaded and spake it as constantly, that he would never returne but die soone after. Both which had like indeede to have come to passe. For, in truth he never came againe to Rome: and within some few dayes, neere unto Tarracina, in a certaine part of his mannour house (built especially for his owne lodging), and called Spelunca, as hee sat there at supper, a number of huge stones from above chaunced to fall down: whereby many of his guestes at the Table and servitours there waitinge were crushed and squized to death; but hee himselfe beyonde all hope escaped.

40

Having made his progresse over Campania, when he had dedicated a Capitol at Capua, and the Temple of Augustus at Nola, which hee pretended to have beene the motive of his journey, he betooke himselfe to Capreæ, delighted especially with that Iland because there was but one way of accesse unto it and the same by a small shore and landing place: as being otherwise enclosed round about, partly with craggy rockes and steepe cliffes of an exceeding height, and in part with the deepe sea. But soone after, when the people called him home, and uncessantly besought him to returne, by occasion of an unhappie and heavy

[1] Adopted.   [2] Naturall.

202

TWELVE CÆSARS

accident, wherby at Fideny xx thousand folke[1] and more, at a solemn fight of sword players perished by fall of an Amphitheater, he passed over into the maine and firme land, permitting all men to come unto him : the rather, for that when he first set forth and went out of Rome, he had given streight commandement by an Edict that no man should trouble him, and all the way voided as many as were comming towards him.

41

Being retired againe into the said Isle, he cast aside all care verily of Common weale; so farre forth as never after he did so much as repair and make up the broken decuries of horse men : hee chaunged no militarie Tribunes nor Captaines: no nor any presidents and Governours of Provinces. He held Spaine and Syria both, for certaine yeares, without Consulare Lieutenantes: hee neglected Armenia and suffered it to bee overrunne and possessed by the Parthians; Mæsia to be wasted and spoyled by the Dakes and Sarmatians, as also Gaule by the Germanes, to the great shame and no lesse daunger of the whole Empire.

42

To proceede, having now gotten the libertie of this secret place, and being as one would say remooved from the eyes of people: at length hee poured foorth and shewed at once all those vices which with much a do for a longe time he had cloked and dissimuled. Of which I will particularize and make relation from the very beginning. In the Campe when hee was but a newe and untrained souldier, for his excessive greedinesse of wine bibbing, hee was for Tiberius named Biberius[a]; for Claudius, Caldius; for Nero, Mero. After being Emperour, even at the very time when hee was busie in reforming the publike manners and misdemeanour (of the Cittie) he spent with Pomponius Flaccus and L. Piso one whole night and two dayes in gluttonie and drunkennesse[2], unto the former of these twaine he presently gave

TIBERIUS NERO CÆSAR

[1] Strangers that conflowed thither to see the showes. [2] In eating and drinking.

THE HISTORIE OF

TIBERIUS NERO CÆSAR the governement of the province Siria: uppon the other hee conferred the Provostship of Rome, professing even in all his letters and writings, That they were most pleasant companions and friends at all assaies. To Sex. Claudius[1] a *senex* fornicatour and prodigal dingthrift, who had in times past been by Augustus put to ignominie and shame, yea and by himselfe some fewe dayes before rebuked before the Senate, he sent word, that hee would take a supper with him: uppon this condition, that he altered nothing, nor left ought out of his ordinarie and customed manner: and namely, that wenches all naked should serve at the Table. He preferred one to be a competitour for the Questorship, who was a most base and obscure person, before others that were right noble gentlemen: onely for carousing and drinking up at a banquet, a whole Amphor[b] of wine when he dranke[2] unto him[2]. Unto Asellius Sabinus he gave 200000 Sesterces for a diologue of his making, in which he brought in a combate or disputation, betweene the Mushrome, the Ficedula[c], the Oister, and the Thrush[d]. To conclude, he instituted a new office, forsooth, *a voluptatibus*[3e], wherein he placed Priscus a gentleman of Rome, and one who had beene Censor.

43

But during the time of his private abode in Capreæ, he devised a roome with seates and benches in it, even a place of purpose for his secret wanton lusts. To furnish it there were sought out and gathered from all parts, a number of young drabbes and stale Catamites, sorted together: such also as invented monstrous kinds of libidinous filthinesse, whom he termed *Spintriæ:* who being in three rankes or rewes linked together should abuse and pollute one anothers bodie before his face: that by the verie sight of them he might stirre up his owne cold courage and fainting lust. Hee had bed chambers besides, in many places, which he adorned with tables and petie puppets: representing in the one sort, most lascivious pictures, and in the other as wanton shapes and figures. He stored them likewise with the bookes of

[1] Or Sestius Gallus.   [2] Or tendered it unto him.   [3] For the devising of newe pleasures, etc.

TWELVE CÆSARS

47

All the whiles he was Emperour, neither built he any stately workes: (for the verie temple of Augustus[1], and the reedification of Pompeius Theatre which onely and none else he had undertaken, after so many yeares he left unfinished) nor exhibited so much as one solemne shew unto the people: and at those which were by any other set out, he was very seldome present; and all for feare least some thing should be demanded at his hands: and namely after that he was compelled once to manumise the Comædian Actius[2]. Having releeved the want and povertie of some Senatours, because he would not helpe more of them, he denied to succour any other than those, who alledged before the Senate good and just causes of their necessities. By which deede of his, he frighted the most part upon a modestie and bashfulnesse in them: and among the rest, one Ortalus, the nephew of Q. Hortensius the professed Oratour, who being of a very meane estate had begotten foure children, by the meanes and perswasion of Augustus[3].

48

As touching his publike munificence, he never shewed it but twice: once, when he purposed and published a free lone for 3 yeares of an hundred millians of Sesterces: and againe, when unto certaine Land-lords of faire houses and tenements, which situate upon mount Cælius were consumed with fire, he restored the full price and worth of them. One of these Boones he was forced to grant, by reason that the people in great want of monie called earnestly for his helpe: what time as by vertue of an Act of Senate hee had ordained, That Usurers should lay out two (third) parts of their Stock[4] in lands, tenements and appurtenances immoveable[5]: the Debtours likewise make present payment of two parts of their debts; and yet the thing was not done and dispatched accordingly[6]: the other, for to miti-

---

[1] At Rome. [2] An Actour in a Comædie. [3] He had maried a young wife upon hope of maintenance by vertue of the lawes Papia, Poppœa, and Julia. [4] Or patrimonie. [5] That therby their money might come abroad. [6] *i.* debts paid.

THE HISTORIE OF

TIBERIUS NERO CÆSAR

gate the greevousnesse of those heavie times[1]. Howbeit this (later) beneficence of his he so highly prised, that he commaunded the name of Mount Cælius to be changed and called Augustus. The Legacies given by Augustus in his last will unto the Souldiours being once published[2], he never after bestowed any Largesse upon them: saving that among those of the Prætorium[3] hee dealt one thousand Deniers a peece; in and to the Legions in Syria certaine gifts for that they alone among all their Ensignes in the field honoured no image at all of Sejanus[4]. Moreover, he made very seldome any discharges of olde Souldiours[5]: as expecting upon age their death, and by death gaping for some gaine and vantage. Neither succored he the very Provinces with his bountiful hand, except it were Asia, by occasion that certaine Cities therein were by earthquake overthrowne[6].

49

Afterwards, and in processe of time he gave his mind wholly even to rapine and plaine pillage. It is for certaine knowne, that Cn. Lentulus the Augur, a man of exceeding great wealth, for very feare and anguish of mind was by him driven to a loathing and wearinesse of his owne life; and at his death to make no other heire but himselfe. That dame Lepida likewise, a right noble Lady was condemned by him, to gratify Quirinus[7], one that had beene Consull, but passing rich[a] and childlesse[8] withall: who having before time put her away beeing his wedded wife, twenty yeeres after called her judicially into question, and laid to her charge, that long agoe she had bought and provided poison for to take away his life. Besides, as well knowne it is, that certaine Princes and Potentates of Gaule, Spaine, Syria and Greece, forfeited their estates upon so slight a slaunder and impudent imputation, that against some of them nought else was objected

---

[1] For then it was that xx thousand were killed at Fideney by the fall of a Theater. [2] *Publicata*. [3] Or Guard. [4] As of their Generall. [5] With allowance of lands, fees or yearely Pensions for their service. [6] In number 12. Plin. lib. 2, cap. 84; Euseb. *Chronic*. 13. [7] Her husband. [8] And therfore he hoped to be his heire.

but this, that they had part of their substance and wealth lying in money [1][b]: yea and that many Cities and private persons lost their auncient immunities and priviledges, as also their right in mines and mettals, Tolls and customes: and finally that Vonones a King of the Parthians who beeing driven out of his kingdome by his owne subjects, retired himselfe with an huge masse of Treasure into Antiochia, under the protection, as it were, of the people of Rome, was perfidiously stript out of all and killed.

TIBERIUS NERO CÆSAR

50

The hatred that hee bare to his kinsfolke and neere Allies, hee bewraied, first in his brother Drusus by disclosing a letter of his: wherein hee dealt with him about compelling Augustus to restore the common Libertie: afterwards, in others also. As for his wife Julia, so farre was he from shewing any courtesie or kindnesse unto her when she stoode confined (which had beene the least matter of a thousand) that whereas by an Ordinance of her fathers, shee was shut up within one Towne, hee gave straight order that shee should not steppe out of dores, and enjoy the Societie of people and worldlie commerce: nay, hee proceeded so farre, as to bereave her of that little stocke and housholde-stuffe which her Father allowed her: yea, and defrauded her of the yeerely Pension and exhibition for her maintenaunce: and all, forsooth, under a colour of common right and law, because Augustus in his last will and testament had not expresly provided in this behalfe. Being not able well to endure his mother Livia, as chalenging to her selfe equall part with him in power and authority, hee avoided both to keepe ordinary and daily company, and also to entertaine long speech or secret conference with her; because hee might not be thought ruled and directed by her counsailes; which otherwhiles notwithstanding he was wont both to stand in neede of, and also to use. Semblably, he tooke to the very heart the passing of this Act in the Senate, ' That in his stile as he had the title, sonne of Augustus, so this addition should runne withall sonne of Livia.' And therefore it was,

[1] More than by law they might.

THE HISTORIE OF

TIBERIUS NERO CÆSAR

that he would not suffer her to be named *Parens Patriæ*:[1], nor to receive any remarkable honour in open place and by publique decree. Oftentimes also he admonished her to forbeare intermedling in greater affaires, and such as were not meet for women; especially after he perceived once, that when the Temple of Vesta was on fire, she also came thither in person among others, and there encouraged the people and souldiours both, to doe their best and help all what they could, as her manner was to doe in her husbands dayes.

51

By these degrees he proceeded even to secret rancour and malice against her, but chiefly upon this occasion, as men report. She had been very earnest with him many a time to enrole one in the Decuries of the Judges[a] who was made free Denizen and Citizen of Rome: but he denied flatly to choose and admit the party, unlesse it were upon this onely condition, That she would suffer a clause to be written and annexed to the Instrument or Roll[2], in these words, 'This graunt was by my mother wrung and wrested from me.' Whereat she highly displeased and offended, brought forth out of her Closet and Cabinet certaine old letters of Augustus (written) unto her, as touching his perverse, bitter and intollerable manners; and those she openly read. He againe tooke the matter so greevously, that she had both kept those writings so long by her, and also cast them in his dish so spitefully, that some thinke this was the greatest cause of his departure from the Citie. And verily, for the space of three yeeres compleat, during which time hee was absent and his mother living, hee sawe her but once: and that was no more than one day, and very fewe howers of the same. And afterwards as little minde hee had to be by her lying sicke: and when shee was dead, suffering her corps by staying so long above ground (whiles men hoped still of his comming) to corrupt at length and putrifie: after shee was enterred, he forbad that she should be canonized and registred in the Catalogue of Saints: pretending as if she

---

[1] Mother of her Country.   [2] *Quorum nomina*, or such like.

TWELVE CÆSARS

her selfe had given that order. Her will hee annulled, all her friends and familiars, even those unto whom upon her death-bed she had committed the charge of her Funerals, within a short time he persecuted and plagued, yea and one of them, to wit, a worshipfull Gentleman of Rome, he condemned to the pump[1].

TIBERIUS NERO CÆSAR

52

Of his two sonnes, hee loved neither Drusus that was by nature, nor Germanicus by adoption, as a father should doe, as taking offence at the vices of the one[2]. For Drusus was of an effeminate minde; given to a loose and idle life. Therefore was not Tiberius so neerely touched and grieved for him beeing dead; but presentlie after his funerall, returned to his ordinarie and accustomed businesse prohibiting vacation of Justice[3] to continue any longer. Moreover, when the Iliensian Embassadours came somwhat with the latest to comfort him, he, (as if now by this time the memorie of his sorrow had beene cleane worne out,) scoffed at them and made this answere, That hee likewise was sorie in their behalfe for the losse they had of Hector, so noble and brave a Citizen. As for Germanicus, he depraved and disgraced him so, as that not onely he did extenuate and diminish all his worthy exploits as mere vaine and needlesse, but also blamed his most glorious victories, as daungerous and hurtfull to the Common-wealth. Also, for that without his advise, hee went unto Alexandria, (by occasion of an extreame and suddaine famine) hee complained of him in the Senate: yea, and it is verily beleeved, he was the cause of his death, and used the meanes of Cn. Piso, Lieutenant of Syria; who soone after beeing accused of this crime, would (as some thinke) have uttered abroad those directions and warrants that hee had so to doe: but that Sejanus secretly withstood it[4]. For which, Tiberius was oftentimes and in many places

---

[1] Or wheele and bucket: *in Antliam.* Some read, *in Antiliam,* or *Anticyram, i.* an Iland: or else *Latumiam,* a dungeon in the common prison.
[2] Of Drusus. [3] *Iustitium,* as the maner was in any mournfull time.
[4] *Ni Seianus secreto obstaret:* or, *Nisi ea secreta obstarent, i.* but that they were in secret delivered, and therefore could not be proved.

THE HISTORIE OF

TIBERIUS NERO CÆSAR

much blamed[1], and in the night season commonly called upon with this crie and note, *Redde Germanicum, i.* 'Give us Germanicus againe.' The suspition whereof himselfe afterwardes confirmed and made good, by afflicting in cruell manner the wife also and children of the said Germanicus.

53

Furthermore, his daughter in law [2] Agrippina, for complaining over-boldly of him after the death of her husband, he tooke by the hand, and recited unto her a Greeke verse[a] to this effect, 'If thou hast not soveraine Rule and Dominion,' quoth he, 'thinkest thou prety daughter that thou art wronged?' and so vouchsafed her no speech at all after. Also, because upon a time, when shee durst not at supper tast of those appels which he had reached unto her, he forbare to invite her any more; pretending, that she charged him with the crime of attempting her with poison: when as in deede, it was of purpose plotted and packed aforehand, both that himselfe should by the offring of such fruit tempt her, and she againe beware most present and assured death. At the last, having untruly accused her, as if shee minded to flie one while to the Statue of Augustus, and another while to the Armies, hee confined and sent her away to the Isle Pandataria; and as shee railed at him, hee by the hands of a Centurion with whipping and lashing her over the face strucke out one of her eyes. Againe, when as shee was fully determined to pine her selfe to death: hee caused her mouth perforce to bee opened, and meate to be crammed into her throate: yea, and after that by continuance in this minde shee consumed quite away and died in the end, hee inveighed against her in most odious and reproachfull termes: having opined first in the senate, that her birth-day also should bee reckoned among the dismall and unlucky dayes. Furthermore, he expected thankes, as for an high favour done unto her, in that hee strangled her not before with a cord, and so

---

[1] *Increpitum:* others read *inscriptum, i.* This inscription was in many places set upon his Statues. [2] Germanicus his adopted sonnes wife, and daughter to Agrippa and Julia.

TWELVE CÆSARS

flung her to the *Gemoniæ* [1][b], and in regard of such a singular clemencie as this, hee suffred a Decree to passe, That thankes should bee given unto him, and a Present of Golde consecrated unto Jupiter Capitolinus.

TIBERIUS
NERO
CÆSAR

54

Whereas by Germanicus he had three nephewes, Nero, Drusus and Caius; by Drusus one, to wit Tiberius, when he was left destitute and fatherlesse by the death of his children, the two eldest sonnes of Germanicus, namely Nero and Drusus, he recommended to the LL. of the Senate; and celebrated the day of both their Commencements with giving a Congiarie[2] to the people. But no sooner understoode he, that upon New-yeeres-day there had beene publique vowes made by the Citie for their life also and preservation, but he gave the Senate to understand, That such honours ought not to be conferred upon any persons, but those that were experienced and farre stept in yeeres. Thereby, having discovered the inward character and canker of his hart, from that day forward hee exposed them to the slaunders and imputations of all men: when also, by sundry subtile devises hee had wrought so, that they might bee both provoked to give railing taunts, and also beeing so provoked come to mischiefe and destruction, he accused them in his letters, heaped most bitterly upon them hainous reproaches, caused them to be judged enemies to the State, and so hunger-starved them to death; Nero, within the Isle Pontia, and Drusus at the very foote and bottome of Palatium. Men think that Nero was driven to worke his owne death[3], what time as the Hangman[4], as sent by a warrant from the Senate, presented unto him halters and hookes[5]. As for Drusus, kept he was from all foode and sustenance: in so much as hee gave the attempt to eate the very flockes that stuffed the mattrese[6] whereupon hee lay: and the reliques[7] of them both, were so dispersed and scattred abroade, that hardly they could be ever gathered together.

[1] *Scalæ*. [2] Or Largesse. [3] To famish his owne selfe wilfully. [4] Or executioner. [5] To strangle him, and drag him to the *Scalæ Gemoniæ*. [6] Or bed. [7] Bones and ashes which was done by him of spight.

THE HISTORIE OF

55

Over and above his olde friends and familiars, hee had demaunded twenty out of the number of the best and principall Citizens, as Counsailours and Assistants unto him in publique affaires. Of all these, hee could hardly shewe twaine or three at the most alive: the rest, some for one cause and some for another he brought to confusion and killed: among whom (with the calamity and overthrow of many more) was Ælius Sejanus, whom hee had to the highest place of authoritie advaunced, not so much for any good will, as to be his instrument and right hand, by whose ministerie and fraudulent practises he might circumvent the children of Germanicus, and so establishe as heire apparent in succession of the Empire the Nephew he had by Drusus, as his naturall sonne.

56

No milder was he one jote unto the Greeke Professours and Artists, living and conversing daily with him, and in whom hee tooke most contentment. One of them named Zeno, as hee reasoned and discoursed very exactly[1] of a question he asked, What harsh dialect [a] that was, wherein he spake? and when hee answered, It was the Dorick, he confined him for his labour into Cynaria, supposing that he twitted and reproached him for his olde vacation and absence from Rome because the Rhodians spake Dorick. Semblably, whereas his manner was out of his owne daily readings, to propound certaine questions as hee sate at supper: having intelligence, that Seleucus the Grammarian enquired diligently of his Ministers and Servitours, what Authors at any time hee had in hand, and so came prepared to assoile the saide questions, first hee forbad him his house and ordinarie Societie, afterwards hee forced him even to death.

57

His cruell, close and unpliable nature was not hidden, no not in his verie childhood: the which Theodorus Gadaræus

[1] Or curiously.

TWELVE CÆSARS

his teacher in Rhetorick, seemed both at first to fore-see most wisely, and also to expresse and resemble as fitly, when by way of chiding and rebuke hee called him ever and anone *Pelon Haimati Pephuramenon;* i. clay[1] soaked in bloud[2]. But the same brake out and appeared somewhat more, when he became Emperour, at the very beginning: what time as yet he lay for to win the love and favour of men, with a pretence of civill moderation. A certaine Buffon[3] there was, who as a Funerall passed by, had willed the party whose body was carried forth, to report unto Augustus, That his Legacies were not yet payed and delivered, which hee had left for the Commons of Rome[4]. Him, he caused to be haled and brought unto his presence, to receive also the debt which was due: and then commaunded him to be led to execution, and so to relate the truth unto his father (Augustus). Not long after as he threatned to send unto prison one Pompeius a Romaine Knight, for stoutly denying some thing, hee assured him, That of a Pompeius he would make him a Pompeianus, glauncing by this bitter and biting taunt, both at the mans name and also at the old infortunity of that side[5].

TIBERIUS NERO CÆSAR

58

About the same time, when the Pretour came to know of him, whether his pleasure was to holde the judiciall Assizes, as touching the case of Majestie[6], or no? he made answere, That the Lawes must have their course and be put in execution: and in very truth he executed them with extreame rigour. There was one who from the Statue of Augustus had taken away the head, for to set the same upon the Statue of another. The matter was debated in the Senate: and because some doubt arose, Who did the deed? inquisition was made by torture. The party delinquent being condemned, this kind of Calumniation by little and little proceeded so farre, that such points as these also were made capitall crimes:

[1] Or mire.   [2] Clay so tempered becommeth verie strong, tough and stiffe.   [3] A scoffing jester.   [4] *Elato mortuo,* or *clare mortuo,* i. with a loude voice called upon the dead man, etc.   [5] The Pompeiani, that took part with Pompeius against Julius Cæsar.   [6] High treason.

THE HISTORIE OF

TIBERIUS NERO CÆSAR

namely, to have beaten a slave, about the image of Augustus [1]. Item, if a man had shifted his apparell[a] and put on other clothes (about the said Image). Item, to have brought into any privie or brothelhouse his image [2] imprinted either in money or ring. Lastly, to have empaired any word or deede of his, in the least credite and reputation that might bee. To conclude, it cost one his life, for suffering in his owne Colonie, honours to be decreed unto him, upon the same day, that they had in times past beene decreed for Augustus.

59

Many parts besides under the colour of gravity and reformation, but rather in deede following the course of his owne nature, hee used to play, so cruelly and with such rigour, that some there were, who in verses both upbraided by way of reproach the calamities present, and also gave warning of the future miseries, in this manner:

Asper et immitis. Breviter vis omnia dicam?
Dispeream, si te mater amare potest.

Harsh and unkind, (In briefe wilt thou I should say all?) thou art:
God me confound, if mother thine can love thee in her hart.

Non es eques; quare? non sunt tibi millia centum;
Omnia si quæras : et Rhodos exilium est.

No Knight thou art; and why? for hundred thousands none;
(Search all) thou hast in store : and now at Rhodes exil'd do'st wone.

Aurea mutasti Saturni sæcula, Cæsar;
Incolumi nam te, ferrea semper erunt.

Of Saturne King thou changed hast that age resembling gold,
For while thou, Cæsar, liv'st, the world of yron shall ever hold.

Fastidit vinum quia iam sitit iste cruorem :
Tam bibit hunc avide, quam bibit ante merum.

Wine doth he loath, because that now of bloud he hath a thirst,
He drinketh that as greedily, as wine he did at first.

Aspice fœlicem sibi non tibi, Romule Sullam;
Et Marium, si vis, aspice; sed reducem,
Nec non Antoni civilia bella moventis :
Nec semel infectas, aspice cæde manus.
Et dic, Roma perit. Regnabit sanguine multo,
Ad regnum quisquis venit ab exilio[a].

---

[1] Fled thither for refuge as unto a Sanctuarie, or otherwise how so ever.
[2] Either of Tiberius or Augustus. Read Seneca *de beneficiis*, lib. 3, cap. 26.

TWELVE CÆSARS

See Sulla, happy for himselfe, O Romulus not for thee :
And Marius, in case thou wilt, but new returned, see ;
Likewise behold of Antonie those hands in bloud embrew'd
Not once, I meane of Antonie, who civill warres renew'd.
Then say, Rome goes to wrack. And he with blud-shed much wil raign
Who to a Kingdomes-state is come, from banishment againe.

TIBERIUS NERO CÆSAR

Which verses at first, he would have had to be taken and construed as made by them who were impatient of any Lordly rule and absolute dominion at Rome : and as if they had beene framed and devised, not so much with any considerate judgement, as upon Stomach and Choler. And evermore his saying was, *Oderint dum probent, i.* Let them hate me, so long as they suffer my proceedings to passe. But afterwards, even himselfe proved them to be very true and most certaine.

60

Within few dayes after hee, came to Capreæ, when a Fisher-man, suddainly and unlooked for presented unto him (as hee was in a secret place doing somewhat by himselfe) a Barble of an extraordinary bignesse [1], he caused his face to be rubbed all over with the same fish : as put in a fright, no doubt, for that from the backe side of that Iland, he had made meanes thorough the rough thickets and by-wayes, to creepe and get unto him where he was. And when the poore fellow amid this punishment seemed to rejoyce yet, and said, It was happy that he had not offred unto him a lopstar also (which he had caught) of an huge greatnesse, hee commaunded that his face should be grated and mangled likewise with the said Lopstar. A Souldiour, one of his owne guard, for filching and stealing a Peacock out of an Orchard [2] he put to death. In a certaine journey that he made, the Licter wherein he was caried chaunced to be entangled and somewhat stayed with briars and brambles : whereupon a Centurion of the formost cohorts in the Vaward, that had in charge to try and cleere thee waies, he caused to be laid along upon the ground, and there he all to beat him [3] untill he was well-neere dead.

[1] Being skaly and having a couple of barbets. [2] Or garden. [3] With cudgels : which punishment was called *Fustuarium.*

THE HISTORIE OF

TIBERIUS NERO CÆSAR

Soone after, hee brake out into all kindes of cruelty; as one who never wanted matter to worke upon: persecuting the familiar friendes and acquaintance of his owne Mother first, then, of his Nephewes and daughter in lawe, and at the last of Sejanus: after whose death hee grewe to be most cruell. Whereby especially it appeared, that himselfe was not wont so much to be provoked and set on by Sejanus: as Sejanus [1] to serve his turne and feede his humour, seeking as he did all occasions: howsoever in a certaine commentarie which he composed summarily and briefely of his owne life he durst write thus much, That he executed Sejanus, because he had found that hee raged furiously against the children of Germanicus his sonne. Of whom to say a truth, the one himselfe murdred, after he had first suspected Sejanus, and the other, not before he had killed him. To prosecute in particular all his bloudie deedes would require a long time. It shall suffice therefore to reherse in generall the patternes as it were and examples of his crueltie. There passed not a day over his head, no not so much as any festivall and religious holieday, without execution and punishment of folke [a]. Some suffered even uppon Newyeares day. Accused and condemned there were many together, with their children, and very wives. Straight commaundement and warning was given, that the nere kinsfolke of such persons as stood condemned to die, should not mourne and lament for them. Especially rewardes were by decree appointed for their accusers, otherwhiles also for bare witnesses. No informer and promoter was discredited, but his presentment taken. And everie crime and trespasse went for Capitall, and so was received: were it but the speaking of a few simple words. Objected it was against a Poet, that in a tragædie hee had reviled and railed uppon Agamemnon [2][b]; as also it was laide to an Historians [3] charge, for saying, that Brutus and Cassius [4], were

---

[1] *Quam Seianum quærenti occasiones subministrasse.* [2] The soverain Captaine and Generall of the Greekes at Troye. [3] A. Cremutius Cordus: read Seneca *Consolat. ad Marcum*, cap. 22. [4] Who slew Julius Cæsar and were accoumpted *Tyrannoctonoi.*

TWELVE CÆSARS

the last of all the Romains ᶜ. Presently were the Authors and writers punished, and their writings called in and abolished: notwithstanding certaine yeares before they had beene recited even in the hearing of Augustus, with his good liking and approbation. Some committed to ward, were deprived not onely of their Solace and comfort in studying, but also of the verie use of talking with others. Of such as were cited peremptorily by writ and processe to aunswere at the barre, some gave themselves (mortall) wounds at home in their houses (as sure to be condemned, onely to avoyd torments and ignominy) others in the open face and middest of the Court dranke poyson: and yet were they with their wounds bound up, and whiles they yet panted betweene alive and dead, haled away to prison. There was not one executed but hee was throwne also into the *Gemoniæ*, and drawne with the drag. In one day were there twentie ᵈ so throwne and drawne: and among them boyes and women. As for young girles and maidens of unripe yeares, because by aunceint custome and tradition, unlawfull it was to strangle Virgins, first deflowred they were by the hang-man and afterwards strangled ᵉ. Were any willing of themselves to die? such were forced violently to live. For he thought simple death so light a punishment, that when he hard, how one of the prisoners, Carnulius [1] by name, had taken his death voluntarily before, he cried out in these wordes, 'Carnulius hath escaped my hands.' Also in overseeing and perusing the prisoners in Gaole, when one of them besought to have his punishment with speed, he made him this answere: 'Nay marry, thou art not yet reconciled unto me, that I should shew thee such favour.' A certaine Consular writer [2] hath inserted this in his Annales: That upon a time at a great feast (where himselfe also was present,) Tiberius being on a sodaine asked, and that openly with a lowd voyce by a dwarfe standing at the Table among other Buffons [3] and Jesters, Wherefore Paconius being attaint of treason lived so long? for that instant verily chid the partie for his saucie and malapert tongue: but after a few daies wrote

TIBERIUS NERO CÆSAR

[1] Or Calvilius. [2] Who had beene sometime consul, and therefore to be credited. [3] *Inter Copreas.*

THE HISTORIE OF

TIBERIUS NERO CÆSAR

unto the Senate, to take order with all speede for the execution of Paconius.

62

He increased and strained still more and more this crueltie, by occasion that he was galled and fretted at the newes of his sonne Drusus his death: for, having beene of opinion, that he died upon some sickenes and intemperate life, so soone as he understood at length, that he was poysoned and so made away by the villanous practise of his wife Livilla[1] and Sejanus together, he spared not to torment and execute any one whomsoever; so bent and addicted whole daies together to the inquisition and tryall of this onely matter, as that when word came unto him how an host of his an inhabitant of Rhodes (whom by familiar letters he had sent for to Rome) was come, he commanded him out of hand to be put to torture[2], as if he had beene some neere freinde present at the foresaid examination: but afterwards, when his errour was discovered, and seeing how he had mistaken, he caused him also to be killed, because he should not divulge and make knowne the former injury[3]. The place is yet to bee seene at Capreæ of his butcherly carnage: from which he caused condemned persons after long and exquisite torments to be flung headlong before his face into the sea: where were readie to receive them a number of mariners, who with their sprits, poles, and oares should beate and batt their carkasses: to the end that none of them might have any breath or wind remaining in the bodie. He had devised moreover, among other kinds of torment, what time as men by deceitfull meanes had their lode with large drinking of strong wine, sodainely to knit fast and tie their privie members with (Lute) strings, that hee might cause them to swell and be pent in most dolorous paines occasioned at once as well by the streight strings, as the suppression and stoppage of urine. And had it not beene that both death prevented and Thrasyllus[4] also enforced him of purpose, (as men say) to put of some designes in hope of longer life, he would have

[1] Daughter of Germanicus and Agryppina, and wife to the said Drusus.
[2] Among other examinates.   [3] Done unto him.   [4] The Astrologer.

murdred a good many more (as it is fully beleeved) and not spared those verie nephewes of his that remained yet alive; considering he both had Caius in suspition, and also cast of Tiberius, as conceived in adulterie. And it soundeth to truth, that he was minded thus to do. For, ever and anon, he called Priamus happie in that he overlived all his sonnes and daughters.

TIBERIUS NERO CÆSAR

63

But, how amid these prankes he lived not onely odious and detested, but exceeding timorous also and exposed to the contumelious reproches of the world, there be many evidences to shew. That any soothsayers should be sought unto and consulted with a part without witnesses by, he forbad: as for the Oracles neere adjoyning to the Citie of Rome, he attempted to subvert them all. But being terrified with the majestie of those answeres[1] which were delivered at Præneste[2], he gave over: namely, when as he could not finde them, (sealed upp though they were and brought downe to Rome) within the chist until the same was carried backe againe unto the Temple[3]. And not daring to send away and dismisse from him one or two[4] Consulare LL. deputies[5], after hee had offered provinces unto them, he detained them so long, untill after certaine yeares expired, he ordained others to succeede them: whiles the other remained present with him: whereas in the meane time, reserving still the title of the office: he assigned unto them many commissions and matters of charge: and they continually gave order for execution thereof, by the ministerie of their Legates, Livetenants and Coadjutours.

64

His daughter-in-law[6], and Nephewes, after they were once condemned, he never remooved from place to place otherwise than chained and in a close covered licter sowed up fast:

---

[1] Fortunes or chaunces. [2] In manner of a Lottery. [3] Of Fortune at Preneste. [4] L. Ælius Lamia and L. Arruntius. [5] Or Presidents that had beene Consuls. [6] Agrippina, his adopted sonne Germanicus wife and widow, or Livilla before named, wife to Drusus his naturall sonne.

THE HISTORIE OF

TIBERIUS NERO CÆSAR

setting his soldiers to prohibite all passengers that met with them, and waifaring persons travailing by, once to looke backe thither[1], or to stay their pace and stand still.

65

When Sejanus went about seditiously to worke alteration in the state: albeit he saw now that both his birth day was publikely solemnized, and also his Images of gold worshipped everie where, he overthrew him (I must needs say) at length: but with much adoo, by craftie sleights and guile, rather than by his princely authoritie and Imperiall power. For first, to the end that he might dismisse the man in shew of honour, he assumed him to be his Colleague in the fifth Consulship, which in his long absence[2] he had taken upon him for that verie purpose. Afterwards when he had deceived him with hope of Affinitie[3] and the Tribunes authoritie, he complained of the man (looking for noe such matter) in a shamefull and pitious Oration[4]: beseeching the LL. of the Senate among other requests, To send on of the Consuls to conduct him an aged and desolate man with some guarde of soldiours, into their sight. And yet neverthelesse, distrusting himselfe and fearing an uprore[5], he had given commandement, that his nephew Drusus, whom still he kept in prison at Rome: should be set at libertie (if need did so require,) and ordained generall captaine. Yea and whiles his ships were readie rigged and prepared to what Legions soever he ment for to flie, hee stood looking ever and anon from the highest cliffe that was, toward the markes and signes, which he had appointed (least messengers might stay too long) for to be reared a great way of: thereby to have intelligence, as any occurrent (good or bad) fell out. Nay, when the conspiracie of Sejanus was now suppressed, he was never the more secure and resolute: but for the space of 9 monethes next ensuing he stirred not out of the village[6] called Jovis.

[1] Because they shold not aske who was within. [2] For he remained still at Capreæ. [3] To be matched in mariage with on of his neipces. [4] Or Epistle rather written unto the Senat. [5] In Rome, about Sejanus, who was so highly honored there. [6] Or ferme house, in the Isle Capreæ.

TWELVE CÆSARS

66

Beside all this, diverse and sundrie reprochfull taunts from all parts netled and stung his troubled minde. For there was not a person condemned, that reviled him not in all sorts openly to his face, yea and discharged uppon him opprobrious termes by libels laid for the nonce in the verie *Orchestra*[1], with which contumelies verily, affected he was after a most divers and contrarie manner: so that, one while he desired for verie shame of the world, that all such abuses might be unknowne and concealed: otherwhiles, hee contemned the same, and of his owne accorde broached and divulged them abroade. Furthermore, rated he was and railed at in the letters also of Artabanus K. of the Parthians, who charged him with parricidies, murders, cowardise and luxurious riot: who gave him counsell likewise with all speede possible, to satisfie with a voluntarie death the hatred of his Citizens, conceived against him in the highest degree and most justly. At the last, being even wearie of himselfe, in the beginning of such an Epistle as this, hee declared and confessed in manner the verie summe of all his miseries. 'What shall I write? my LL. of the Senate, or how shall I write? Nay, what is it, at a word, that I shall not write at this time? The Gods and Goddesses all plague and confound me utterly at once, feeling as I do my selfe dayly to perish.'

67

Some thinke, that he foreknew all this by the skill he had of future events[1a]: that he foresaw also long before how great a calamitie and infamie both, would one day betide him: and therfore it was, that he refused most obstinately to take upon him the Empire and the name of *Pater Patriæ*, as also stood against the oath, to maintaine his Acts: for feare least within a while after, to his greater disgrace and shame he might be found inferiour, and unworthie of such speciall honours, which verily may be gathered out of the

---

[1] Where the Senatours sat to behold the plaies. [2] For he was wonderfully addicted to the study of Astrologie and such curious Arts.

speech hee made as touching both those points, when he saith but thus: That hee would be alwaies like to himselfe, and never chaunge his manners, so long as he continued in his sound wits. Howbeit, for example sake, provided it would be that the Senate binde not themselves to keepe and ratifie the Actions of any one, who by some chaunce might bee altered. And againe, 'Marie, if at any time,' quoth hee, 'yee shall make doubt of my loyall behaviour and devoted mind unto you (which before it ever happen, I wish my dying day to take me from this minde and opinion of yours, once conceived of me and afterwards chaunged) the bare title of *Pater Patriæ* will adde no honour unto me, but upbraide you either with inconsiderate rashnesse, for imposing that Surname uppon mee, or else with inconstancie, for your contrary judgements of mee.'

68

Corpulent he was, big set and strong, of stature above the ordinarie^a, broad betweene the shoulders and large breasted: in all other parts also of the bodie (from the crowne of his head to the verie sole of his foote) of equall making and congruent proportion. But his left hand was more nimble and stronger than the right: and his joynts so firme, that with his finger he was able to bore through a greene and sound Apple: with a fillop also to breake the head of a boy, yea of a good stripling and big youth. Of colour and complexion he was cleere and white: wearing the haire of his head longe behind, in so much as it covered his very necke: which was thought in him to be a fashion appropriate to his linage and familie[1]. He had an ingenuous and well favoured face: wherein notwithstanding appeared many small tumours or risinges[b]: and a paire of verie great gogle eyes in his head, such as (whereat a man would marvaile) could see even by night and in the darke: but that was onely for a little while and when they opened first after sleepe: for in the ende they waxed dim againe[2]. His gate[3] was with his necke stiffe and shooting forward[4][c]: with a

[1] The Claudii. [2] For such prominent eyes are not commonly quicke of sight. [3] Manner of going. [4] Or downeward into his bosome.

TWELVE CÆSARS

countenance bent and composed lightly to severitie: for the most part he was silent: seldome or never should you have him talke with those next about him: and if hee did, his speech was exceeding slowe, not without a certaine wanton gesticulation and fimbling with his fingers. All which properties being odious and full of arrogancie, Augustus both observed in him, and also went about to excuse and cloke for him before the Senate and people, assuring them, they were the defects and imperfections of nature, and not the vices of the mind. He lived most healthfull: and verily all the time well neere that he was Emperour not once in maner crasie: albeit from that he was thirtie yeares old he governed his helth after his owne order and direction, without any helpe or counsell at all of Physicians [d].

TIBERIUS NERO CÆSAR

69

As little respect as hee had of the Gods, or sence of any religion, (as one addicted to astrologie and calculation of nativities, yea and fully perswaded, that all things were done and ruled by fatall destinie[1]) yet feared he thunder exceedingly: and were the aire or wether any whit troubled, hee ever carried a chaplet or wreath of lawrell about his necke[2]: because that kinde of greene branch is never, as they say blasted with lightning[3].

70

The liberall Sciences of both sorts[4] he loved most affectionatly, in the Latine speech[5] he followed Corvinus Messalla; whom being an aged professour he had observed from his verie youth: but with overmuch affectation and curiositie he marred all and darkened his stile: so as he was thought to do somewhat better *ex tempore*[6], than upon studie and premeditation. He composed also a poem in lyricke verses[a], the title whereof is, *A complaint of D. Cæsars death*[7][b]. Hee made likewise Greeke poemes in

---

[1] The course of the stars.   [2] Or upon his head in maner of a Coronet.
[3] As Plinie reporteth, lib. 2 and 15.   [4] As wel Greeke as Latine.   [5] Prose.
[6] Of a sodaine.   [7] One of Augustus sonnes, yet some expound it of Julius Cæsar, Dictator.

THE HISTORIE OF

TIBERIUS NERO CÆSAR

imitation of Euphorion, Rhianus and Parthenius: in which Poets being much delighted, their writings and Images he dedicated in the publike Libraries among the aunceint and principall authors. A number therefore of learned men strove a vie to put forth many pamphlets of them [1], and to present him therewith. But above all he studied for the knowledge of fabulous historie [2], even unto meere fooleries, and matters ridiculous. For, the verie Grammarians (which kind of professours as we have said, he affected especially) he would assay and appose commonly with these and such like questions: namely, Who was Hecubaes mother? What name Achilles had among the Virgins [3]? What it was that the Mer-maides were wont to sing? The verie first day, (after the death of Augustus) that he entred into the *Curia*, as if he minded once for all to performe the dutie of pietie and religion: following the example of Minos he sacrificed indeede, as the manner was with Frankincense and wine, but without a minstrell, as the said Minos some-time did at the death of his sonne [4].

71

In the Greeke tongue, howsoever he otherwise was readie enough and spake it with facilitie, yet he used it not every where, but most of all forbare it in the Senate house: in so much verily, as when he came to name *Monopolium* [a], he craved leave before hand: for that he was to use a strang and foraine worde; yea and in a certaine decree of the Senatours, when this word *Emblema* [b] was red, he gave his opinion, that the saide word should be changed, and insteede of that strang terme some Latine vocable sought out: and if such an one could not be found, then to utter and declare the thing, though it were in more words and by circumlocu-tion. A certaine Greeke souldier also, being required for to depose and deliver his testimonie, he forbad to make answere, unlesse it were in Latin [c].

---

[1] *De hiis*, haply of their doing. [2] Wherein many tales or fables are in-serted. [3] The daughters of King Lycomedes in the Isle Scyros where hee faigned him selfe to bee a maiden. [4] Androgeus.

TWELVE CÆSARS

72

TIBERIUS NERO CÆSAR

All the time that he was retired and lived from the Cittie of Rome, twice and no more he assaied to returne thither: once he came by water embarked in a gallie[1], as farre as to the hort-yards and gardens adjoyning to the *Naumachia*[a]: but he had set guardes along the banks of Tibre, for to void and put backe such as went forth to meete him. A second time, by the streete or part way Appia, so farre as the 7 miles end from Rome[2][b]: but when he had onely seene the walles a farre of, without approching neerer unto the Citie hee returned. For what cause he did so at first[3], it was not certainely knowne: afterwardes, affrighted he was with this prodigious picture and straung sight[4]. Among other delights he tooke great pleasure in a Serpent Dragon[c], which, when according to his usuall manner, he would have fed with his owne hand and found eaten by pismires, he was warned thereupon to beware the violence of a multitude. In his returne therefore speedily into Campania he fell sicke at Astura: but being eased a little of that maladie he went forward as farre as to Circeii: and because he would give no suspicion of sickenesse, he was not onely present himselfe at the games exhibited by the garison souldiers there, but also, when there was a wild bore put foorth into the open shew-place for to be baited, he launced darts at him from above, where he was: and presently therewith, by occasion of a convulsion in his side, and for that hee had taken the cold aire upon an exceeding heat, he fell backe by relapse into a more dangerous disease[d]. Howbeit, he bare it out a pretie while: notwithstanding that after he was come downe so farre as to Misenum, he pretermitted nothing of his ordinary and daily manner, no not so much as his feasting and other pleasures: partly upon an intemperate humour of his owne, and in part to dissimule and palliate his weakenesse. For, when Charicles his Physician, who by vertue of a pasport was licensed to depart and be absent, went foorth from the table and tooke hold of his hand to kisse it, he supposing

[1] With three ranks of oares.   [2] *Ad septimum lapidem.*   [3] When he came by the River.   [4] When he journied by land.

THE HISTORIE OF

TIBERIUS NERO CÆSAR

that he had felt his pulse [1], desired him to stay and sit downe againe, and so drew out the supper longer. Neither gave he over his usuall custome, but even then standing in the midst of the banquetting roome with a lictor [2] by him he spake to every one by name [3] as they tooke their leave.

73

Meane while, when he had reade among the Acts passed in the Senate that certaine prisoners were enlarged and dismissed, but not so much as once heard: concerning whom he had written very breifly and no otherwise than thus, that nominated they were by an appeacher: chafing and frowning hereat, as if he had beene held in contempt, he fully purposed to go againe into Capreæ [4], as one who lightly would attempt nothing, but where he was sure enough and without all daunger. But being kept backe, as well by tempest as the violence of his disease that grew still uppon him, hee died soone after in a village [5] bearing the name Luculliana [6a], in the 78 yeare of his age, three and twentieth

A.U.C. 790.

of his Empire, and the seventeenth day before the Calends of Aprill [7]: when Cn. Acerronius Proculus and C. Portius Niger were Consuls. Some thinke that Caius [8] had given him a poyson of slow operation: which should by little and little consume him. Others are of opinion, that when hee desired meat in the remission of an ague fit wherein hee had swowned (it was denied him [9]) and therewith a pillow [10] throwne uppon his face to smudder him and stop his breath. Some againe, that it was when comming soone to himselfe, he called for his Ring which was plucked from his finger whiles he fainted. Seneca writeth that perceiving

---

[1] *Venas*, for *Arterias* by the trope *Catachresis*, for they onely beat.
[2] Who waited uppon him, or upon whom he leaned.   [3] *Valere dicentes*, or as they saluted him, after the Greeke phrase, *Chairein Kaieuprattein. Gaudere et bene rem gerere* — Horat.: All haile and faire cheere you.
[4] With full intent as it should seeme to bee revenged of the Senate.
[5] Or manner house.   [6] Of Lucullus, who either built it, or there dwelt.
[7] 16 of March.   [8] Caligula, Emperour after him.   [9] Some leave out this clause, and read thus, as he desired meat, etc., a pillow was, etc.
[10] Or cushin.

TWELVE CÆSARS

himselfe drawing on and readie to die[1], he tooke of his Ring, as if he minded to give it unto some one, and so held it a pretie while: then afterwardes did it uppon his finger againe: and so keeping down and griping close his left hand[2], lay still a long time without once stirring: but sodainely calling for his gromes and servitours, when none made aunswere, rose up, and not farre from his pallet, his strength failing him, fell downe dead.

TIBERIUS
NERO
CÆSAR

74

Upon the last Birth-dayes-feast of his that ever he saw, him thought as hee lay a sleepe, that Apollo Temenites (an Idol of exceeding bignesse and most artificially wrought) which was newly brought from Saracose to be set up in the librarie of his new temple, assured him, That he could not possibly by him be dedicated. And some few daies before his death, the watch-tower that gave light[3] at Capreæ by an earthquake fell downe in the night: and at Misenum, the ashes remaining of the embers and coales brought in to heate his refection parlour, being quenched quite and continuing cold a long time, suddainly brake forth into a light fire, at the shutting in of the evening, and so shone out a great part of the night and gave not over.

75

The people joyed so much at his death, that running up and downe at the first tidings thereof, some cried out in this note, '(Fling) Tiberius into Tiberis'[4]: others in their prayers besought the Mother Earth and the infernall Gods to vouchsafe him now dead no place, but among impious wretches: and a sort there were, who threatned his lifelesse carkasse the Drag and the *Gemonia*: as who, over and above the remembrance of his former cruelty in times past, were provoked to anger with a fresh outrage newly committed. For whereas by an Act of Senate it was provided, That the

---

[1] *Intellecta defectione.* Some expound this of the slinking away of his familiars and those that were about him. [2] Upon which he ware the ring. [3] Unto sea men and passengers by night. [4] *Tiberium in Tiberim.* Into Tiberis with Tiberius.

TWELVE CÆSARS

TIBERIUS NERO CÆSAR

execution of condemned persons should be put off unto the tenth day after (sentence given), it happened so, that the day on which some of them were to suffer, fell out to be the very same, wherein newes came of Tiberius death. These poore soules, notwithstanding they piteously called for mans help (because in the absence yet of Caius no man was known, who might (in such a case) be repaired unto and spoken with) the Gaolers, for that they would do nothing against the Constitution aforesaid strangled them and flung their bodies into the *Gemonia*. Heereupon, I say, the peoples hatred against him encreased, as if the Tyrants cruelty remained still after his death. His corpes, so soone as it began to bee removed from Misenum, notwithstanding the most part cried with one voice, To carie it rather to Atella[a], and there to half-burne it[b] in the Amphitheatre[c], yet was brought to Rome by the Soldiours and burnt in a publick funerall fire.

76

A two-fold will[1] he made two yeeres before: the one written with his own hand: the other by his freed-man: but both of them were of the same tenour: and signed he had them with the seales of most base persons. By vertue of which will and testament, he left coheires and equall in portion Caius his nephew by Germanicus, and Tiberius by Drusus. These he substituted and appointed to succeed one another. He gave legacies also to manie more, and among the rest unto the vestall Virgins, and to the Souldiers of all sorts in generall: as also to the commons of Rome by the poll: yea and to the Masters of everie Street by themselves severally.

[1] He meaneth I suppose a counterpaire indented.

ANNOTATIONS

ANNOTATIONS UPON
C. JULIUS CÆSAR DICTATOR

1

^a CAIUS CÆSAR, hee died sodainly at Pisæ in Italy, as hee put on his shooes in a morning, when hee was newe risen. Plin. *Natur. Hist.* lib. 7, c. 53.

^b *Flamen Dialis, i.* the great Priest of Jupiter. Three Flamens there were at Rome, by the first Institution: *Dialis* of Jupiter, *Martialis* of Mars, *Quirinalis* of Romulus; and these were the principall: unto whom (in processe of time) 12 more were adjoyned, attending all upon severall Godds and Goddesses. Carol. Sig. *de ant. Jure Rom.* lib. 1, cap. 19.

^c *Ut repudiaret.* In the civill Lawe, wee observe a difference betweene *Repudium* and *Divortium. Repudium*, when the man rejecteth and casteth off the woman betrothed only unto him before mariage in this forme, *Conditione tua non utor.* And in this wise Cæsar and Cossutia parted before. *Divortium*, when hee putteth her away after shee is his wedded wife, with these solemne words: *Res tuas tibi habeto*, or *Res tuas tibi agito.* Howbeit, in this place *Repudiare* is to be taken in this latter sense, for Cornelia was his wife, and had borne him a daughter. Paul. *Modestin Caius.*

^d I take it, that he meaneth such inheritances, as are not *Testamentariæ,* but *Legitimæ*: 1. Which when one dieth intestate, fall unto the children first, and for default of them, to the Agnati and Gentiles, *i.* to the next of kinne, and to the name. These are called with us, the Right heires at common Law. *Vide* Car. Sigon. *de Judiciis*, lib. cap. 4. *De antiq. jur. civ. Rom.* lib. 1, cap. 7.

^e The principall of them was, Cornelius Phagitas, a Freed man of Sulla, unto whom Cæsar gave two talents, for to escape his hands. See cap. 74, and Plutarchus.

^f It belonged unto these Votaries and Nunnes of Vesta, to goe betweene parties offended, and make reconciliation. See more hereof Alex. ab Alexandr. *Genial die*, lib. 5, cap. 12.

2

^a Young gentlemen of noble bloud, the better to bee trained up in martiall feats, and the knowledge of any Province affaires, were wont

TWELVE CÆSARS

CAIUS JULIUS CÆSAR

to attend the LL. Deputies there, and to be entertained with them in the same pavilion, as familiar companions. Cic. *orat. pro Cœlio et Plancio.*

[b] Libertines were such properly, as of bondmen were manumised and made Free, although Sueto. elsewhere, to wit in *Cl. Cæs.* nameth the children of such, Libertines; by which it appeareth that hee confoundeth them with *Ingenui, i.* Freeborne.

[c] Clients have a relation to their Patrones: and as these were *Patritii* and Nobles, so the other were Commoners. And such a mutuall and reciprocall entercourse of duetie was betweene them, that as the Patrons were ready to instruct in the knowledge of the lawes, to defend and protect their Clients, who had put themselves into their patronage: so these were bound to attende their Patrons when they went abroad into the city and returned home, to relieve them with their purse in the bestowing of their daughters etc. And lawfull it was for neither of them to enforme, to depose, to give their voices, or to side with adversaries, one against another, without the note and guilt of treachery and perfidious prodicion.

[d] Made of oken branches, or of Ilex, or Esculus, bearing mast, in defect of the Oke for saving the life of a citizen. Although Generals of the field were honoured therewith, in other respects.

3

[a] Who being Consull with Q. Catulus Luctatius, went about to repeale and anull all the Actes of Sulla late deceased, and so kindled a newe civill warre.

4

[a] By the death of Lepidus, whom his Colleague Catulus drave out of Italy into Sardinia, where he dyed, as some write, of a violent Rheume: or as others, with a deepe thought that he tooke, upon intelligence that he had of his wives adultery, in which melancholy he pyned away. Plutarch.

5

[a] These Tribunes Militarie, call them Colonels over a thousand footmen, whereupon they tooke that name first, to wit, when the Romaine Legion consisted of 3000 according to the three ancient Tribes, *Rhamnium, Lucerum* and *Tatiensium*: or High Marshals, as Budæus would have them to be, considering the execution of their office in the campe, not much unlike to our Kn. Marshals in these daies; some by vertue of an Act or Lawe preferred by Rutilus Rufus, were chosen in the Armie by the L. Generall, and named *Rutuli* or *Rufuli*, others by the voices of the people in their publick assemblyes for Elections called *Comitia,* and for distinction sake, named *Comitiati*. And such a Tribune Militarie was Cæsar in this place.

ANNOTATIONS

b *Rogatione Plotia.* A bill preferred, and the same as a Lawe not yet enacted, was called *Rogatio,* (as one would say) *Interrogatio*: for that the people were demaunded and asked their opinions in this forme of words: *Velitisné, jubeatisné Quirites,* etc. : Is it your will and pleasure, yee citizens of Rome, that such a thing should passe, or no? And of him who proposed the same, it tooke the name.

8

a By the Latine Colonies, are meant here those beyond the Po, which being before endowed *Latinitate, i.* with the freedome of Latium, stood not therwith contented, unlesse they might be *donati civitate, i.* enjoy the Franchises and Freedome of Rome.

10

a *Commitium* was one part of the *Forum Romanum,* wherein stood the *Rostra,* and the people used to assemble for election of Magistrates, for making of Lawes, and hearing of publike Orations.

11

a Sulla, in the time of his proscription and outlawing of the adverse faction of C. Marius, ordained two talents for every one that killed any of the proscribed and brought him his head, not sparing master or father : but that the servant might kill his master and the sonne his father ; nay hee made it death if they saved any such.
b Of Cornelius Sulla.

12

a T. Labienus. Cicero and Hortensius pleaded for him.
b For, to kill a Tribune of the Commons, who were *Sacrosancti* and *Inviolabili,* would beare the Action *Perduellionis.* And that was laide to Rabirius a Senatour his charge, although indeede hee slewe him not, but one Scava : mary, when he was killed, hee caused his head, in most ludibrious manner to be caried about.
Now was the crime *Perduellionis,* all one with treason against the Common wealth, or a principall person of State : or else Felonie in some high degree.
c The liberty of appealing unto the people, was graunted by Tullus Hostilius the third king of the Romaines, as appeareth by Livius, in the case of Horatius, for killing his owne sister.

13

a Q. Lutatius Catulus, and P. Servilius Isauricus.

15

a Cæsar envying such an honour unto Catulus, as to reedifie and dedicate the Capitol consumed with fire, a peece of worke that Sulla the Dictatour tooke in hand but finished not, and the onely thing

TWELVE CÆSARS

CAIUS
JULIUS
CÆSAR

wherby his felicity was not compleat, would have put him by it and conferred it upon another: and therefore put the matter in question before the bodie of the people, there to bee discussed and debated, whether it were their minde and will that Catulus should doe it, or some other.

b A Lawe is said to be promulged, after it is once proposed for to bee considered upon, untill it be fully enacted: during which time, reasons were alledged for the convenience thereof, or otherwise; and free it was for any man who had a voice to impugne or allowe it.

c *Optimates* and *Populares*, were in the citie of Rome opposite either against other, and are lively described by Cicero in his Oration, *pro Sextio*, in these wordes. *Duo genera in hac civitate semper fuerunt eorum, qui versari in rep. atque in ea se excellentius gerere studuerunt. Quibus ex generibus, alteri Populares, alter, Optimates et haberi et esse voluerunt. Qui ea quæ faciebant, quæque dicebant, multitudini jucunda esse volebant, Populares: qui autem ita se gerebant, ut sua consilia optimo cuique probarentur; Optimates habebantur. Item. Quis ergo est Optimas? quis? De numero si quæris innumerabiles, neque enim aliter stare possemus. Sunt principes consilii publici. Sunt qui eorum sectam sequuntur. Sunt maximorum Ordinum homines quibus patet Curia, Sunt municipes Rusticique; Roma, Sunt negotia gerentes, sunt etiam Libertini Optimates.* Wherby it appeareth, that those were counted *Optimates*, not simply of noble birth, and of great wealth, etc.: but were they *Patritii*, *Equites*, or *Plebeii*, if they stoode for good thinges, or favoured those that so did; nay, whether they were Burgesses of Free Burroughes, yeomen of the country following husbandry, Merchants and Tradesmen, or very Libertines, so they affected good causes, they were reckoned in the number of *Optimates*. On the other side, as many as aymed onely at this, to please and content the multitude, were they never so well borne or otherwise qualified, they went in the rancke of *Populares*; so that it seemeth, that *Populares* were the *Forensis factio*, that Livie writeth of, and whome Q. Fabius reduced all in to the foure *Tribus urbanas*; and *Optimates*, the *Tribus rusticæ*, wherein was *integer populus, fautor et cultor bonorum*. Thus much of the strickt signification of this worde *Optimates*. But for as much as commonly fewe of the Nobilitie and Gentry of Rome were Popular, and as fewe of the Communaltie favourers of the best things usually; by these *Optimates*, or the better sort, are ment the *Patritii* and Gentlemen.

d Upon the Kalends of January, *i.* the first day of the yeare, the Consuls entred their officie, on which day attended they were obsequiously by those better sort of the citizens and their friends, waiting upon them, when they went up into the Capitoll for to Sacrifice, and home againe. On this day likewise it appeareth, that Cæsar began his Pretorshipp.

16

a This purple Robe bordered, called *Prætexta*, was a Garment not proper to the Pretors onely, but to other Magistrates also. Em-

234

ANNOTATIONS

brodered it was or garded about with purple. For Plinie writeth, that Lentulus Spinter Ædile Curule, wore in his Robe, purple of a duble die, called thereupon, *Dibapha*. And thereupon it was called in Greek περιπόρφυρος. And not onely citie-Magistrates, but Priestes and children of gentle birth used the same. Setting aside the border of purple, it was otherwise white.

CAIUS JULIUS CÆSAR

b By *Curia* simply without any adjunction, is ment *Curia Hostilia*, as witnesseth Alex. ab Alexandro. *i.* A statly place built by K. Tullius Hostilius in the *Forum Romanum*, neere unto the *Rostra* : where, as in the Parliament house assembled the Senators ordinarily to consult upon the affaires of State. For, other places there were, under the name of *Curia*, wherein likewise the Senat met together, as *Curia Pompeii*, in which Cæsar was murdered, *Divi Augusti*, etc., but then they had their addition. I am not ignorant, that other *Curiæ* there were for the Pontifies and Priestes. To say nothing how the people was divided into *Curisa, id est*, Parishes, and in every of them was a *Curia*, and a superintendent or Curate called *Curio*.

17

a Superiour Magistrates, bee the Consuls, Pretours and Censors, the rest as Ædiles, Questors, were accounted inferiour, etc.

18

a Crassus is named for one, who entred into a bond for him of 830 talents, what time Cæsar deeply indebted, said, *bis millies et quingenties centena millia numum sibi adesse oportere, ut nihil haberet, id est*, that 250 millions of sesterces would but set him cleare with the world.

b By the Lawes, none might make suit for a tryumph, but whiles they remained absent without the citie, nor for a Consulship except they were present as private persons within the citie. In these streights, Cæsar made choyce to be Consul, and gave over his right to a triumph, for the victorie obteyned in Spaine over the Calleci and Lusitanes.

19

a The manner was at Rome, that they who sued for Magistracies should for the obteining of the peoples voices and suffrages make promise of certaine summes of money to be distributed amonge them, and such as were appointed to deale the saide Largesse, they called *Divisores*. Now, for that the Election of Consuls passed by *Comitia centuriata*, that is, by the assembly of the people, by their centuries or Hundreds according as Serv. Tullus first ordeyned them, therefore was this money to bee devided amongst them, as they gave their voices.

b Provinces signifie three things, the countries conquered or yeilded, and the same governed by Roman Deputies : and this is the proper and primative signification thereof, also the Region wherein any Roman Generall by commission from the state maketh warr : and last of all,

TWELVE CÆSARS

CAIUS JULIUS CÆSAR

what publick function or affaires soever is to be administred. In which sence it is heere taken.

^c Either for the cutting downe of trees for the best commodities. or els for a gaurd to be kept neare unto them, to suppresse the outrage committed by theeves, haunting the same and robbing and spoyling passengers.

^d To amend the waies and beaten pathes, where, either wayfairing men or beastes shoulde passe with more ease. And verily these were base matters and requiring no great forces to bee performed: and so by consequence, the Consuls employed therein could compasse no greate projects and therefore lesse to be feared.

^e This societie bred the Civill warre that after ensued, betweene Ceasar and Pompeius unto which the Poet Lucan alluded writing thus.

Tu causa malorum
Facta tribus dominis communis Roma.

20

^a As well to avoide tedious canvassings and consultations as to provide for the historie and memoriall of every matter.

^b One of the Consuls onely had the twelve Lictors going before him, with the rods and axes: to witt, each of them their moneths, by turnes one after the other, *Ne si ambo fusces haberent duplicatus terror videretur*. As Livie writeth: An ordinance as auncient well neere, as the first institution of Consuls.

^c Accensus, an officer attendant upon Magistrate, so named *ab acciendo, id est*, of giving summons to any for appearance, or of calling any to the Magistrate.

^d Great indulgences, immunities and priviledges were graunted by the Romanes unto those that had *jus trium liberorum*: but as Appian writeth more particularly to the explication of this place, there assembled 20000 together, craving maintenance and foode every man, for three children and more that they had.

^e Publicanes were they that either for a certaine rent tooke to ferme the publicke revenewes of the City, whether it were corne, pasturage, customes, impostes, etc., or undertooke by the grosse to make provision for the state, or to build and repaire any citie-workes, etc.

21

^a This was not *more maiorum*, for then his sentence should have bene demaunded first, that by the Censors was elected *Princeps Senatus, id est*, President of the Counsell: but extraordinarily, as appeareth by Aul. Gel. *Noct. Attic.* lib. 4, cap. 10, and lib. 14, cap. 7.

22

^a For as Livie testifieth, lib. 38. The Romanes triumphed oftener over the Gaules, than over all the world beside.

ANNOTATIONS

ᵇ Which Vatinius a Tribune of the Commons proposed in the behalfe of Julius Ceasar, that for five yeares together, hee should (without casting lots, and the Senates decree), governe Cisalpine Gaule, together with Illyricum : contrarie to the Lawe Sempronia, which provided that such Provinciall Governours, or LL. Deputies, should yearely bee chosen by the Senate. Carol. Sigon. lib. 2, cap. 1, *de antiquo jure provinciarum.*

CAIUS
JULIUS
CÆSAR

ᶜ Cisalpina Gallia, is that, which lay betweene Italy and the Alpes, divided into Cispadana and Transpadana, according to the site thereof, either on this side, or beyond the river Po : it caried the name likewise of Togata, either because it was much inhabited by the Romanes, or for that unto this Province the Romane Robe *Toga* was graunted, or els in regard that the saide Province was more civill and peaceable, than the other called Transalpina.

ᵈ Comata Gallia, a part of Gallia Transalpina, lying beyond the Alpes, from Italy toward Spaine : so called for the long haire that they wore : and συνεκδοχικῶς put for the whole Transalpine Province, like as Brachata, one part of the said Province, so called of a certaine kinde of apparell, is taken for the whole and confounded with Comata.

ᵉ This terme, which they commonly use, who threaten such as they contemne, may bee drawen to an obsceene and filthy sense, not heere to bee named : and albeit Ceasar hereby was galled to the quick, as privie to himselfe, of the passive abuse of his body with K. Nicomedes, yet in his answere thereto, he turned it to another signification.

ᶠ Warlike women, so called (as some write) of their paps which they did cut off and sear, therby to bee more expedite and nimble in fight, and to shoot at greater ease. See Strabo, Justin. Q. Curtius, Herodotus, etc.

23

ᵃ For, if his Questour or Treasurer had beene condemned, it would have beene a shrewde precedent for his conviction also in the same cause.

24

ᵃ Who stoode in Election for the Consulshippe : so called of the whited robe, which they put on, who sued for such Magistracies and places of Honour. For whereas the ordinarie gowne that Romaine citizens daily wore, was white of it selfe, against such a time they made it whiter with chalke : so that a difference there was betweene *Toga alba,* and *candida,* whereupon they were called *Candidati,* as appeareth by Macrobius, and T. Livius, lib. 4 *ab urb. condita.*

ᵇ Supplication, was a solemne Honour done unto the Lord Generall of a Province upon some notable victorie. For the manner was, that LL. Governours, after they were by their Souldiers salute by the name of Emperour, *i.* Soveraigne commanders, should send their Letters dight with Lawrell unto the Senate, wherin they required both to be stiled by the saide name, and also to have solemne processions made by

TWELVE CÆSARS

CAIUS
JULIUS
CÆSAR

the people in the Temples, and thanksgiving unto the Gods for their good successe, which solemnity, at the first continued but one day, as T. Livius reporteth in the 304 yeare after the foundation of Rome: but processe of time, it grewe to 4 and 12. And at length, Ceasar obtained it for 15, yea and 20 daies together, as Plutarch testifieth in his life, and himselfe in his owne *Comentaries*, of the Gauls warre.

26

ᵃ *Super HS. millies*. This character HS. standeth for a Silver coyne in Rome, which is the three halfe pence, farthing, cue, the 4 part of *Denarius* : and is called *Sextertius quasi sesquitertius* : as one would say, valuing two brasen Asses and the halfe of a third : so common a peece of money there, that *Numus* put absolutely alone, standeth for it and no other coine : so that *Millies sestertium* and *millies nummum* are both one. Now if the Romaine Denier bee valued at vii d. *ob.* with us, and 100 Deniers arise to one pound starling : this summe here set downe, that is to say, a Sesterne multiplyed by the Adverbe *Millies*, amounteth by just account unto 781250 li. starling. And thereto for the overdeale or surplusage *ducenties sestertium*, which is one 5 part of the former summe, it maketh up 937500 li. sterling. A thing that may be thought incredible, but that we reade that Ceasar himselfe saide, hee was 250 millions in debt when he went into Spaine, and P. Clodius, whom Milo slewe, dwelt in a house, the purchase whereof cost him almost 15 millions. No marvell therefore, if so many houses, which Cæsar must needs buy for the plot of ground aforesaid and in so populous a city, cost not so little as a hundred millions.

27

ᵃ The dole given by a Prince or great man unto the people, was properly called a Congiarie, which word tooke name of the measure *Congius* among the Romaines, consisting of 6 *Sextarii*, and is answerable to our gallon : by which Oyle or wine was given. Howbeit καταχρηστικῶς, any such publicke munificence, in mony or otherwise is so called : and in this place, by it are ment other gifts bestowed upon private persons.

28

ᵃ In some copies, wee reade, *Quando nec plebisicito Pompeius postea abrogasset*. To this sence : That Cæsar beeing absent, was not eligible by vertue of an Act made by Pompeius to that effect, considering he had not abrogated the same by any ordinance of the people, but onely of his owne authority corrected it after it stood upon record in the city chamber.

30

ᵃ This hath reference unto his violent dealing with his fellowe Consull Bibulis. See before in the 20 chapter.

ANNOTATIONS

33

ᵃ The fourth finger next unto the little one, honoured especially with a golde ring, for that there is an evident arterie from the heart reaching unto it. Gellius. But Plinie alledgeth another reason.

ᵇ He would doe any thing rather than his souldiers so well deserving at his hands, should not bee satisfied: such a credit caried the ring upon a Romaines finger.

ᶜ Which is the State and worth of a Romaine knight or gentleman according to this verce of Horace: *Si quadringintis sex, septem millia desint, Plebs eris*, etc., and amounteth to 3125 li. starling.

34

ᵃ As if Petreius, Afranius, and Varro had no skill in martiall feats.

ᵇ He meaneth Cn. Pompeius, for his militarie knowledge and warlike exploytes surnamed *Magnus, i.* the Greate: whose principall power was now overthrowne at Ilerda in Spaine.

37

ᵃ *Lychnuchos Gestantibus*, bearing either young men that caried Linckes, Torches, and cresset lights: or els braunches and candle stickes, resembling them, and holding the said lights. Some reade, *Lychnos gestantibus, i.* bearing lights: but to the same affect.

38

ᵃ *Super bina HS., i. Sestertia*: that is to say, 15 li. 12s. 6d.

ᵇ *Quaterna Sestertia, i.* 31 li. 5s.

ᶜ *Vicena quaterna millia*, 187 li. 10s. By which reckning, hee gave unto horsemen foure times as much as to footemen. Looke in the marginall note to the text, and you shall finde this donative much more: which may seeme incredible: but consider what provinces hee spoyled, and what pillage hee made, in regard whereof hee was called of the Greekes χρηματυποιὸς ἀνήρ.

ᵈ *Denos modios*, in round reckoning may goe for ten peckes or hoopes with us.

ᵉ *Totidem libras, i.* so many pynts, with the better.

ᶠ *Trecenos nummos, i.* 46s. 10d. ob. ⎱ Which being put together make 100 *Denarii* or Drachemes, that
ᵍ *Centenos, i.* 15s. 7d. ob. ⎰ is, one *Mina*, and amount in all to 3 li. 2s. 6d.

ʰ *Bina millia nummorum, i.* 15 lib. 12s. 6d.

ⁱ *Quingenos sestertios, i.* 3 l. 18s. 1d. ob.

39

ᵃ *Regionatim urbe tota.* Rome, as Plinie witnesseth, was divided into 14 regions, and every one of these had their severall Stage Playes by themselves.

TWELVE CÆSARS

CAIUS
JULIUS
CÆSAR

^b The Games *Circenses*, I take to be so called of the Greet Cirque or Shewplace, wherein they were performed: and not of swordes, wherewith they were environed, as one would say, *Circa enses*. Indeede these games resembled the Olympick in Greece by Elis, where the runners with chariots were hemmed in of the one side with the running river, and of the other with swordes pitched pointwise, that they should hold on the race directly, and not swerve aside without danger. Herein were performed running with horses and chariots, justing, tilt, and turnement: baiting and chasing of wild beasts, etc.

^c *Pyrrhica:* Of some, thought to bee the same that *Enoplia* was, a kinde of Moriske daunce, after a warlike manner in harnois, devised in Creta first by Pyrrhus. Plin. lib. 7 *Nat. Hist.* cap. 56. In which young gentlemen were trained to exercise all parts of the body by sundry gestures as well to avoide all venues and defende themselves, as to annoy and offend the enimie.

^d This Decimus Laberius was a poet also, that kind which wrote wanton Poems or lascivious Comœdies called *Mimi*. For, howsoever in all Stage Playes, there is represented a lively imitation in gesture and voice of others, yet in these *Mimi*, these same are done after a more licentious manner and without all modest reverence, even in unseemely and filthy arguments: as Ovid testifieth in these words, *imitantes turpia Mimi.* It seemeth therefore, that as well the Poemes as the Authours and Actours be called *Mimi*.

^e *Orchestra*, is here taken for the most commodious place in the Theatre, wherein the Senators and Nobles of Rome were allowed to sit and behold the Stage Playes, apart from the people. For so the Poet Juvenal understandeth it in these words, *Similemque videbis Orchestram et populum*.

As touching this *Orchestra* and the Poet Laberius above named, Seneca in his second booke of *Controversies*, and third controversie, reporteth thus. Julius Cæsar, at the solemnitie of his Playes, brought Laberius forth to act upon the Stage: and when he had made him a gentleman, or Knight of Rome, willed him to take his place among them of that degree, but as he came toward them, they all sat so close and neere one another, that there was no rowme for him. Now by the way, you must understand that Cicero then in place, had gotten himselfe an ill name, for that hee was no fast and faithfull friend, either to Pompeius, or to Ceasar, but a flatterer of them both. Againe, Cæsar at that time had chosen many unto the range of Senatours, partly to supply and make up their number, which during the late civill warres was much diminished, and in part to gratifie those who had well deserved of him and the side. Cicero therefore alluding to the extraordinary number of newe Senatours, sent unto Laberius as hee passed by, this word merily, *Recepissem te nisi angustè sederem, i.* I would have taken you to mee and give you a place, but that I sit my selfe very streight. Then Laberius returned this pleasant answere backe unto him, *Atqui solebas duabus sellis sedere, i.* And yet you

ANNOTATIONS

were wont to sit upon two stooles, skoffing at him for his double dealing with Pompeius and Ceasar.

ᶠ The Troy fight, was in warlike manner on horsbacke, brought by Æneas into Italy. The manner whereof is described by Virgil, *Æneid*, 5.

ᵍ These Goales called in Latine *Metæ*, above which the horses and chariots ranne, were in fashion broad beneath and sharpe above, in manner of Pyramides, Steeples or cocks of hey, and for their mater, of wood first, or of soft gritstone, but afterwards of marble and laid over with gold. Concerning this Cirque why Cæsar enlarged it and brought water round about it, reade Plinie, 8 lib. cap. 7 and 36 lib. cap. 15 *Naturall Hist.*

ʰ To try maisteries in footemanshippe, leaping, flinging the coit or hammer, darting and wrestling: which Game was called Pentathlon, of those five kindes of exercises.

ⁱ *In minore Codeta*, which was a place on the further side of Tiberis, so called of certaine plots of young springs or shootes there growing which resemble horsetailes. Some reade *In morem cochleæ*, that is, narrow beneath and broad above, like to the shell of a periwincle or such like fish.

40

ᵃ This day is called *Bissextus*, and falleth out to bee the fift day before the end of Februarie, to wit, the sixt before the Calends of March, by interposing whereof wee say twise Sext Calend *Martii*, of which day our leape yeare hath the name *Bissextilis*.

41

ᵃ Which by the first institution were 300, and by occasion of the late troubles much impaired.

ᵇ *Patritios allegit.* For those that were *Plebei generis*, might bee Senatours: or els, as some expound it, he advanced divers to the degree and ranck of the *Patritii*.

ᶜ All but Consuls, Prætors and Censors, were counted inferiour Magistrates.

ᵈ For the Censors with the publicke Notaries ordinarily tooke this reviewe, and that in *Campus Martius*, and *Villa publica*.

ᵉ By reason of so great a number receiving corne from the State, the purveyance hereof stoode the city yearely as Plutarch writeth in a thousand two hundred and fiftie talents.

42

ᵃ For they might discontinue out of Italy eleven yeares. Plutarch.

ᵇ Such were called *Comites*, or *quasi ex cohorte Prætoria*, as it were gentlemen of the privie chamber.

ᶜ *Noverum tabularum.* To wit, when the olde bonds being cancelled, and therby former debts remitted, new obligations were made.

TWELVE CÆSARS

CAIUS JULIUS CÆSAR

^d *Parricidis, i. Parenticidis,* such as kill father, mother, brother, sisters and such like, nere in bloud, as also, any other man or woman wilfully, according to the Lawe of K. Nume, *Si quis hominem liberum sciens monti duit parricida esto.*

43

^a *Repetundarum convictos.* Such governours as by way of extortion pilled and polled the Provinces which they ruled: who after their time expired, were many times called judicially to their answeres.

^b Many Lawes there were called *Sumptuariæ* and *Cibariæ*, to restraine the excesse at the table, as namely Fannia, Licinia, Æmilya, Julia, etc. Read Aul. Gell. *Noct. Att.* lib. 2, cap. 24, Macro. *Saturnal.* lib. 3.

44

^a Of whom Terentianus writeth thus, *Vir doctissimus undecunque Varro.*

^b Isthmus is a narrow straite or foreland by Corinth, five miles over, lying betweene the two seas Ionium and Ægeum, or as Plinie writeth, lib. 4, cap. 4, betweene the two Gulfes Corinthiacus and Saronicus. The cutting through whereof, was attempted before by K. Demetrius, and afterwards by C. Caligula and Nero, but without effect.

^c Which Crassus before him had not done; and therefore was overthrowne.

45

^a *Comitiali Morbo*, so called, for that the assemblies of the people called *Comitia*, were dissolved and broke up by occasion thereof, in case any one among them fell downe of that disease, according as Q. Serenus Semonicus hath testified in these verses, cap. 57.

> *Est morbi species subiti, cui nomen ab illo est,*
> *Quod fieri nobis suffragia justa recusant.*
> *Sæpe etenim membris acri languere caducis,*
> *Concilium populi labes horrenda diremit.*

As also for that, they who were subject thereto, fell into a fit thereof ordinarily at such assemblyes, if they were crossed in their suites and businesses there. Cornelius Celsus calleth it *Morbum maiorem, i.* a great sicknesse. It is named likewise ἱερὸν νόσημα, *i.* the sacred disease, either because it affecteth the heade, which is the most honorable place of the body and the seate of the Soule, or in regard of the greatnesse thereof, which the Græcians express by the ἱερόν. Also *Epilepsia*, for the sodaine invasion of it. *Herculeus Morbus*, either for the strength of the malady, whereby a man is forced to fall, or because Hercules was troubled therewith. Plinie nameth it, *Senticus*, for the hurt that it doth unto the bodie: others *Caducus*, for that upon it, men fall to the ground. It is called moreover *Lunaticus*, of the Moone: because it keepeth time with the course of the Moone, or apprehendeth

ANNOTATIONS

them that are borne in the change thereof, as the same Serenus reporteth in these verses:

CAIUS
JULIUS
CÆSAR

Huc quoque commemorant dubiæ per tempora Lunæ,
Conceptum talem, quem sæpe ruina profudit.

Lastly Hippocrates nameth it *Pædicon, i. puerilem morbum,* for that children bee subject thereto: whereupon some tearme it, *Mater puerorum.*

ᵇ This manner of going so loosely girt, might signifie a dissolute and effeminate wanton. Hereupon Cicero made choyce in the civill warre to take part with Pompeius against Ceasar: and when one asked him how it came to passe, that in siding with Pompeius hee was so much overseene, for that hee had the worse, this answere hee made, *Præcinctura me decepit, i.* deceived I was by that loose girding of his.

49

ᵃ Cæsar derived his pedegree from Jülus, the sonne of Æneas, whose mother was Venus.

ᵇ The grace which is in the Latine cannot be expressed well in English, because the word, *Subegit,* carieth a double sence, the one signifieth the conquering of a nation, and so it is taken in the former place, as it is applyed to Gaule: the other, the wanton abuse of the bodie: in which acception it is to bee understood in reference to Ceasar, abused by K. Nichomedes.

50

ᵃ In the twofold sense likewise of these two words, *Tertia* and *Deducta,* lyeth the pleasant grace of this conceipted speech.

By the one, may be understoode, that a third part of the price was deducted: by the other Cicero ment, That her daughter Tertia was brought by her to his bed.

51

ᵃ This Distichon, or ii verses, which his souldiers after their licentious manner in the Tryumph chaunted may thus be Englished.

Looke to your wives, yee cytizens, a lecher bald wee bring.
In Gaule Adultery cost thee gold, heere 'tis but borrowing.

For, as hee borrowed of other men, so hee lent or paide as much againe, in that his owne wife Pompeia, as is thought, was kept by P. Clodius.

52

ᵃ Such a vessell as this named here *Thelamegos,* and by Seneca, 7 lib. *de Beneficiis, Naviscubiculata,* Ptolomæus Philopater, as witnesseth Athenæus, had, which caried in length halfe a furlong¹, in bredth 30 cubites, and in heigth little lesse then 40.

¹ *Semistadium.*

TWELVE CÆSARS

CAIUS JULIUS CÆSAR

^b *Impudicitiæ.* I observe, that both in this Authour and also in other approved writers, *Impudicitia*, is properly and peculiarly taken for that abhominable uncleannesse onely, which is named Sodomie: like as *Pudicitia*, for the integritie of the bodie, and clearenesse from that detestable filthinesse. And so, *Pudicus* and *Impudicus* are to bee understoode.

54

^a Which commeth to 23 pound, 8 shillings, 9 pence, and is not much more than halfe the worth. According to Budeus it was 7 pound *dim* of Silver for one of Gold.

^b For it was esteemed a great honour to be called Allies and Associates, or stiled Kings, by the people of Rome.

56

^a *Anticatones.* Whereas Cicero had written in the prayse of Cato (*Uticensis*) he wrote two bookes against the said Cato, which he called *Anticatones.*

61

^a Venus, surnamed Genitrix, *i.* Mother, Cæsar honoured, as the goddesse from the which he was descended, by Jülus or Ascanius, her nephew.

62

^a The principall ensigne or standerd of the Romane Legion was an Ægle of Silver, reared upon a Speare toppe, the poynt whereof beneath was sharpe, and fastened into the ground: and the same stood within a little shrine, not to bee remooved, but when the Armie was on foote.

64

^a Dion, lib. 42, and Appian, *Civil.* 2, report this otherwise: namely, that he forsoke the said Coat armour (it clogged him so much), and so the Ægyptians got it.

68

^a *E viatico suo.* Albeit *viaticum* properly signifyeth the store and provision set by for a journey, yet heere it is put for the wealth and the substance of a souldier: like as in Horat. lib. 2, *Epist.* 2.

*Luculli miles collecta viatica multis
Aerumnis,* etc.

In which sense, ἐφίδιον likewise in Greeke is taken.

^b Plinie calleth it *Lapsana*, lib. 19, cap. 8, *Natural. Histor.* A kinde of wilde worte or cole.

^c To be tithed, *i.* everie tenth man to suffer death. Appian.

^d Which ordinarily consisted of 550 footemen, and 66 horse,

ANNOTATIONS

whereof ten went to a Legion. Some, I wot well had more, some fewer. But for this place it may suffice, that it was the tenth part of a Legion.

CAIUS JULIUS CÆSAR

70

a *Quirites, i.* Romane Citizens. As freed now from their alleageance, which by their military oath they were bound unto.

71

a Which was a great abuse offered, among the Barbarians, who set great store by their beards, and suffered them to grow very long.

76

a *Thensa* or *Tensa et ferculum*, a Chariot of Silver or Yvorie, with a frame in it sustaining the Images of the gods, which was drawn in most solemne and stately manner unto the Pulvinar.
b *Pulvinar.* A bed loft, or place where certaine rich beds were made for the said Images to be laid upon.
c *Flamin.* A certaine priest, bearing the name of that god, for whose service he was instituted. As *Dialis* of Jupiter, *Martialis* of Mars, *Quirinalis* of Romulus, etc. Cic. 2 *Phil.* saith that M. Antonius was Flamen to Julius Cæsar.
d *Luperci*, were certaine young men, who at the licentious feast, *Lupercalia*, instituted to the honour of Pan Lycæus, otherwise called Inuus, by Romulus and Remus, ran up and downe naked in the Citie of Rome. A new kind of these *Luperci* ordained Cæsar, of his owne name called *Juliani.* At this feast *Lupercalia*, M. Antonius played the part of a Lupercus, at which solemnitie, when Cæsar sat in a Throne of Gold, arayed in a purple robe, the said M. Antonius attempted to doe upon his head the royall Band, called a Diademe. Cicero.
e Whereas, before it was called *Quintilis*, he named it *Julius.*
f This was Caninius Rebitus: of whose Consulship, there go divers jestes, as namely these, whereof Cicero was the Author. A vigilant Consull we have had of Caninius, who in all his Consulship never slept winke. Also, A consull we have had so severe and Censar-like, as that during his Consulship, no man dined, no man supped, no man so much as once slept. Likewise Pithalus said of him, Heretofore we had *Flamines Diales*, and now wee have Consuls *Diales*, playing upon the æquivocation or double sense of the word *Dialis*, which being derived of Διός, *i.* Jupiter, signifieth his *Flamin*: but of *Dies, i.* a day, betokeneth a day Consul or *Flamin.*

77

a According to Lucane, *Omnia Cæsar erat.* Cæsar was all in all.
b Well knowne it is that Sulla was passing well learned both in Greeke and Latine. But in that he resigned up the absolute power of his Dictatorship, which he tooke upon him, for an hundred and

TWELVE CÆSARS

CAIUS JULIUS CÆSAR

twentie yeares, that is to say, for ever; Cæsar said he was no Gramarian, *quia nescivit dictare, quod munus est Grammatici*: alluding to the ambiguous word *dictare*, *i.* to endite, or give precepts as Grammarians doe to their schollers, as also, to commaund absolutely, whereof it may seeme that Dictator tooke the name.

78

a Who were in number 10.

b Or, if I may for Pontius Aquila: spoken by way of a scornefull *Ironia*.

79

a *Plebeio*, and not *Plebi*, for the commons could not endure that name, as may appeare by Ciceroes words in his second *Philippica* or invective against M. Antonius: Thou shewedst the Diademe. The people all over the common place gave a groane thereat. Thou wert about to set it upon his head, to the great griefe and sorrow of the people, hee rejected it, with as great joy and applause of theirs.

b The name Optimus Maximus, wherewith the auncients styled Jupiter, signifieth most bountifull and most powerfull: wherein it is observed that Bountie goeth before Power: because as M. Tullius writeth, it is better and more acceptable to doe good unto all, then to have power over all.

c In Ægypt: a renowmed Citie, built by King Alexander the Great: for the pleasant site much commended, and therefore might bee affected by Cæsar: at which, there is no day almost through the yeare, but the Inhabitants behold the Sunne shining cleare upon them: and which Ammianus calleth *Verticem omnium civitatum*, *i.* The chiefe of Cities.

d Ilium, a Citie where Troy stood: the Citizens whereof, as Strabo writeth, Cæsar in memoriall of his progenitors from thence descended, and namely, from Jūlus or Ascanius the Sonne of Æneas, had indowed with many franchises and immunities, and therefore it caried some likelihood, that he ment there to make his abode.

e These *Quindecim-viri*, or fifteene men, were instituted in the daies of Cornelius Sylla with this addition *Sacrorum*: unto whose charge it appertained to see that Sacrifices and Divine service, that supplications, and processions, expiations, and ceremoniall rites should bee duely performed, as also to peruse the bookes and prophesies of Sibylla. At first they were but two, called *Duumviri*, afterwards x. under the name of *Decemviri sacris faciendis*. Alex. ab Alex. lib. 3, *Genial. dierum*. cap. 16.

80

a *Bonum factum*. A forme of preface which in olde time they use, *boni omnis causa*, before their Edictes and decrees, etc., so commonly, as that these two Capital letters B. F. did betoken the same as ordinarily, as S. C. stand for *Senatus consultum*. It had the same use, as *In nomine Dei* with us.

ANNOTATIONS

ᵇ Some take these *Brachæ*, whereof Brachata Gallia, a part of Transalpine Gaule, tooke name, for frize rugges striped with sundrie colours, which may resemble Irish mantles; but I suppose them to be a kinde of course breches, much like to the Irish trousses, but that they are more full.

ᶜ By rising up unto him, and shouting or applauding as he passed along.

ᵈ *Utinam viveres.*

ᵉ   *Brutus quia Reges ejecit consul primus factus est:*
    Hic, quia consules ejecit, Rex postremò factus est.

ᶠ Certaine bridges there were for the time made, upon which the Tribes passed when they gave their voyces in *Campus Martius*, at their solemne Leets and assemblies for Election of Magistrates.

81

ᵃ Some take it to bee the same that Regulus, or Trochilus, thought to be the Wren, and is likewise named King of Birdes, in Greeke βασιλεύς, ominous therefore unto Cæsar, seeking to be king.

82

ᵃ This is diversly reported by authors. The occasion of which varietie ariseth upon the affinitie of these names, Cassius and Casca. For as there were two Cassii at this action, so likewise were there two Servilii brethren, both surnamed Casca. By Alter Cassius or Casca, therefore, you may understand one of the two brethren, or the second of them. For some write, that the one Casca gave him in the necke a wound, but not deadly, whereupon Cæsar caught hold of his dagger, crying out, *Scelerate Casca quid agis?* i. What meanest thou, O wicked Casca? and then Casca called unto his brother for helpe, who came in, and gave him his deathes wound, in the breast under the chanell bone. Plutarch.

ᵇ Albeit, *Graphium* doth signifie a writing punch (or steele or wier), otherwise called *Stylus*, wherewith they wrote in hard matter, as wood, or barke, before the use of our parchment and paper, as also our pen made of a quill or other substance, as brasse, etc., in which sense it is taken in that verse of Ovid, *Amor. lib. 1, Eleg. 11*:

   Quid digitos opus est graphium lassare tenendo?

And probable it is that Cæsar sitting in counsell was not without such a writing instrument: yet both Dominicus Marius upon the foresaid verse, and Perottus also the author of *Cornucopia*, expounding this place of Suetonius, takes *Graphium, pro pugiunculo*, i. a little poyniard, poinado, or pocket dagger. And hapely therwith Cæsar wounded Cassius or Casca (whether you will) being more readie at hand, hanging at his girdle, than the style or steele aforesaid, which by all likelihood was yet in the case or sheath, called *Graphiarium*,

CAIUS
JULIUS
CÆSAR

TWELVE CÆSARS

CAIUS JULIUS CÆSAR

considering Cæsar was but new set. But I leave the exposition of this place, *in medio.*

c Valerius Max. under the title of *Verecundia,* commendeth this maydenlike modestie of Cæsar, who notwithstanding that he was maskared with 23 wounds, for manhood sake forgot not to hide his nakednesse, and to die in decent manner: but as Euripides writeth of the virgin Ladie Polixena.

πολλὴν πρόνοιαν ἔσχεν δυσχήμως πεσεῖν.

Where, by the way it may be noted, that the Romanes wore not trusses or breches, as we doe, to cover those inferior and secret parts.

d This may have reference to that which is reported before, how in his youth, he loved Servilia, the mother of this Brutus: for his age falleth out to agree fitly with that time: in so much as he was commonly thought to be a sonne of his. And yet this attribute *Fili,* may sort well with the familiaritie that was betweene them.

Some read Καί σὺ εἶς ἐκείνων, *i.* And art thou one of them?

83

a *Virgini Vestali Maximæ.* That Nun or Vestall virgin, who in age and dignity excelled the rest, and was the Mistresse as it were, and governesse of them, they called *Maxima*: much like unto the Ladie Abbesse or Prioresse in our daies.

84

a The argument whereof was the deciding of the contention betweene Ajax and Ulysses, about Achilles Armor.

b For, some of these who tooke part with Pompeius, he had pardoned.

c *Quicquid præterea ad manum aderat.* Others read, *ad donum aderat*: understanding thereby those giftes which they brought as offerings to his Ghost, and be called *Inferiæ.*

88

a Which is counted one of the Climacterich years, in which it falleth out that 7 is multiplied by 8, which two numbers, as Cicero hath observed, 6 *de Rep.*, be complete. A revolution fatal to Scipio Africanus the yonger, to Virgil also and Plinie.

b Appian writeth, that it was in a sodaine uprore of the people burnt to the ground.

c To signifie, that upon that day, The father of his countrie was killed.

ANNOTATIONS

OCTAVIUS
AUGUSTUS
CÆSAR

ANNOTATIONS UPON
OCTAVIUS AUGUSTUS CÆSAR

3

ᵃ *Inter divisores, operasque campestres.* This was thought to bee but a base occupation, namely, to give among the Tribes, such sums of money as the *Candidati,* or those that stood in election for offices promised and pronounced for the buying of voices. The name also grew to be odious, howsoever Plautus in *Aulul.* calleth them *Magistros Curiæ.* Likewise all such servitours as otherwise gave attendance in *Campo Martio,* and thereby gat a living, whom he termeth here *operas campestres,* were but of meane reckoning.

5

ᵃ *Regione Palatii.* In old time Rome was divided into foure principall regions or quarters: *Suburrana, Equilina, Collina,* and *Palatina.*

ᵇ The manner in old time was, that the newe borne babe should be set up on the bare ground to cry and call upon the Goddesse Ops, who so gently had received it. And the Goddesse forsooth, that helped to lift it up againe, was called Levana, *i. a Levando.* Augustin. Macrob.

8

ᵃ The Virile robe was the ordinary Romane gowne, all white without purple, which they wore when they came to be past 16 yeares of age.

ᵇ To wit, bracelets, chaines and collars, Speare staves without iron heads, trappings, chaplets and guirlands, etc.

ᶜ This was the Triumvirate, so much spoken of: during which, M. Antonius, M. Lepidus, and Augustus ruled joyntly together.

12

ᵃ Marcus Brutus.

ᵇ Hee meaneth Cicero, as appeareth by an Epistle of D. Brutus unto Cicero in these words, *Narravit mihi, etc., ipsum Cæsarem (Augustum) nihil sane de te questum nisi dictum quod diceret, te dixisse laudandum adolescentem, ornandum, tollendum : se non commissurum ut tolli possit.* In which words, as also in this place of Tranquillus, there is an æquivocation or doubtfull sense in this Verbe *Tollendum*: which in one signification, is in manner æquivalent with *laudandum* and *ornandum*; and betokeneth, to bee advanced, extolled, or lifted up: and so is to be taken in good part: but in another, it is all one with *tollendum de*

TWELVE CÆSARS

OCTAVIUS AUGUSTUS CÆSAR

medio, or *occidendum, id est*, to be dispatched out of life : or killed. In which sense Cicero ment it, and Augustus tooke it, namely in ill part. Much like to this, you shall reade in Nero, *sustulit hic matrem, sustulit ille patrem*. The grace lieth in the ambiguitie of the Latine word *tollendum*, which cannot in English be so well delivered.

13

ᵃ The *Egnatii*, as Appian witnesseth.

14

ᵃ Which by the Lawe Julia, *Theatralis*, and Roscia, were allowed for the knights or Gentlemen of Rome, whose estate was valued not under 400000 Sesterces. The lawes abovesaid, were promulged by Augustus Cæsar, and L. Roscius Otho a Tribune of the Commons. And these 14 Seates named *Equestria* were the next unto the stage after the *Orcestra* arising by degrees and staires, as it were higher and higher, and so farther of. Above which in the upper and more remote scaffolds sat the common people, and thereupon they were called *Popularia*. Howbeit, for all the lawe Roscia, many Commoners of good wealth and credit, used to sit indifferently in the said 14 formost seats, untill the other Lawe Julia was enacted, which distinguished the orders more precisely. Carol. Sigon. *De Antiq. Jur. Civ. Rom.* lib. 2, cap. 19.

16

ᵃ When in stately Pompe, the sacred chariot *Thensa*, with the images of the Gods in it, was devoutly drawen according to the solemne manner.

ᵇ A coast-towne of Italy affronting Sicile, from whence it is a very short cut over sea : so called by the Greekes, as if even there a breach was made by the sea, dividing Italie from Sicilie which before time was a part of the continent or mainland : and no mervaile of that Name : since that Maritime Region, wherein Locri stood, was in times past called *Magna Græcia*.

ᶜ In that hee put downe in his will the children which he had by Cleopatra a stranger and barbarian borne, which also were begotten in bastardie, as well as if they had beene naturall Romanes and legitimate, hee faulted in common civilitie, but much more, when hee proceeded to call the sonnes that he had by her, Reges Regum, *i.* the King of Kings. As absurd also and immodest hee shewed himselfe, when having by her at one birth two twinnes, the male infant he surnamed Sol, *i.* the Sunne, and the Femall, Lunà, *i.* the Moone.

ᵈ In the custodie of the Vestall Nunnes, or Votaries, as Julus Cæsar had done before him : of such integritie and so good conscience they were thought to be, as things of greatest weight were committed unto them in trust.

ᵉ This forename, Titus cannot truly be given to any of the *Domitii*, if that bee true which is written of them afterward in Domitius Nero, cap. 1.

ANNOTATIONS

^f But in the behalfe of M. Antonius, considering he was their Patrone and Protector. For other foraiu States and Cities usually were shrouded under the favour of Gentlemen at Rome. In which regard, he laid not to their charge that they had not sided with himselfe, but rather taken part with their Patron Antonii: considering that nere bond wherewith such Protectors and Clients or Dependents were linked together: which Dionysius supposeth to bee almost as ancient as Rome it selfe, and almost æquall to that of Allies, yea and kinsfolke in bloud.

OCTAVIUS AUGUSTUS CÆSAR

^g A Promontorie or Cape in Epirus, shooting into the Bay Ambracium, in the view whereof the sumptuous Armada of Antonie and Cleopatra was defaited.

17

^a These Psylli are people in Affricke supposed to have bodies of a singular vertue to kill serpents, as also a speciall skill in sucking foorth venome out of the wound made by their sting. Yet Cornelius Celsus, lib. 5, cap. 27, is of opinion, that they have no principall gift or cunning in this feate above other men, but more boldnesse rather, confirmed by use and practise. For the venome of a serpent, saith hee, hurteth not by being tasted, but as it is infused by a wound, which he proveth by those poysons that the French use especially in hunting. And therefore a verie Snake or Adder it selfe, may bee eaten safely, how ever the sting is deadly: and if whiles it lyeth astonied or benummed (the cast wherof these Monte-bankes or juglers have by meanes of certaine medicines) one put his finger into the mouth thereof, and be not bitten or stung withall, there is no spettle or slimie humours there to doe harme. So that whosoever else, by example of these Psylli shall sucke any wound inflicted by a Serpent, he shall doe it safely, and cure besides, the party that is stung. Provided alwaies, that hee have no sore or ulcer, in gummes, palate, or any part of his limmes.

^b Some thinke this kinde of Aspis which shee used, was *Pytas*, others *Hypnale*[1]; for that the sting brought drowsinesse upon her: and Lucane called it *Aspida Somniferam*. But common it is unto all the sortes to kill by sleepe and stupefaction without paine, some sooner, some later: but all within the space of 6 houres: so that *Hypnale* may seeme to be a generall attribute to them all.

18

^a As if hee counted those Ptolemees dead, who left no memorable actes behinde them: and Alexander, a King still, or worthie alone to be called King, whose memoriall was yet so fresh and lively.

19

^a For that one of his parentes was a Parthine, that is to say, a stranger of Illyricum, and the other a Romane.

[1] Solinus.

TWELVE CÆSARS

OCTAVIUS
AUGUSTUS
CÆSAR

20

a. Warres take the name of those that bee vanquished. As, *Gallicum bellum*, *Germanicum*, *Dalmaticum*, etc., in which Gaule, Germanie, and Dalmatia be subdued.

b. Some take this bridge to be a kinde of fabrick or skaffold reared for the assault of the towne Metulium, and not an ordinarie bridge built over some river.

21

a. This temple, as appeareth afterwards, hee had vowed in the Philippian warre, which hee undertooke in revenge of his Father Julius Cæsars death, and therefore dedicated it unto Mars, Revenger.

22

a. The Temple of Janus Quirinus, or Quirini, because it was first founded by Romulus, Numa Pompilius his successor ordained to be set open in time of warre, and shutte when there was peace. Whereupon Janus was termed under a two-folde name, Patucius and Clausius. Once it was shutt in the said Numa his reigne; and a second time, after the first Punick warre ended, when M. Atilius, and T. Manlius, or Mallius, were Consuls. At all times before and after it stood open, untill Augustus Cæsars daies; during whose Empire it was thrice shut. First, upon the defeature of Antonius and Cleopatra before Actium. Secondly, after his victorie in Spaine over the Cantabri. Last of all, when all nations (in manner) of the earth by occasion of his victories, grew to an universall peace. About which time our Saviour Jesus Christ, Immanuel, that True Peace-maker betweene God and us, was borne. Thus Orosius reporteth, and readeth, *ter*, not *tertio*. Howbeit Livie seemeth to acknowledge, but once, namely, upon the Actiack victorie.

b. Ovation was a kinde of petie triumph: wherin the Captaines victors rode not in a Chariot, nor wore a Coronet of Laurell, but of the Myrtle. It tooke the name *ab ovibus*, *i*. Sheepe Sacrificed, or rather all the voyce, *Ovoe*, which the Soldiours in their acclamations resounded.

23

a. The Romane Armie consisted of Legions, who were all Romanes, and of *Auxilia*, *i*. aids, and those were of Allies and confederate nations.

b. This day, was *Ante diem quartum non Sextil*, *i*. the second daye of August. Which was also that verie daye of the moneth, wherein the Romans in times past suffered the desasterous overthrow at Cannæ.

24

a. By which the people of Rome wonne their immortall fame, and conquered the whole world: as Cicero saith: *Pro Murœna*.

252

ANNOTATIONS

OCTAVIUS AUGUSTUS CÆSAR

ᵇ December, Januarie, and Februarie.
ᶜ Thereby disabling them for being serviceable souldiers.
ᵈ These Publicanes, so called for that they fermed their Cities revenewes, as Customes, Tolles, Imposts, etc., were likewise Knightes or Gentlemen of Rome, and by being so earnest to buy out one of their owne sort, were thought to favour him, and minded presently to dismisse him at liberty: which was contrary to his intent.

25

ᵃ For his Uncle and Predecessor Julius Cæsar, had taken up that familiar terme of *Commilitones*, by occasion of so many troubles that followed him, and therefore was driven to speake his Souldiers fayre.

ᵇ Libertines were those who having beene bond were made free or manumised: and these were not capable of *Militia Romana*, but in time of great extremitie and desperate cases.

ᶜ It seemeth by this, that these *vallare* and *murall* coronets were made of some other matter than Silver and Gold. Yet Aul. Gell., lib. 5, cap. 6, writeth that both these, as also the *Navale*, were of gold. Now, the *Vallare* or *Castrensis* coronet, (for they were both one) resembled *vallum*, i. the Rampier a palaisade about a Camp, made *ex vallis*, i. stakes or pales sharpened at the head, wherewith the banke or mure was the better fortified, and hee received it as an honorable reward, who first mounted the said palaisade, and entered the Camp of his enemies. The Murall, was fascioned like to the battlements of a wall, given likewise unto that souldier, who approached the enemies wall first, skaled, and climbed over it into the Citie. As for these *Phaleræ*, albeit they be commonly taken for the ornaments or trappings of horses, yet it appeareth that they be the ornaments of the men themselves: and as well they as Torques were, *Tralatitia militum dona*, i. ordinarie and common gifts bestowed upon good souldiers. See Juvenal, *Satyr. ult.*: *Ut læti phaleris omnes, et torquibus omnes.*

ᵈ Such as he called before *Manipulares* and *Gregarios*: although in other authors, *Caligati* stand for all manner of souldiers.

ᵉ In Latin *Festina lentè*: much to this sense in our English tongue: No more hast then good speed: for, The soft fire makes sweet malt. This proverbe the same Augustus expressed also in his coines, wherein hee stamped together with lightning or a thunderbolt, the God Terminus, representing by the one, Celeritie; and by the other, Stayednesse. Like as Titus Vespasianus the Emperour joyned an Anchor and a Dolphin together in his coine, to the same purpose.

ᶠ A verse of Euripides, in the Tragedie *Phœnissæ*, i. A warie Captaine is better than a venterous.

ᵍ It was the Apophthegme of Cato, Soone enough is that done, which is well done.

26

ᵃ By the law *Annaria*, that L. Julius, or Villius rather promulged, required it was, that a Consull should not be under the age of 43.

TWELVE CÆSARS

OCTAVIUS
AUGUSTUS
CÆSAR

Yet for their worthinesse and demerits, some attaine to that dignitie, under 30.

b Like unto this was the speech of that Centurion, who being sent by Julius Cæsar Dictator, for to have the time of his government and conduct of an Armie in the province proroged, standing before the doore of the Senate house, and taking knowledge that it would not be granted, shooke his sword hilt with his hand and said, *Hic prorogabit,* i. This then shall proroge it.

29

a Three such Halles there were in Rome, wherein Judiciall courts were held, and causes pleaded. 1. *Romanum,* which was so much frequented with Lawyers and their Clients, that Cato Censorius delivered his opinion, that it should bee paved with Calthrops, to keepe out that rabble which hanted it. 2. *Cæsareum,* that Cesar Dictator built, and adjoyned thereto the Temple of Venus Genitrix. 3. Augusti, whereto was annexed by him one Temple of Mars Revenger. For, another he erected in the Capitoll, after he had regained from the Parthians, the Roman Standerds and militarie ensignes, which they wonne from Crassus.

b An Amphitheater, and a Theater, differs as the full Moone from the halfe, or a compleat roundle from a semicircle.

30

a Pliny writeth, that Rome was devided into foureteene Regions, or wards, and into more than a thousand streets.

31

a Augurs were certaine Priests employed about the observation of Birds, and from them out of their learning gave directions. In number at first they were but three belonging unto the three ancient tribes of Rome. In processe of time there was a Colledge or convent of them to the number of 24, namely, in the daies of Sulla Dictator: so that I doubt not but among these were some appointed for this ministerie eyther about the Goddesse Salus, i. Health or safety, unto whom there was likewise a Temple built, or else in the name and behalfe of the people, *Captare Augurium salutis,* which as Dio maketh report, was in this manner: That they should call unto God for safetie, if he would permit: as if it were not lawfull to crave it at the Gods hands, unlesse they first granted it. And one day every yeare was chosen for this buisinesse, in which no Armie did set forth to warre: no man warre against them, nor toke weapon in hand to fight: a thing that could not be, during the late troubles and civill warres. No merveile therefore, if this function being forelet, was now taken up againe by Augustus, when by occasion of peace, he did shut the Temple of Janus. And as this function was called *Augurium,* so I see no reason but the very Augurship or Sacerdotall dignity it selfe in this

ANNOTATIONS

place might be named *Augurium*, in the same forme, that presently after, the Flamenship or Priesthood belonging to Jupiter, is named *Fluminium*: and this I take to be the meaning of our Author.

OCTAVIUS AUGUSTUS CÆSAR

b Which were solemnized once in an hundred, or as some say, an hundred and ten yeares.

32

a By which addition, there were in the yeare 230 Law-daies or pleadeable.

33

a *More maiorum* ordained it was, that a Paricide, should first be beaten with rods, and then, sowed within a lether male or budge togither with a dog, a cocke, a viper, and an ape, and so throwen into the sea or some running water.

b Whereof Cornelius Sylla was the Author intituled: *de falsis*, or *Testamentaria*.

34

a Many lawes went under the title *Sumptuaria*, to represse the immoderate expense in apparell, and belly-cheere especially: as namely, Fannia, Didia Oppia, Cornelia, Julia, as well Cæsaris as Augusti. But in the time of Tiberius Cæsar, notwithstanding he did what he could to keepe them in force, yet they were all abrogated.

b *Lex Julia, Cæsaris et Augusti, de Adulteriis et Pudicitia*. For albeit the law Scatinia[1], provided against the later, to wit *Pæderestie*, yet the penaltie thereof by vertue of the said law was but *Pecuniaria, i.* a mony matter. Whereas by Julia it was *Capitalis, i.* worthie of death. And, that Augustus established and inforced this law against Incontinencie, it may appeare by this, that Sextus Aurelius reprooved him: because being himselfe given to lasciviousnesse, yet he was a most severe and sharpe chasticer of that vice: as also by that answere of a young man, whom he for committing adultery with his daughter Julia smote with his owne hands. Who thereupon cried out, Νόμον ἔθηκας, ὦ Καίσαρ, *i.* Thou hast made a lawe O Cæsar. Now as touching the foresaid law Scatinia, it was so called (as Valerius Maximus writeth) by occasion of one Scatinius[2] a Tribune of the commons, who against kinde had abused a sonne of Marcellus, and was therefore condemned accordingly.

c *De ambitu*. Of which there were divers, namely, Acilia Calpurnia, Aufidia, Bæbia Æmilia, Cornelia Fulvia, Maria, Pompeia, Pætilia, Tullia and Julia, Cæsaris and Augusti.

d *Lex papia poppæa, de maritandis ordinibus*, wherof, there were many branches and chapters, not only respecting this conjunction of the Gentrie and commons: but also concerning penalties to be laid

---

[1] Or Scantilia.   [2] Or Scantinius.

TWELVE CÆSARS

OCTAVIUS AUGUSTUS CÆSAR

upon those that neglected mariage, and rewards due to such as lived in wedlocke and begat children, etc.

35

a The badges that distinguished Senatours from others, were their Robes purfled or embrodered with broad studs of purple like naile heads, called thereupon *Laticlavi*, and shoes with peakes resembling the horned tips or pointed ends of the moone, named therefore *Calcei lunati*, in token of their auncient Nobilitie, as some interpret it.

b These solemne feastes at which Senators were allowed to be present, were *Epulum Jovis* otherwise called *Cæna Dialis* within the capitoll: likewise *Cæna Triumphalis Pontificialis*, and *Auguralis*, *i.* the sumptuous suppers to the honour of Jupiter, at triumphes, given by the Pontifies and Augurs.

c The first day of everie moneth.

d The 15 of March, May, July, and October, the 13 of the rest.

36

a A judiciall court there was at Rome called *Centumviralis Hasta*, for that it consisted of certaine Commissioners or judges named *Centumviri*, *i.* The Hundred men. Before whom were debated civill matters and causes betweene citizen and citizen, of no great importance. Chosen these were out of everie Tribe three: and those were in all 35, which number doth arise to 105, but in round reckoning they went for an hundred.

38

a What these ornaments and badges were, T. Livius reporteth in the 30 booke of his *Romane Historie*: to wit, a crowne of Gold, and a faire golden Boll: a curule, Ivorie chaire, with a staffe likewise or scepter of Ivory: a long Robe embrodered of sundrie colours, and a rich coate of Needle worke representing the Date tree.

b This solemne shew or Riding of Roman Gentlemen, was upon the Ides: the 15 day of *Quintilis*, alias July yearely. Instituted first by Fabius Rutilianus in the honour of Castor and Pollux, who appeared unto the Romans, at the battell neere the Lake Regillus, what time they atchived a noble victorie. They rode from the Temple of Honour, as some write, or as others, of Mars without the walles, through the Forum, and by the Temple of Castor, up into the Capitall, dight with chaplets of Olive braunches, as Plinie writeth, lib. 15 *Natur. Hist.*

40

a By this it appeareth, that ordinarily he might not bee a Tribune of the commons, who was not a Senator: for albeit this be a Plebian Magistrate, yet might a commoner be a Senator.

b Whereupon, Suidas thinketh, *Annonas* to take their name, *quasi* ἀνὰ τὰς Νώνας διδόμεναs, *i.* because corne was wont to be dealt among the people, upon the Nones of everie moneth, namely, the seventh

ANNOTATIONS

day of March, May, July and October, and the fifth of the rest: whereas indeed *Annona* is derived *ab anno, i.* the yeare, *quasi annalis alimonia, i.* the yeares provision of food.

OCTAVIUS AUGUSTUS CÆSAR

c It seemeth that Augustus held of two Tribes: to wit, Scaptia, unto which the Octavii belonged, and wherein he was borne: and Fabia, by his adoption into the familie of the Julii.

d For, howsoever the Romane habit was the Gowne, yet permitted were they, upon necessitie, namely to save the said gowne in foule wether, or to defend themselves from cold, to cast over it a cloake in any frequented place of the Citie, as were the Forum, *i.* the common pleading courtyard or Market place, and the Circus, *i.* the Shew place.

44

a For the ordinarie Roman Gownes were white and faire kept.

b Of these spectacles and games, some were *Matutini*, some *Meridiani*, and other *Pomeridiani*: according as they were exhibited, in the morning, at noone, and after-noone.

45

a These were called likewise sacred Games, as Stage-playes, Gymnicke Exercises, and Masteries in Musicke, in Neroes time.

b They tooke that name of a spatious Gallerie or walking place called *Xystos*, wherein they were woont to exercise in winter time.

46

a Colonies, were Towne-ships in Italy and other Provinces planted with Romane Inhabitants. In which *Decuriones*, as one would say Aldermen, had the same authoritie as Senators in Rome.

47

a Hereupon, some Provinces were called *Cæsaris*, or *Præsidiariæ*: namely, which were ruled by the Emperours sole appointment, and had strong Garrisons placed in them: others, *Populi*, and they were named *Prætoriæ, Consulares*, or *Proconsulares*, governed by Pretors, Consuls, or their Vicegerents.

50

a There is a kinde of Munkey or Marmoset in Æthiopia, going under the name of Sphinx, in Plinie. The Poets also faine, that a certaine monsterous beast so called, sometimes did haunt the Citie of Thebes and the Territorie about it: which from a rocke proposed ridales unto the passengers. This monster by their report, caried the resemblance of three creatures, to wit, a Foule, a Lion, and a mayden, according to these verses of Ausonius.

> *Terruit Aoniam volucris, Leo, virgo, triformis*
> *Sphinx: volucris penna, pedibus fera*[1], *fronte puella.*

[1] *Leo.*

TWELVE CÆSARS

OCTAVIUS
AUGUSTUS
CÆSAR

A three-shap'd Sphinx, Bird-Lion-Maid,
  Aonian land did fright,
In wing a foule, in feete a beast [1],
  In face a virgin [bright].

Plinie writeth in the last booke of his *Naturall Historie*, That Augustus used at the beginning to signe with this Sphinx engraven upon his Signet. 'And verily,' quoth he, 'in the casket of his mothers Jewels two of these he found, so like, that one could not be discerned from the other. And as hee was woont to weare the one wheresoever he went, so in his absence during the civill warres with Anthonie, his friends that menaged his affaires at Rome, sealed with the other, those missives and edicts which passed in his name. And from hence it came, that those who received any such letters or edictes conteyning matter of difficultie, were wont merily to say, that the said Sphinx came ever with some hard riddle or other, which could not be assoiled. Whereupon Augustus to avoid the obloquie that arose by his Sphinx gave over sealing therewith, and signed alwaies after with the image of King Alexander the Great,' etc.

51

[a] This humanitie and affable courtesie termed by Sueton. *Civilitas*, was reproved in Alexander the Emperour by his mother and wife both, as not beseeming the Majestie of a Prince: for they told him many times, that thereby he caused his Imperiall power and dignitie to be the more contemptible: Yea, but it is by that meanes, quoth he, both surer, and like also to last the longer.   Lamprid. in *Alexandro*.

53

[a] This name *Dominus* among the Romans, like as Sir with us, was diversly used. In the sense of imperious and Lordly commaund, as wee sometime take [Lord] it was odious: as having a relation to *Servus* a slave or villaine. To mollifie therfore the harshnesse of the word, they used to terme housholders or masters of families, *patresfamilias*, in steed of *Dominos*, as also houshold servants *familiares*, and not *servos*. Otherwise they used it by way of flatterie or faire speech, as appeareth in the chap. 21 of Claudius following. Hence it is, that lovers call their sweet hearts, *Dominas*, i. Mistresses. Also if a man speaketh unto one, whom he eyther knoweth not, or hath forgotten, he saith, *Domine*, i. Heere you, Sir, according to that Epigram in Martiall.

Cum te non nossem, Dominum Regemque vocabam.
Al while that I you kenned not, I cald you L. and King [2].

Last of all, by way of scorne and derision. And so, the same Martial testifyeth in this Distichon.

[1] Lion.   [2] Or Sir.

ANNOTATIONS

Cum voco te dominum, noli tibi, Cinna, placere, OCTAVIUS
Sæpe etiam servum sic resaluto meum. AUGUSTUS
When I O Cinna call you sir, joy not, I you advise, CÆSAR
For even my servant I salute oft times no otherwise.

In which manner we speake unto our servant, or any other in contempt, by this terme sirrha : to say nothing of sir knave. No mervaile therefore, if Augustus could not abide this word *Dominus* so doubtfully taken, and seldome in good sense.

 ᵇ If you read [*adoperta*], *i.* close and shut, it may have reference to this, That he tooke not state upon him, nor sought the peoples applause : which accordeth to his other behaviour reported before. If [*ad aperta*], *i.* open, it sheweth likewise his courteous cariage and affabilitie : as who was readie to accept of petitions and requests : a thing right commendable in a Prince, as it is written of King Artaxerxes surnamed Mnemon, how riding in a Carroch with his Queene, he commaunded her to draw open the curtaines thereof, that he might the better attend upon his subjects. And this agreeth as well with that which followeth of Augustus. And hereto I rather encline.

 ᶜ He looked not for their attendance at home in his owne house, neyther would he be thought to have conferred with any one privately, as touching the publike affaires.

 ᵈ It is generally a received opinion, that within seven naturall daies such voluntarie abstinence from food is not mortall, as Plinie writeth in his eleventh booke, who reporteth also, that many have continued fasting more than eleven daies. Which I easily beeleeve. For, in mine owne knowledge I may be bold to report, that a Bitch lived so long, and yet died not, nor miscaried the whelps within her. Some meloncholicke persons therefore, may within the Latitude of Health endure so long, yea and those likewise who are fraught top-full with a ballanse of crud and cold humours, which may engender a quartaine ague as well as melancholie doth. For, I doubt not, but in such chronicke diseases occasioned and maintained by grosse matters, one may abide above eleven daies without all manner of food. Yet Aulus Gellius saith, that beyond seven daies wilfull abstinence, a man is not able to live.

55

 ᵃ For, as Ulpian testifyeth, l. 18, *de Testamento*, a law there was, that whosoever to the infamie of any person published a Libell eyther in his owne or another mans name, yea without name at all : if he be convict thereof, shall be *Intestabilis*, *i.* disabled both for making a will himselfe, and also for to be a witnesse unto another mans.

56

 ᵃ By these Candidates, he meaneth eyther such as himselfe recommended unto the people for any office, as Cæsar his predecessor did before him, and those were called *Cæsaris Candidati*, or else his especiall friends whom he laboured for.

TWELVE CÆSARS

OCTAVIUS AUGUSTUS CÆSAR

[b] Plinie, lib. 35, cap. 12, writeth, that Cassius his accuser charged him to have killed 130 guestes, with one platter of poisoned meat.
[c] Certaine souldiers there were going under the name of *Scutarii*, as Paulus Diaconus witnesseth in his supplement upon Eutropius writing that Valentinian of a Tribune or Colonell over these *Scutarii*, became Emperour.

64

[a] Germanicus was the sonne of Drusus, and Antonia the younger. Now, had Drusus for his mother, Livia the wife of Augustus, and Antonia for hers, Octavia the sister of Augustus.

[b] In all bargaines of sale, and alienations, the solemne and ceremoniall forme at Rome was this, that five witnesses at the least, Romane Citizens and of lawfull age, with one other beside, of the same condition called *Libripens*, (because he held a payre of balances, etc.) the chapman or buyer should come with a peece of Brasse coyne in his hand, and say, (for example sake, if it were a boundslave to bee bought and sold) these words, 'This man or woman, I avouch by the law of the Romans to be mine, and bought I have him or her, for this peece of brasse, and with this brasen balance,' and therewith, striking the said ballance give the brasen peece unto the other partie that is the seller, by which imaginarie kind of chaffering, things were alienated, and their property changed.

[c] So ordinarie it was to traine up youth in swimming, and in Grammer[1], of which the one had relation to the exercise of the bodie, the other of the minde, that of such as had no bringing up at all, arose this proverbe, μέτε νεῖν, μέτε γράμματα.

65

[a] Caius was sent by Augustus with an armie to suppresse the troubles and insurrections in the East-parts: where he was stabbed treacherously, with a knife or short skeene, by one who presented unto him a supplication, of which wound he died afterwards. A. Lucius likewise he sent into Armenia, recommending him unto the Gods in these words, that they would vouchsafe him as welbeloved as Pompeius, as valorous as King Alexander, and as fortunate as himselfe.

[b] These he adopted, because they were out of the tuition of their fathers (deceased) in the common Hall or Forum, before the high priestes, and with consent of the people, by vertue of the law *Curiata*. And this was properly called Adoption. Wheras, sufficient it was to adopt others above named with the assent of their fathers, by the formall bargaine of saile called *Mancipatio*.

[c] Certaine questours there were named also *Candidati Principis*: whose office it was to read such missives or letters in the Senate.

[d] Happily, this he did to know thereby, whether she had beene naught of her bodie with them or no, considering wee learne out of

[1] Reading and writing.

ANNOTATIONS

naturall philosophy, that commonly children resemble their parents in complexion, favour, and markes. Howbeit, this Julia is reported to have brought forth children, all like unto M. Ægrippa, her husband, so long as he lived, notwithstanding she was knowen to be a common strumpet. But beside her answere to that point, unto those who made a wonder at it, which ye may see in Macrob. *Saturnal.* lib. 2, cap. 5, read the pleasant and wittie Epigram of Sir Thomas Moore, upon the like example.

OCTAVIUS
AUGUSTUS
CÆSAR

ᵉ Alluding to a place of Homer, *Iliad* 3, wherein Hector curseth his brother Caris, and after some approbrious terms saith thus,

αἴθ' ὄφελές τ' ἄγονός τ' ἔμεναι, ἄγαμός τ' ἀπολέσθαι

Would God, thou had'st of women ne're bene borne:
Or else had died thy wedding day beforne.

Which verse, by inversion of words and using one of them in a contrarie sense, Augustus transferred unto his owne person. For it is to be noted, that ἄγονός heere in Homer hath a passive signification, and soundeth, as much, as μὴ γεννηθείς, *i.* not borne, whereas Augustus taketh it in the active, for one that is childlesse, or hath begotten no children [1].

ᶠ These Cancers be certain tumors or swellings, hard and unequal of their nature which be called Scirrhes, and of an ugly aspect, as arising from unnaturall melancholy, breeding, as Cornelius Celsus writeth, for the most part in the superiour region of the bodie, about the face, nose, eares, lips, and womens breasts. Which our Author heere and the Greeke writers name *Carcinomata*, for the resemblance of the Crab-fish crooked cleies, which the blacke or swart veines all about them doe represent, or because they be hardly or uneth remooved, if they once take to a place, no more than the said fish when it setleth to a thing and claspeth it. Untoward to be healed, and commonly the worse for all the cure done unto them. These Cancers, if they become ulcers once are termed Wolves. In regard of which properties, aptly compared Augustus those ungracious Impes of his breed, unto them, as being foule Eyesores, disteining his honour, and by no discipline of his corrigible [2].

ᵃ According to that sage precept of Solon, τοὺς φίλους μὴ ταχὺ κάτα, *i.* Be not hasty in making any thy friends, and the saying of Hecuba in Euripides,

οὖς ἔστ' ἐραστής, ὅστις οὐκ ἀεὶ φιλεῖ.

No friend, I say,
Who loves not ay.

[1] Or is unable for generation.
[2] [This Note refers to the following words of the original:—' Nec aliter eos appellare, quam tres vomicas, aut tria carcinomata sua.' Omitted in the *Princeps.*—ED. *T.T.*]

TWELVE CÆSARS

OCTAVIUS AUGUSTUS CÆSAR

Which two rules Propertius elegantly comprehendeth in one verse,

Amare
Nec cito desisto, nec temere incipio
Late ere I love, as long ere I leave.

[b] Æsope gave this lesson, τῇ γυναῖκι μηδέποτε πιστούσης ἀπόρρητα, i. Commit no secrets to a woman. And as for this Mæcenas, he was noted to be *Uxorius*, more than he should, and one, who (albeit his wife was a shrew and readie to goe from him every day) soone admitted attonements and reconciliations. Wherupon Seneca in his morall Epistles said, That having but one wife, yet he maried a thousand times.

68

[a] Every word almost in this verse carieth a double construction, without the understanding wherof, all the grace is lost. For, *Cynædus* in one sense, betokeneth one of the Galli, Priests of the Goddesse Cybele, named also *Ops Mater deum*, and *Tellus*, even the very Earth. Which priests were gelded or disabled for generation, and tooke that name of the river Gallus, the water wherof drunken, caused men to be evirate and effeminate. Now, the maner of these priestes in the divine service of the said goddesse, was to bear the Taber or tamper upon the Timbril, which is expressed here in these words, *Orbem digito temperat*. For that the Timbrill is round and circular, to signifie the Globe of the earth symbolyze by Cybele. And in this sense, may the verse literally be interpreted: but, beside this signification, *Cynædus* betokeneth a wanton Pathick or Catamite, who suffereth himself against nature to be abused. *Orbis* also is put, for the habitable world, and *digito temperat*, is as much to say, as He hath the world at a becke, or at his commaund, as if the same were ruled by Augustus Cæsar, who was noted for that abhominable filthinesse. And in this latter sense did the people of Rome expound the said verse, and apply it unto him.

70

[a] Of twelve Gods and Goddesses together: alluding to those six select Gods, and as many Goddesses whom antiquitie in heathenesse honoured above the rest: whose names Ennius the Poet comprised in these two verses,

> Juno, Vesta, Minerva, Ceres, Diana, Venus, Mars,
> Mercurius, Jovis[1], Neptunus, Vulcanus, Apollo.

Answerable to which number hee entertained sixe yong women attired like Goddesses, and six boyes (Catamites) in habit of Gods, as his guests at this supper.

[b] I doubt, the first verse of this Hexasticon is not perfect, for, I doe not please my selfe in the translation of it.

[1] Jupiter.

ANNOTATIONS

^c Neyther is it certaine what this Mallia should bee. Some read Manlia, as if it were the name of a chamber within the Castell or Citadyll of the Capitall, which this banqueting place of his did counterfeit, and then we must admit the figure *Prosopopœa*. Others take Mallia to be the name of some woman, imploied in the furnishing and setting out of such a supper.

OCTAVIUS
AUGUSTUS
CÆSAR

^d For Augustus not onely sate heere among the rest in the person of Apollo, but also would sometimes be thought Phœbus, otherwhiles Phœbus his sonne.

^e For, it is not unknowne what adulteries the Poets talke of, betweene Jupiter and Alcmena, etc., betweene Mars also and Venus.

^f No marvaile, if Jupiter Capitolinus, with other Gods and Goddesses, being before possessed of the Capitall, abandoned their shrines and chappels, when they saw such in place.

^g Wherein Tormentors whips and scourges were to be sold: and there-upon he tooke that name of Tortour (like as before he is surnamed Sandaliarius, and Tragædus) which Augustus seemed now to verifie in himselfe, whipping and plauging the people with hunger, as he did.

71

^a In which moneth the feast *Saturnalia* was kept, and much libertie tolerated of gaming, feasting and reveling.

^b In this game called in Latine *Lusus talorum*, or *Talarius*, there is some resemblance of our dies, but that the *Tali* have but foure faces or sides, and therefore yeeld foure chaunces and no more. Of which the first is named *Canis* or *Canicula*, answering as some thinke to our *Ace*, and is the worst of all. The opposite unto it, they termed *Venus* or *Cous*, and is accompted the best, as which may stand for our *Sise*. The third bare the name of *Chius*, proportioned to *Trey* with us: and the last *Senio*, and is as much as *Quatre*. For in these *Tali* or cockall bones there is no chance of *Deux* or *Cinque*.

^c *Quinquatrus* or *Quinquatria*, were certaine festivall holidaies held for five daies together in the moneth March to the honour of Minerva. See Ovid *de Fast.*, Var., Macro., Aul. Gell.

72

^a For pleasure therein he called it Syracusæ, comparing it to that beautifull Citie in Sicily, and because it served his turne for meditations and inventions, he gave it the name τεχνόφυον.

74

^a Employed, as it should seeme in his civill warres. Certaine soldiers there were attending upon the Prince under the name of *speculatores*, whose service he used, in spying and listening. In Greeke such were named 'Οπτῆρες, σκεποὶ and κατάσκοποι. Also in doing execution upon condemned persons, and in sending of letters unto the

TWELVE CÆSARS

OCTAVIUS AUGUSTUS CÆSAR

Senate, as Lævinus Torrentius hath observed verie well in his Annotations upon Caius Caligula.

76

a *Sabbatis Ieiunium servat.* If Sabbats be put for weeks, as the manner of the Jewes was to speake, according as the Publicane saith in the Gospell after Saint Luke, νηστεύω δὶς τοῦ Σαββάτου, and as it appeareth in other places of the Evangelists, true it is, that Suetonius or Augustus reporteth of the Jewes, as also if by Sabbaths are meant other of their festivall and solemne daies. But if you take it for the seventh or last day of the week, it is altogether untrue, and to be imputed unto the errour and ignorance of Suetonius and the Romanes, in the Jewish rites and ceremonies. For seeing them religiously to keepe the said seventh day or Sabbat holy, whereupon they were commonly called *Sabbatarii,* and observing withall their fasting, generally it was thought of straungers that they fasted upon the Sabbat. Also for their devout fasting against the feast of the Passover, called by themselves sometime the great Sabbat, as also by forainers, as it appeareth by Horatius, lib. 1, *Serm. Sat.* 9, in this peece of verse, *Hodie tricesima Sabbata,* etc., they imagined that the Jewes fasted everie Sabbat. And in truth, reckon from September (at which moneth the Jewes in one computation begin their yeare) 30 weeks forward, you come unto their *Pascha*: according to which time wee Christians also doe celebrate our feast of Easter. This onely is the difference betweene us and them, for that they observe the *Neomenia* or new moone at the spring Æquinox, and solemnize their passover in the next full moone, and wee, the Lords day or Sonday after the said full.

78

a It seemeth, he tooke but a light repast: not putting off his shoes, as the maner was, at full meals.

b Some copies have, *retectis pedibus,* making (*re*) to be ἐπιτατικόν, as if he meant, verie well covered (contrarie to the use of that word *retegere,* which otherwise signifieth, to uncover) like as *recondere, i.* to lay up verie fast and sure. Others, *retractis, i.* with his feete somewhat drawen or pulled up to him: in the same sense as Cornelius Celsus useth *paulum reductis, qui fere jacentibus habitus est,* as hee saith, which is the ordinarie forme of lying, when as men be in health. Lastly, some read, *reiectis, i.* Let downe or stretched out to the full length.

c Casabonus interpreteth, [*Lecticulam lucubratoriam*] a pallet or low bedde made for the nones, to rest and studie upon.

79

a By whose report, he wanted not much of the ful height of men, to wit, nere six foot, according to Vegetius. Above which stature the grouth is somewhat giantlike.

ANNOTATIONS

80

^a *Ad Impetiginis formam.* The second kinde whereof, as Cornelius Celsus writeth, (for willingly do I often cite him as the Roman Galene, in explication of a Roman writer) *Varias figuras habet, i.* resembleth many and sundre formes, lib. 5, cap. 28.

^b This infirmitie of his was a kinde of gout, which the Greeke writers call *Ischias*, and is commonly named Sciatica. As for the remedie or palliative cure rather (for easement of paine) with sand: it may be meant eyther of some fomentations with linnen bagges wherein was sand; for, Cornelius Cæsar writeth, that Millet seed, salt, and sand, or any of them put within a linnen cloath, and so applied to the affected place, cure the said disease: or of walking in sand by the sea side, or else of tumbling and wallowing therein: which remedie Q. Serenus Samonicus in this verse: *Nec non et tepidis convoluere corpus arenis*, etc., hath prescribed and experience verified.

^c Cato in his *Husbandrie*, and Plinie, lib. 17, cap. ultimo, maketh mention of curing the Sciatica with a clift of a green cane or reed, but there must be forsooth, a charme go with all, and so, it reposeth dislocations or bones out of joynt. Indeed, both Dioscorides, and also Galene, attribute unto the rinde or barke of Cane-rootes, and to their ashes a desiccative vertue: whereby, they are found good for such dislocations, and so may cure the Articular disease likewise, called Sciatica, which differeth not much from a dislocation, of the huckle-bone.

^d Plinie reporteth 3 cap. lib. 25, That the disease of the bladder, and especially the Strangurie, *i.* pissing drop-meale, occasioned by gravell, (which I take heere to be meant) is of all others most dolorous.

81

^a This accordeth to an observation of Cornelius Cels.: *Qui secundis aliquando frustra curatus est, contrariis aliquando restituitur, i.* The patient whose cure devised by art, and according to the rule of Physicke, sometime speedeth not well, recovereth otherwhile by a course of meanes quite contrarie.

^b Which the Greekes call *Periodicall*: as the Quartane Ague and other intermittent fevers be so termed, because their fits returne upon certaine daies. The falling sicknesse likewise, keeping time with the moone, whereupon some name it *Lunaticus*. And gouts, which are most busie in the spring and the fall, etc.

^c Toward the end of September. An unequall season of the yeare, wherin commonly, the mornings and evenings be cold, and the Noone tides hotte, whereby many diseases are occasioned. But as touching the Birth-day heere mentioned, Valerius Max. and Plinie report, That Antipater Sidonius the Poet every yeare upon the day of his Nativitie onely felt the accesse of an Ague. Whereof he died in the end, after he had lived to a gret age.

TWELVE CÆSARS

OCTAVIUS AUGUSTUS CÆSAR

^d No marvaile if in cacochymicall bodies, such as his was, the humors which lay still and quiet all Winter, began to spread and swell in the spring, causing Distentions and Ventosities: especially in that place where they were gathered and laid up as it were in store, to doe a mischiefe when the time came.

82

^a *Fæminalibus et tibialibus.* In steede of our Breeches and Stockings, the Greeks and Romans used in those daies certaine loose cloathes in manner of Swathling bands to cover and lap their nakednesse. And long it was, ere they tooke to anie such, unlesse it were upon occasion of some disease. Witnesse heereof Philip King of Macedonia who as Plutarch [saith], when he sate in Port-sale of certaine slaves or captives, was admonished by one of them to let downe his upmost garment for to hide his shame. Julius Cæsar also himselfe, being deadly wounded, was carefull to let fall the lap of his gowne[1] for to cover his privie parts when he should fall. In processe of time they tooke to wearing the cloathes aforesaid in lieu of *Braccæ, i.* Breeches, which the French and other barbarous Nations used: but they did so in Winter onely. For, otherwise they went ordinarily in those parts without trusses: covering all as mannerly as they could with their loose upper garment, which upon a small occasion were readie to flie open.

^b Partly, to make a noise, and so to procure sleepe, and in part to refresh and coole the Ayre.

^c As well to coole him as to drive away gnats, for want of curtaines or a canopie, which thereof tooke the name in Greeke κωνωπεών or κωνωπεῖον. Now the manner of this winowing or making wind was for the better and daintier sort, with plumes of peacocks tailes, much like to the fannes of feathers used in these daies as well as in old time, but for the meaner, with beasts tailes.

^d From Rome to Præneste or Tibur, is about one hundred *Stadia*, if then you reckon 125 pases to a *Stadium*, it commeth to 12 miles and an halfe. Cato Censorius was of another minde, who said he repented when soever he went to any place by water if he might by land.

^e The abstinence wherof in some measure is good for those that have feeble joynts, and be remembred otherwhiles with any gout, as Augustus was yet, a thing that Physicians in old time could hardly bring their patients unto, so ordinarie it was in those daies to bath.

^f Which, the wanton and delicate Ladies of Rome, as Plinie writeth, used of silver.

83

^a *Ad pilam.* Whereas there were divers kinds of bals to play with, it seemes, that he meaneth in this place that, which of all other was least and hardest, as being stuffed with haire, whereupon it tooke the

---
[1] Which usually was cast over the shoulder.

ANNOTATIONS

name: the same no doubt that our Tennis Ball is sent to and fro with **OCTAVIUS** the Racket. Named likewise it was *Trigonalis*, of a Tennis court **AUGUSTUS** within the baines, three square walled: from which wals the ball **CÆSAR** did rebound. Of this ball, and the exercise thereof, Galen wrote a Treatise.

ᵇ *Folliculum.* By *Folliculus* is meant a kinde of wind hand-ball covered with lether: having within it a bladder puffed up with wind, the softest and lightest of all others, smitten, not with a racket as the other, nor with the palme of the hand, as that which they called *Paganica,* filled with woole, flocks or yarne, but driven with the clutched fist, whereupon it tooke the name *Pugillatoria.*

ᶜ So Turnebus expoundeth it. But Isaacus Casaubonus understandeth thereby, *Segestrie* or *Segestrium,* in Greeke στεγαστρὸν, a light blanquet or quilt.

ᵈ By this, is meant a play, that children used, and not that game of hazard resembling dice, at which, hee saide before, they played γεροντικῶς.

ᵉ For ought that I can gather out of the sundry conjectures of expositours, these *Ocellati* made of silver or ivorie, resemble the game of young Gentlewomen called of some *Trol-Madame*: or else that pastime of boyes named nine holes.

85

ᵃ Besides the pretie allusion unto the fabulous historie of Ajax, Torrentius hath observed in the word *Spongia,* a double signification: to wit, a spunge called *Deletilis,* which writers had at hand, eyther to wipe and wash out what misliked them, or to blurre and blot the same, according to these of the Poet Ausonius,

Aut cunctis pariter versibus oblinat
Fulvam lacticolor spongia sepiam.

Whereupon Martialis saith of it,

Utilis hæc quoties scripta novare voles:

and also a sword. Which addeth the better grace unto the conceit, considering that Ajax fell upon his owne sword. But in this latter sense, I have not yet found *Spongia* taken, in any approved author.

86

ᵃ Augustus taxed Mæcenas for being *Cacozelos,* and found as much fault with Tiberius, because he was *Antiquarius.*

ᵇ By these words μυροβρεχεῖς *Cincinnos* Augustus noteth the affectate forced phrases, and curious ynkehorne termes as it were, of Mæcenas, *Cuius oratio,* as Seneca reporteth of him, *Epist.* 94, *æque soluta est, ac ipse discinctus.* His manner of stile might be compared to those haires of his, curled with crisping pins and besmered with odoriferous oiles, which Cicero calleth *capillos calamistratos et*

TWELVE CÆSARS

OCTAVIUS
AUGUSTUS
CÆSAR

delibutos. Neither do I thinke that Augustus reprehendeth Mæcenas for using these words, μυροβρεχεῖς cincinnos, because it is his owne manner in writing to enterlace Greeke with Latin, and besides, no *Cacozelon* is therein to be found. But his over curious termes and new devised phrases he so calleth, for that Mæcenas was wont in trimming and tricking up himselfe to be somewhat womannish.

c Augustus in a certaine Epistle unto Mæcenas by expressing his owne nice and delicate phrases, after a sort derideth them, and dehorteth him thereto, in these words: *Vale mel gemmeum Medulliæ ebur ex Hetruria, laser Aretinum, adamas supernas, Tiberinum Margaritum, Cilviorum Smaragde, Iaspi figulorum, Berylle Porcennæ, carbunculum Italiæ,* καὶ ἵνα συντιμῶ πάντα μαλάγμα *Mæcharum.* In which words, as in a mirror he might see himselfe.

d As if he should say, 'Never a barrell better herring.' There was neyther of them better than other, as offending both waies. The Asiatick Orators were Cacozeli, Cimber, Atticus and Veramius, *Antiquarii.* So that, it was meere folly and vanitie to make any doubt, whether of them to imitate, being all starke naught.

89

a This Sphærus was a deep Scholler and great Humanitian as we speake, and whom the Greekes call *Philologon.* Under him Augustus became πολυμαθής, *i.* skilfull in historie, antiquities, etc., like as, under Areus he learned philosophy.

b The principall Authors whereof Horatius comprised in this verse,

Eupolis atque Cratinus Aristophanesque poeta.

In this manner of Comedie the vices of men and women were represented and taxed upon the stage over-boldly, and plainly to their discredit. For which it grew to be offensive, and was laid away a long time.

c Who was Censor in his time, and perswaded in his orations that al men of what degree soever should be compelled to marie for procreation of children.

90

a Plinie, lib. 2, cap. 55, *Nat. Hist.* writeth, that it never lightneth above five foot within the ground. Fearfull persons therfore thinke such deepe caves most safe.

91

a By this custome and gesture, as the argument and circumstance of the place naturally importeth, he thought to intreat the goddesse Nemesis for to spare him: Nemesis I say, whom the Heathen imagined to attend with an envious eye, upon all excessive prosperitie. To avoid therefore adverse afterclaps, which this spitefull goddesse might bring upon him, unlesse they were pacified, Augustus thus debased himselfe superstitiously, and in some sort, seemed to abridge

ANNOTATIONS

his owne felicitie. Much after the manner of Polycrates that rich tyrant who to be excused from this Nemesis, flung into the sea a jewel, with a precious stone of inestimable price.

OCTAVIUS
AUGUSTUS
CÆSAR

92

a *Nundinæ* among the Romans were those daies in every moneth whereon they kept fayres and markets. It should seeme therefore, that he held the day after them ominous and of unlucky presage, as we say in our proverbe, 'A day after the faire,' or else because he had sometime not sped very well, when as he did set out in his journey upon such a day.

b *Nonis*, quasi, *non is*, which literally osseth as much as, You go not. Much like to that in Plinie 15 lib. cap. 19, when M. Crassus was readie to embarke in that infortunate expedition into Parthia where he was slaine, a fellow cried certaine figs to be sold with this note, *Cauneas, Cauneas* (for of that kinde were those figs) which ossed thus much unto him, as if in short speech he had cried *Cave ne eas, cave ne eas, i.* Take heede you go not this voyage.

93

a An Idoll resembling an Oxe, which the Ægyptians worshipped as a God for Serapis.

b He did this, as it should seeme in policy, because he would not be thought addicted to the Jewish sect. For otherwise it appeareth as well by his gracious Indulgences granted unto them, as his own testimonie in Edicts and commissions, wherin he giveth unto their God [the true and onely God] the attribute of ὑψὸς, and instituted for ever certaine Holocausts, or whole burnt offerings, to wit, two lambs and one bul, to be offered unto that soveraigne and most high Diety.

94

a Some have expounded this of our Saviour Christ, King, not of Rome onely, but also of all the world, who tooke our nature upon him, and was borne in the daies of Augustus Cæsar.

b The like conception by a serpent is reported of Olympias the mother of king Alexander the great, of Pomponia likwise the mother of Scipio Africanus.

c This broad seale wherewith were signed letters Patents and other publike Instruments, caried a stamp representing the Citie of Rome: and being thus put into his bosom, prefigured that he one day should have the governement of the state and commonweale.

d Symbolizing thereby, that the Citizens of Rome, who before time might not lawfully be scourged were in danger to loose their liberty in that behalfe.

95

a Or, when he stood the first time for to be Consull. For, the

269

TWELVE CÆSARS

OCTAVIUS
AUGUSTUS
CÆSAR

maner was of the Candidats or Competitours of the Consulship, the night before the Election day to lie without the Citie abroad in the open ayre: and afterwards earely in the morning to sit in a chaire made of one entier peece within the precinct of a certaine place therefore appointed (which thereupon was called *Templum*) and there, to wait and expect untill some God presented unto them a good and fortunate signe.

96

ᵃ *Cum augeri hostias imperasset.* The manner was of the Painims if they could not speed of their Gods favour at the first sacrifice, to kill more beasts still, untill they saw some tokens thereof: which in the Southsayers learning was called *Litare*. Thus did Paulus Æmilius for 20 together, and obtained no warrant of happie successe before he had slaine the one and twentieth. Yet some write, that Sacrifices are then said *Augeri*, when together with the beasts, there is use of *Salsa molæ*, i. meat and salt. Which kind of Ostes be called *Mactæ*, quasi, *magis auctæ*.

ᵇ Significant names both, and osses of victorie. Eutichus, importeth Luckie or Fortunate: Nicon, Victour or Conquerour.

97

ᵃ This solemnitie of purging the Armie everie five yeares was instituted by King Servius Tullus, and celebrated with the Sacrifice of a Swine, a Sheepe and a Bull, named thereupon *Suovetaurilia*. Heereupon, the revolution of five yeares, they called *Lustrum*. This function or office belonged afterwards to Generals of the field: like as the expiation and purging of the people unto the Censours. And this maner of *Lustrum* is here meant. Carol. Sigon. *Ascon*.

ᵇ Writings or Instruments signed, conteyning the said vowes: whereby they bound themselves, as it were, by obligation to pay and performe the same. Oftentimes also they fastened them with waxe unto the knees of those Gods or Idols unto whom they nuncupated those vowes, according to that verse of Juvenal, *Satyr.* x.

Propter quæ fas est genua incerare Deorum.

ᶜ *Præter consuetudinem.* Suetonius seemeth heere to forget himselfe, writing that Augustus contrarie to his olde wont embarked by night, having reported before, that it was his manner so to doe. Torrentius would salve all, expounding it thus, that his hastie and long journey (for it was a good stretch from Astura to Beneventum) was contrarie to his wonted manner. But to speake, what I thinke, his journey now by night, was occasioned by a gale of winde that served well for Beneventum, and hath no reference at all to his accustomed travaile. Some would read, (*pro consuetudine*) i. after his usuall maner, but they respect not the scope of our Author, whose purpose in this place is to put downe certaine particulars that were ominous and presaging his death. Among which, this may be reckoned

ANNOTATIONS

for one, That he did a thing now, repugnant to his ordinarie guise. A point, I wis, observed too much even now a daies by those that are superstitiously given. Although, I am not ignorant, that of this observation, in sicke folke, there may be a naturall reason rendered out of Phisicke.

OCTAVIUS AUGUSTUS CÆSAR

98

ᵃ *De navi Alexandrina*. By *Navis* he meaneth as I suppose, *Classis* (by the trope *Synecdocie*), *i*. the whole fleete, like as by the same figure, *classis* signifieth a ship. For one vessell alone arrived not into that haven of Puteoli, fraught with marchandise, considering that the same is by other writers named πορευτικὸς στόλος, and *Comeatus*. Yea, and by the figure *Catachresis*, Martial calleth it *Niliacus cataplus*, which properly betokeneth the fleet when it is arrived. Neyther is it like that Mariners and Passengers out of one ship onely saluted Augustus in this wise.

ᵇ *Quadragenos aureos*. Every such peece was worth fifteene shillings starling and better, aunswerable to our Spurre Roials.

ᶜ These commodities were thought to be Drugs and Spices of all sorts, webs or clothes in Say, Books, Paper, Glasses of sundrie fashions, teere of flaxe, hirds, or Tow, sindall or fine linnen, twisted yarne and threed of divers colours, Babylonian and Ægyptian cloath, well favoured bondslaves, and of good education, etc.

ᵈ *Vicinam capreis insulam*. Yet some read otherwise, *Vicinam capreas insulam, i*. The Iland Capreæ neere adjoyning, as if Augustus had abode all this while in the skirt and coast of Campania, or in some other of the neighbour Ilands. But I incline rather to the former exposition.

ᵉ The Citie of Ease and Idlenesse.

ᶠ This Masgabas, seemeth by his name to have beene an Africane, whom Augustus had made Constable as it were of that place, and ruler over a Companie, that he sent thither to dwell, after he had purchased it of the Neapolitanes. And for that Augustus had in mirth given him the name of Founder, he was so reputed, and his yeares minde after his death solemnized accordingly.

ᵍ *Morbo variante*. I take it, he meaneth that which Celsus calleth *Alvum variam*, and other Physitians *Egestiones varias*, namely when in a fluxe the excrements and humors be of divers colours, an argument that nature is not able to concoct them being so irregular, and therfore, somtimes a deadly figure. Or, it may be expounded thus, That otherwhiles he seemed to be better and on the mending hand, and thereupon more venterous. Then read, *Morbo variante tamen*, etc.

ʰ Celebrated everie five yeares after the Græcian manner, and called Gymnicke, because the masteries therein, were performed by Champions for their better agilitie well neere naked.

100

ᵃ This was a speciall honour and indulgence granted by a singular

TWELVE CÆSARS

OCTAVIUS AUGUSTUS CÆSAR

priviledge, for otherwise it was against the custome and lawes of the Romans to bring a dead bodie into a sacred place, or into the Citie, for feare of polluting and profaining it.

[b] The Senatours and Gentlemen of Rome wore rings of Gold, the Commoners of Iron.

[c] The chiefe Colledges and Societies, at this time were compted foure, that is to say: The Pontifies or chiefe Priests, the Augures, the Septem-virs, or seven wardens called *Epulones*, for that to them belonged the charge of providing the sacred feasts, the sumptuous suppers of the Pontifies, named *Cœna adjiciales*, as also the stately Tables, in the honour of Jupiter and other Gods, and fourthly, of the *Quindecimvirs, sacris faciundis*, i. Fifteene overseers of the Sacrifices. Afterwards adjoyned there was to these a fifth, *Augustalium Sodalium*, erected by order from Augustus, and others in process of time by his precedent.

[d] This *Rostra* was the publicke pulpit for Orations, standing in the common Market place, called *Forum Romanum*: so called for that it was beautified with the beake-heads of ships (named in Latine, *Rostra*) which in a memorable fight at Sea, the Romans wonne from their enemies. Neere unto which were certaine shops called *Veteres Tabernæ*: and absolutely *veteres*, for distinction of others, knowen by the name of *Novæ*, i. the new shops. Yet some are of opinion, that in this place our Author meaneth *Rostra vetera*, i. the olde pulpit: to put a difference betweene it and another named *Nova*, i. the New.

[e] You must thinke, that the dead bodie to be burnt in a funerall fire, was set therein so, as the ashes and bones thereof remained apart by themselves from the rest. Otherwise, the ashes of wood, the bones likewise of horses and other beasts sometimes burnt therewith, should have the honour due unto the said dead corps. Some are of opinion that it was lapped in a linnen sheete of the flaxe called *Asbeston*, which would not bee consumed with fire.

[f] The sumptuous Tombe that Queene Artemisia built for her husband Mausolus King of Caria, and reckoned one of the seven wonders of the world, was called *Mausoleum*, after his name. Whereupon, al such costly and stately monuments are so named; and more particularly, that of Augustus. Of which you may read more, 5 *Geograph. Strabonis*, for the better explanation of this place.

101

[a] *Depositum apud se.* Some read, *apud se, sex virgines vestales*, as if sixe of these Vestall virgins had the custodie thereof, or at leastwise brought the same forth, being committed to them all: and the seventh, named *Maxima*, the Prioresse as it were, and governesse of the rest, were left behinde.

[b] This hath a reference unto the *As*, or pound waight Romaine consisteth of 12 ounces, which standeth for the base and rule of many other things: and namely heere for the entiere inheritance that

ANNOTATIONS

OCTAVIUS AUGUSTUS CÆSAR

Augustus disposed of by his last will and testament. For, two third parts of 12 he gave unto Tiberius: and another third part unto Livia, which made up the whole.

c This was against the law *Voconia*, which expresly provided, That no man should endow a woman in more then the fourth part of his goods. So that if a man died seized of one hundred thousand pounds, his wife might not enjoy the thirds, but onely 25000 pounds and no more. Howbeit Augustus had a speciall indulgence and dispensation for this Lawe.

d Albeit Tiberius had beene long before adopted his sonne, and thereby may be thought to have assumed the names of his civil father, into his stile: yet this surname onely of Augustus, would not be communicate with him, but left it as hereditarie after his decease; as apeareth in Tiberius. As for Livia, after Augustus his death she was commonly called Julia Augusta: how ever some writers retaine her olde name Livia, and others againe in Augustus his life name her Julia: by the figure *Prolepsis*, because she caried that name after he was dead.

e In most copies of Suetonius you find this reading, *Legavit populo Romano quadringenties, tribubus tricies quinquies*. In which words there may be thought a Tautologie: for that the people of Rome and the Tribes (which were in number 35) be all one. Therefore, some learned men have thought good to leave out the later clause wholly, or at leastwise, the word *Tribubus*. Others againe would have heere two legacies to be implied, the one of foure millens given generally in common to the whole bodie and people of Rome, the other of three millenes and one halfe, to be distributed among the Tribes in particular, or to the poorest persons in everie Tribe according to the discretion of their *Vicimagistri*. And these, put a distinction betweene *populus* and *plebs*, which *plebs* is heere understood under the name of *Tribubus*. But I leave it indifferent, although I am not ignorant, that sometimes *Populus* and *tribus* be confounded and put the one for the other, as also that *tribus* stand for the vulgar and meaner sort of the people onely, expresly distinct from *Populus, Equites* and *Senatores*, which the Poet termeth *Sine nomine turbam*: and T. Livius not unaptly, *Ignota capita*.

f Which amounteth by the computation of Budæus to three thousand and five hundred Myriades.

TWELVE CÆSARS

TIBERIUS
NERO
CÆSAR

ANNOTATIONS UPON
TIBERIUS NERO CÆSAR

1

^a It seemeth that in his owne Native countrey, where the Inhabitantes before time were descended from the Greeks, he had to name Atta Clausus: and being once incorporate among the Romans, changed it, into Appius Claudius. Now, *Atta* savoreth of the Greeke word ἄττειν, which is in going, not to set the sole of the foote firmly upon the ground, but rather lightly to tread as it were, on tiptoe. Heereupon, as Festus noteth, they that have that imperfection in their feete, whereby they can go no better, be called *Attæ*: which was the occasion, that one of the said house tooke that name first, and so his posteritie after him. Like as among the Romanes, of another accident, arose the name Agryppa first: for that one was borne into the world with his feete forward. And these additions, whether they were forenames or surnames in the beginning, it skilleth not: for surnames in continuance of time came to be forenames, and contrariwise.

^b If you have recourse unto the Originall, Nero is as much as Νεύρων, or Νευρώδης, *i. Nervatus* or *Nervosus*: that is to say, well compact of nerves and sinewes: and such are strong.

2

^a Seneca reporteth in his booke *De Brevitate Vitæ*, cap. 12, That this Claudius perswaded the Romanes first, to go to sea, and embarke: whereupon he was styled *Caudex*, which in our Latin is as much to say, as the framing, and joyning together of many plants or ribs of timber, which is the very Periphrases of a Barke.

^b One of his predecessours who had a Jurisdiction there, gave it that name, as having built likewise a Forum or Hall of Justice there, whereupon the Inhabitants of it and the territour thereabout, owing service to that court, as Clients and dependants to that Family, afforded this Claudius a meete place for him of Innovation and usurping unlawfull dominion.

^c Observing signes from Birds, by their feeding, flying or otherwise, that might give him warrant to go forward with the favour of the Gods, in his Enterprise.

^d Adoptions by order of Law, should follow the course of Nature, whereby the sonne, cannot be elder than the Father. The cause why he sought thus extraordinarily to bee adopted a commoner, was that he might be chosen Tribune of the Commons.

ANNOTATIONS

^e The usuall manner in Rome was, that those persons who were arrested for criminall causes, during all the time of their trouble and triall, should chaunge their apparell, and in steed of gownes which were faire and white, put on others sullied and foule, thereby to moove mercie and compassion of the people. Whereupon such *Rei* were called *Sordidati*.

^f These Tribunes of the commons as may appeare in T. Livius were *sacrosancti, i.* Unviolable, and such as no violent hands might bee laid upon.

3

^a So called, of *Salinæ*, the salt pits or salt houses. For being Censor he set an impost upon salt, and thereby augmented the revenewes of the State, little to the benefit or contentment of the people.

4

^a For the manner was, that Governours of provinces, who (as they were) so would be counted also, more courteous than others, should unrequested allow some of their lectors unto all Roman Senators that repayred unto them, for to doe them honour: Cic. *Ep. ad Cornificium*.

5

^a In token of his nativitie there, which as they gave out, was borne to the good *urbis et orbis, i.* Of Rome and the whole world besides, for so, by way of flatterie they magnified their Princes.

6

^a Some read, *Luctuosam, i.* sorrowfull, in regard of many hurts and dangers.

^b When a chariot is drawne by a teeme of foure steeds all in one ranke or affront, as we may see them pourtraited upon divers coines, it must needs bee that the two middle are joyned or yoaked as it were to the spire pole running betweene them: and these be called σύγιοι. The other two then are without, the one on the left, and the other on the right side, called παρήοροι in Greeke, and in this place by our Authour Funales, because they are guided and ruled by a cord, or some reines or cheine in lieu thereof. And say, that these *quadrigæ* or foure steeds drawe two by two in files, one payre before the other: those which be next unto the chariot be aptly called *Jugales*, and those before them beyond the spire, *Funales*, of which, Tiberius rode upon one and Marcellus upon the other.

10

^a According to the vulgar speach, *Nimia familiaritas parit contemptum*.

14

^a These dice were called *Tali*, because at first they used with such cockall bones named *Tali* to play: but afterwards they were made of

TIBERIUS
NERO
CÆSAR

TWELVE CÆSARS

TIBERIUS NERO CÆSAR

Ivory, gold, etc. Among many sorts of sorceries and divinations, one there was by these bones or dies, and the wisards that professed their cunning in it, were termed 'Ἀστραγαλομαντεῖς.

 b For the greater light to this place, and better proofe of Thrasillus skill, Dion reporteth, that when Tiberius intended verily to throw him downe headlong, he perceived him by his countenance to be much troubled and disquieted in minde, whereupon he demaunded the cause thereof, and then Thrasyllus answered, that by speculation of the Stars he foresaw some present daunger to himselfe, and so Tiberius durst not proceede to execute this intent of his.

17

 a *Septa*, was a place in Mars Field railed about at first like a sheepe Pen: whereupon it was called *Ovilia*. But afterwards mounded with Marble stone, beautified also with stately galleries and walks, within which cloysture and precinct, the people oftentimes assembled about Election of Magistrates and other publicke affayres: yea and with wares which were there set out to be sold. As Alex. ab Alexandro witnesseth.

19

 a Some read *Bructero,* of which name there is a nation, as well as of the Rhutaine in Gaule. Others, *Rutero,* as if he meant one of those horsemen or riders in Germanie, which at this day be called Rutters.

20

 a A long robe embrodred and garded with purple, a cassocke branched with Date tree worke, a rich mantell of sundry colours. A chaplet of Laurell, a staffe and chaire, both of Ivorie. Liv. lib. 30.

21

 a By this ænigmaticall speech, Augustus compareth the state of the people of Rome, unto the miserable case of one, whom some savage and cruell beast hath gotten betweene his teeth, not devouring and dispatching him at once, but there holdeth and cheweth him a long while in exceeding paine: alluding to the secret malice, and dreaming nature withall of Tiberius.

 b It should seeme that in adopting him, he used these very words, *Hoc Reipub. causa facio, i.* This doe I for the common-wealthes sake.

 c Alluding to this verse of Ennius in the commendation of Qu. Fabius Max.

> *Unus homo nobis cunctando restituit rem.*
>
> One man alone by sage delay
> Restor'd our state fall'n to decay.

 d In the tenth booke of his *Iliads,* where Diomedes in making

ANNOTATIONS

choise of Ulysses, to exploit a peece of service with him, giveth him this praise.

TIBERIUS NERO CÆSAR

23

ᵃ The Tribunes of the commons had power to call a Senate, but not whensoever they would, without a speciall Decree graunted by the Nobles.

25

ᵃ The cohort or band of Souldiers which were of the Princes Guard, were called *Prætoriani*, taking that name of *Prætorium* which signifieth the Lord Generals Pavilion in the campe, his Royall Pallace in Rome and else where. As also the Lord Deputies house of Estate in any Province. Now those Souldiers that gave attendance and served in this place about the Prince or Governour, were intertained in better condition than the rest, because their wages was greater, and the time of their service shorter. For Augustus had set downe their terme twelve yeares, whereas the rest, before they could be discharged, were to serve sixteene.

ᵇ It may be thought, that *Germaniciani* as well by the Grammaticall Analogie of the letter, as also by some circumstance of this verie place, import a reference unto Germanicus the son of Drusus disceased. Like as *Vitelliani, Flaviani*, etc. But the learned observe, that as an Armie lying encamped or in Garrison, in Germanie, is properly in Latin called *Germanicus,* so the Soldiours of the said Armie be fitly named *Germaniciani.*

26

ᵃ These solemnities were exhibited about the midst of November, whereas the other, named *Romani*, were held in the beginning of September.

ᵇ It is to be noted, that the name of *Imperator* in the Roman Historie is taken three waies: First, for him, who by commission or warrant from the State, hath the conducting of an Armie: and in this sense, it hath relation to Souldiers, and is all one with Lord Generall of the field, or a commaunder, etc., and the same that *Prætor* was in olde time. Secondly, for a Victor or Conquerer, namely when such a Generall or chiefetaine hath by martial prowesse atchieved many valiant exploits, and put to sword such a number of enemies, as the law setteth downe. For then the souldiers were wont to salute him by the name of *Imperator*, i. Conquerour. Lastly for a Soveraigne Prince, King and Monarch. In the first acception, it is a meere Relative, in the second a surname, in the third and last, the forename of all the Romane Emperours, to wit, from Julius Cæsar forward. Who although they wore not the Crowne and Diademe, were neverthelesse absolute Princes, Soveraignes, Kings and Monarches. The want of this distinction may breed some trouble in the readers of the Romane Historie.

TWELVE CÆSARS

TIBERIUS NERO CÆSAR

ᶜ Made of Oke branches, or in default thereof, of some other tree bearing mast: which garland by the first institution, was given to that souldier, who in battell had rescued a Citizen of Rome and saved his life. And afterwards, it, together with the Laurell, beautified the gates of the Cæsars Palaces, although some of them were bloodie Tyrants, and made no spare of their citizens and subjects lives.

30

ᵃ The manner was, if Prince or Senatour were caried in his Litter, usually supported by eight bond-servants, and thereupon called *Octophoron*, to have a companie of Citizens in their gownes going before, and accompanying him by his side, as also certaine servitours to carie his curule chaire of ivory behinde.

31

ᵃ This free embassage, called *Libera legatio*, was granted many times to such, as being desirous eyther to travell and see forraine countries, or to fly, for avoiding of daungerous troubles at home: therby to be better intertained abroad, and with the more honest colour, to conceale the occasion of their departure, and absence as if they were sent from the state, about the affayres onely of Common-weale.

32

ᵃ It was not ordinarie with the Emperours to accompanie the corpes unto the funerall Fire: but onely to vouchsafe their presence at the Funerall Oration in the Forum or common place. This therefore may be attributed unto Tiberius his civill humanitie.

ᵇ It appeareth by Dion, that they had omitted to subscribe the clause which went in this forme, *Vota facimus pro te, Imperator*, i. We make our vowes (and pray) for thee O Emperour.

33

ᵃ Causes were heard judicially, and Justice ministred, eyther from a superiour place as the Tribunall, or beneath upon the even and plaine ground, *de plano*, as the Lawyers speake, so that there were a Chaire or seat for the judge to sit upon. And the said place of Justice wheresoever, eyther *pro tribunali*, or *de plano posita sella*, is properly called *Ius*: as Carolus Sigonus hath observed, lib. 1, cap. 5, *de Judiciis*. Whereupon commeth the usuall phrase, *In ius vocare*. It seemeth therefore, that Tiberius would come into the *Comitium* or Hall of Justice, and take his place, sometime within the Tribunall (for it was a spacious rowme) or else sit in his Curule chaire of Ivory beneath, as a moderator, which is expressed heere by the terme *de plano*.

34

ᵃ As Marchpanes, Tarts, Gingerbreed, Custards, Sugred Bisket, and generally all manner of pastrie-conceits, wrought with honie or sugar.

ANNOTATIONS

The workeman is called *Dulciarius*, and the things, *Bellaria Mellita*, or *Pemmata*. Toyes not onely needlesse, but hurtfull also to the bodie, according to that in Aulus Gellius, lib. 13, cap. 11, *Noct. Attic. ex varone*. *Bellaria ea maxime sunt millita quæ mellita non sunt* : Πέμμασι γὰρ πέψει, *societas infida, i*. Such junkets sort not well with Concoction¹.

TIBERIUS NERO CÆSAR

35

a Diverse Statutes there were sharpely punishing the adulterie of Matrones or maried wives. An Act likewise passed in the Senate, that no Person of Knights degree or above, should play upon the stage, performe sword-fight, or combat with wild beastes for hire. Providing all to preserve the honour of wedlocke entire, and to maintaine the reputation of Knighthood and Nobilitie. Those shamelesse dames therefore, of whom Suetonius writeth in this place, eyther because they would be thought unworthie to be reckoned within the censure of Law, or as Tacitus writeth, deemed to have abidden punishment enough in making profession of so base a trade and life : these lewde persons likewise, and unreclaimable unthrifts suffering themselves thus to appeare noted with infamie, and that upon record, made accompt, both the one and the other not to be obnoxious or liable unto the statutes and acts aforesaid.

b The manner was at Rome, for Tenaunts to remoove and flit out of one house into another, upon the first day of July, like as with us, at the feastes of Saint Michaell and the Anunciation of the Virgin Marie : which are the ordinarie rent daies.

36

a Josephus, lib. 18, *Antiquit. Judaic.* writeth that Tiberius sent 4000 of them into Sardinia, an Iland in Summer time especially, verie intemperate and unwholsome, as may appeare by that pretie Epigram of Martialis, wherein he opposeth the healthie Citie Tibur, to the pestilent Isle Sardinia.

Nullo fata loco possis excludere, cum mors
Venerit, in medio Tibure Sardinia est.

No place exempt from fatall death, for when our time is come,
Mid Tibur, will Sardinia be found of all and some.

38

a This Callipides, who gave occasion of this By-word, was a famous Stage-player, or one of these *Mimi*, counterfaiting other mens gestures, as Beraaldus supposeth. See Plutarch in *Apophtheg. Laconic.*

42

a Biberius, *a bibendo, i.* of drinking. Calius, *a Calda*, or *Calida, i.* hote. Mero of *Merum, i.* strong wine. An elegant Agnominiation :

¹ Or digestion.

TWELVE CÆSARS

TIBERIUS NERO CÆSAR

whereby is shewed, that he loved to drinke wine hote, which is right delicate, and goeth downe more merily.

ᵇ The Italicke Amphor conteyneth 48 *Sextarii*, everie Sextarius 20 ounces *Mensurales*, which is a wine pinte and halfe of our measure with the better. By which reckoning he dranke at one meale a rundlet of ten wine gallons well neere.

ᶜ A Bird that feedeth upon grapes and figges especially, whereupon it tooke the name. In Autumne or the latter end of Summer it is so called: at other times *Melanocoryphos*, or *Atricapilla*, of the blacke cop, or hair-like fethers that it carieth upon the head.

ᵈ Of this Bird for the daintie flesh of it Martiall made this Epigram,

Inter aves, turdus, si quis me judice certet,
Inter quadrupedes, gloria prima Lepus.

Of fethered foules, if I may judge, the blackbirde is the best,
Among four-footed beasts the Hare surpasseth all the rest.

ᵉ To invent and devise new pleasures.

43

ᵃ Alluding partly to the Isle Capræa, and in part eyther to *Capra* in Latin, a goat, or to Καπρός in Greek, a wild bore, and that member, *Quo viri sumus.*

49

ᵃ Seneca reporteth thus, lib. 2, de *Benefic.* cap. 27, *Quater millies sestertium suum vidit*, i. He saw of his owne, 400 millions of Sesterces.

ᵇ Provided it was by an auncient law, and the same revived by Jul. Cæsar Dictator, that no person should in silver or gold possesse above 60 *sestertia*, that is, three score thousand *sestertii*. This also may have a relation to that order set downe by him a little before, That monied men and usurers should lay out two third parts of their stocke in lands and houses, etc.

51

ᵃ As we say, to make him Justice of Quorum, etc: for the *decuries* of Judges were they *Quorum nomina*, were written in the Commission Roll.

53

ᵃ The Greeke verse is red thus, Εἰ μὴ τυραννεῖς, θύγατερ, ἀδικεῖσθαι δοκεῖς, or Εἰ μὴ τυραννεῖς, τέκνον, etc.

ᵇ *Scalæ Gemoniæ.* A place at Rome upon the Aventine hill, into which the dead bodies of malefactors were dragged and throwen with shame.

56

ᵃ They speake the Greeke language generally throughout all Greece,

ANNOTATIONS

yet not after one manner. For in divers parts were different kindes of Greeke called Dialects, to wit, Attick, Ionick, Æolick, etc. Like as with us in Great Britaine a common English tongue goeth wel neere throughout the whole Iland, albeit there is a diversity perceived between the Scottish or Northren English, and the Southerne, betweene the Cornish and the Kentish, etc.

TIBERIUS
NERO
CÆSAR

58

^a In so doing the bodie must needes be bared and some shame discovered which being an Impietie before the sacred Images of the Gods, was made Treason also before the Emperours Statue, unto whom divine honours were exhibited.

59

^a The last Hexastichon or 6 verses, seemeth to make one entier Epigram by it selfe. Every *Distichon* before, carieth a severall sense. And as for the first two, they seeme to have a reference to the time, whiles he abode in Rhodes, before he was *Sui Iuris*.

61

^a At which times, both among the Greekes and Romans also, the manner was to forbeare Execution, yea and to ease prisoners of their yrons.
^b As if under his person he had offered abuse unto the Emperour Tiberius.
^c He would say, The courage and generositys of the Romans died with them, seing that none arose to recover their libertie oppressed and trode under foote by this Tyrant Tiberius.
^d Rather, two hundred and twentie. For Tacitus, lib. 6, *Annal.* reporteth, that all the suspected complices of Sejanus were killed, *Iacuit immensa strages, omnis sexus, omnis ætas,* etc.
^e The like hypocriticall Religion was practised during the bloudie proscription in the Triumvirate. A young Gentleman nobly borne, because he might not be killed lawfully, *prætextatus, i.* under age, and wearing still his embrodered garment *prætexta,* hee commaunded to put on his virile gowne, and so he was murthered. Appian. Dio.

67

^a For wonderfully addicted he was to the studie of Astrologie, and such curious Arts.

68

^a The full stature of men in Italy, was six foot wanting two ynches, if men grew higher than sixe they were accompted exceeding tall, if to seven, (and to that height men may grow, as Varro, Gellius and Solinus doe write) they went for Giants. So that in Musters yong men were chosen soldiours, five foote high and ten ynches, which was called *Iusta Statura.*

TWELVE CÆSARS

TIBERIUS NERO CÆSAR

ᵇ Some read *subiti*, and not *subtiles*, to signifie that such pimples continued not, but arose and fell at times, much like to those that the Physitians call *Hidroa, Sudamina*, or *papulas sudorum*, according to Plinie, proceeding of heat or sweat, if the humours be sharpe.

ᶜ Such be termed in Greeke βυσαυχένες. And if we may beleeve the Physiognomie delivered by Aristotle: they be by nature deceitfull and wilie, given to circumvent, entrap and supplant others.

ᵈ Cornelius Celsus, among other good rules and precepts of Health, writeth thus, *Sanus homo qui et bene valet et suæ spontis est, nullis obligare se legibus debet, ac ne medico neque alipta egere*, etc. But give he what directions he will, and let us say what wee can to this point, that men and women may be Physicians to themselves, such is there misgovernment in diet and otherwise, that Physitians shall never want imployment. And as touching thirty years of age, Tacitus addeth moreover and saith, That he[1] was wont to mock those and hold them to be fooles, who after the said yeares had neede of other mens instructions, to know what was good or hurtfull for their bodies. Whereupon might arise our English proverbe, A foole or a physician.

70

ᵃ Such as were sung to the Harpe. In which kinde Pindarus excelled among the Greekes, and Horace among the Romans.

ᵇ One of Augustus [adopted] sonnes. Yet some read Julius Cæsar.

71

ᵃ A word usuall with us in these daies, for who knoweth not that Monopoly is, when one man engrosseth some commoditie into his owne handes, that none may sell the same but himselfe, or from him?

ᵇ It signifieth in this place a peece of workmanship set upon a cup or other vessell of Gold or Silver to garnish the same, so fitted, as it may be put to, or taken away at our pleasure. The auncient Poets in Latin called such devises *Insertas*.

ᶜ Contrarie to Augustus Cæsar, whose manner was ever and anone in his speeches and writings to interlace Greeke words and sentences.

72

ᵃ A place neere the river Tiberis, so called of a Navell fight exhibited sometime there, by Julius Cæsar Dictator, within a spatious pit receiving water for that purpose.

ᵇ In the port high waies from Rome, the manner of the Romans, was at everie miles ende to pitch downe a great stone, and according thereto were the miles reckoned, like as with us in some places there stand crosses of wood or stone to that end.

ᶜ *i*. A creeping Dragon. Which implieth, that there be others winged, or at least wise supposed to flie, in the common opinion of men. For the attribute, *Serpens*, signifieth Creeping. Now, because

[1] Tiberius.

ANNOTATIONS

all of them use most so to do, the general name of Dragons, goeth under Serpents. And as for the word Dragon, it is given to the whole kinde for their quicke sight, comming of *Draco*, in Latine, and δράκων in Greeke, ἀπὸ τοῦ δρακεῖν, i. of seeing.

TIBERIUS NERO CÆSAR

ᵈ *Recidiva peior radice*, say the Physitians. The relapse unto a former disease is more dangerous, than it was before.

73

ᵃ It tooke the name of L. Lucullus, the Lord thereof.

75

ᵃ A towne in Campania where he tooke so great delight, and a place infamous for the licentious life of the inhabitants, whereupon grew the name of those lascivious and filthie Comedies, *Atellanæ*. A place I say suiting well to his beastly behaviour. As if he had beene unworthie to be conveyed to Rome, the Citie which so long before he had abandoned.

ᵇ As poore begger bodies were wont to be served in hast, by the common bearers, and not fully burnt with leasure.

ᶜ Where malefactors ordinarily were burnt.

EDINBURGH
T. & A. CONSTABLE
Printers to Her Majesty
1899

www.ingramcontent.com/pod-product-compliance
Lightning Source LLC
Chambersburg PA
CBHW030746230426
43667CB00007B/860